DIFFICULT ATHEISM

Crosscurrents

Exploring the development of European thought through engagements with the arts, humanities, social sciences and sciences

Series Editor
Christopher Watkin, University of Cambridge

Editorial Advisory Board

Andrew Benjamin
Martin Crowley
Simon Critchley
Frederiek Depoortere
Oliver Feltham
Patrick ffrench
Christopher Fynsk
Kevin Hart
Emma Wilson

Titles available in the series

Difficult Atheism: Post-Theological Thinking in Alain Badiou, Jean-Luc Nancy and Quentin Meillassoux by Christopher Watkin

Politics of the Gift: Exchanges in Poststructuralism by Gerald Moore

Visit the Crosscurrents website at www.euppublishing.com/series/cross

DIFFICULT ATHEISM

*Post-Theological Thinking in
Alain Badiou, Jean-Luc Nancy
and Quentin Meillassoux*

Christopher Watkin

EDINBURGH UNIVERSITY PRESS

© Christopher Watkin, 2011, 2013

First published in hardback by Edinburgh University Press 2011

Edinburgh University Press Ltd
22 George Square, Edinburgh EH8 9LF

www.euppublishing.com

Typeset in 10.5/13 Sabon
by Servis Filmsetting Ltd, Stockport, Cheshire

A CIP record for this book is available from the British Library

ISBN 978 0 7486 4057 7 (hardback)
ISBN 978 0 7486 7726 9 (paperback)

The right of Christopher Watkin
to be identified as author of this work
has been asserted in accordance with
the Copyright, Designs and Patents Act 1988.

Contents

Acknowledgements	vii
Abbreviations	viii
Series Editor's Preface	xii
Introduction: Atheisms Today	1
1. The God of Metaphysics	22
2. The God of the Poets	58
3. Difficult Atheism	95
4. Beyond A/theism? Quentin Meillassoux	132
5. The Politics of the Post-Theological I: Justifying the Political	168
6. The Politics of the Post-Theological II: Justice	206
General Conclusion: How to Follow an 'Atheism' That Never Was	239
Bibliography	244
Index	277

For Alison, with all my love
BB

Acknowledgements

I owe a debt of gratitude to those who very kindly read all or part of this book in its latter stages, saving my blushes on a number of points and improving the text in countless ways. I would like to register particular thanks to Frederiek Depoortere, Emma Gilby, John O'Brien, Joeri Schrijvers and Kenneth Watkin. I would like to thank Ian James and Martin Crowley for providing feedback and encouragement at an early stage in the project's life, along with three anonymous readers for Edinburgh University Press who offered incisive and detailed feedback on the first chapter at a critical point in the book's development, and to two anonymous readers for *French Studies* whose invaluable comments on arguments from the second chapter led to a substantial re-write. The problems that no doubt still remain are all my own.

My gratitude goes to Carol Macdonald at Edinburgh University Press for the care and professionalism with which she has handled the project from start to finish. I am grateful to the Master and Fellows of Magdalene College, Cambridge, and the President and Fellows of Murray Edwards College, Cambridge, for their encouragement with the project at every phase.

My profoundest admiration is reserved for Alison, who has lived with my tinkering away on this book at unconventional hours with a grace and largeness of spirit that speak of a greater love than I can here express. 'We love because he first loved us.'

Abbreviations

BADIOU

15T	'Fifteen Theses on Contemporary Art'
19R	'Dix-neuf réponses à beaucoup plus de questions'
2M	*Second Manifeste pour la philosophie*
AMP	*Abrégé de métapolitique*
AP	*Ahmed le philosophe*
APBE	'Author's preface' in *Being and Event*
APTW	'Author's preface' in *Theoretical Writings*
ASR	'Afterword: some replies to a demanding friend'
BE	*Being and Event*
BF	'Beyond formalisation'
BN	'Being by numbers'
BOE	*Briefings on Existence*
C	*Conditions*
CCBT	'Can change be thought?'
Cen	*The Century*
CH	*The Communist Hypothesis*
Circ1	*Circonstances 1*
Circ2	*Circonstances 2*
Circ3	*Circonstances 3*
Circ4	*Circonstances 4*
Circ5	*Circonstances 5*
Con	*Conditions* [English translation]
ConM	*Le Concept de modèle*
CT	*Court Traité d'ontologie transitoire*
D	*Deleuze: La Clameur de l'être*
Del	*Deleuze: The Clamor of Being*
DP	*Monde contemporain et désir de philosophie*
E	*L'Ethique*
EE	*L'Être et l'événement*

Eth	*Ethics*
HJD	'Homage to Jacques Derrida'
HOI	*Handbook of Inaesthetics*
IT	'L'Investigation transcendantale'
LM	*Logiques des mondes*
LW	*Logics of Worlds*
M	*Manifeste pour la philosophie*
M&P	'Mathematics and philosophy: the grand style and the little style'
Man	*Manifesto for Philosophy*
MetP	*Metapolitics*
MOS	*The Meaning of Sarkozy*
NN	*Le Nombre et les nombres*
NuN	*Number and Numbers*
ONTS	'Ours is not a terrible situation'
OPI	'Ontology and politics: an interview with Alain Badiou'
OR	'L'Offrande réservée'
OTP	*On the Truth Process*
PAF	'Préface' in *Après la finitude*
PE	*La Philosophie et l'événement*
PLN	'Peut-on penser le nouveau en situation?'
PLP	*Peut-on penser la politique?*
PMI	*Petit Manuel d'inesthétique*
PND	'Politics: a non-expressive dialectics'
Pol	*Polemics*
PoP	'Politics and philosophy'
PoPa	*Pocket Pantheon*
PP	'Philosophy and politics'
PPP	*Petit Panthéon portatif*
S	*Le Siècle*
SA	'The subject of art'
SP	*Saint Paul: La Fondation de l'universalisme*
SPe	*Saint Paul: The Foundation of Universalism*
SR	'Some replies to a demanding friend'
TC	*Théorie de la contradiction*
ThS	*Theory of the Subject*
TS	*Théorie du sujet*
TW	*Theoretical Writings*
W	*L'Antiphilosophie de Wittgenstein*

MEILLASSOUX

AF	*Après la finitude*
AfF	*After Finitude*
HE	'Histoire et événement chez Alain Badiou'
ID	'L'Inexistence divine'
NE	'Nouveauté et événement'
PV	'Potentiality and virtuality'
SD	'Spectral dilemma'
SR	'Speculative realism: presentation by Quentin Meillassoux'
TES	'Temps et surgissement ex nihilo'
TWB	'Time without becoming'

NANCY

ADC	*L'Adoration: Déconstruction du christianisme* II
AfS	'Answering for sense'
AL	*L'Absolu littéraire*
BSP	*Being Singular Plural*
BST	'Between story and truth'
BTP	*The Birth to Presence*
CA	*La Communauté affrontée*
CalP	'Calculation of the poet'
CC	'The confronted community'
CD	*La Communauté désœuvrée*
CM	*La Création du monde, ou, la mondialisation*
Com	'La Comparution'
Comp	'La Comparution/The compearance'
Cor	*Corpus*
Corp	*Corpus* [English translation]
CP	*Chroniques philosophiques*
CWG	*The Creation of the World, or, Globalization*
DDC	*La Déclosion: Déconstruction du christianisme* I
DisDC	*Dis-Enclosure: The Deconstruction of Christianity*
DLD	*Des Lieux divins*
EF	*The Experience of Freedom*
EL	*L'Expérience de la liberté*
ES	*Ego sum*
ESP	*Être singulier pluriel*
FP	'The future of philosophy'
FT	*A Finite Thinking*
GOI	*The Ground of the Image*

GT	*The Gravity of Thought*
HIN	*Hegel: L'Inquiétude du négatif*
HRN	*Hegel: The Restlessness of the Negative*
IC	*L'Impératif catégorique*
InC	*The Inoperative Community*
LA	*The Literary Absolute*
Mu	*Les Muses*
Mus	*The Muses*
NMT	*Noli me tangere*
NMTe	*Noli me tangere* [English translation]
ODP	'Of divine places'
OP	*L'Oubli de la philosophie*
PC	*Philosophical Chronicles*
PD	*La Pensée dérobée*
PF	*Une Pensée finie*
PHS	'Postface' in *L'Homme sans*
Poids	*Le Poids d'une pensée*
PSC	'Philosophie sans conditions'
PWC	'Philosophy without conditions'
RP	*Retreating the Political*
RS	*L'"il y a" du rapport sexuel*
RSAV	'Responsabilité – du sens à venir'
SM	*Le Sens du monde*
SW	*The Sense of the World*
TD	*The Truth of Democracy*
UJ	'Un Jour, les dieux se retirent . . .'
VD	*Vérité de la démocratie*

Series Editor's Preface

Two or more currents flowing into or through each other create a turbulent crosscurrent, more powerful than its contributory flows and irreducible to them. Time and again, modern European thought creates and exploits crosscurrents in thinking, remaking itself as it flows through, across and against discourses as diverse as mathematics and film, sociology and biology, theology, literature and politics. The work of Gilles Deleuze, Jacques Derrida, Slavoj Žižek, Alain Badiou, Bernard Stiegler and Jean-Luc Nancy, among others, participates in this fundamental remaking. In each case disciplines and discursive formations are engaged, not with the aim of performing a pre-determined mode of analysis yielding a 'philosophy of x', but through encounters in which thought itself can be transformed. Furthermore, these fundamental transformations do not merely seek to account for singular events in different sites of discursive or artistic production but rather to engage human existence and society as such, and as a whole. The cross-disciplinarity of this thought is therefore neither a fashion nor a prosthesis; it is simply part of what 'thought' means in this tradition.

Crosscurrents begins from the twin convictions that this re-making is integral to the legacy and potency of European thought, and that the future of thought in this tradition must defend and develop this legacy in the teeth of an academy that separates and controls the currents that flow within and through it. With this in view, the series provides an exceptional site for bold, original and opinion-changing monographs that actively engage European thought in this fundamentally cross-disciplinary manner, riding existing crosscurrents and creating new ones. Each book in the series explores the different ways in which European thought develops through its engagement with disciplines across the arts, humanities, social sciences and sciences, recognising that the community of scholars working with this thought is itself spread across diverse faculties. The object of the series is therefore nothing less than to examine and carry forward the unique legacy of European thought as an inherently and irreducibly cross-disciplinary enterprise.

Christopher Watkin
Cambridge

Introduction: Atheisms Today

> Lightning and thunder require time; the light of the stars requires time; deeds, though done, still require time to be seen and heard. This deed is still more distant from them than most distant stars – *and yet they have done it themselves.*[1]

> Dieu est mort, mais l'homme n'est pas, pour autant, devenu athée.[2]

There is a new move in French philosophy today to come to terms with the death of God more rigorously than ever, and it cannot be understood under the banner of 'atheism'. No longer can we think in terms of a monolytic atheism or of a single agenda of thinking 'without God', for what we see developing is a plurality of perhaps incommensurable approaches to thinking after God. We must not mistake this for a return to God after God, or for the growth of a new postsecular or postreligious philosophy; it is a thinking that tries more fully than ever to have done with God, that tries to remake itself fundamentally as 'without God', and on this basis moves beyond the simple term 'atheism'. This new thinking casts doubt on the claims of all previous atheisms to be without God and its contours indicate the possible future trajectory of French philosophy more broadly. This book will comparatively analyse its different branches and ask whether French thought has yet attained a thinking that is truly without God.

THE OLD GAME: IMITATIVE AND RESIDUAL ATHEISMS

As a prolegomenon to understanding this novelty, we shall begin by briefly sketching two dominant tendencies in post-Enlightenment French atheism, tendencies that are by no means mutually exclusive. The first tendency, to which we shall assign the name 'imitative atheism', merely replaces 'God' with a supposedly atheistic placeholder such as 'Man' or 'Reason', explicitly rejecting but implicitly imitating theology's categories of thinking, changing merely the terms in which those categories are articulated. The placeholder might furnish the reason and the end – the Alpha and the Omega – of the world, provide the source of Truth or Value, or stand god-like like a divinity outside the flux of intramundane becoming. Imitative atheism is inaugurated by Enlightenment humanism's more or less explicit substitution of Man for God, shifting onto human shoulders the weight of (almost literally) holding the universe together:

> Pourquoi n'introduirons-nous pas l'homme dans notre ouvrage, comme il est placé dans l'univers? Pourquoi n'en ferons-nous pas un centre commun? Est-il dans l'espace infini quelque point d'où nous puissions, avec plus d'avantage, faire partir les lignes immenses que nous nous proposons d'étendre à tous les autres points?[3]

This move is itself foreshadowed in the Cartesian cogito, where the cogito apes God in being distinct and detached from the world which it contemplates. The poster girl of imitative atheism is the 'goddess of reason' (by many accounts in fact Sophie Momoro, wife of artist Antoine-François Momoro) installed on the altar of Notre Dame cathedral in November 1793 by decree of the Convention Nationale.

In the nineteenth century imitative atheism is given most vivid form by Auguste Comte's secular 'religion of humanity', with man as its New Supreme Great Being,[4] and complete with chapels and its own catechism. Ludwig Feuerbach similarly inscribes Man in the place of God, arguing in his *Essence of Christianity* that 'Man – this is the mystery of religion – objectifies his being and then again makes himself an object to the objectivised image of himself thus converted into a subject'.[5] In this 'anthropotheism' Man is not only the guarantor of truth, but also of freedom, justice and dignity:

> If human nature is the highest nature to man, then practically also the highest and first law must be the love of man to man. *Homo homini Deus est*: – this is the great practical principle: – this is the axis on which revolves the history of the world.[6]

Notwithstanding Feuerbach's atheistic intention in taking the position that 'God become man merely reveals man become God',[7] his understanding of a Humanity that takes the place of God cannot but be parasitic on theological categories; it may be explicitly atheistic but it cannot be implicitly without God.

Imitative atheism assumes that Truth or Justice can be grounded by appealing to Man in the same way that Platonic thinking appeals to the Ideas and Augustinian Christianity to the Mind of God. Imitative atheism has flung wide its gates to welcome in theology's Trojan horse. As the ship's captain who scours the main with his telescope and affirms that there are no lenses on the high seas, this parasitic atheism can be blind in the midst of its own insight to the conditions of possibility of its own affirmations.

Care, however, should be taken to distinguish imitative atheism from the casual use of religious or theological terms within an atheistic context. If a philosopher uses terms such as 'miracle', 'faith' or even 'God', it does not necessarily follow that her thought is imitative. An atheism is parasitic upon theology only when it deploys concepts that cannot be accounted for in exclusively atheistic terms but require assumptions proper to theology, whether or not those concepts happen to carry theological labels. This, of course, raises the question of what assumptions are proper to theology. This is a question that receives different, often contradictory answers; it will be one focus of the studies in this book.

The twentieth century in France saw a widespread rejection of this parasitic atheism on the grounds of its complicity with the theological and religious paradigms it seeks to replace. Raymond Aron denounces the 'secular religion' of communism in which 'l'eschatologie marxiste attribue au prolétariat le rôle d'un sauveur collectif',[8] and its combination of prophetism and scholasticism that produces a new set of theological virtues: 'foi dans le prolétariat et dans l'Historie, la charité pour ceux qui souffrent et vont triompher demain, l'espérance en l'avenir radieux d'une société sans classes'.[9]

The existentialism of the mid twentieth century marks a significant moment in the rejection of imitative atheism. Albert Camus struggles in the tension between an old imitation and a new refusal of parasitic thinking:

> Je continue à croire que ce monde n'a pas de sens supérieur. Mais je sais que quelque chose en lui a du sens et c'est l'homme, parce qu'il est le seul être à exiger d'en avoir. Ce monde a du moins la vérité de l'homme et notre tâche est de lui donner ses raisons contre le destin lui-même.[10]

Camus's absurd holds itself in the impossible breach of imitative atheism, claiming concepts to which it knows it has no right; it is 'le péché sans Dieu'.[11] His thought adumbrates the second tendency within post-Enlightenment atheism, a tendency that arises in part as a critique of imitative atheism. This second tendency seeks, in rejecting all that might be considered parasitic upon theology, to elaborate with more rigour an atheism that is truly without God. It takes inspiration in part from the displacement of the Cartesian cogito by Heideggerian *Dasein* in the 'Letter on humanism' and *Being and Time*.[12] The cogito imitates a deity who sits outside the world it objectively observes, and if such a God is no longer believed in, then the Man made in his image must be renounced also.

This second current of atheism, a renunciation of any imitation of the dead God, is pressed among others by Maurice Blanchot in his reading of Camus. The renunciation of any pseudo-theological redemption of the human condition issues in an ascetically meagre consolation, the iconic moment of which is the end of Camus's *Mythe de Sisyphe*:

> Je laisse Sisyphe au bas de la montagne! On retrouve toujours son fardeau. Mais Sisyphe enseigne la fidélité supérieure qui nie les dieux et soulève les rochers. Lui aussi juge que tout est bien. Cet univers désormais sans maître ne lui paraît ni stérile ni fertile. Chacun des grains de cette pierre, chaque éclat minéral de cette montagne pleine de nuit, à lui seul, forme un monde. La lutte elle-même vers les sommets suffit à remplir un cœur d'homme. Il faut imaginer Sisyphe heureux.[13]

We must imagine Sisyphus happy? This is an empty, impersonal imperative, a weak affirmation of a value that has become aware of its groundlessness. Having heroically renounced any theologically redemptive eschatology, Sisyphus can only gather the meagre crumbs of finding happiness in his relentless torture. Blanchot presses the necessity of renouncing all redemption in *Le Mythe de Sisyphe* and *L'Homme révolté*:

> Du moment que, de toutes mes forces, je m'attache comme seul possible à un univers où ma présence n'a aucun sens, il faut que je renonce totalement à l'espoir; du moment que, envers et contre tout, je maintiens ma volonté de voir clair tout en sachant que l'obscurité ne diminuera jamais, il faut que je renonce totalement au repos; du moment que je ne puis que tout contester sans donner à rien, même à cette contestation, une valeur absolue, il faut que je renonce à tout et même à cet acte de tout refuser. Absence totale d'espoir, insatisfaction consciente, lutte sans fin, telles sont les trois exigences de la logique absurde; elles définissent désormais le caractère de l'expérience qui consiste à vivre sans appel.[14]

Blanchot sees in Camus an ongoing unwillingness to embrace the atheistic absurd, a manipulation of the absurd into an atheism that once more imitates theology:

> « Il faut imaginer Sisyphe heureux. » Heureux? Voilà qui est vite écrit. [. . .] C'est que lui-même n'est pas fidèle à sa règle, c'est qu'à la longue il fait de l'absurde non pas ce qui dérange et brise tout, mais ce qui est susceptible d'arrangement et ce qui même arrange tout. Dans son ouvrage, l'absurde devient un dénouement, il est une solution, une sorte de salut.[15]

This call to systematic renunciation exemplifies the second tendency in post-Enlightenment atheism, a tendency that we shall call 'residual atheism', an atheism that seeks, with a heroic or despairing asceticism, to make do with the meagre residue left over after the departure of God, Truth, Justice, Beauty and so on. Residual atheism traces its genealogy through Heidegger's *Dasein* to Nietzsche's pronouncements of the death of God. Nietzsche's madman in the marketplace is speaking to unbelievers,[16] the imitative atheists who do not yet realise their continued parasitism on the God they reject. In *The Gay Science* Nietzsche warns of the extent to which modern thought still relies on the God it has replaced:

> It is still a *metaphysical faith* upon which our faith in science rests – that even we seekers after knowledge today, we godless anti-metaphysicians still take our fire, too, from the flame lit by a faith that is thousands of years old, that Christian faith which was also the faith of Plato, that God is the truth, that truth is divine. – But what if . . . God should prove to be our most enduring lie?[17]

It is imitative atheism's 'faith in Plato' that must be challenged, the faith in the 'heavenly place' (*topos ouranios*) of Truth, Justice, and Meaning, the Ideas that, in parasitic atheism, radiate out in 'immense lines' as from Diderot's Man.[18] Thought in the wake of Nietzsche is no longer warranted in evoking a suprasensory world as the custodian of Truth. The Ideas of which the suprasensory God was guarantor cannot survive the death of that God, a death that, though it has happened, still lies in the future for an unsuspecting humanity:

> Much less may one suppose that many people know as yet *what* this event really means – and how much must collapse now that this faith has been undermined because it was built upon this faith, propped up by it, grown into it; for example, the whole of our European morality.[19]

In resisting imitative atheism, Nietzsche's own position is deprived of the certainties and horizons of the Platonic or Judaeo-Christian suprasensory by the death of God. In addition to morality, the Christian eschatological and redemptive view of history must be jettisoned, along with the Platonic idea of truth, and hypostatised Reason and Meaning, which cannot survive the washing away of the horizon that comes with the death of God: ' "Reason" in language – oh, what an old deceptive female she is! I am afraid we are not rid of God because we still have faith in grammar.'[20]

Nietzsche has been received in France as rejecting the certainties, truths and values of imitative atheism's parasitism upon theology, with a recognition that the place of God is not occupied by man, but empty, and with a realisation that parasitic atheism's naïve humanism is nothing more than the assumption that 'la *nature humaine* avait pour attributs la vérité et la justice, comme d'autres espèces ont pour elles la nageoire ou l'aile.'[21] In denying itself the Truths and Values of the suprasensory, this post-Nietzschean residual atheism cuts a somewhat ascetic figure. To be sure, Nietzsche's rhetoric around the death of God is itself far from ascetic. It leaves us as 'free spirits' upon whom a new dawn has shone.[22] Nevertheless, deprived of the eternal truths previously underwritten by God, 'Man alone among the animals has no eternal horizons and perspectives'.[23] Far from triumphantly acceding to God's vacated throne, Man finds himself unable to survive the divine demise. The rhetoric of Progress and Reason gives way to a recognition that 'Nietzsche a mis en évidence ce fait primordial que, la bourgeoisie ayant tué Dieu, il en résulterait tout d'abord un désarroi catastrophique, le vide et même un appauvrissement sinistre.'[24] Instead of an idolatrous humanism, this ascetic atheism issues in the death of Man:

> A tous ceux qui veulent encore parler de l'homme, de son règne ou de sa libération, à tous ceux qui posent encore des questions sur ce qu'est l'homme en son essence, à tous ceux qui veulent partir de lui pour avoir accès à la vérité, à tous ceux en revanche qui reconduisent toute connaissance aux vérités de l'homme lui-même [. . .] on ne peut qu'opposer un rire philosophique c'est-à-dire, pour une certaine part, silencieux.[25]

Even so, this asceticism does not succeed in disengaging residual atheism from the parasitism it denounces. In limiting itself to the sensory world *as opposed to* the suprasensory, the immanent *as opposed to* the transcendent, residual atheism finds itself – just like imitative atheism – defined in terms of that which it seeks to escape. This is the thrust of Heidegger's critique of Nietzsche in 'Nietzsche's word: God is dead'.[26] For Heidegger, the very way in which Nietzsche understands the death of God inscribes it ineluctably in terms of reference dictated by the theology of the God whose death is being declared. Glossing Nietzsche's parable of the madman in *The Gay Science*, Heidegger warns us not to forget 'what is said at the beginning of the passage that has been elucidated: that the madman "cried incessantly: I seek God! I seek God!"'[27] The madman's cry 'God is dead' is not a simple cry of triumph but a lament, issuing in his *requiem aeternam deo*. The problem for Nietzsche, as far as Heidegger is concerned, is that 'the terms "God" and "Christian god" in Nietzsche's thinking are used to designate the suprasensory world in general',[28] and Nietzsche himself parasitises that Platonic-Christian dichotomy of, on one hand, the 'suprasensory' or 'true and genuinely real' world of Ideas and Ideals, and on the other hand the sensory world which is by contrast 'changeable, and therefore the merely apparent, unreal world'. The madman's cry concerns this Platonic world of Ideas: 'The pronouncement "God is dead" means: The suprasensory world is without effective power. It bestows no life. Metaphysics, i.e., for Nietzsche Western philosophy understood as Platonism, is at an end.'[29]

However Nietzsche may insist on the inaccessibility of the suprasensory, the division into sensory/suprasensory is itself already a theological move: 'if God in the sense of the Christian God has disappeared from his authoritative position in the suprasensory world, then this authoritative place itself is still always preserved, even though as that which has become empty'.[30] Nietzsche's sensory universe is still complicit, therefore, with Kant's determination in the Preface to the second edition of the *Critique of Pure Reason* (1787) to 'deny knowledge in order to make room for faith'.[31] The problem for Nietzsche is that in his residual atheism the sensory is limited by the suprasensory that has been swept away. Not only is it thereby denied Truth, Meaning and Justice, but the boundaries of the sensory stand now as a *de facto* limit beyond which philosophy cannot stray and therefore outside which it is unable to secure its atheism. If for Kant 'the principles of [reason's] natural use do not lead at all to any theology',[32] then conversely theology remains untouched either by the empirical or by the rational, and post-Kantian philosophies struggle to exorcise the same theological ghost.

It is not only Nietzsche who runs the risk of making room for God, however. Any philosophy that limits itself in respect of the sensory/suprasensory or rational/mystical dichotomies, or that remains silent on the question of God, is implicitly, if not explicitly, re-inscribing Kant's 'making room'. Such a re-inscription is Wittgenstein's famous 'whereof one cannot speak, thereof must one be silent',[33] or Husserl's insistence in *Ideas 1* that the transcendence of God is 'suspended': 'Naturally we extend the phenomenological reduction to include this "absolute" and "transcendent" being. It shall remain excluded from the new field of research which is to be provided, since this shall be a field of pure consciousness.'[34]

In seeking to wipe away the theological suprasensory, residual atheism struggles to articulate itself in terms other than as the negative residue of theology's plenitude or a renunciation, along with theology, of truth and goodness. It is not hard to mount a theological critique of this residual atheism at the point of its insistence on immanence, for '[c]'est par référence à la transcendance et par l'exclusion de celle-ci hors de sa structure interne que l'immanence a été définie'.[35]

Jacques Derrida presents us with a sophisticated version of ascetic atheism. From his early writings onwards Derrida resists his thought being understood as a residue of metaphysico-theological structures:

> on n'aurait pas fait un pas hors de la métaphysique si l'on n'en retenait qu'un nouveau motif du « retour à la finitude », de la « mort de Dieu », etc. C'est cette conceptualité et cette problématique qu'il faut déconstruire. Elles appartiennent à l'onto-théologie qu'elles contestent. La différance est aussi autre chose que la finitude.³⁶

It is in this very resistance to the conceptuality of theology's problematic, however, that Derrida's thought opens itself to the charge of asceticism, for in the process of avoiding one asceticism, namely the retreat into finitude as opposed to the infinite, it opens itself to the charge of a second asceticism, namely quietude and inactivity. An ascetic reticence before the *passage à l'acte* and before the decision are to be seen in Derrida's later qualification of the notion of universal justice as a demand, horizon or surprise and an absolute dissymmetry with the present: justice, if there is such a thing, can never be here and now and it is utterly unforeseeable, a justice that is 'to come', always to come.³⁷ Can atheism claim that a certain action is or is not just, without the judgment immediately dying the death of a thousand qualifications? Derrida remains ascetically open to justice to come, without knowing if there is such a thing, and his anti-parasitic re-working of atheism is vulnerable to the accusation that justice can no longer determine ethical and/or political decisions. Badiou's despair at the deconstructive position is indicative of those who express exasperation with this asceticism:

> « Une pensée tout entière à venir! » Comme est irritant le style post-heideggérien de l'annonce perpétuelle, de l'à-venir interminable, cette sorte de prophétisme laïcisée ne cesse de déclarer que nous ne sommes pas encore en état de penser ce qu'il y a à penser, ce pathos de l'avoir-à-répondre de l'être, ce Dieu qui fait défaut, cette attente face à l'abîme, cette posture du regard qui porte loin dans la brume et dit qu'on voit venir l'indistinct! Comme on a envie de dire: « Écoutez, si cette pensée est encore tout entière a venir, revenez nous voir quand au moins un morceau en sera venu! » (OR 15–16)³⁸

It is hardly surprising, then, that this ascetic atheism leaves the door open for a 'theological turn' in French phenomenology,³⁹ a 'return to religion' or the 'return of religion' that 'has become perhaps the dominant cliché of contemporary theory'.⁴⁰ This theological turn can be understood as theology's colonisation of residual atheism by exploiting its gesture of 'making room'. In the case of Emmanuel Lévinas, the exploitation of 'making room' is the evocation of an Alterity that comes 'd'un pays où nous ne naquîmes point'.⁴¹ This position is quite at home with the ascetic strategy of excluding religious language from philosophy's rational or empirical domain, indeed its alterity relies on such an exclusion. Similarly, Lévinas is in no way compromised by the suggestion that it is meaningless to talk of God at all, but re-affirms such meaninglessness in a quasi-mystical register:

> Les questions relatives à Dieu ne se résolvent pas par des réponses où cesse de résonner, où s'apaise pleinement, l'interrogation [. . .] On se demande s'il est possible de parler légitimement de Dieu, sans porter atteinte à l'absoluité que son mot semble signifier.[42]

What is more, this is a non-ontological theology quite at peace with the death of the God of metaphysics, for we have moved 'vers une pensée peut-être déjà post-métaphysicienne'.[43] More than merely leaving the door open for the return of the theological, however, ascetic atheism finds itself quickly consumed by the unfolding narrative of the God whose death it hails; it is dialectised as a necessary renunciation of the God of metaphysics in preparation for a non-metaphysical faith:

> Si le titre « signification religieuse de l'athéisme » n'est pas vain, il implique que l'athéisme n'épuise pas sa signification dans la négation et la destruction de la religion, mais qu'il libère l'horizon pour quelque chose d'autre, pour une foi susceptible d'être appelée [. . .] une foi post-religieuse[44]

To deny the Being of God is simply to hold that God gives himself to be known according to a 'more radical horizon' than Being;[45] it is not to condemn God to nonbeing but to save God from Being and to announce the co-option of atheism by a post-religious or post-secular faith. Furthermore, the death of God understood as a rejection of the suprasensory is easily co-opted as an articulation of Christ's death on the cross, as Merleau-Ponty notes in *Le Primat de la perception*:

> L'idée nietzschéenne que « Dieu est mort » est déjà contenue dans l'idée chrétienne de la mort de Dieu. Dieu cesse d'être objet extérieur pour se mêler dans la vie humaine; et cette vie n'est pas simple retour à une solution intemporelle[46]

This systematic occupation of residual atheism's territory by a returning post-religious or post-secular theology is demonstrated by Jean-Luc Marion in *Dieu sans l'être* and *L'Idole et la distance*.[47] To affirm the Being of God for Marion is merely to affirm the God of Being, the God who gives himself according to the horizon of Being,[48] and it amounts to claiming not that God has attained Being but that Being has attained God, that Being defines the first and the highest of the divine names.[49] Though God for Marion undoubtedly is, his relation to Being does not radically determine him. To free God from being is to affirm that the absolute God is 'défait de tout rapport, donc aussi de tout rapport pensable, qui le lierait à un absurde « autre que lui ».'[50] The 'death of God', in so far as it is the death of the God of Being, serves merely to liberate the God who gives himself as *agapē* from the idolatry of radically determining God as Being, for the 'death of God' sets forth a contradiction: that which dies does not have any right to claim, even when it is alive, to be 'God'.[51] And in so far as this idol is summarily dispatched, 'the death of God' understood as the death of the God of being expresses the death of the 'death of God' itself.[52] Not only is the 'death of God' no threat to any God worthy of the name, and in this case to the God who gives himself as *agapē*, it is in addition a positive succour to the true religion which has always sought to rid itself of idols, the God of Being chief among them. With this move, a certain post-religious theology has colonised ascetic atheism, incorporating atheism's moves within its own trajectory:

> now, when Nietzsche says that god is dead, as a matter of fact he is only developing this extreme point introduced to the world by Christianity of the historicity of history. In other words, no structure, no objective on eternal god, *just as Christianity has always said*.[53]

This Christianity of the death of God has succeeded in colonising residual atheism with the argument that 'real religiosity relies on secularisation'.[54] Furthermore, the death of God is seen to be the enemy not of religion but of atheism itself, for 'the end of metaphysics and the death of the moral God have liquidated the philosophical basis of atheism',[55] if atheism consists in denying those particular deities. We find that a transformed religious discourse has effectively come to occupy the territory of the atheism which sought to resist it:

> The idea of some kind of postsecular moment emerges precisely from what Nietzsche calls the 'death of god' because it's the death of any version of monism or reductionism, including secularism. Nietzsche fancied himself a prophetic voice, but he didn't see that coming.[56]

Atheism is left defending the Maginot line of rationality while the postsecular tanks rumble on behind its lines.

Despite his antipathy to the 'theological turn', Dominique Janicaud's position in *Le Tournant théologique de la phénoménologie française* does nothing to address this theological colonisation of the death of God. Janicaud argues for an expulsion of the question of God outside the field of legitimate phenomenological enquiry[57] against Lévinas's reinscription of Husserlian phenomenological rigour,[58] and for an affirmation of the 'insurmountable difference' between phenomenology and theology.[59] But this does nothing more than reaffirm residual atheism, along with all its problems. Such an atheistic phenomenology has no means to engage with and resist theological discourse. If 'la phénoménologie a été prise en otage par une théologie qui ne veut pas dire son nom',[60] then it is also true that a phenomenology refusing to speak the language of theology is equally prey to a God it has explicitly given itself no means to engage. Such a phenomenology may be agnostic, but can never be atheistic. Once more, residual atheism finds itself unable to refute the turn to religion; in fact it is the very seedbed in which the turn can take root and bloom.

To the extent that ascetic atheism confines itself to the sensory domain bequeathed to it by theology, it is irrelevant whether theological language be labelled 'irrational' or 'nonsense', or whether God's existence be denied; atheism will never be rid of God because it can only ever chase God to the borders of the rational, or the sensory. Ascetic atheism is condemned to a perpetual game of defence, always beating the bounds of its own territory (whether that be the limit of the sensory or of the rational) but never able to pursue the theological intruder beyond those bounds. In seeking to rid herself of God the would-be atheist has only succeeded in proofing God against her own attacks. Furthermore, atheism has consigned itself to playing the role of religion's ascetic poor relation, prone to define itself in terms of what it lacks (no Truth, no Goodness, no 'eternal horizons and perspectives' . . .). The dirty secret of residual atheism is that under the guise of heroically repelling the religious intruder it is in fact an abject accommodation to religion's terms of engagement.

Parasitism keeps the fruit of the Platonic-Christian structure, but does nothing to attack its root. Asceticism destroys the root, but denies itself the fruit of Truth, Goodness and Justice. What is more, neither parasitism nor asceticism – this Scylla and Charybdis of modern atheism – succeed in taking full account of the death of God, for both rely upon the dichotomy of the sensory and suprasensory, and both are open to being occupied or colonised by theology. A dissatisfaction with this situation is motivating a search for a new atheism in French thought, an atheism that can combine the fruit enjoyed by parasitism with the uprooting of theological categories attempted by asceticism.

THE NEW GAME: POST-THEOLOGICAL INTEGRATION

If thinking without God is to move beyond the impasse of parasitism and asceticism it cannot simply produce – to adopt a Lyotardian idiom – a new move in atheism's old game of the sensory and the suprasensory. It cannot simply take religion's categories for its own, but neither can it afford to leave religion alone, expelled merely beyond its own sensory or rational bounds. It must learn from the postsecular colonisation of atheism in order not to resist but to occupy theism's territory, re-deploying theism's notions in its own cause, just as the postsecular co-opts atheism to do its own work of denouncing idols. Only this will provide an escape from being theology's parasitic or ascetic poor relation. It is this project of escaping theism's shadow, we will argue, that makes sense of French philosophy's attempt, in the opening decades of the third millennium, to follow the death of God more rigorously than before.

It might at first blush appear that the opening of the twenty-first century has seen one more 'turn to religion', not by writers confessing an affinity to some version of theology but by those seeking to be rid of God. Much has been written on the apostle Paul by recent Continental thinkers,[61] and the early 2000s saw a cottage industry of books and articles on religion by Slavoj Žižek.[62] In France, Alain Badiou has revisited the death of God in his the prologue to his *Court Traité d'ontologie transitoire*, crystallising themes developed ever since his early *Théorie du sujet* and still deployed in his most recent interviews. In 2010 Jean-Luc Nancy published the second volume of his deconstruction of Christianity, *L'Adoration*, reworking ideas that stretch back to his early 'Des lieux divins' (1987). As yet less well known than Badiou or Nancy but rapidly receiving the wider readership and following that his audacious thought deserves, Quentin Meillassoux lays claim to a unique position in current debates about God. His *Après la finitude* begins to unfold arguments that, in the as yet unpublished 'L'Inexistence divine', blossom into the most sustained direct engagement with and rejection of atheism in recent years, as Meillassoux indicts all existing atheisms as complicit with theology. Our aim in the chapters that follow is not to provide an exhaustive map of this new direction in thinking, but to explore in depth the writing of Badiou, Nancy and Meillassoux, the three key writers who, in three different ways, are seeking to move the contemporary debate beyond parasitic and ascetic atheism, and who provide three radically different ways of thinking without God, forcing us to re-cast 'atheism' as only one of a new palette of terms that express the complexity of how French thought is seeking to follow the death of God.

In the pages that follow we shall use the term 'post-theological' as an umbrella term for different ways of thinking after God.[63] The prefix 'post-' is merely an indication of chronology: to think in the West today is to think after God, with concepts and a tradition bequeathed by theology and theologically informed thinking, and even if the aim of such thinking is to be atheological it cannot avoid the task of disengaging itself from the theological legacy.[64] The common impulse of the three post-theological philosophies we shall consider is that they seek 1) to move beyond imitative and residual atheism in order fundamentally to re-think philosophy without God or the gods and without parasitising any assumptions dependent on them (hence post-theological, not merely post-theistic), while nevertheless 2) refusing ascetically to renounce the notions associated with such gods – namely, truth and justice – relinquished by residual atheism. A thinking radically without God is integrated with a retention of the notions otherwise associated with God. These two ideas taken together account for our characterisation of thinking after atheism as a 'post-theological integration'. It is this integration that makes the new post-theological thought truly new: it is a turn to religion in order to turn the page on religion. In the chapters which follow we shall attempt to evaluate whether these integrating approaches succeed.

Above all, we must not see these thinkers as performing a new 'theological turn' or 'return of religion'. Badiou has short shrift for such a notion, arguing that the 'return of religion' is merely a mask for the contemporary decomposition of politics (*PE* 40) and the notion that the world is consumed by a violent quarrel between free-thinkers and men of the cloth is obsolete and absolutely astounding (*PE* 41). As for Nancy, the 'return to religion' is just as decrepit and insipid as any other 'return' (*DDC* 129/*DisDC* 85), and in fact there is no return of the religious but only the contortions and turgidity of its exhaustion (*DLD* 33/*ODP* 136). It is also incorrect, we shall argue, to paint Nancy as a defender of sceptical agnosticism in contrast to Badiou's supposedly materialistic atheism. The terms 'agnostique' and 'agnosticisme' do not significantly appear in Nancy's work, although he does argue that atheism is the only possible contemporary *ethos*, or way of holding oneself in the world (*DDC* 30/*DisDC* 17). Nancy, we shall argue, recognises that atheism is fatally compromised by asceticism and parasitism, and requires a new direction.

There is a further twist in the new post-theological integration: its frequent foregrounding of religious ideas, language and themes. Much has been made of Badiou's use of the terms 'grace' and 'faith', 'hope' and 'love' and Nancy's deconstruction of Christianity, especially in its second volume, is conspicuous in its recourse to a number of terms drawn from a religious lexicon: 'spirit', 'agapic love', 'praise', and of course 'adoration' itself. As for Meillassoux, the prevalence of religious and theological terms is even more striking: 'conversion', 'immortality', 'incarnation', the 'Child of man' and even the 'philosophical God' tumble approvingly off the pages of 'L'Inexistence divine'. There are two errors to avoid in trying to make sense of this peppering of religious terms. The 'parasitic' reading is that this theological vocabulary indicates the same old reliance on religious forms of thinking that we encounter in Comte and Feuerbach, such that post-theological integration is living off the borrowed religious capital of imitative atheism, and is therefore a fortiori ripe for the same postsecular colonisation. The 'ascetic' interpretation is that that the prevalence of religious vocabulary and ideas in these thinkers is a complete irrelevance, a semantic blip of no interest to a serious study of their thought. It is our argument in the pages that follow that neither the 'parasitic' nor the 'ascetic' way of trying to account for these religious and theological terms is adequate to make sense of what is at stake in post-theological thought for Badiou, Nancy or Meillassoux. What post-theological integration attempts is not to oppose theism but to occupy it, not to expel theism but to ingest it, taking terms and patterns of thought previously associated with theism and re-inscribing them in a way that is not to be confused either with parasitism or with asceticism.

Three questions will guide our exploration of this post-theological integration. First, how do Nancy, Badiou and Meillassoux seek to articulate a new position or positions beyond the problems of parasitism/asceticism? Secondly, can one coherent understanding of what it means to think without God emerge from Nancy, Badiou and Meillassoux, or do they develop different, perhaps incommensurable approaches to the post-theological? Thirdly, do the different approaches to a post-theological integration in fact succeed in avoiding the problems identified with parasitism and asceticism? Do they succeed in occupying religion's territory without letting the religious Trojan horse into their own camps? Though our own position will inevitably become clear in the course of the discussion, our aim throughout will be to respect the maxim *audi alteram partem*. The reader's pardon is begged in advance for the failures there will no doubt be in this respect.

The six chapters of our study fall into three groups of two. Chapters 1 and 2 interrogate Badiou's and Nancy's reception of the death of God. Taking our lead from Badiou's distinction in the prologue of his *Court Traité d'ontologie transitoire*, the first chapter addresses the death of the God of the philosophers, and the second chapter looks at the death of the God of the poets. In Chapter 1 we encounter a fundamental differend between Badiou's 'Platonism of the multiple' and Nancy's 'deconstruction of Christianity' which will structure much of the debate that follows. In the second chapter we show the central importance for Badiou's post-theological integration of the motif of the

Idea and the assertion that 'nothing is inaccessible', and for Nancy of the double movement of dis-enclosure's 'yet without' and the relation between sense and signification.

Chapter 3 moves from considering the place of the death of God in Badiou's and Nancy's thought to interrogating their articulations of atheism per se. Entitled 'Difficult Atheism', this third chapter is a comparative study of Badiou's axiomatic atheism and Nancy's re-inscription of faith as the 'nothing at all' of reason, without which reason cannot be what it is. While Nancy moves away from the language of atheism to 'atheology', we argue that neither Badiou nor Nancy unproblematically secures a position that is 'without God', and that they develop divergent post-theological positions that cannot easily be reconciled with each other.

In the fourth chapter, 'Beyond A/theism', we invite Quentin Meillassoux into the discussion. Meillassoux goes further than Nancy in distancing himself from 'atheism', rejecting both theism and atheism in favour of 'philosophy'. Distinct from both Badiou's axiomatic atheism and Nancy's 'faith that is nothing at all', Meillassoux defends the bold claim that his position relies not on a decision or on a moment of faith but on a demonstration. Meillassoux's position is startling for its willingness to colonise religious terms and ideas, and he claims to be articulating for the first time a thinking that enjoys all the 'benefits' of religion without being beset by any of the problems attendant on what we are calling imitative and residual atheisms. Furthermore, Meillassoux's philosophy poses an explicit challenge to Badiou's atheism and an implicit critique of Nancy's atheology. We argue that, for all its boldness, Meillassoux's move beyond atheism does not succeed in freeing itself from the shadow of religion.

In the final two chapters we move to consider a case study of post-theological integration, namely how it proposes to think and act politically without falling either into parasitism or asceticism. In asking the question 'What politics are possible after God?', our main concern in the fifth chapter is to see how Meillassoux, Badiou and Nancy lay claim to ethical and political imperatives without partaking in a re-theologisation of the political. The final chapter focuses on the idea and politics of justice, and on the different ways in which our three thinkers understand justice in terms of their respective post-theological integrations. We consider Meillassoux's audacious claim to bring justice for both the living and the dead, and examine the similar way in which Badiou and Nancy articulate the place of capital and communism in their notions of justice, contrasting Badiou's communist hypothesis with Nancy's ontological communism. The investigation of justice also allows us to ask whether the political positions that each thinker adopts are a necessary consequence of their post-theological thought, and whether any one particular political position or set of positions can be said to flow from their thinking.

In the conclusion we return to the central concern of the inadequacy of 'atheism' to capture current complexities in French thought. We argue that the term is too blunt an instrument with which to make sense of the diversity of current approaches to thinking in the wake of the death of God, and that it would avoid much confusion to stop using it as a blanket term to refer to thinking without God. We also argue that the future of post-theological thought will be determined by its ability to account for the choice for one fundamental philosophical orientation over another.

'Deeds, though done, still require time to be seen and heard', warned Nietzsche's madman,[65] and his admonition echoes through the chapters of *Difficult Atheism*. The death of God still requires time to be fully seen and heard, but it is not that this death itself is slow in reaching contemporary thought, rather that contemporary thought is still straining to do justice to it. The process of understanding how philosophy in the twenty-first century continues to come to terms with the death of God is important for French philosophy's re-negotiation of the religious legacy and for the future shape of that philosophy more broadly. This book is a contribution to that process.

NOTES

1. Nietzsche, *The Gay Science*, p. 182.
2. Jean-Paul Sartre, *Critiques littéraires*, p. 153. 'God is dead, but man has not, for all that, become atheistic' (author's translation).
3. Diderot, *Œuvres complètes*, ed. Jane Marsh Dieckmann, vol. 7, pp. 212–13.

   > Why will we not introduce man into our work, in the same way he is placed in the universe? Why do we not make him a common centre? Is there any point in infinite space from where we can, with greater advantage, send out the immense lines that we propose to stretch to all other points? (author's translation)

   This passage is cited by Stefanos Geroulanos in *An Atheism that is not Humanist* (p. 13), a fine analysis of the relation between humanism and atheism to which the present volume owes a debt.
4. The New Supreme Great Being is discussed at length in Comte, *System of Positive Polity*.
5. Feuerbach, *The Essence of Christianity*, p. 52.

6. Feuerbach, *The Essence of Christianity*, p. 341.
7. Feuerbach, *The Essence of Christianity*. p. 335.
8. Raymond Aron, *L'Opium des intellectuels* (Paris: Calmann-Lévy, 1955), p. 78. 'In Marxist eschatology, the proletariat is cast in the role of collective savior' (Aron, *The Opium of the Intellectuals*, p. 66).
9. Aron, *L'Opium des intellectuels*, p. 278. 'Faith in the proletariat and in history, charity for those who suffer today and who tomorrow will inherit the earth, hope that the future will bring the advent of the classless society' (Aron, *The Opium of the Intellectuals*, p. 267).
10. Camus, *Lettres à un ami allemand*, pp. 72-3.

 > I continue to believe that the world has no ultimate meaning. But I know that something in it has meaning, and that is man, because he is the only creature to insist on having one. This world has at least the truth of man and our task is to provide its justification against faith itself. (Camus, *Resistance, Rebellion, and Death*, p. 22)

11. Albert Camus, *Le Mythe de Sisyphe* (Paris: Gallimard, 1942), p. 60; 'sin without God' (Camus, *The Myth of Sisyphus*, p. 38).
12. Heidegger, *Being and Time*; Heidegger, 'Letter on humanism', pp. 189-242.
13. Camus, *Le Mythe de Sisyphe*, p. 168.

 > I leave Sisyphus at the foot of the mountain! One always finds one's burden again. But Sisyphus teaches the higher fidelity that denies the gods and raises up rocks. He, too, concludes that all is well. The universe henceforth without a master seems to him neither sterile nor futile. Each atom of that stone, each mineral flake of that night-filled mountain, in itself forms a world. The struggle itself towards the heights is enough to fill a man's heart. One must imagine Sisyphus happy. (Camus, *The Myth of Sisyphus*, p. 99; translation altered)

14. Blanchot, *Faux pas*, 1975, p. 69.

 > From the instant that, with all my strength, I link myself as the only possibility to a universe where my presence has no meaning, I must completely renounce hope; from the instant that, toward and against everything, I maintain my will to see everything clearly, knowing that the obscurity will never diminish, I must completely renounce rest; from the instant that I can do nothing but question everything without giving anything, even this questioning, an absolute value, I must renounce everything, even this act of refusing everything. Total absence of hope, conscious dissatisfaction, endless struggle, those are the three demands of absurd logic; from now on they define the character of the experience that consists of living without appeal. (Blanchot, *Faux Pas*, trans. Charlotte Mandell, p. 56)

15. Blanchot, *Faux pas*, 1975, p. 70.

   'One must imagine Sisyphus happy.' Happy? That is easy enough to write [. . .] It is because he himself is not faithful to his rule, because in the long run he makes of the absurd not that which disturbs and breaks everything but that which is amenable to arrangement and which even arranges everything. In his work the absurd becomes a denouement; it is a solution, a kind of salvation. (Blanchot, *Faux Pas*, trans. Charlotte Mandell, p. 57; translation altered)

16. 'As many of those who did not believe in God were standing around just then, he provoked much laughter' (Nietzsche, *The Gay Science*, p. 181).
17. Nietzsche, *The Gay Science*, p. 344.
18. See note 3.
19. Nietzsche, *The Gay Science*, p. 279.
20. Nietzsche, *The Anti-Christ, Ecce Homo, Twilight of the Idols, and Other Writings*, p. 170.
21. Maurice Merleau-Ponty, *Signes* (Paris: Gallimard, 1960), p. 368; 'human nature had truth and justice for attributes, as other species have fins or wings' (Merleau-Ponty, *Signs*, p. 355).
22. Nietzsche, *The Gay Science*, p. 181.
23. Nietzsche, *The Gay Science*, p. 192.
24. Bataille, *Écrits posthumes, 1922–1940, Œuvres complètes*, vol. 2, p. 102. 'Nietzsche revealed this primordial fact: that once the bourgeoisie had killed God, the immediate result would be catastrophic confusion, emptiness, and even a sinister impoverishment' (Bataille, *Visions of Excess*, p. 38).
25. Foucault, *Les Mots et les choses*, pp. 353–4.

   To all those who still wish to talk about man, about his reign or his liberation, to all those who still ask themselves questions about what man is in his essence, to all those who wish to take him as their starting-point in their attempts to reach the truth, to all those who, on the other hand, refer all knowledge back to the truths of man himself, [. . .] we can answer only with a philosophical laugh – which means, to a certain extent, a silent one. (Foucault, *The Order of Things*, pp. 342–3)

26. Martin Heidegger, 'Nietzsche's word: God is dead', in *The Question Concerning Technology and Other Essays*, pp. 53–114.
27. Heidegger, 'Nietzsche's word', p. 111.
28. Heidegger, 'Nietzsche's word', p. 61.
29. Heidegger, 'Nietzsche's word', p. 61.
30. Heidegger, 'Nietzsche's word', p. 69.
31. Kant, *Critique of Pure Reason*, p. 117.
32. Kant, *Critique of Pure Reason*, p. 586.
33. Ludwig Wittgenstein, *Tractatus Logico-Philosophicus*, trans. C. K. Ogden (New York: Barnes and Noble, 2003), p. 157.

34. Husserl, *Ideas Pertaining to a Pure Phenomenology*, p. 134.
35. Henry, *L'Essence de la manifestation*, p. 349. 'Immanence has been defined by reference to transcendence and through the exclusion of the latter from its internal structure' (Henry, *L'Essence de la manifestation*, p. 281).
36. Derrida, *De la Grammatologie*, p. 99.

    it would not mean a single step outside of metaphysics if nothing more than a new motif of 'return to finitude,' of 'God's death,' etc., were the result of this move. It is that conceptuality and that problematics that must be deconstructed. They belong to the onto-theology they fight against. Differance is also something other than 'finitude' (Derrida, *Of Grammatology*, p. 68)

37. Derrida, *Force de loi*, p. 60; Derrida, 'Force of Law', p. 27.
38.

    'A thinking that is entirely to come!' How irritating is this post-Heideggerian style of the perpetual announcement, of the interminable to-come; this sort of secularised prophecy never ceases to declare that we are not yet in a position to think what is to be thought, this pathos of having-to-respond to being, this God who is lacking, this waiting before the abyss, this posture of gazing far into the mist and saying that we see the indistinct approaching! How we long to say: 'Listen, if this thinking is still entirely to come, come back and see us when at least a piece of it has arrived!' (author's translation)

39. See in particular Hent de Vries, *Philosophy and the Turn to Religion* (Baltimore: Johns Hopkins University Press, 1999), and Janicaud, *Le Tournant théologique de la phénoménologie française* [*Phenomenology and the 'Theological Turn'*].
40. Critchley, 'Mystical anarchism', p. 272.
41. Lévinas, *Totalité et infini*, p. 22; 'from a land not of our birth' (Lévinas, *Totality and Infinity*, p. 33).
42. Lévinas, *De Dieu qui vient à l'idée*, p. 8.

    Questions relative to God are not resolved by answers in which the interrogation ceases to resonate or is wholly pacified. [...] One wonders whether it is possible to speak legitimately of God without striking a blow against the absoluteness that this world seems to signify. (Lévinas, *Of God who Comes to Mind*, pp. xi–xii)

43. Marion, *Réduction et donation*, p. 7; 'toward a thought that is perhaps already postmetaphysical' (Marion, *Reduction and Givenness*, p. 1).
44. Ricœur, *Le Conflit des interprétations*, p. 431.

    If the title 'The Religious Meaning of Atheism' is not nonsensical, it implies that atheism does not exhaust its signification in the mere negation and destruction of religion but that, rather, it opens up the horizon for something else, for a type of faith that might be called [. . .] a postreligious faith. (Ricœur, *The Conflict of Interpretations*, p. 436; translation altered)

45. Jean-Luc Marion, 'Preface to the English edition', in *God Without Being*, p. xxiv.
46. Merleau-Ponty, *Le Primat de la perception et ses conséquences philosophiques*, p. 72.

    Nietzsche's idea that God is dead is already contained in the Christian idea of the death of God. God ceases to be an external object in order to mingle in human life, and this life is not simply a return to a non-temporal conclusion. (Merleau-Ponty, *The Primacy of Perception*, p. 27)

47. Marion, *Dieu sans l'être, L'Idole et la distance*.
48. Marion, 'Preface', in *God Without Being*, p. xxiv.
49. Marion, 'Preface', in *God Without Being*, pp. xix–xx.
50. Marion, *L'Idole et la distance*, p. 185; 'undone from any relation and therefore also from any thinkable relation, which would tie it to an absurd "other than it"' (Marion, *The Idol and Distance*, p. 141).
51. Marion, *L'Idole et la distance*, p. 16; *The Idol and Distance*, p. 1.
52. Marion, *L'Idole et la distance*, p. 16; *The Idol and Distance*, p. 1.
53. Vattimo, 'A prayer for silence', p. 91; GV's italics.
54. Vattimo, 'A prayer for silence', p. 95.
55. Vattimo, *After Christianity*, p. 17.
56. Caputo, 'On the power of the powerless', p. 133.
57. Janicaud, *Le Tournant théologique*, p. 86; *Phenomenology and the 'Theological Turn'*, p. 99.
58. Janicaud, *Le Tournant théologique*, p. 28; *Phenomenology and the 'Theological Turn'*, p. 38.
59. Janicaud, *Le Tournant théologique*, p. 89; *Phenomenology and the 'Theological Turn'*, p. 103.
60. Janicaud, *Le Tournant théologique*, p. 31; 'phenomenology has been taken hostage by a theology that does not want to speak its name' (Janicaud, *Phenomenology and the 'Theological Turn'*, p. 43).
61. A cluster of texts in recent years has brought Paul up the philosophical agenda. See: Giorgio Agamben, *The Time That Remains: A Commentary on the Letter to the Romans* (Stanford: Stanford University Press, 2005); Badiou, *Saint Paul: La Fondation de l'universalisme* [*Saint Paul: The Foundation of Universalism*]; Daniel Boyarin, *A Radical Jew: Paul and the Politics of Identity* (London: University of California Press, 1994); Jacob Taubes, *The Political Theology of Paul*; John D. Caputo and Linda Martin Alcoff (eds), *St Paul Among the Philosophers* (Bloomington: Indiana University Press, 2009).
62. See Žižek, *The Fragile Absolute*; *On Belief*; *The Puppet and the Dwarf*; as well as extended treatments of religious themes in other texts, notably *The*

Parallax View, not to mention the numerous articles and interviews on themes such as faith, fundamentalism, the suffering God and divine love, and Žižek's self-definition as a 'fighting atheist'.
63. The term 'post-theological' has been employed by the theologian Stanley James Grenz to indicate what he perceives to be the theological consequences of a 'post-Christian' and 'postmodern' culture. See Grenz, *Renewing the Center*. David Crownfield equates the term to a *via negativa* and Mark Taylor's 'atheological erring'; see Crownfield, 'Extraduction', in *Lacan and Theological Discourse*, p. 162. Scattered English references elsewhere, and references in French to the *post-théologique*, tend to mean either 'atheistic' in the traditional sense, or postmodern. In these pages we are using the term with quite a different meaning.
64. To use the term 'atheology' would confuse this umbrella term with Nancy's atheology, and to use 'atheism' would confuse it with Badiou's atheism. 'Post-theological' is a neutral term intended to predispose to neither a Nancean nor a Badiousian reading.
65. Nietzsche, *The Gay Science*, p. 182.

1. *The God of Metaphysics*

> On dit fort bien que si les triangles faisaient un Dieu, ils lui donneraient trois côtés.[1]

> Mathematics is the science in which we never know what we are talking about, nor whether what we are saying is true.[2]

'Je prends au pied de la lettre la formule «Dieu est mort». [. . .] Dieu, c'est fini. Et la religion aussi, c'est fini' (*CT* 12).[3] This striking intervention in the prologue of Badiou's *Court Traité d'ontologie transitoire* is not merely a claim that the moral God is dead, much less that the death of God is one move in a wider Christian dialectic. By claiming that God is dead Badiou is doing more therefore than echoing Nietzsche's madman. For Badiou as for Heidegger, Nietzsche's claim that God is dead is not yet without God, for the theistic schema of the sensory and the suprasensory still dominates Nietzsche's thought.[4] In other words, there remains in Nietzsche's thinking the Pascalian infinite abyss that can be filled only with an infinite and immutable object.[5] When pressed, therefore, Badiou maintains a position more radical than Nietzsche's: 'Mon propos n'a rapport à aucune religion, et c'est pourquoi il peut librement les traiter toutes comme schèmes de l'esthétique historiale. Dieu n'est pas même mort, pour moi (ce mort est encore l'interlocuteur constant de Nietzsche)' (19R 262).[6]

Badiou concurs in his analysis of the death of God, so he tells us, with Jean-Luc Nancy's assertion that the death of God is irreversible (*CT* 12/*BOE* 23). But this moment of supposed agreement between Badiou and Nancy belies the fact that, despite the respect they demonstrate for each other's work, their readings of the 'death of God', present to us two radically divergent attempts to move beyond atheism's impasse of parasitism (seeking to be rid of God in ways that assume or require God) and asceticism (renouncing, along with God, the notions of truth, goodness and beauty that he underwrites). The stakes of this antagonism are double: not only do the arguments that pass between Badiou and Nancy shape our sense of what the death of God can mean for the future of post-theological thought, as well as for philosophical ethics and politics, but in addition they stage *en abyme* an encounter the stakes of which will do much to direct the future of Continental thought itself: the encounter between philosophies of finitude and philosophies of the infinite.

Starting from Badiou's account of the death of God, this chapter begins our exploration of the contrasting treatment of theological themes in Badiou and Nancy, and also opens a concurrent investigation into the scope for staging a productive encounter between Nancean finitude and the Badiouian infinite.[7] We begin to explore how Nancy and Badiou understand finitude and the infinite differently, to probe the reasons for – and consequences of – their divergent understandings, and to ask to what extent they may eventually be commensurable. Our intention is to resist sliding into either a Nancean or a Badiouian position – though our sympathies will no doubt be evident and we make no pretence of disguising them – and to seek instead to vindicate the hypothesis that bringing Badiou's and Nancy's thinking into conversation will be productive for our understanding of each of the two thinkers, the current possibilities of post-theological integration, and the possible futures of French thought.

1.1 THE DEATH OF THE GOD OF METAPHYSICS

Peter Hallward is surely correct in his emphatically ambiguous comment that '[n]o one, perhaps, has taken the death of God as seriously as Badiou',[8] a seriousness manifest not least in the care with which Badiou disambiguates the different meanings of 'God is dead'. In the prologue to *Court Traité d'ontologie transitoire* he identifies three 'major gods' (*dieux capitaux*, CT 22/BOE 30), each requiring its own mode of despatch: the God of religions, the God of metaphysics and the God of the poets. For the God of religions it is sufficient merely to declare that he is dead; the God of metaphysics must be brought to an end by a thinking of infinity disseminated in multiplicity rather than gathered in the One, and the God of the poets is expunged by breaking the poetic disposition to think in terms of the Romantic loss and return of the divine (*CT* 23/ *BOE* 31). While the death of the God of religions is considered a historical datum and – somewhat problematically – receives little further mention from Badiou, there is so much at stake in his treatment of the gods of metaphysics and the poets that we need to take them one at a time, and slowly. The present chapter will consider Badiou's account of the death of the God of metaphysics, while Chapter 2 will examine the death of the God of the poets.

Badiou's God of metaphysics[9] is the God of Aristotle, an intellectual agent separate from the material world, a set of operations that completes the Aristotelian theory of substance by accounting for the relationship between matter and form, and between the one and the many. It is the Prime, Unmoved Mover that, in its immobile eternity, remains completely indifferent to that which it moves (*CT* 15/*BOE* 25). It is the conceptual God of Descartes, the placeholder of the infinite, the glue bonding mathematical truths to the world of extension, or the (Kantian) big Other as guarantor of the validity of judgments. In short, it is a god-as-principle (*dieu-principe*, *CT* 18, 19/*BOE* 28).[10]

Badiou identifies the supposed transcendence of the God of metaphysics as a construct of the philosophical identification of the One with infinity, made possible by philosophy's adherence to the disastrous notion of finitude. That is to say, since at least as far back as Galileo and Descartes, God has occupied the inaccessible and impregnable position of being the only actual infinity (*CT* 10/*BOE* 22), a position which residual atheism endorses through its denial that there exists an actual infinite. Badiou cites Leibniz as the emblematic exponent of this position in his assertion that '« Il appartient à l'essence du nombre, de la ligne, et d'un tout quelconque, d'être borné. » Et « le vrai infini à la rigueur n'est que dans l'absolu, qui est antérieur à toute composition, et n'est point formé par l'addition de parties »' (*CT* 115).[11] Furthermore, metaphysics can be defined as the enframing of Being by the One (*arraisonnement de l'être par l'un*, *CT* 26/*BOE* 34). Once more Badiou turns to Leibniz for the paradigmatic formulation of this position, for it is Leibniz who establishes the norm of the reciprocity of being and the One in the maxim '« Ce qui n'est pas *un* être n'est pas un *être* »' (*CT* 26; AB's emphasis).[12]

Given that the God of metaphysics is a god-principle it is misplaced, Badiou insists, to suggest that this God is dead, for that would imply that it was once alive, or is capable of life, which as a principle it is not.[13] The God of metaphysics is properly neither 'alive' nor 'dead'. However, in so far as it entertains no relationship either with life or with death, from the point of view of life and religion it is perfectly dead (*CT* 16/*BOE* 26), dead since the beginning, and no religion can nourish its faith on this non-existent corpse (*CT* 14/*BOE* 25). The god-principle, a pseudonymous deity of many guises, has not been quashed, merely chased into ever remoter corners of the philosophical landscape: it is holed up in actual infinity by Descartes and Galileo, relieved of its providential oversight of the world by the Enlightenment, transmuted into the figure of 'man' in the imitative atheism of post-Cartesian humanism (*S* 237/*Cen* 168), evicted from actual infinity by Georg Cantor, and sequestrated in projections of familial organisation by Feuerbach and psychoanalysis (*CT* 10–11/*BOE* 22). It is clear, then, that the demise of the god-principle of metaphysics is no swift affair.

1.1.1 The Birth of Philosophy

The tool which Badiou employs both to have done with the God of metaphysics and to loosen the infinite from the grip of the One is mathematics, and he finds a model for its employment in the birth of philosophy, which he traces to Plato. In contrast to the poetic form that allows Parmenidean thought to maintain its discourse in the proximity of the sacred, for his part Badiou insists that philosophy can only begin with a desacralisation, installing a regime of discourse that provides its own, resolutely worldly, legitimation. Philosophy began in Greece because there alone the matheme allowed for the interruption of the sacred mytheme (*C* 95/*Con* 37).[14] The philosophical miracle of Greece is to be ascribed not to the mythic and poetic richness of that culture, nor to its poetry's grasp of the sacred, but rather to its *interruption* of sacred cosmogonies and opinion by secularised and abstract thought, and truth (*M* 14/*Man* 34): 'la mathématique est le seul point de rupture avec la *doxa* qui soit donné comme existant, ou constitué. La singularité absolue des mathématiques est au fond leur existence' (*C* 167).[15]

For his own part, Badiou describes his recourse to mathematics in terms that resemble those of a crusade:

> it is by donning the contemporary matheme like a coat of armour that I have undertaken, alone at first, to undo the disastrous consequences of philosophy's 'linguistic turn'; to demarcate philosophy from phenomenological religiosity; [...] to identify generic multiplicities as the ontological form of the true. (M&P 16–17)

It is by recourse to the matheme that Badiou seeks to have done with residual atheism's implicit assumption of a domain beyond its own purview.

Although the Platonic interruption of the mytheme by the matheme took place within a given historico-cultural context, Badiou insists that it must not be viewed in a historicist perspective. In the essay 'Le (Re)tour de la philosophie elle-même' (*C* 57–78/*Con* 3–22), he expands on five propositions concerning the relation of philosophy to history, five propositions which will provide the framework for our comparison of Nancy and Badiou in this chapter. They amount to an attack on what Badiou sees as the danger of inscribing philosophy within a finite historical horizon. Philosophy today is paralysed by its relation to its own history (proposition 1) because philosophy no longer knows whether it has a place of its own, scattered and subordinated as it is in a host of disciplines including art, poetry, science, political action and psychoanalysis, with the desultory consequence that philosophy has become little more than its own museum (C 57/Con 3). It therefore becomes imperative for philosophy to break decisively with historicism (proposition 2), which means that philosophy's self-presentation must in the first instance make no reference to its history; its concepts must be presented without having to appear before the tribunal of their historical moment, for it is philosophy which judges history, and not the reverse (C 58/Con 5). If philosophy is thus to be freed from the vicissitudes of historicism it must be defined in a historically invariable way (proposition 3), and in a way that distinguishes it from sophism (proposition 4), where Badiou understands the emblematic contemporary sophism to be the Wittgensteinian reduction of thought to the ascetic dichotomy of language games and pure, silent 'indication' (C 60/Con 6, cf. W 55–7). So philosophy as understood by Plato is both possible and necessary (proposition 5) in the face of the modern sophism of Nietzsche, Wittgenstein, Vattimo and Rorty.

For Badiou, the sundering of philosophy from mathematics is a state from within which our contemporary situation cannot fully prosecute the agenda of the death of God:

> L'embarras contemporain quant au thème de la mort de Dieu, sinon dans son énoncé, du moins dans son effectivité, doit être renvoyé à ceci que le délaissement de la pensée mathématique par la philosophie livre l'infini, dans le médium de l'Histoire, à un nouvel avatar de l'Un. (C 164)[16]

In order to crush odious superstition, we must turn to the solid, secular eternity of the sciences (C 164/TW 26), and forge a wholly new relation for mathematics and philosophy (C 165/TW 27). Badiou's prognosis is categorical: finitude is constitutive of the residual atheism that always leaves room for God: 'Athées, nous n'avons pas les moyens de l'être, tant que le thème de la finitude organise notre pensée' (C 164),[17] and, conversely, '[l]a thèse de l'infinité de l'être est nécessairement postchrétienne' (EE 162).[18] However, it is far from clear that the thesis of the infinity of being is indeed necessarily post-Christian. Was not Georg Cantor, the pioneer of set theory and the mathematician to whom Badiou credits the 'genuine killing' of God (C 303/Con 225), himself a

Catholic who saw no necessary tension between his transfinite numbers and his faith? For Cantor, God is neither finite nor infinite. If such a God were to feature in a given philosophy, Badiou could gain no purchase on it by his insistence on the infinity of being. Such a God is sketched by Adam Drozdek,[19] who, starting from the position that, for Augustine, 'all infinity is certainly made finite to God',[20] concludes that the Augustinian God 'is neither finite nor infinite and his greatness surpasses even the infinite'.[21] Like Virgil's reed, when one god is plucked another grows in its place;[22] there are potentially as many gods of the philosophers as there are philosophers.

Drozdek sees an affinity to Augustine's position in the Cantorian 'absolute infinite', which Cantor situates beyond the finite/infinite dichotomy. After distinguishing between the bad infinite of endless succession and the actual infinite, Cantor subdivides the latter into the transfinite and the absolute infinite.[23] The absolute infinite is beyond the dichotomy of the finite and the infinite; by contrast with the transfinite, the absolute infinite cannot be surpassed in cardinality by ever greater infinities, and again unlike the transfinite it cannot be determined by mathematics: 'It belongs particularly to speculative theology to investigate the absolute infinite and to determine what can be humanly said about it. On the other side, the questions about the transfinite belong chiefly to the domain of metaphysics and mathematics.'[24]

The Cantorian absolute infinite, if it is admitted, would prove deadly to Badiou's prosecution of the death of God, for the transfinite multiplication of infinities and the position that 'the One is not' would no longer be sufficient to foreclose the possibility of the god-principle of metaphysics. For Badiou's position to hold, there can be nothing that is beyond or otherwise than the dichotomy of the finite and the infinite; if there were it would reinscribe Badiou's mathematising move as an ascetic atheism, placing God beyond the purview of the mathematical infinite, serenely untouched by any set-theoretical proclamation that 'the One is not'. The absolute infinite opens an alternative reading of Badiou's recourse to mathematics, not this time as the triumph of post-theological thinking but rather as a fact that 'can be used by theologians [to substantiate] that God simply must surpass all infinities and in this sense he is not infinite – he is the Absolute'.[25] Such a God, outside the finite/infinite dichotomy, would simply not be thinkable set-theoretically.

Not surprisingly, therefore, Badiou gives short shrift to the Cantorian absolute infinite. He ascribes it to 'la folie de sauver Dieu, c'est-à-dire l'un, de toute présomption absolue du multiple' (*EE* 54),[26] and dismisses the move as a mathematical god of the gaps. Furthermore, Zermelo-Fraenkel axiomatised set theory provides Badiou with a mathematically orthodox alternative to Cantor's absolute infinity.[27] ZFC indeed furnishes possible, but not necessary, grounds to reject Cantor's absolute infinite, and a complete account of Badiou's foreclosure of residual atheism through his rejection of the Cantorian absolute infinite in favour of ZFC requires an axiomatic move, namely that 'nothing is inaccessible' to set-theoretical counting as one.[28] It is not the recourse to set theory itself that secures Badiou's post-theological thinking,[29] but the particular version of set theory he chooses; Badiou can only escape the possibility of ascetic atheism through axiomatic decision. We shall scrutinise this reliance on axioms further in Chapter 3.

1.1.2 *The Multiple And The Infinite*

The mathematical rupture from the mytheme takes the form, in Badiou's own thinking, of the radically new understanding of multiplicity and infinity brought about by set theory. What the death of God demands, Badiou argues, is a thinking of the infinite on the basis of a multiplicity that is no longer derived from a prior One: 'Du Dieu de la métaphysique, il faut achever le parcours par une pensée de l'infini qui en dissémine la ressource sur l'étendue entière des multiplicités quelconques' (*CT* 22).[30]

Much of twentieth century French thought is an attempt to think just such a multiplicity, but for Badiou all previous endeavours fall short. Derridean *dissémination*, the Lyotardian *différend*, Lacan's 'dispersive punctuality of the real' and the virtual/actual distinction in Deleuze[31] all seek to elaborate an ontology beginning with a multiple irreducible to any One, but do so, for Badiou, in an 'impure' way. In each case the multiple is the multiple *of* something, or in other words what is presented as multiple is something other than presentation itself (*EE* 38/*BE* 30); presentation makes reference to some substantial difference outside itself.[32] To these various expressions of 'impure' multiplicity Badiou contrasts his own pure or 'inconsistent' multiplicity which cannot be defined (*CT* 31/*BOE* 37) and which is reduced, in the absence of any immanent unification, to the sole predicate of its multiplicity (*CT* 34/*BOE* 40).

For Badiou inconsistent multiplicity is the 'phantom' of the count (*EE* 66/*BE* 53). Nothing can be known about the inconsistent multiplicity that is counted as one, other than that it is not one. Furthermore, it can only be retroactively assumed (*EE* 65/*BE* 52) to be not-one in the wake of the axiomatic decision that one-ness itself is only ever the result of a counting-as-one (*EE* 33/*BE* 25). The recourse to inconsistent multiplicity is the result of a decision on Badiou's part, a decision intended to allow him to elaborate an ontology in which God – as the metaphysical One – is not simply absent, peripheral or irrelevant, but strictly impossible.[33]

Though the 'inconsistent multiplicity' that is presented in the count as one of being is not one, it is important to note that, for Badiou, it is not strictly multiple either: 'Est-ce à dire que l'être n'est pas non plus multiple ? A la rigueur, oui, car il n'est multiple qu'autant qu'il advient à la présentation' (*EE* 32).[34] It is therefore not correct to say that, for Badiou, pure being is multiple; it is the presentation of being that is multiple: what *presents* itself is always multiple, but *what* presents itself is neither one nor multiple. Being itself is simply inaccessible outside its presentation as multiple. Badiou passes through this point only briefly in the first meditation of *L'Être et l'événement*, but Peter Hallward clarifies the idea as he glosses Badiou's inconsistent multiplicity, insisting that any determination of being as multiple 'would reintroduce a kind of one beyond the multiple or reduce the sphere of the multiple itself to a kind of bounded unity. Pure multiplicity must not itself be made to consist.'[35] But this purity of being occupies a problematic place in Badiou's thought. The 'multiplicity' of this inconsistent multiplicity is arrived at in a roundabout manner, through a deduction from the decision that the One is not, namely that '*if* the one is not, only what is not one, or multiple, can be'.[36] In a move from which it is hard to dispel all shadows of begging the question, the retroactive reasoning is that '[t]he one is not, precisely because ones, unifications, come to be as results'.[37] This is the final reason why Badiou's mathematics must be axiomatic; there is no other way to eradicate the one and, with it, the God of metaphysics.

Inconsistent multiplicity can be secured only by recourse to mathematics, and its implications are given ontological purchase by Badiou's equation of ontology with mathematics. The meta-mathematical statement 'ontologie = mathématique' (see, for example *EE* 12/*BE* 6, *CT* 55/ *BOE* 59) is not a thesis about the world, but about discourse (*EE* 14/ *BE* 8); it does not mean that, for Badiou, ontology is nothing but the language of mathematics, but rather that set-theoretical mathematics provides us with a way to speak of being qua being, that is, of pure multiplicity. But how can Badiou hold this equation of ontology and mathematics? Badiou can jump the gap between formalised mathematics and ontology by virtue of his understanding of the one point at which formalised mathematics asserts existence, namely the void or empty set. The empty set is the one point of contact between mathematics and ontology, unifying matheme and *logos*. Even though inconsistency cannot be intuited or accessed directly it is not correct to assert that inconsistency does not exist; we must rather say: inconsistency is nothing (*EE* 67/*BE* 54). There is no intuition of this nothing (or, more precisely, of this void), but there is nevertheless a 'being of nothing', that Badiou calls the unpresentable (*l'imprésentable*) (*EE* 67/*BE* 54). Every ontological situation has its unpresentable: that which does not appear in the situation because it is not counted as one. Once Badiou has asserted that all countings as one are modalities-according-to-the-one of the void (*EE* 70/*BE* 57), it follows that the only thing that exists is the void (*EE* 71/*BE* 58). The empty set of set theory, from which all other sets can be constructed, is to a set as, ontologically speaking, the unpresentable is to a situation. Both ontologically and set-theoretically speaking, all that exists is the void in its infinite modalities.

Yet this alone does not secure for the matheme an ontological reach. The second element of Badiou's link between ontology and mathematics is that the empty set is the object of an axiom (*EE* 73/*BE* 60). Inconsistency cannot be intuited or presented, and there is no definition of the multiple, so the existence of the empty set can only be the object of an axiom. It is by virtue, then, of the axiom of the empty set, that Badiou seeks to justify his equation of ontology and mathematics. We shall explore the place of axioms in Badiou's thought in more detail in Chapters 2 and 3.

For Badiou, the pure multiplicity of being after the death of God can have only one name: mathematical set theory (*NN* 86/*NuN* 65). Nevertheless, it is far from clear why 'ontology = mathematics' should be the same as 'ontology = ZFC set theory'. As Quentin Meillassoux points out in his critique of Badiou in 'Nouveauté et événement', not all mathematical perspectives are equally compatible with Badiou's philosophy of truth and the event (*NE* 41). In fact, only the doctrine of the generic will do, to the exclusion of the axioms of constructability or large cardinals.[38] For Badiou, the history of mathematics must be subordinated to thinking the event. To say that mathematics = ontology is to give to ontology a history, but in order truly to affirm that mathematics has a history, we would need to consider truth and event themselves as notions that could be historically superseded (*NE* 43). In the words of Jean-Michel Salanskis, ZFC set theoretical mathematics is for Badiou the right ontology (*la bonne ontologie*), the one that allows us to think being as multiple,[39] and thereby to banish the God of metaphysics identified with the One.

As for the infinite, Badiou argues that reserving the category of 'actual infinity' for God in Western monotheistic thought brought no radical break with Greek finitism. Infinity – or 'infinitude', as we can call this monotheistic infinite, to distinguish it from Badiou's actual infinity[40] – is ascribed not to the natural world but to the divine One, preserving the finitude of natural being (*EE* 163/*BE* 144). Badiou's critique of infinitude is a critique of ascetic atheism, for infinity is merely the transcendent region of being-as-a-whole and does not threaten the essential thesis of the finitude of being. In fact, it relies upon it, as it secures a dwelling place for the divine beyond the finite limits of being. A theology of the infinite is perfectly compatible with an ontology of the finite (*EE* 161/*BE* 143), and so it remains that 'the only really contemporary requirement for philosophy since Nietzsche is the secularisation of infinity' (*BN* 86). This is a necessary requirement not least because Badiou identifies the infinite as a site for the re-insinuation of the one (*C* 164/*TW* 27).

The 'desacralising' remedy for this latent unity is the set-theoretical actual infinite, an infinite which is flat (as opposed to transcendent), plural (as opposed to unique), local (as opposed to universal) and natural (as opposed to divine) (*CT* 22/*BOE* 30; *LM* 121/*LW* 111; *C* 164/*Con* 99; *EE* 169/*BE* 150). Badiou admires and adopts Richard Dedekind's (1831–1916) definition of the infinite: '« Un système S est dit infini quand il est semblable à une de ses parties propres; dans le cas opposé, S est dit un système fini »' (*NN* 51).[41]

This definition of infinity is simple, primary and positive: an infinite system has the positive characteristic of a biunivocal correspondence between itself and one of its own parts. By comparison with this simple, affirmative elegance, finitude is secondary, rare, complex and lacking; the finite is that which lacks a biunivocal correspondence with one of its own parts. The finite is that which is not infinite (*NN* 25/*NuN* 36), the negation or limitation of the simple and positive multiple (*C* 176/*Con* 110; cf. *NN* 110/*NuN* 85; *EE* 179/*BE* 159). The difficulty for philosophy therefore is not in thinking the infinite, but in thinking the finite.

The confusion in which philosophy finds itself today over the implications of the death of God, if not over its pronouncement, is therefore due to philosophy's own decoupling from mathematics, leaving the infinite trapped in a historicism that makes it a new avatar of the One (*C* 164/*TW* 27). By contrast, set theory admits an infinity of infinities, completing the Cantorian project of a total dissemination and dis-unification of the concept of the infinite (*EE* 305/*BE* 277), and foreclosing the 'forme retournée ou détournée de la finitude, d'un horizon inappropriable, ou innommable, de divinité immortelle' (*C* 164).[42] We simply do not possess the capacity to be (post-theological) atheists so long as the theme of finitude governs our thinking (*C* 163/*TW* 26).

The great achievement of mathematics for Badiou is to have 1) rendered the infinite primary, more commonplace and easier to manipulate than finitude and 2) irrevocably separated the concept of infinity from the divine or quasi-divine One. The primacy and ubiquity of the infinite also allow Badiou to make the claim that the death of God, far from ascetically robbing us of actual infinity and consigning our thinking thereby to an interminable finitude, in fact delivers us to the omnipresent infinity of thought, leaving finitude itself simply as a vestige of the tyranny of the sacred (*NN* 110/*NuN* 86). Though we lose with the death of God the divine actual infinite, we gain an infinity of infinites.

We might question to what extent the primacy of the infinite over the finite is a secularising move. Adam Miller argues that the position whereby 'finitude is derived from the pure multiplicity proper to infinity' is common to Badiou and St Paul.[43] For Paul, the infinite gift of grace whereby 'Jesus demonstrates that God's commitment to us is infinite and that it holds nothing in reserve' is contrasted to the finite debt of sin where 'we are sinfully engaged in the suppression of the truth about our dependence on God's grace because *we* mistook that grace for a debt'.[44] But Miller surely equivocates over 'infinity', for the divine infinite of Paul cannot be equated to the post-Cantorian dissemination of the infinite in multiplicity.

The thesis of the infinity of being, like the empty set, is necessarily axiomatic, for 'sans cette décision, il restera toujours possible que l'être soit essentiellement fini' (*EE* 167),[45] and a finite being is open to the mystical apophaticism of ascetic atheism. Badiou's verdict on the set-theoretical conjunction of the multiple and the infinite is categorical: in giving rise to a thought in which the infinite is irreversibly separated from every instance of the One, mathematics has in fact accomplished the programme of the death of God (*C* 175/*Con* 110). In summary, Badiou claims to have comprehensively despatched the God of metaphysics along with its support in ontological finitude. Now we turn to Nancy, and to his very different account of the death of the God of metaphysics. We will soon find that Badiou's philosophy of the infinite also faces accusations harbouring latent and undisclosed theological assumptions.

1.2 THE METAPHYSICS OF THE DEATH OF GOD

In his discussion of the death of God in the prologue to the *Court Traité*, Badiou refers approvingly to Nancy with the words 'Dieu, c'est fini. Et la religion aussi, c'est fini. Il y a là, comme Jean-Luc Nancy l'a fortement énoncé, de l'irréversible' (*CT* 12).[46] There are two candidate passages in the Nancean corpus that refer to the religious in such terms, but both of them challenge Badiou's wider point about the birth of philosophy. We begin our discussion of Nancy by quoting them both in context and at length:

> Il n'y a pas de retour du religieux : il y a les contorsions et les boursouflures de son épuisement. Que cet épuisement fasse place à un autre souci des dieux, à leur errance ou à leur disparition infinie, ou encore à pas de dieu, c'est une autre affaire: c'est une tout autre question, ce n'est rien dont on puisse s'emparer avec les pinces du religieux, *ni du reste avec celles de l'athéisme*. Pas de dieu: ce serait, ou ce sera, sans rapport avec l'athéisme – du moins avec *cet athéisme métaphysique, pendant du théisme, et qui veut mettre quelque chose à la place du dieu nié ou réfuté*. (DLD 33; author's emphasis)[47]

> Le « retour du religieux » dont on parle tant, et qui désigne un phénomène réel, ne mérite pas plus d'attention qu'aucun autre « retour ». Dans les phénomènes de répétition, de reprise, de relance ou de revenance, ce qui compte n'est jamais l'identique mais le différent. Car l'identique perd d'emblée son identité dans son propre retour, et *la question devrait bien plutôt se poser sans cesse à nouveaux frais, de savoir ce que la « sécularisation » peut désigner et désigne inévitablement d'autre qu'un simple transfert de l'identique*. (DDC 9; author's emphasis)[48]

If the death of God for Nancy is irreversible, then it is not to the obvious benefit either of atheism or of secularisation, and it is around these initial dissonances between Nancy's and Badiou's accounts that we propose to begin the dialogue between them. We shall see that Nancy elaborates a very different account of the death of the God of metaphysics from Badiou's, one that discerns in Badiou's atheism a certain parasitism, but that cannot escape the same charge itself. We shall begin to discern two very different ways to appropriate the death of God that are vying to shape the future of Continental thought, for despite his rejection of Badiou's atheism, Nancy still characterises his thought as atheistic, though not without hesitation.[49] In order to understand why these disagreements matter, we need to consider what Nancy says about metaphysics, the God of metaphysics, and the death of the God of metaphysics.

Nancy's 'Philosophie sans conditions' details his response to some aspects of Badiou's early philosophy in *L'Etre et l'événement*. In a remarkable interweaving of different levels of argument, the paper sets a meditation on the nature of metaphysics *en abyme* inside the question of the possibility of Badiou and Nancy sharing 'cet espace commun dans lequel sont possibles de telles hétérotopies, et dans lequel elles sont mêmes nécessaires' (PSC 65).[50] Both elements of Nancy's argument develop out of propositions from Badiou's 'Le (Re)tour de la philosophie elle-même' (C 57–78/*Con* 3–22). Nancy's resistance to the way in which Badiou dispatches the God of metaphysics focuses on Badiou's second proposition, namely that philosophy must break decisively with historicism or, in other words, that philosophy does not have historical conditions (PSC 66–7/PWC 40). The question of the possibility of a heterotopic relation[51] between Badiouian and Nancean philosophy takes issue with the third proposition, namely that philosophy must be defined in a historically invariable way, with Nancy insisting that 'la définition de la philosophie doit admettre sa propre démultiplication' (PSC 66).[52] Furthermore, Nancy's two concerns are intertwined: the question of how metaphysics constitutes itself is, as we shall see, vital to the possibility of Nancy's heterotopic philosophical relation to Badiou.

Nancy focuses his engagement with Badiou predominantly on one passage from 'Le (Re)tour de la philosophie elle-même', taken from the section dealing with Badiou's first proposition, which we quote here in full, maintaining Nancy's ellipses and insertion:

> L'idée dominante [dans la veine heideggérienne] est que la métaphysique est historiquement épuisée, mais que l'au-delà de cet épuisement ne nous est pas encore donné. [. . .] La philosophie est alors prise entre l'épuisement de sa possibilité historiale et la venue sans concept d'un retournement salvateur. La philosophie contemporaine combine la déconstruction de son passé et l'attente vide de son avenir. Tout mon propos est de rompre avec ce diagnostic. [. . .] *La philosophie doit rompre, de l'intérieur d'elle-même, avec l'historicisme.* (C 58, as quoted in PSC 69)[53]

Nancy discerns here a double misunderstanding on Badiou's part, first in relation to the 'exhaustion of the historical possibility' of metaphysics and 'the deconstruction of its past', and secondly regarding 'the non-conceptual arrival of a salutary overturning' and 'the empty expectation of its future'. It will take us this chapter and the next to tease out all the vast consequences of Nancy's response to this supposed double misunderstanding. This chapter will consider the deconstruction of philosophy's past in relation to the God of metaphysics, and Chapter 2 will reflect on the empty expectation of its future in terms of the God of the poets.

1.2.1 The 'Death' of God and the 'End' of Metaphysics

Nancy's reading of Badiou on the history of philosophy culminates in the following argument: not to recognise the historicity of metaphysics, far from being a final break with the God of metaphysics, is itself an onto-theological move, and so the 'God of metaphysics' and Badiou's atheism in fact share a particular situation in, and view of, history. In other words, Nancy is accusing Badiou's atheism of a certain parasitism upon the God he is trying to banish. To track how the argument builds to this conclusion, we need to follow three steps.

The first step concerns the relation between history and metaphysics, and the status of any claim that metaphysics is finished. In 'L'Offrande réservée',[54] a paper devoted to Nancy's finite thinking, Badiou reads Nancy as endorsing the Heideggerian announcement of the end of philosophy, an announcement which itself forms a programme of thought (OR 17). This reading is inexact. Nancy's preferred articulation is not that philosophy-as-metaphysics is finished, but that it is exhausted, and that this exhaustion is what is indicated by the 'death of God' (OP 64-5). Nancy clarifies that we only say that metaphysics has 'ended' 'pour dire qu'elle épuise ce qui prétendrait achever aussi bien sa rétrospection que sa prospection. L'une et l'autre doivent être inachevables, elles doivent être l'inachèvement même, conformément à l'essence de la philosophie' (PSC 73).[55]

To say that metaphysics is exhausted is not the same as saying that it has ended, because what metaphysics has exhausted *is* its end. For Nancy, metaphysics is understood, in terms of its history, as the double postulation of a step back into the immemorial and a step forward into unarrival (*l'inadvenir*) (PSC 73/PWC 48), and the end of metaphysics is thus the end of the possibility this sort of self-grounding: it cannot exhaustively account for its own origin (i.e. 'complete its retrospection') or exhaustively predetermine its own end (i.e. 'complete... its prospection'). The end of metaphysics, the exhaustion of its self-completion, is nothing other than the opening of metaphysics.

In this context (step two), Nancy's reading of the 'death of God' comes as a direct challenge to Badiou's account of the ahistorical condition of philosophy:

> Ce qui fut nommé « mort de Dieu », et plus tard « fin de la métaphysique », ou même « fin de la philosophie », a consisté à mettre au jour ceci : il n'y a pas de condition première ou dernière, il n'y a pas d'inconditionné qui fasse principe ou origine. Mais cet « il n'y a pas » est inconditionné, et voilà, si j'ose dire, notre « condition humaine ». (CP 12-13)[56]

The meaning of the 'death of God' is just this: that there is no historically unconditioned intervention – in terms either of *archē* or *telos* – which can rescue philosophy from its historical content, apart from the minimal condition of the 'there is no' itself. In other words, on Nancy's reading Badiou's account of the ahistorical condition of philosophy undermines Badiou's own account of the death of God, which is precisely the thesis that Badiou claims it secures. But why would that be so, when Badiou is not claiming mathematics – ahistorical or not – to be of divine origin, nor arguing that his Platonism resolves to some crude substance dualism with a divine world of Ideas?

The problem for Nancy is this: Badiou divorces the history of metaphysics from the metaphysics of history, and presumes to speak of the end of the former as if it had no impact on the latter. For Nancy this is a mistake because metaphysics cannot be thought independently of history, far less exhausted within history. In Nancy's own words, 'l'épuisement de la métaphysique [. . .] n'est historique que pour autant qu'il est lui-même, précisément, l'épuisement de la possibilité historique elle-même (ou du sens de l'histoire)' (PSC 69).[57] The exhaustion of metaphysics cannot be something that happens within a historical narrative that precedes and succeeds it, of which it forms but one chapter among many. The exhaustion of metaphysics has implications for 'history' as such, because what is exhausted *is* history 'as such', history in so far as it has an origin and a *telos*. The exhaustion of metaphysics cannot be merely an exhaustion within history; it must inevitably be the exhaustion of history.

There are two further nuances that need to be brought to an understanding of the relation between philosophy and history for Nancy: the idea of exhaustion 1) is itself metaphysical and 2) constitutes historical possibility proper. First, exhaustion is itself metaphysical because it is only by virtue of a history that posits its own principle and end (i.e. a metaphysical history) that it is possible to speak of 'exhaustion' at all, for what is exhausted (in the sense of fulfilled) is precisely the approximation to history's *telos* (PSC 70/PWC 42). Secondly, exhaustion constitutes historical possibility proper because it is metaphysics' own construal of history that it build towards a *telos*, so exhaustion is itself a metaphysical idea. We can begin to see why the view Badiou is imputing to Nancy, namely that philosophy or metaphysics has ended, could not in Nancy's own terms be the straightforward end that Badiou suggests, but must be a problematic statement irreducibly in tension with itself. This is our first encounter with a misprision on Badiou's part of the meaning of deconstruction, which we shall explore at greater length below.

Whereas Badiou is seeing philosophy and historicism as separable – hence the second proposition of 'Le (Re)tour de la philosophie elle-même', that philosophy must decisively break with historicism – Nancy is maintaining that historicism is a construction of philosophy as metaphysics, that historicism is philosophy's own product. It follows from this Nancean argument that to disengage philosophy from historicism would be to disengage philosophy from 'philosophy', from philosophy-as-metaphysics, in other words it would be to envision a different philosophy, which in turn would be to concede the point that there are, after all, heterotopic definitions of philosophy, and not just one definition of philosophy as Badiou maintains in proposition 3. So Nancy is using proposition 2 of 'Le (Re)tour de la philosophie elle-même' to undermine proposition 3: Badiou cannot *both* say that there is only one philosophy *and* try to disengage philosophy from historicism. Badiou holds that philosophy must break with historicism from within itself (C 58/Con 4), but Nancy's reply is that metaphysical philosophy can only break with historicism by breaking *from* itself, by becoming incommensurable with itself, other than itself.

The third step in the Nancean argument is that this Badiouian relation to history – upon which his dispatch of the God of metaphysics relies, let us remember – is not merely metaphysical, but also Christian. The Christian faith, Nancy argues, is an experience of its own history, the experience of God's plan of salvation, from which it follows that 'la dimension de l'histoire en général, en tant que dimension occidentale, est fondamentalement chrétienne' (*DDC* 212).[58] This does not amount to claiming that all history is Christian history, or that all historians have the whiff of incense about them. Western history is *fundamentally* (though not necessarily *essentially*) Christian in that the relation it assumes between metaphysics and history conforms to the pattern of a Christian eschatology.

In his analysis of the complicity of parasitic atheism with theology, Nancy evokes the 'Christmas projection', according to which 'une naissance pure et simple du christianisme [. . .] un beau jour, advient et change tout' (*DDC* 121).[59] It is in repeating this 'Christmas projection' that our tradition remains Christian: 'toute notre tradition, aussi peu chrétienne qu'elle se veuille, maintient toujours quelque chose de la « projection de Noël » : à un moment donné, « ça » a lieu, et l'on se retrouve ensuite en état chrétien' (*DDC* 121).[60]

Badiou's account of philosophy's ahistorical condition, crucial as it is for his reading of the death of God, is in Nancy's eyes just such a Christmas projection, for it suggests that, at a given moment, the matheme interrupted the mytheme: 'that' takes place, philosophy is born. Philosophy itself may be ahistorical, but Badiou nevertheless requires it to effect a rupture with the mytheme at a particular historical moment. Nancy begins his essay 'La déconstruction du christianisme' with the question 'en quoi et jusqu'à quel point tenons-nous au christianisme ?' (*DDC* 203).[61] In Badiou's case, it appears that Nancy's answer would be: up to and including the point of the death of God. It is to this extent that Badiou's death of God is, on Nancy's reading, a very Christian demise.

So, for Nancy, the way that Badiou frames the proposition that 'God is dead' categorically and literally – 'Je prends au pied de la lettre la formule « Dieu est mort » [. . .] Dieu, c'est fini. Et la religion aussi, c'est fini' (*CT* 12)[62] – re-inscribes itself into metaphysical onto-theology, into the same arche-teleological structure from which it is ostensibly seeking to extricate itself. Bluntly, the charge is that Badiou is bootstrapping the death of God, for:

> On se prend alors à se demander s'il y a quelque discours sur Dieu qui peut s'écarter, si peu que ce soit, de celui de Hegel (fût-il revu), c'est-à-dire du discours de la philosophie, ou encore de *l'onto-théologie (qui culmine dans l'ontothéologie dialectique de la mort de Dieu)*. (DLD 5; author's emphasis)[63]

In other words, theism and atheism – we might use the contraction a/theism – are of a pair, two species of the same genus, reliant on the same logic and differing only in the small matter of either affirming or negating. The discourse of ontotheology is not only confounded by the death of God, but also culminates in it (it is the latter of these two propositions that, on a Nancean reading, Badiou fails to appreciate). A true break with ontotheology cannot therefore be by the way of a self-grounding, ahistorical assertion of the death of God, for such an assertion is parasitic on the ontotheology it seeks to deny. If ontotheology is to be non-parasitically overcome, it is its arche-teleological structure that must be disrupted. This is what Nancy seeks to achieve with his 'deconstruction of Christianity'.

1.2.2 *The Deconstruction of Christianity*

Nancy's own account of the death of God avoids being caught in the parasitic double bind in which Badiou – on Nancy's reading at least – finds himself. In the 'deconstruction of Christianity', deconstruction is understood not only as exhaustion but also as opening and possibility:

> « Déconstruire » signifie dès lors désassembler ce qui s'est édifié sur les commencements pour laisser venir ce qui se creuse sous eux. C'est donc d'un même geste ébranler (non détruire) l'édifice de la tradition philosophique (ou métaphysique) et l'auto-positionnement historique de cette tradition. (PSC 72)[64]

The exhaustion or evacuation of the fullness of history (in terms of its truth or salvation, that is to say of any self-sufficient *archē* or *telos*) opens possibilities not in terms of a re-inscription of the Platonic (or Pauline or Augustinian) moment of the birth of philosophy, but an opening of the beginning itself onto its own anteriority: to deconstruct is not to begin again, but to show that the beginning was already an 'again'; it is to seek the history of the beginning, to ask 'quelle provenance trouver à ces commencements?' (PSC 72).[65] This is one aspect of what Nancy sees in the deconstruction of Christianity, his own response to the death of God.

Nancy is at pains to stress that 'deconstruction' should not be equated with 'destruction', but is rather 'le geste d'une ouverture ou d'une réouverture en direction de ce qui doit avoir précédé toute construction' (DDC 116).[66] The deconstruction of Christianity is therefore double, its two senses captured by its double genitive. It is the deconstruction *of* Christianity (subjective genitive) in so far as 'la question est de savoir si nous pouvons, en nous retournant sur notre provenance chrétienne, désigner du sein du christianisme une provenance du christianisme plus profonde que le christianisme lui-même' (DDC 208),[67] and it is the deconstruction *of* Christianity (objective genitive) in so far as 'le christianisme lui-même, le christianisme comme tel est dépassé, parce qu'il est lui-même et par lui-même en état de dépassement' (DDC 206),[68] a 'self-surpassing' that transforms Christianity 'itself' (NMT 10 n.4/NMTe 108 n.4).[69]

The double genitive also exposes Nancy's deconstruction of Christianity to a danger against which it cannot secure itself, namely that it will prove to have been all along a Christian hyperbole,[70] and therefore once more parasitic upon the God whose death it articulates. This is the worry voiced by Derrida in *Le Toucher*; for Derrida the deconstruction of Christianity is as necessary as it is impossible. It is necessary because only Christianity can do the work of deconstructing itself; it is impossible because if only Christianity can deconstruct Christianity then '[l]a déchristianisation sera une victoire chrétienne'.[71] The problem is that, given Christianity's structure as dis-enclosure, a 'deconstruction of Christianity', if such a thing were possible, would have to begin by divesting itself of the Christian tradition of *destructio*.[72] In other words, in deconstructing Christianity Nancy imitates Christianity, ot at least cannot conclusively be said not to imitate Christianity.

Nancy's position is complicated by a further danger, however, for Nancy's approach to escaping this theo-logic of parasitic imitation is itself a theological move, another instance of what Nancy would call the Christmas projection: 'Il n'y a pas ici à être indemne, sauf, sauvé, à chercher un salut ou une immunité hors du christianisme. Ces valeurs seraient encore chrétiennes'.[73] In other words, Nancy is either parasitic on a Christian deconstruction of Christianity or on a Christian salvation from Christianity, and to the extent that he avoids the one parasitism he falls into the other. In seeking to avoid the imitation of the Christmas projection, Nancy exposes himself to the inevitability of another but equally theological imitation.

Nancy is aware of this danger of seeking to bootstrap his way to post-theological thinking, and in *L'Adoration* he mounts a defence against this charge by claiming to be faithful to something in Christianity deeper than Christianity itself, for which God is only the 'front man' (*ADC* 31–2). It is the movement of self-surpassing that is crucial for Nancy's purposes, he claims, not that this self-surpassing happens to be, in this instance, Christian:

> Du christianisme, il faut extraire ce qui nous a portés et qui nous a produits: il faut, si c'est possible, extraire du fond plus profond que celui de la chose religieuse ce dont la religion aura été une forme et une méconnaissance. (*ADC* 40)[74]

Indeed, Nancy is not interested in Christianity for itself, for any religious, moral, spiritual or salvific virtue (*ADC* 39), and the self-surpassing he discerns only in some currents of the Christian tradition (most prominently the Reformation, *ADC* 50–1) is deeper than religion itself. This is a classic move of what we are calling post-theological integration: rather than either parasitically adopting or ascetically renouncing theological notions, Nancy is seeking to retain the fruit of deconstruction while rejecting Christianity as its incidental husk, wresting deconstruction from Christianity's grasp by suggesting that Christianity is itself only one instance of a more fundamental self-surpassing gesture. Nevertheless, this move does not free Nancy from Derrida's charge of Christian hyperbole, for the very move of discerning in Christianity a truth deeper than itself once more repeats a Christian move, namely the opposition between the outward appearance and the heart (*kardia*) and a preference for the latter. In this, Nancy's defence against his deconstruction of Christianity becoming a Christian hyperbole is once more a repetition of Christianity's own movement of self-deconstruction. Though he discerns and seeks to avoid Badiou's imitative recourse to the Christmas projection, Nancy's own thinking is inevitably implicated in parasitic imitation.

Notwithstanding this powerful critique, Nancy's 'deconstruction of Christianity' is a movement which transforms the Christianity from which it cannot escape. Nancy describes this transformation, the objective genitive of the 'deconstruction of Christianity', in the following terms: 'non seulement le christianisme se détache et s'excepte du religieux, mais il désigne en creux, au-delà de lui, le lieu de ce qui devra finir par *se dérober à l'alternative primaire du théisme et de l'athéisme*' (*NMT* 10)[75]

According to this analysis, the deconstruction of Christianity would be less a parasitically atheistic account of the death of God and more a deeper rejection of the a/theism binary per se, for it not only deconstructs Judaeo-Christian theism but it also deconstructs the logic of opposition in which theism dictates the terms of its own negation; it disrupts not only the content of theism – to speak somewhat reductively for a moment – but also its form, the formal conditions in which 'theism' can either be affirmed or negated:

> Il n'y a pas même « athéisme » ; « athée » ne suffit pas! c'est la position du principe qui doit être évidée. Il ne suffit pas de dire que Dieu s'absente, se retire ou bien est incommensurable. Il s'agit encore moins de placer un autre principe sur son trône – Homme, Raison, Société. Il s'agit de prendre à bras-le-corps ceci: *le monde repose sur rien* – et c'est là le plus vif son sens. (*ADC* 48; J-LN's italics)[76]

Nevertheless, the way in which Nancy's deconstruction of Christianity proceeds with the 'religions of the book' bears striking similarities on some levels to Badiou's reading of the death of God, for the deconstruction of Christianity 'répond toujours à ceci: le dieu « Un » n'est précisément plus « un dieu »' (*NMT* 10).[77] Both Nancy and Badiou prosecute the death of God by displacing the One, but whereas Badiou proceeds through a Platonism of the multiple, Nancy pursues a deconstruction of the origin of Christianity. This difference between, on one hand, atheism pursued in terms of a retroactively assumed inconsistent multiplicity in accordance with which the One is not (because all ones are countings-as-one) and, on the other hand, a/theism disrupted by a deconstruction of the One God that finds non-foundation at the origin of monotheism itself, outlines the shape of a contrast between Nancy and Badiou, between the infinite and the finite, that will prove to be of crucial importance as we move through the following chapters. For now, let us note that both Nancy and Badiou understand the death of God in terms of having done with the One, but for Badiou this is achieved with a philosophy of the infinite cast as a Platonism of the multiple, and for Nancy it is achieved with the finite thinking of the deconstruction of Christianity.

In contrast to Badiou's account which privileges the moment of mathematisation, the interruption of the mytheme by the matheme, as the singular moment of philosophy's birth, Nancy argues in *La Création du monde* that when metaphysics arrives in the West it comes as the result of a number of different influences, including the flight of the gods, 'départ dont le monothéisme est en Occident le premier nom, en soi déjà gros de la «mort de Dieu»' (CM 123).[78] Rather than discounting the Platonic moment, Nancy's account of the death of God co-opts it as a factor alongside that of monotheism: 'et l'on pourrait ajouter: que fait Platon, sinon tresser ensemble la tragédie et le monothéisme, juste avant que le judaïsme hellénistique puis le christianisme ne parachèvent le travail?' (CM 123).[79] This allows Nancy to posit a contemporaneity (or at least a 'cohistoriality') of philosophy and monotheism, notwithstanding their 'enormous differences' (RSAV 192).

For Nancy it is an inextricable mix of Hebrew, Greek and Roman influences which forms both the West and the Christianity that is inseparable from it (DDC 207/DisDC 142). When Nancy argues that the death of God is a necessarily Western phenomenon he is not echoing the more straightforward point made by André Glucksmann and John Caputo, that the decline of religion in Western countries is not replicated in other parts of the globe,[80] but the more complex contention that the death of God is constitutively and inevitably Western, that the death of God is not only *in* the West, it is *of* the West (DLD 47–8/ODP 148). All this does not mean, however, that outside the West God is 'still alive'. Where there still is an 'elsewhere' of the West, Nancy clarifies, the gods were long since exhausted in the excess of signs and powers, clergy, clans and castes, and in scrupulous observances (DLD 47–8/ODP 148). It does mean, however, that the consummation of the death of God not only negates the religious forms and structures of Western thought (the death of God, we might say, as an objective genitive); it also completes them (subjective genitive). In other words, simply asserting the death of God, however that is done, will always re-inscribe itself in the same structures it is seeking to surpass and leave behind. In his *Genealogy of Nihilism* Connor Cunningham argues persuasively that ' "radical" death of God theologians are reactively constituted by onto-theology, which is to say they propagate a "conservative" theology'.[81] It seems hard to escape the conclusion that Nancy's reading of Badiou places him also among the conservatives in so far as he uses the tools of onto-theology (metaphysical self-positing and pre-destination) to despatch the God of onto-theology. It is Badiou's failure to accept this complex, *impure* genesis of the West and its philosophy that leaves him, on Nancy's reading, with a conservative and parasitic a/theism in tension with itself. In Nancy's eyes, 'seul peut être actuel un athéisme qui contemple la réalité de sa provenance chrétienne' (DDC 205).[82] But of course, an 'atheism' that does contemplate its Christian origin is not free from God either.

The constraints of a review article go some way to excusing Chris van Rompaey of stripping away layers of nuance as he simply suggests that

Nancy 'misrepresents important elements of Badiou's project'[83] at this point. Such a flattened reading falls short not only of the painstaking development of Nancy's response to Badiou in 'Philosophie sans conditions' but also of Badiou's own writing on Nancy. Critiquing Nancy's account of Platonism-monotheism sketched above, van Rompaey suggests that Nancy 'blurs what for Badiou is a crucial distinction' between the 'generic form' of the emergence of the discourse of philosophy amid the structures of a crumbling mythico-religious world, and the 'articulated content' of wresting that discourse 'from the clutches of the poem so as to constitute an independent, "properly" philosophical mode of enquiry'.[84] However, only if we have decided a priori that Badiou's 'crucial distinctions' are beyond question can this be a 'misrepresentation'. Nancy is not misrepresenting Badiou here, but rather challenging the neat dichotomy of form and content and the tidy separation of influences upon which van Rompaey's reconstruction of Badiou relies. Rather than being 'based on the assumption that Badiou's claims are other than they actually are',[85] Nancy's critique is rather based on the argument that Badiou's claims are actually other than he thinks they are.

So to accomplish the death of the God of metaphysics by a quintessentially metaphysical gesture (the self-positing of an origin) takes with one hand only to give back with the other; it dispatches metaphysics with the help of metaphysics; it establishes not post-theological thinking but a parasitic a/theism. Or so Nancy's argument goes. But now it is Nancy's turn to be inexact, for Badiou is not simply claiming that the Platonic moment of the interruption of the mytheme by the matheme is the self-positing origin of philosophy. Rather, he is claiming that the definition of philosophy is ahistorical, that *qua philosophy* it has no historical origin, and that the Platonic rupture with the mytheme is merely one historical instantiation of philosophy's ahistorical definition.

This does not necessarily mean, however, that Nancy's critique is rebutted. The critique can still be made to work if it is taken to be challenging the possibility of ahistoricity itself, not simply the metaphysics of the Platonic philosophical moment. Any philosophy issuing a historical claim (for Badiou's claim is also historically situated, let us not forget) for the ahistoricity of philosophy's definition might be asked to provide some substantiation for that claim in terms of historical instances which demonstrate the sort of philosophy that fits the ahistorical definition. If the privileged historical instance of this definition of philosophy is shown not to fit the definition after all – as is the thrust of Nancy's argument for the complexity of the Platonic moment – that has consequences for the definition itself, or at the very least for the claim that this sort of philosophy has ever in fact existed.

For his part, Badiou accuses Nancy's finitude (philosophy has no ahistorical, 'eternal' definition) of amounting to the reintroduction of the One, and therefore of the God of metaphysics, into the heart of his thinking. Borrowing from a Lacanian register, Badiou argues that finitude is the 'master signifier' of Nancy's philosophical discourse (OR 14). In other words, finitude is not simply the 'with' of being-with that Nancy claims at all, but rather it inevitably becomes a term that names and gathers multiplicity. Finitude is Nancy's master signifier in two senses: 1) because it is charged with naming thinking itself (OR 17), and 2) because it issues an injunction and a duty: the contemporary call to an ethics is the call 'à conserver et à augmenter l'accès de l'existence à son propre sens inappropriable et sans fondement' (*PF* 34, quoted by Badiou on OR 19)[86] which Badiou interprets as the call to maintain thought in the responsibility of finitude. Noting that, in *Une Pensée finie*, Nancy affirms that he is concerned with nothing but finitude, Badiou concludes '[n]ous tenons ici l'aveu de la souveraineté signifiante de « finitude », de l'Un qu'elle impose au texte' (OR 18).[87] Finitude absorbs the totality of Nancy's positive vocabulary – *sense, the meaning (sens) of being, the responsibility of sense, existence, freedom, thought* – and the task of philosophy for Badiou is to unravel these terms so that their absorption in finitude is made clear (OR 19). What is more, Badiou sees this as a Hegelian move on Nancy's part, for Hegel is the 'grand master' of the re-absorption of terms in an essential recapitulation under an ultimate name. In the same way that he accuses Deleuze of a 'Platonism of the virtual' (*D* 69/*Del* 46), Badiou's charge against Nancy might be characterised as a 'Platonism of finitude', with finitude raised to a transcendental category that names thinking as such.

Nancy's master signifier is exposed, without imposing its presence, and this is what Badiou calls Nancy's 'offrande réservée' (OR 20, 'reserved/private offering'). But it is hard to see this as anything other than a misreading of Nancean finitude. It is not that finitude is in reserve, that it does not 'impose its presence' as Badiou claims, but rather that it has no presence to impose. Finitude is not a positive shared attribute, but the sharing-in-common of finite existence irreducible to a possession 'commune à tous, propre à aucun, impropriété commune communicante jamais communiquée ou communiée' (*SM* 111).[88] Badiou is reading finitude as if it were a variant of his own inconsistent multiplicity that had tipped its hand too much. If the deconstruction of Christianity amounted simply to the exhaustion (qua end) of signification, then finitude would indeed act as a parasitic placeholder for onto-theological meaning. However, Nancy's is not a finitude in reserve; it is a finitude in common, and it does not bestow sense upon existence from outside, it is (nothing but) the 'with' of being-with. The differend here comes down to the difference between Badiouian axioms and Nancean singular plurality. It is a crucial distinction for our investigation of post-theological integration: can either of these approaches yield thinking that is neither ascetic nor parasitic, and does the difference between the two approaches necessarily fracture our understanding of the coherence of post-theological thinking?

As we explore this difference in the coming chapters, one further relatively simple but important distinction between the approaches of Badiou and Nancy must be borne in mind: Badiouian thought is dichotomising, whereas Nancy works to deconstruct dichotomies. Badiou's decision for multiplicity is secondary, for the way that he handles inconsistent multiplicity relies on a more fundamental decision, namely that the dichotomy of the One and the multiple utterly exhausts the possibilities of being. This is the heart of Badiou's philosophical atheism: the dichotomy that the One (understood as theological) and the multiple (understood in terms of Badiou's inconsistent multiplicity) are the 'properly primordial duality of being',[89] or in other (and perhaps less potentially misleading) words, that if being is not one in the theological sense, it must therefore and inevitably be multiple in Badiou's set-theoretical sense. But must it? Nancy's philosophy of finitude challenges both the retroactive construction of inconsistent multiplicity and its grounding assumption that being, if it is not one, must be pure multiplicity.

For Nancy it is not accurate to suggest, with Peter Hallward, that the 'only genuine alternative' to Badiou's ontological atheism 'is indeed, as Lévinas understood with particular clarity, to accept instead that ontology itself is incoherent and so cannot fulfill the role of first philosophy – a move that prepares the way for an effective dismissal of philosophy by religion.[90] The ontology of being-in-common that Nancy elaborates inhabits, as we shall see below, precisely the place between religion and Badiou's atheism that Hallward's dichotomy denies. Nancy's is not an ontology that denies the death of God, but that seeks fully to embrace it:

> L'ontologie du « commun » et du « partage » ne serait pas autre chose que l'ontologie de l' « être » radicalement soustrait à toute ontologie de la substance, de l'ordre et de l'origine. La « mort de Dieu » n'est pas accomplie, ni surmontée, tant que nous n'en sommes pas là. (Com 57)[91]

Nancy's ontology too is 'pure', so to speak: pure of any substantial relation, a pure sharing of finitude where finitude is nothing that is possessed. Nancy explicitly distances himself from Lévinas's naming of God, characterising it as an infinite and non-thematisable revision of Hegel's bad infinity, giving to the incomplete the dignity of divinity. The death of God, as we have seen, can all too easily become a dialectic ontotheology (*DLD* 5/ODP 113), and Nancy sees the Hegelianism revised by Lévinas and the declaration of the death of God as equally onto-theological, equal and opposite so to speak, and his intention is to disrupt both of them. In other words, Lévinas for Nancy is no genuine alternative to Badiou at all, for they both inhabit the same site of thought (onto-theology) in equal and opposite ways: the only genuine alternative is to find a true alternative to this non-alternative.

Hallward is right in claiming 'we know that Badiou takes it for granted that all genuinely contemporary philosophers agree that pure being as being (as opposed to being-this-or-that) must be thought as multiple *rather than* one'.[92] We also know that a thinking that challenges this dichotomy, like Nancy's singular plural, will always fly under Badiou's 'genuinely contemporary' radar. Yet we must stress once again that this does not allow Nancy to emerge from the debate triumphant. The search for such an alternative is once more caught in the bind identified by Derrida between a parasitic deconstruction and a parasitic redemption of the death of God. Neither Baidou nor Nancy articulate the death of God in a way immune from imitative parasitism.

Badiou's forcing of dichotomies (like one/multiple) is explicit and intentional. In describing the conjunction of Platonic philosophy and modern mathematics, he lays down as a principle that every thought (and therefore mathematics, because mathematics is thinking), takes decisions from the point of the undecidable but must maximally extend the principle of choice in those decisions:

> Les contraintes de la construction [. . .] doivent être au contraire subordonnées aux libertés de la décision pensante. C'est pourquoi le platonicien ne verra rien à reprendre, pour peu que les effets de pensée soient maximaux, au libre usage du principe du tiers exclu et, par voie de conséquence, du raisonnement par l'absurde. (*CT* 103)[93]

Badiou's excluded middle is the reverse engineered condition of the maximally extended principle of choice that his philosophy demands. He employs a similarly pragmatic reasoning in his critique of Derrida, arguing that the Derridean refusal of metaphysical dichotomies

> does not suit tempestuous times, when everything is submitted to a law of decision, here and now. [. . .] The (Maoist) truth of those years insisted that 'one can be divided into two'. This statement expresses poetically the metaphysics of radical conflict rather than the patient deconstruction of oppositions. (*HJD* 43)

Badiou's taste for dichotomy and the excluded middle comes from the 'tempestuous times' in which he and Derrida were writing, as much as from an ahistorical philosophical necessity.

CONCLUSION

At the end of this first chapter we are presented with two very different accounts of the death of God. For Badiou, the only way to consummate the death of God is by a rejection of ascetic humility before the divine infinite through a recourse to the Cantorian transfinite which finally leaves the God who lurks beyond finitude's ascetic horizons and limits with nowhere to hide. This requires the retroactive and axiomatic positing of a pure, inconsistent multiplicity and the equation of mathematics with ontology, by virtue of which the multiple is preserved as generic in the formal language of set theory. Nancy's finite thinking is not only impotent finally to banish God, but it reintroduces the One in its very midst through its gathering of thinking under the single term of finitude. Nancy, following the path of a finite thinking, is powerless to extricate himself from finitude's irreducible religiosity.

Whereas for Badiou we simply do not have the means to be atheist so long as the theme of finitude governs our thinking (C 164/TW 26), for Nancy the death of God will not be realised by any thinking that repeats the Christmas projection in its rejection of God (DDC 121/ DisDC 145). We must move beyond the a/theism dichotomy because the dichotomy itself is irremediably parasitic on the thought it seeks to deny. While Badiou reads Nancy's thought as an ascetic atheism, denying itself the resources of the infinite, Nancy sees Badiou's as harbouring elements of the parasitic in its Christmas projection. Nevertheless, both thinkers are seeking to move beyond the impasse of parasitism and asceticism in elaborating a post-theological integration, Nancy by arguing that we must extract from Christianity something deeper than religion which religion itself misunderstands (ADC 40), and Badiou by occupying the ground of actual infinity with a rigorously secularised transfinite. Neither of these positions can, in the final account, however, banish the ghost of parasitism.

For Nancy, it is the ahistorical infinite in Badiou's thought that is theologically problematic, and for Badiou it is Nancy's finitude that is to be resisted on pain of reintroducing God. In Montesquieu's *Lettres persanes*, Rica quips that, if triangles invented a god, that god would doubtless have three sides: the god is formed in the image of his human creators. When it comes to the death of God, things might seem little different: God is dispatched in an image appropriate to the philosophy that claims to follow his death, and the claim is made that only this philosophy, in each case, can adequately respond to that death.

Underlying the disagreements about finitude and the infinite, unity and the multiple, is the fundamental question of the possibility of heterotopic sites of thought in contemporary French philosophy and, more specifically for our purposes, the question of heterotopic understandings of the death of God and heterotopic post-theological integrations. What can be made of the 'difference' between Badiou's axioms and Nancy's singular plurality, between the Badiouian infinite and the Nancean finite? Can philosophy after the death of God still meaningfully employ the notion of a common space of thought and, if it does, is that employment itself necessarily 'religious'? This is precisely the question that is raised in the engagement between Nancy and Badiou qua engagement, and it is why the future of French thought, as well as that thought's relation to the religious legacy of the West, plays itself out *en abyme* in the question of the finite and infinite responses to the death of God. We develop our treatment of these questions now by observing that, when it comes to the God of the poets, Nancy and Badiou have much more in common than we have seen so far in our treatment of metaphysics.

NOTES

1. Montesquieu, *Lettres persanes* (Paris: Garnier, 1965), p. 124. Letter LIX, Rica to Usbek: 'It has been well said that if triangles were to create a god, they would give him three sides' (Montesquieu, *The Persian Letters*, p. 129).
2. Bertrand Russell, 'Recent work on the principles of mathematics', *International Monthly*, 4 (1901), p. 84.
3. 'I take the formula "God is dead" literally. [. . .] God is finished. And religion is finished, too' (*BOE* 23).
4. See Martin Heidegger, 'Nietzsche's word: God is dead', in *The Question Concerning Technology and Other Essays*, p. 69.
5. Blaise Pascal, *Pensées* [Lafuma] 425/[Brunschvicg] 148.
6. 'My position has no relation with any religion, and that is why it can freely treat them all as schemata of historic esthetics. God is not even dead, for me (this dead God is still Nietzsche's constant interlocutor).' Author's translation.
7. It is true that both Nancy (notably in *HIN* and *VD*) and Badiou (in *LM* and *2M*) have recently elaborated a fuller account of the relationship between the finite and the infinite in their work, one of the consequences of which is to problematise the terms 'philosophy of the infinite' and 'philosophy of finitude'. We will treat this important shift and its consequences

in Chapter 2. Nevertheless, we will fail to understand what is at stake in this complication of the relationship if we have not first worked through the Badiouian infinite and Nancean finitude as presented in the current chapter.

8. Hallward, *Badiou: A Subject to Truth*, p. 7.
9. The term 'dieu de la métaphysique' (God of metaphysics) is relatively stable throughout Badiou's œuvre. He only once mentions the 'Dieu des philosophes' (God of the philosophers) (*SP* 50/*SPe* 47), and then only when quoting Pascal, and he makes no reference to the 'god of onto-theology' as such. Other than this, traits of the god of metaphysics are reflected in Badiou's characterisation of the god of Descartes who is required as guarantor of the truth (*EE* 237/*BE* 214; *CT* 12/*BOE* 23), and the watchmaker god of Voltaire (*EE* 237/*BE* 214).
10. Badiou's *Dieu-principe* resonates with Pierre Magnard's 'fonction dieu' (God-as-function): not the true God but god qua truth (Magnard, *Le Dieu des philosophes*, p. 16).
11. Leibniz, *Nouveaux Essais sur l'entendement humain II* (Paris: Garnier-Flammarion, 1966), ch. 17, p. 1. 'It belongs to the essence of number, line and some such whole to be bounded.' And the 'true infinite, strictly speaking, is only in the absolute, which precedes all composition and is not formed by the addition of parts.' G. W. Leibniz, *New Essays on Human Understanding*, ed. P. Remnant, J. Bennett, K. Ameriks and Desmond M. Clarke (Cambridge: Cambridge University Press, 1996), p. 157, quoted in *BOE* 104.
12. '"What is not truly *one* being is not truly a *being* either"' (G. W. Leibniz, 'Letter to Arnauld' (30 April 1687), *The Leibniz–Arnauld Correspondence*, ed. and trans. H. T. Mason (Manchester: Manchester University Press, 1967), quoted in *BOE* 34.
13. In this way Badiou avoids, in relation to the god of metaphysics, an ambiguity in Nietzsche's pronouncements on the death of God. See Eric von der Luft, 'Sources of Nietzsche's "God is Dead!"': 'Ironically, Nietzsche's theology could be termed "apophatic." In proclaiming that God has died, indeed, has been killed, he seems to suggest that God was once alive' (p. 270).
14. The term mytheme (*mythème*) originates from Claude Levi-Strauss's 1955 'La structure des mythes', in *Anthropologie structurale* (Paris: Plon, 1958), pp. 227–55, where it is used of the constituent building blocks of myths. Matheme (*mathème*) is a Lacanian coinage. Part of Lacanian algebra, mathemes have no univocal meaning but serve the transmission of psychoanalytic concepts (see Jacques Lacan, *Le Séminaire, livre XX, Encore, 1972–73*, ed. Jacques-Alain Miller, Paris: Seuil, 1975, p. 100). Badiou's use of the term stresses the uniquely formalised, rigorous non-hermeneutic 'language' of mathematics, antinomy of the poem, its truth the antinomy of knowledge (*C* 55).
15. 'Mathematics is *the only point of rupture with doxa that is given*

    as existent or constituted. The absolute singularity of mathematics is basically its existence' (*Con* 102).
16. 'When it comes to the effectiveness, if not the proclamation of the death of God, the contemporary quandary in which we find ourselves must be ascribed to the fact that philosophy's neglect of mathematical thinking delivers the infinite, through the medium of history, over to a new avatar of the One' (*TW* 27; translation altered).
17. 'We do not have the wherewithal to be atheists so long as the theme of finitude governs our thinking' (*TW* 26).
18. 'the thesis of the infinity of being is necessarily post-Christian' (*BE* 143).
19. Drozdek, 'Beyond infinity: Augustine and Cantor'. The present discussion is indebted to Frederiek Depoortere's treatment of Drozdek's thesis in *Badiou and Theology*.
20. Augustine, *The City of God*, book XII, ch. 19, p. 527.
21. Drozdek, 'Beyond infinity', p. 133.
22.
>   At last we touched upon that lonely shore
>   that never yet has seen its waters sailed
>   by one who then returned to tell the tale.
>   There, as another willed, he girded me.
>   Oh, miracle! When he pulled out the reed,
>   Immediately a second humble plant
>   Sprang up from where the first one had been picked.
>   (Dante Alighieri, *Purgatory*, trans. Mark Musa,
>   London: Penguin, 1985, p. 5)

23. Drozdek, 'Beyond infinity', p. 138.
24. Georg Cantor, *Gesammelte Abhandlungen mathematischen und philosophischen Inhalts* (Berlin: Springer, 1932), p. 378; quoted by Jané, 'The role of the absolute infinite in Cantor's conception of set', pp. 384–5.
25. Drozdek, 'Beyond infinity', p. 138.
26. 'the folly of saving God – the one, that is – from any absolute presumption of the multiple' (*BE* 43; translation altered).
27. Though there is no space to elaborate it here, the reader is directed to Reynhout, 'Alain Badiou: hidden theologian of the void?', and the appendix in Hallward, *Badiou: A Subject to Truth*, for a presentation of ZFC in relation to Badiou's thought.
28. 'Every atheist philosophy posits that nothing, in principle, is inaccessible. Hegel is decisive on this point: the whole of the real is rational. My own thesis is not that the Inaccessible is accessible. It is that there is nothing inaccessible' (letter to Peter Hallward, 19 June 1996, quoted in Hallward, *Badiou: A Subject to Truth*, p. 320).
29. Though Badiou does not describe his own thinking as 'post-theological', it is a true description of his system in the sense in which we defined the term above. In order to avoid confusion between 'atheism' as a general

term for thinking without God and 'atheism' as Badiou's characterisation of his own thought, we shall call Badiou's thought 'post-theological' in contexts where what is meant is the impetus he shares with Nancy and Meillassoux in moving beyond imitative and residual atheism. 'Atheism' will be reserved for Badiou's thought in contradistinction to Nancy's atheology and Meillassoux's philosophical divine.

30. 'Regarding the God of metaphysics, thought must accomplish its course in the infinite. The latter disseminates thought's reserve over the entire expanse of manifolds' (BOE 31).
31. The examples are taken from Hallward, *Badiou: A Subject to Truth*, p. 81.
32. Hallward mistakenly says that, in CT 141, Badiou claims that 'the "death of god" enabled the conception of pure multiplicity as without One' (Hallward, *Badiou: A Subject to Truth*, p. 393 n.39). Badiou does not in fact attribute pure multiplicity to the death of God explicitly, but to 'la crise de l'idéalité métaphysique de l'un' (CT 141) ('crisis in the One's metaphysical ideality', BOE 25).
33. The attempt to render the God of metaphysics impossible is complicated by the proliferation of forms that such a God can take, however. It is by no means clear that dispensing with the One deposes the Trinitarian God of Christian theology. John Milbank uses Badiou's insistence on the retroactive inaccessibility of pure multiplicity to argue that there is no internal necessity to Badiou's identification of inaccessible inconsistency with pure multiplicity:

> Certainly, one can agree with Badiou that, as already for Plato, and as in Trinitarian theology (as he notes!) the One is later than the Many and emerges only as their unity. Nevertheless, because there is only ever any specific 'set' of the manifold by virtue of its unity, one might still decide, in divergence from Badiou's fundamental decision, to accord to unity a retroactive primacy (as indeed in the case of Trinitarian theology). (Milbank, 'The shares of being', p. 22, accessed January 2010)

Inaccessible inconsistency may, but by no means must, be multiple.

34. 'Does this mean that being is not multiple either? Strictly speaking, yes, because being is only multiple inasmuch as it occurs in presentation' (BE 24). Graham Harman raises a similar problem, questioning whether Badiou's inconsistent multiplicity is really multiple:

> For me, the problem is [. . .] is the inconsistent multiple in Badiou really multiple? It doesn't really seem to do anything other than haunt our current count, our current situation. But the proper multiple would actually need to interact apart from the subject. (Harman, 'Speculative realism', pp. 382–3)

Badiou's problem is the difficulty of holding both that inconsistent multiplicity is multiple, and that it is directly inaccessible. Either it is not truly inaccessible, or it is not verifiably multiple.

35. Hallward, *Badiou: A Subject to Truth*, p. 82.
36. Hallward, *Badiou: A Subject to Truth*, p. 82.
37. Hallward, *Badiou: A Subject to Truth*, p. 82.
38. The generic is a term Badiou borrows from Paul Cohen, and which he esteems indispensible for his own philosophical account of the event (*EE* 23/*BE* 6). The generic for Badiou is infinitely subtracted from the subsumption of the multiple under the One of a concept; it is a superabundance of being that evades the clutches of language (*C* 184–5/*Con* 118). The generic subset contains 'a little of everything' such that no predicate can gather all its terms (*C* 184/*Con* 117). Truths for Badiou (be they scientific, amorous, political or artistic) are without exception generic in this way. A 'constructible' subset of a set, by contrast, admits of a clear description, and the axiom of constructability simply states 'all sets are constructible', which Badiou glosses as 'all multiplicity is under the law' (*PND* 6). 'Large cardinals' require axioms supplementary to those of ZFC set theory and are as abyssally removed from aleph zero – the smallest infinite set, being the cardinality of the set of all natural numbers – as it is from finite multiples. Because large cardinals are 'inaccessible' in this way, they are prey to an ascetic atheism. In Badiou's succinct summary: 'Le constructible déplie l'être des configurations du savoir. Le générique, avec le concept du multiple indiscernable, rend possible que soit pensé l'être d'une vérité. Les grands cardinaux approximent l'être virtuel que requièrent les théologies' (*EE* 314). 'The constructible unfolds the being of configurations of knowledge. The generic, with the concept of the indiscernible multiple, renders possible the thought of the being of a truth. The grand cardinals approximate the virtual being required by theologies' (*BE* 284).
39. Salanskis, 'Les mathématiques chez x avec x = Alain Badiou', p. 83.
40. For a discussion of the difference between infinity and infinitude, see Bandres, 'Badiou et l'atomisme ancien', p. 49.
41. 'A system S is said to be *infinite* when it is similar to a proper part of itself. In the contrary case, S is said to be a *finite* system' (*NuN* 36). Badiou is quoting Richard Dedekind, *Les nombres. Que sont-ils et à quoi servent-ils ?*, trad. J. Milner and H. Sinacoeur (Paris: Seuil, 1978), p. 93; Richard Dedekind, *The Nature and Meaning of Numbers*, in *Essays on the Theory of Numbers* (La Salle, IL: Open Court, p. 190; reprinted New York: Dover, 1963), § 64.
42. 'inverted or diverted form of finitude, of a non-appropriable or unnameable horizon of immortal divinity' (*TW* 26).
43. Miller, *Badiou, Marion and St Paul*, p. 154.
44. Miller, *Badiou, Marion and St Paul*, p. 43.
45. 'without this decision it will remain for ever possible for being to be essentially finite' (*BE* 148; translation altered).
46. 'God is finished. And religion is finished too. As Jean-Luc Nancy has strongly stated, there is something irreversible here' (*BOE* 23).

47.
> There is no return of the religious: there are the contortions and the turgescence of its exhaustion. Whether that exhaustion is making way for another concern for the gods, for their wandering or their infinite disappearance, or else for no god, that is another matter: it is another question altogether, and it is not something that can be grasped between the pincers of the religious, *nor indeed between those of atheism*. No god: this would be, or will be, unrelated to atheism – at least to that metaphysical atheism that is the counterpart of theism, and that wants to put something in the place of the god that has been denied or refuted. (ODP 136)

48.
> The much discussed 'return of the religious,' which denotes a real phenomenon, deserves no more attention than any other 'return.' Among the phenomena of repetition, resurgence, revival, or haunting, it is never the identical but the different that invariably counts the most. Because the identical immediately loses its identity in returning, the question should rather be asked, ceaselessly and with new risks, what an identical 'secularization' might denote, inevitably, other than a mere transferal. (*DisDC* 1; translation altered)

49. Nancy equivocates on the term 'atheism'. On occasion he treats it as a symmetrical concomitant of theism which, like theism, needs to be deconstructed. The deconstruction of monotheism points the way to 'un avenir du monde qui ne serait plus ni chrétien, ni anti-chrétien, ni monothéiste ni athéiste ou polythéiste, mais qui s'avancerait précisément au-delà de toutes ces catégories' (*DDC* 54); 'a future for the world that would no longer be either Christian or anti-Christian, either monotheist or atheist or even polytheist, but that would advance precisely beyond these categories' (*DisDC* 34).

Elsewhere, he seeks to retain a re-defined notion of atheism:

> Aussi longtemps que nous ne prenons pas en compte, sans réserve, le mondial comme tel, nous ne sommes pas quittes des démiurges et des créateurs. Autrement dit, nous ne sommes pas athées. Être athée ne signifie plus nier un divin qui s'est de lui-même résorbé (et cela ne peut donc peut-être plus s'appeler « athéisme »). Cela signifie: ouvrir le sens du monde. (*SM* 239)

> As long as we do not take into account, without reserve, the worldly as such, we have not gotten rid of demiurges and creators. In other words, we are not yet atheists. Being an atheist is no longer a matter of denying a divine instance that has reabsorbed itself into itself (and this can perhaps therefore be called 'atheism'). It is a matter of opening the sense of the world. (*SW* 158)

It is in order to clarify this and other equivocations that we have insisted on 'post-theological' for the second of these two senses, a sense which Nancy himself concedes may need to be abandoned.

50. 'this common space in which such heterotopias are possible, or indeed necessary' (PWC 39).

51. Heterotopia (*hétérotopie*) is a complex term coined by Michel Foucault in 'Des espaces autres' to refer to a real, localisable space, one of the features of which can be that it has 'le pouvoir de juxtaposer en un seul lieu réel plusieurs espaces, plusieurs emplacements qui sont en eux-mêmes incompatibles' (Michel Foucault, 'Des espaces autres', at: http://foucault.info/documents/heteroTopia/foucault.heteroTopia.fr.html, accessed January 2010); 'The heterotopia is capable of juxtaposing in a single real place several spaces, several sites that are in themselves incompatible' (Michel Foucault, 'Of other spaces (1967), Heterotopias', trans. Jay Miskowiec, at: http://www.foucault.info/documents/heteroTopia/foucault.heteroTopia.en.html, accessed January 2010). It is on this feature of finding a common space for the otherwise incompatible that Nancy is wishing to draw with his use of the term.

52. '[t]he definition of philosophy must allow for its own multiplication' (PWC 39).

53.

> The dominant idea [in the Heideggerian tradition] is that metaphysics has reached a point of historical exhaustion, but that what lies beyond this exhaustion has not yet been given to us [. . .]. Philosophy is then caught between the exhaustion of its historical possibility and the non-conceptual arrival of a salutary overturning. Contemporary philosophy combines the deconstruction of its past with the empty expectation of its future. My entire thesis is to break with this diagnosis [. . .] Philosophy must break with historicism from within itself. (Con 3–4, as trans. Ray Brassier, quoted in PWC 42; translation altered)

54. Badiou, 'L'Offrande réservée'.

55.

> when we say that metaphysics has 'ended' we only say that it exhausts whatever would presume to complete its retrospection as well as its prospection. The former and the latter must be unachievable, they must be the unachievable as such, in conformity with the essence of philosophy. (PWC 44)

56.

> What was called 'the death of God' and later 'the end of metaphysics,' or even 'the end of philosophy,' consisted in bringing to light the following: there is no first or last condition; there isn't any unconditioned that can be the principle or the origin. But this 'there isn't' is uncondi-

tioned, and there you have, if I dare say so, our 'human condition' (*PC* 5; translation altered)

57. 'the exhaustion of metaphysics is historical only insofar as it is the exhaustion of historical possibility as such (or of the meaning of history)' (*PWC* 42).
58. 'the dimension of history in general, as a Western dimension, is fundamentally Christian' (*DisDC* 146).
59. 'a pure and simple birth of Christianity, which one fine day comes along and changes everything' (*DisDC* 145).
60. 'our whole tradition, as unchristian as it would like to be, still retains something of the "Christmas projection": at a given moment "that" takes place, and we find ourselves thereafter in a Christian condition' (*DisDC* 145).
61. 'How and to what degree do *we hold* to Christianity' (*DisDC* 139).
62. 'I take the formula "God is dead" literally. [...] God is finished. And religion is finished, too' (*BOE* 23).
63.

> One thus finds oneself wondering whether any discourse on God can deviate, however slightly, from that of Hegel (even if revised), that is to say from the discourse of philosophy itself, or of *ontotheology (which culminates in the dialectical ontotheology of the death of God)*. (ODP 113; translation altered)

64.

> 'To deconstruct' means to disassemble that which has been erected over the beginnings so as to allow what has been hollowed out beneath them to arrive. Thus, it is at once to undermine (rather than destroy) the edifice of philosophical (or metaphysical) tradition and the historical auto-positioning of that tradition. (*PWC* 43–4)

65. 'what provenance can we ascribe to these beginnings?' (*PWC* 44).
66. 'the gesture of an opening or reopening in the direction of what must have preceded all construction' (*DisDC* 189; translation altered).
67. 'the question is to find out whether we can, by revisiting our Christian provenance, designate from the heart of Christianity a provenance of Christianity deeper than Christianity itself' (*DisDC* 143; translation altered).
68. 'Christianity itself, Christianity *as such*, is surpassed, because it is itself, and by itself, in a state of being surpassed' (*DisDC* 141).
69. Roberto Esposito uses the same subjective/objective genitive structure to make a different point in relation to the 'specifically Christian character of all the "deaths of God" that have followed each other over time.' These deaths, he argues, are 'precisely and always *of* God, both in the objective and subjective genetive senses; all these deaths belong to him after all,

or rather "before all", since the beginning, in the figure of God dying on the cross' (Esposito, 'Chair et corps', p. 157; author's translation). It will become clear in this chapter and the next why we prescribe severe limits to this 'Christian atheism' reading of the death of God.
70. Derrida, *Le Toucher*, p. 249/ *On Touching*, p. 220.
71. Derrida, *Le Toucher*, p. 68; 'Dechristianization will be a Christian victory' (*On Touching*, p. 54).
72. Derrida, *Le Toucher*, p. 74/*On Touching*, p. 60.
73. Derrida, *Le Toucher*, p. 248; 'This is not about being free from harm, safe, and saved, seeking one's salvation or immunity outside of Christianity. These values would still be Christian' (*On Touching*, p. 220).
74. 'We must extract from Christianity what has carried us and what has produced us: we must, if possible, extract, from the depths deeper than those of the religious thing, that from which the religion will have been a form and a misreading' (author's translation).
75. 'not only does Christianity detach and exempt itself from the strictly religious, but it also marks out intaglio, beyond itself, the place of what will finally have to abandon the simplistic alternative of theism or atheism' (*NMTe*, p. 108 n.4).
76.

> There is not even 'atheism'; 'atheist' is not enough! What we need to hollow out is the positing of a principle. It is not enough to say that God absents himself, withdraws or again is incommensurable. Much less is it a case of placing another principle on his throne – Man, Reason, Society. It is a case of grasping this with both hands: the world rests on nothing – and that is its most vivid sense. (Author's translation)

77. 'always corresponds to the following: the "One" god is no longer precisely "one god"' (*NMTe*, p. 108 n.4).
78. 'a departure whose initial name in the West is monotheism, already pregnant with the "death of God"' (PWC 46).
79. 'and one could add, what did Plato do if not weave together tragedy and monotheism just before Hellenistic Judaism, and then Christianity completed their work?' (*CWG* 85).
80. Glucksmann makes the point that God is only dead in Europe. In America and even more in the rest of the world Christianity is on the increase, as are Islam and other religions (see Glucksmann, *La Troisième mort de dieu*, p. 259). Caputo makes a similar observation, suggesting that

> While something like that [the death of God: author] might be happening in Western Europe, nothing of the sort has happened in the United States, not to mention South America, the Middle East, Asia, Africa, or the post-Soviet Eastern Bloc. Sociologists who wrote about the 'secularisation' of America in the 1960s were soon sent scurrying back to the

drawing board to write about its 'desecularisation.' (Caputo, 'Atheism, a/theology and the postmodern condition', p. 270)
81. Cunningham, *Genealogy of Nihilism*, p. 101.
82. 'the only thing that can be current is an atheism that contemplates the reality of its Christian origins' (*DisDC* 140; translation altered).
83. Van Rompaey, 'A question of fidelity', p. 354.
84. Van Rompaey, 'A question of fidelity', p. 354.
85. Van Rompaey, 'A question of fidelity', p. 354.
86. 'to conserve and to augment the access of existence to its own inappropriable and groundless sense' (*FT* 18).
87. 'We take from this the admission of the signifying sovereignty of "finitude", of the One that it imposes on the text' (author's translation).
88. 'common to all, belonging to none, as a common impropriety, communicating yet neither communicated nor communion' (*SW* 68; translation altered).
89. Hallward, 'Consequences of abstraction', in *Think Again*, p. 6.
90. Hallward, *Badiou: A Subject to Truth*, p. 62.
91.
> The ontology of the 'common' and 'share' would not be other than the ontology of 'being' radically removed from all ontology of substance, or order and origin. The 'death of God' is neither accomplished nor surmounted as long as we have not reached that one point. (Comp, p. 374; translation altered)

92. Hallward, 'Depending on inconsistency', p. 12; author's emphasis.
93.
> The constraints of construction [...] must be, on the contrary, subordinated to the liberties of thoughtful decision. This is the way the Platonist will see nothing to change, provided the effects of thought be maximal, regarding free use of the law of the excluded middle and consequently of the *reductio ad absurdum*. (*BOE* 95; translation altered)

2. The God of the Poets

Everything to be true must become a religion.[1]

The God of metaphysics is not the final, nor the most tenacious, of the gods Badiou seeks to despatch in his assault on the latent theology of finite thinking. Haunting the thought even of those who claim to have deconstructed the God of metaphysics is the third of Badiou's three 'chief deities': the God of the poets. For a finite thinking the God of the poets remains perfectly intact after the God of metaphysics is 'finished' (*CT* 18–19/*BOE* 28), for the motif of finitude is 'comme la trace d'une survivance, dans le mouvement qui confie la relève du Dieu de la religion et du Dieu métaphysique au Dieu du poème' (*CT* 20).[2]

The God of the poets is neither the God-principle of Western metaphysics nor the 'living God' of religions. It is the God(s) – or divine principle(s) – of Romanticism, whose most acute expression is found, Badiou argues, in the poetry of Friedrich Hölderlin (*CT* 18/*BOE* 28). This God is the poetic principle of the enchanted world, and it is neither dead nor alive but rather withdrawn. It follows that the God of the poets cannot be mourned, like the God of religions, nor critiqued, like the God of metaphysics; its persistence is felt in terms of a nostalgia, a melancholic and endlessly disenchanted anticipation of its improbable return that leaves thinking in a state of paralysed suspense (*CT* 19/ *BOE* 29) that Badiou gives the name 'Romanticism'. This nostalgia for a lost presence is a symptom of an ascetic atheism that suffers in the absence of the God it denies, and it is an asceticism that renders Nietzsche's anti-Christianity for Badiou merely a reversal of romanticism (*un romantisme retourné*, 19R 262). Romanticism is still the site of our thinking today, Badiou insists, and this fact renders the theme of the death of God ineffectual (*C* 162/*Con* 97).

In Badiou's genealogy, Hegel prepares the way for the romantic gesture in philosophy (C 166/*Con* 100) through the decisive cutting adrift of mathematics from philosophy (see C 159–62/*Con* 94–7). Whereas Plato sought to expel from his academy all who were not geometers, now the poem finds itself at the heart of 'philosophy', and the matheme is expelled (C 163/*Con* 98). Hölderlin's singular contribution to the Romantic schema is his powerful poetic evocation of the flight of the gods 'when the Father had turned his face from the sight of us mortals',[3] the flight that issues in the attitude of an endlessly anticipated return that Badiou identifies as the characteristic disposition towards the God of the poets. It is through poetic mediation, through the 'new religion' of poetic *Dichtung*,[4] that the gods can return to earth (*EE* 285/ *BE* 257). Notwithstanding the inaugural contribution made by Hegel, and the distinctly Hölderlinian motif of the withdrawal of the gods, the greatest Romantic with whom Badiou takes issue is Heidegger. For Heidegger, even though advances in technology have brought to completion Nietzsche's death of God, there is yet a new advent of the 'holy', a 'truly divine God' that remains after the death of the *causa sui*, a God before whom one can kneel, sing and dance.[5] For Badiou, to recognise the death of the God of religions and the end of onto-theology and yet to await this divine salvation is only to have advanced two thirds of the way to a truly contemporary post-theological thought.

Badiou does not set himself up in utter opposition to Heidegger and the flight of the philosophers to poetry, literature and art, and indeed his own mathematical interruption of the mytheme relies on Heidegger's distinction between truth and knowledge.[6] Rather, he sees Heidegger's way of understanding the relation of philosophy to poetry as a great opportunity almost taken. Badiou's assessment of Heidegger has three aspects, two positive and one negative (C 97/*Con* 39–40). First, Heidegger quite legitimately re-establishes the autonomous function of poetic thinking in the face of philosophical imperialism. Secondly, he shows the limits of an approach which would simply separate poetry and philosophical argument; but thirdly he fails to recognise the originality of the Greek interruption of the poem by the matheme, and so he cannot but restore the sacred authority of poetic speech that locates authenticity in the flesh of language. So Heidegger falls back into a discourse of the sacred.

Badiou's reconstruction of Romanticism has two main facets: the open infinite and incarnation. What Badiou calls the Romantic infinite is the correlate of the Romantic notion of finitude (C 162/*Con* 97). At its limit, finitude opens onto an infinite as an endlessly receding horizon beyond which the gods have withdrawn, in a structure that in our present analysis we are identifying as residual and ascetic. This infinite does not escape historicity, but simply marks the horizon of finitude's own historicity (C 162/Con 97). Furthermore, Romantic finitude's opening onto the infinite is unable to have done with the sacred or the divine, for it cedes the territory of the infinite to a mystical and inaccessible alterity: '[t]ant que la finitude reste la détermination ultime de l'être-là, Dieu demeure' (C 163).[7] God remains precisely *in absentia*, God's withdrawal leaving an ascetic state of abandonment and dereliction before an inappropriable or unnameable horizon (C 164/Con 99). The openness of finitude to the infinite is inextricable from openness to the promise and the poetico-political disposition towards the return of the gods, and the re-enchantment of the world:

> Que notre exposition à l'être soit essentiellement finie, qu'il faille toujours revenir à notre être-mortel, est ce à partir de quoi nous n'endurons la mort du Dieu vivant qu'à soutenir, sous de multiples formes, l'indistincte promesse d'un sens retiré, mais dont la « venue en retour » n'est pas forclose. (CT 20)[8]

The failure to foreclose this return leaves us powerlessly waiting for the divine and vulnerable to the promise of such an infinite God to fill the lack that finitude suffers with regard to the inaccessible infinite to which it is open (C 175/Con 176). In other words, finitude and the open infinite are ineradicably complicit with an asceticism that can never be rid of God.

This paradigm of finitude and its open infinite issues in the Romantic conception of art as incarnation, the descent of the infinite-true into finitude (PMI 23/HOI 11), the appearing of the absolute in the world. In this thoroughly Christian schema, the artist, possessed of genius, becomes the sacrificial mediator of spirit and matter, his works attesting the incarnation of the infinite in a way that leaves Romanticism unable to escape the sacred (S 217/Cen 154). Incarnation, however, simply drowns and quashes the Idea in a flood of materiality. After the pattern of the tortured body of Christ, the pattern of incarnation in the twentieth century is the tortured body of the Idea (S 166/Cen 116). More than this, incarnation for Badiou is evil. The terrorist states of the twentieth century laboured under the falsehood that justice can be captured 'in the solidity of a body' (PP 132).

Badiou's overcoming of the God of the poets articulates itself around these two themes of a finitude open to the infinite and incarnation, and they are also the themes that will guide us through this chapter. Both Badiou and Nancy argue that incarnation and the open infinite are to be overcome by their post-theological thinking, but each seeks to avoid them in different ways. Seeking most keenly to avoid an ascetic atheism,

Badiou affirms a conception of poetry in terms of the Idea, whereas Nancy, more wary of the danger of parasitic atheism, rewrites the open and incarnation in terms of singular plural sharing and the double gesture of the deconstruction of Christianity.

2.1 THE DEATH OF THE GOD OF PRESENCE

2.1.1 *The Open, the Infinite and the Art of the Idea*

Badiou's response to finitude's open infinite is the infinity of the matheme. The limit of the Open is a denial of the regime of counting (*NN* 104–5/*NuN* 81) because finitude and the limit are foreign to the infinite multiplicities of mathematical ontology which know no limit. Openness is the possibility of the return of the gods, as opposed to the 'firmness of the multiple' (*CT* 28/*BOE* 35), and so if philosophy is to be rigorously atheist and if we are to establish ourselves serenely in the irreversibility of the death of God (*CT* 20/*BOE* 29), we must deliver infinity from the metaphorics of the Open (*C* 165/*Con* 100). Finitude's openness to salvific return (*C* 58/*Con* 4) can only be disciplined by passing it through the sieve of mathematics (*LM* 583/*LW* 558; see also *C* 166–7/*Con* 111).

As a concomitant to the rejection of the Romantic open infinite, it is necessary, Badiou maintains, in following through the implications of the death of God, to envision a new type of poetry (see *CT* 19–20/*BOE* 28–9). Badiou by no means rejects poetry *tout court*; the rupture of mathematics, let us remember, is not with the poem itself but with the mytheme (19R 263–4). Envisioning a new type of poetry comes down for Badiou to developing a new paradigm for the relation between philosophy and poetry, or between philosophy and art more broadly.[9]

For the Badiou of *Petit Manuel d'inesthétique* there are three extant schemata for understanding the relationship between art and philosophy. The didactic schema either condemns or instrumentalises art, putting it under philosophical surveillance and leaving it with a role illustrating and elucidating philosophical positions. In the didactic schema the truth of art comes from outside art, and art itself becomes a sensory didacticism, the 'goodness' of which is seen only in its consequences for the polis. The second schema is Romantic, according to which art, truth's real body, is alone capable of truth (*PMI* 12/*HOI* 3). Evoking Lacoue-Labarthe and Nancy's *L'Absolu littéraire*, Badiou characterises the Romantic body of art as a glorious body, and art itself in this schema, as we have seen, as incarnation (*PMI* 12/*HOI* 3). Seeking to position itself between both the didactic and romantic schemata, the third schema is classical, stressing the ethical purposes of art: to please and to produce catharsis. Art is itself incapable of truth, and should not be thought of in terms of truth but in terms of verisimilitude, this demarcation of its territory from that of philosophy bringing about a truce between them. In the classical schema, philosophy only trespasses onto artistic territory in the guise of the aesthetic, offering its opinions on the rules of pleasing. Our age, according to Badiou, is characterised by its failure to produce any new schema.

In moving towards his own fourth schema of the relation between philosophy and art, Badiou shuns the dichotomy between philosophies that place themselves under the auspices of the poem (in the wake of Heidegger) or the matheme (the various branches of analytic philosophy), affirming that '[o]ne of the peculiar characteristics of my own project is that it requires both the reference to poetry and a basis in mathematics' (APTW xvi), or elsewhere 'I use mathematics and accord to it a fundamental role', but 'I also use, to the same extent, the resources of the poem' (APBE xiv).

While he rejects poetry that is nothing more than the melancholic guardian of finitude or a gesture towards a mystical silence that inhabits the limit of language (CT 21/BOE 29), in the *Court Traité* Badiou sets down two conditions for a poetry that would break with finitude for the actual, mathematical infinite: 'Qu'il se dévoue à l'enchantement de ce dont le monde, tel quel, est capable; qu'il discerne au point même de l'impossible la surrection infinie des possibilités invisibles' (CT 21).[10]

Transposed into the discourse of mathematics, this means that poetry is to serve as an indication of as yet uncounted multiples in a situation (or of the indiscernible in a world, to use the language of *Logiques des mondes*), and it is to serve as a reminder of the infinity of possible countings-as-one of the pure multiplicity that is counted in any situation.

In a characteristically dichotomising gesture, Badiou identifies just two types of poetry. The first is poetry as an appearance of the coming presence of being. The second, which seeks as its support not the Greek concept of nature as *phusis* but the Platonic Idea, decouples being from appearance and essence from existence through the matheme subtracted from all presence (EE 143/BE 125). Poetry for Badiou does not speak being, but connotes the void of a situation. It is, we might say, not the guardian of being but the guardian of a truth, in Badiou's sense of a truth as (in EE) a hole in knowledge, 'cette consistance minimale (une partie, une immanence sans concept) qui avère dans la situation l'inconsistance qui en fait l'être' (M 90).[11] Indeed, in *Le Nombre et les nombres* Badiou states categorically that '*Tout poème* cherche à déceler et à porter aux lisières formelles de la langue le vide latent des référents sensibles' (*NN* 200; author's emphasis).[12] The way in which poetry accomplishes this can be understood by considering its relation to philosophy.

Inaesthetics, Badiou's proposed fourth schema for relating philosophy to art, refuses to consider art merely as an object for philosophy. Instead,

> Par « inesthétique », j'entends un rapport de la philosophie à l'art qui, posant que l'art est par lui-même producteur de vérités, ne prétend d'aucune façon en faire, pour la philosophie, un objet. Contre la spéculation esthétique, l'inesthétique décrit les effets strictement intraphilosophiques produits par l'existence indépendante de quelques œuvres d'art. (*PMI* 7)[13]

For inaesthetics philosophy does not do art's thinking for it; art itself thinks, and its thinking is atheistic. The manifesto which Badiou lays down for contemporary poetry is a post-theological manifesto:

> L'impératif du poème est aujourd'hui de conquérir son propre athéisme, et donc de détruire de l'intérieur des puissances de la langue, la phraséologie nostalgique, la posture de la promesse, ou la destination prophétique à l'Ouvert. [. . .] c'est la poésie elle-même qui procédera, qui procède, depuis au moins le début du siècle, à la mise à mort de son propre Dieu. (*CT* 19–20)[14]

An indication of what this means for poetry in particular and art more generally can be gleaned from the three brief examples of Lucretius, Valéry and film. Given Badiou's post-theological agenda for poetry, it is perhaps little surprise that among the poems he praises most highly is *De Rerum Natura*, the work of 'the magnificent figure of Lucretius' (*CT* 28/*BOE* 35). Badiou's Lucretius is a figure in whom 'la puissance du poème, loin de garder dans la détresse le recours à l'Ouvert, tente plutôt de soustraire la pensée à tout retour des dieux, et à l'établir dans la fermeté du multiple' (*CT* 28).[15] Notice here that it is the poem *itself* that tries to establish thinking within the firmness of the multiple. Lucretius' poetry is not merely illustrative or exemplary, it itself seeks to establish the thinking of the multiple.

Badiou insists that Lucretius – the only thinker who was also an immense poet – and his poem – this singular fusion of poetry and philosophy that gives the lie to the whole Heideggerian reconstruction of metaphysics after Plato (*C* 105/*Con* 46) – elaborate a materialist thinking which positively *demands* its poetic exposition. But what is it about poetry that forces this demand? To explain, Badiou turns to the beginning of book IV of *De Rerum Natura*, where Lucretius undertakes to argue, in the teeth of Plato, for the legitimacy of the poem as the means of exposition for his philosophy (C 105/*Con* 46). Badiou singles out three functions of poetry for Lucretius. First, to illumine: Lucretius points out that his poem treats an obscure theme, and the presentation of this obscurity of being requires the luminous verses of poetry. Secondly, to persuade: Lucretius is wrenching the mind of his readers from the tight reins of religion, and in order to secure this rupture a certain force of speech is necessary, a force that can be readily granted by the poetic muse. And finally, to sweeten: the naked truth, Lucretius admits, appears somewhat sad. There are no gods to enchant the world or to reward virtue and punish evil. The place of philosophy, the place where truth is spoken, can, if viewed from a distance, seem a melancholy sort of place, and this deficit of pleasure must be supplemented by a lateral pleasure, procured by 'sweet poetic honey' (C 105–6/*Con* 47).

So the poem does not merely illustrate the void, it draws the reader towards the void, and that in three ways: 1) by sugaring materialism's bitter pill, 2) by wresting sense from the talons of religion, and 3) by what Lucretius calls the glorious linguistic body of the poetry shining its oblique light in such a way that it shows forth the unpresentable void of Lucretian thought. The poetry itself is advocating for Lucretius's Epicureanism. Nevertheless, Badiou insists, there is still a distance between philosophy and poetry. The language and the charm of the verses are only in the position of a supplement. Lucretius excuses his poetry as a sop to the reader who, looking at Epicureanism from afar, needs to be coaxed to come close before she can appreciate it properly. It is striking that, whereas poetry needs such an apology in Lucretius's eyes, philosophy needs no such justification: Epicurus is simply praised in *De Rerum*, not defended. What is driving the Lucretian poetry is the truth of an atomistic universe, a truth that is forced poetically, through illumination, persuasion and sweetening.

The role that Badiou gives to poetry in the case of Lucretius is as a servant of the Idea, in two senses. First of all, and more generally, the poetry of *De Rerum Natura* serves Epicurean atomism in the three ways detailed above. In addition, however, the universe of atoms and void set forth within the poem is amenable to a reading in terms of Badiou's own pure multiplicity (the difference being that Badiou's own thought does not recognise two principles, atoms and void, but only one, multiples), and it is within a frame of such multiplicity that a Badiouian truth, or Idea, can appear.[16] It is in this predisposition to multiplicity and to the Idea that poetry can 'conquer its own atheism'.

We can further see how Baidou reads poetry as a means of conquering its own atheism if we turn to a discussion of Valéry in which he glosses the following lines from 'Au Platane':

> – Non! dit l'arbre. Il dit *Non!* par l'étincellement
> De sa tête superbe,
> Que la tempête traite universellement
> Comme elle fait une herbe.[17]

Badiou develops his reading of these lines in terms of the connection between the chance inherent in a situation and the eternity of an event in his own philosophy, arguing 'N'est-ce pas à cette connexion que pense Valéry quand le platane répond furieusement à qui veut le réduire à son apparence particulière?' (2M 96).[18] He continues, 'Entendons, dans "tempête", l'action événementielle, et dans la "tête superbe", l'incorporation du platane aux conséquences universelles de la tempête, à la venue au monde d'une vérité' (2M 96).[19] All the weight of the reading here is in the 'Entendons . . .'. Badiou is seeking to understand 'Au Platane' in terms of his notion of truth in a way that performs the same sort of simplification that we saw in the previous chapter in relation to the birth of philosophy as the interruption of the mytheme by the matheme. It is important to recognise what Badiou is seeking to achieve here. He is not proposing a general theory of art or an engagement with historical approaches to Valéry, but a selective approach concerned only with 'some works of art' (*PMI* 7/*HOI* xiv) and concerned to read those selected works in terms of the post-theological agenda he sets for poetry:

> je pense que les événements littéraires opèrent pour la philosophie, mais que quand la philosophie les met en condition de son propre développement, elle opère des opérations malgré tout de sélection, de changement ou de transformation qui à mon avis ne sont pas des falsifications mais ce sont quand même des déplacements. (PLN 88–9)[20]

Inaesthetics 'simplifies' the reading of poetry in the same way that Badiou's account of the history of philosophy simplifies the Platonic moment to what in *Logiques des mondes* he calls a 'point' of a world's transcendental. A little clarification: a 'world' can be an epoch, moment in artistic or cultural development, battle or culture.[21] The transcendental of a world is its capacity to attribute different intensities of existence to what is within the world. The 'point' of a world's transcendental is the appearing of the infinite totality of the world before the instance of a decision (*LM* 614–15/*LW* 591). A point filters the nuances of a world's transcendental, producing a binary choice. In a similar way, an inaesthetic reading of poetry does not try to give a global account of a poem or an œuvre but to discern, isolate and if necessary force an interpretation of those moments which figure the Badiouian truth, or Idea. It is an 'engaged' approach to art, an approach that asks always after its effects for thought and whether it 'conquers its own atheism'.

This is what Jean-Jacques Lecercle calls a 'strong reading', an 'assertive and critical' mode of engaging with a text[22] defined as 'a construction whereby a philosopher constructs himself by constructing his Other',[23] and a reading he recognises entails a certain violence[24] in reading for the content of the text while showing no interest in signifiers[25] and resulting in a provocative intervention, not an interpretation.[26] That in addition Badiou's way of reading includes 'translation (of the text into the language of the theory) and modeling (of the theory by the text) which is a form of intervention (the text reads the theory that reads it)'[27] does little to redress the balance of power between Badiou's thought and the texts which it subjects to its strong reading, not least as a result of the very carefully chosen corpus of works with which Badiou engages, what Lecercle calls his 'happy few'.[28] Similarly unconvincing is the notion that the texts Badiou reads, texts that of course antedate his readings, have plagiarised him 'in anticipation'.[29] In a telling metaphor, Badiou frames philosophy as the procuress of the true:

> La philosophie a dès lors comme rapport à l'art, comme à toute procédure de vérité, de le montrer comme tel. La philosophie est en effet l'entremetteuse des rencontres avec les vérités, elle est la maquerelle du vrai. Et de même que la beauté doit être dans la femme rencontrée, mais n'est nullement requise de la maquerelle, de même les vérités sont artistiques, scientifiques, amoureuses ou politiques, et non pas philosophiques. (*PMI* 21)[30]

Philosophy, then, is the procuress of the true because it draws attention to artistic (or scientific, or amorous or political) truths and does not bring forth any truths of its own. Furthermore, if philosophy is truth's pimp, then art, as a truth condition, must be one of philosophy's whores.

As Badiou's ontology in the first *Manifeste* was dubbed a 'Platonism of the multiple', so in the *Second Manifeste* his logic is called a 'materialism of the Idea' (2*M* 67), where an Idea is the mediation between the individual and the subject of a truth, that in terms of which a faithful subject incorporated into a truth process represents the world to itself, or that which orients the life of a human animal/individual according to the Truth (2*M* 119). A similar premium on the Idea, or on 'truth' as Badiou uses the term, is prominent in his approach to film. He recommends passing through normative judgment (which says 'this is good') and through diacritic judgment ('this is better') to what he calls an axiomatic attitude, asking 'what are the effects of this or that film for thought?' (*PMI* 131/*HOI* 85). The axiomatic approach understands a film as that which exposes the passage of the Idea according to shot and editing (*PMI* 133/*HOI* 86). Cut, framing, movement, colour, actors, sound and so on are to be considered only to the extent that they contribute to the apprehension of an Idea in its impure presentation in the film (*PMI* 131/*HOI* 85). Given this rigorous focus on the film as vehicle of an Idea, it is perhaps not then surprising that Badiou identifies the main difficulty of speaking axiomatically about film to speak of it *as* film (*PMI* 132/*HOI* 86), rather than as the impure presentation of an Idea. The focus on the Idea does ensure, however, that Badiou's secularising manifesto for art is prosecuted. Rather than a finite, sacred art whose limit is open to an infinite horizon, Badiou's inaesthetics strives in its selective and 'displacing' approach to art to think an art that figures the Idea on the ground of multiplicity. What we have in the case of inaesthetics is a focus on art as a secularised rejection of the romantic paradigm and an evaluation of art as a function of the extent to which, and efficiency with which, it prosecutes this agenda.

2.1.2 *Presence, Incarnation and Idea*

The second front that Badiou opens in his attack on the irreducible religiosity of romanticism and post-Heideggerian poetic ontology is the collusion between a philosophy of finitude and the theology of incarnation. Just as Badiou identifies two types of poetry, the Romantic poetry of openness to the infinite to-come and the poetry of the Idea that connotes the void and produces truth, so also he discerns two opposed notions of incarnation, two ways of constructing the relation between the finite and the infinite in relation to art and the body, one Romantic and one subtractive. The paradigmatically Romantic conception of art is as the descent of the infinite, the ideal, into the finite body of the work (*S* 218/*Cen* 159), through the mediation of the sacrificial artist who, working by the 'spirit', imparts to the canvas forms that attest to the incarnation of the infinite (*S* 216/*Cen* 153–4). The price that must be paid for this incarnational paradigm, however, is a sort of generalised Christianity (*S* 218/*Cen* 155). Badiou rejects this incarnational paradigm complicit with the sacred and the Romantic infinite; the great question of contemporary art is how not to be Romantic (15T).

Not being Romantic brings problems of its own, however, for in rejecting the romantic notion of incarnation a post-theological art also rejects the essence of artistic activity – namely the relation between the finite and the infinite – and embarks on the destruction of art in its complete 'disinfinitisation'. To renounce the infinite altogether would be an ascetic approach, figuring the only possible infinity as a religious infinity and subsequently denying all infinity, and with it all art, to post-theological thought. Badiou's approach is rather to move beyond the oscillation between a Romantic subjectivity that possesses the infinite within itself and the nihilistic sacrifice of the infinite that would liquidate the notion of art as thinking (S 218/Cen 155); this can only be done by seeking a non-Romantic way of relating the finite to the infinite in art.

It is Hegel who is Badiou's guide along the way, in his discussion of the 'good' and 'bad' infinite in the discussion on 'Quantity' in the *Logic*.[31] The way in which Badiou appropriates Hegel's thought on the infinite is predicated on a re-definition of the essence of the finite. In Hegelian terms, the finite is what exceeds itself in itself, or what, in going beyond itself to the Other, remains in the element of the Same, where there is no alteration of itself, merely an iteration. The essence of the finite, in other words, is not that it is limited or circumscribed, but that it is a repetition (S 222–3/Cen 157). With this understanding of the finite in place, Badiou notes that Hegel's 'bad infinity' (*das schlechte Unendliche*) is the interminable repetitive series, for example the unending succession of natural numbers, or in Schelling's more colourful illustration, the English national debt, where one loan is repaid by another ad infinitum.[32] It is a sterile repetition that never escapes the finite.

Hegel's innovation is to discern an infinite within this finite sterile repetition itself. Considered in terms of its *result*, this endless repetition of adding one can be nothing other than a finite 'bad infinite', but the *action* of adding one, considered apart from the repetition of its result, is actually infinite, a Hegelian 'good infinite'. The finite (qua 'bad infinite') and the 'good infinite' are not opposed, rather, the good infinite is to be found within the bad infinite; the good infinite is immanent to the movement of the repetitive bad infinite, and the actual infinite is the *quality* of finite *quantity* (S 223/Cen 157): the act of self-exceeding is taken up in itself, exceeding the quantitative sphere to become qualitative, a pure quality of the finite itself (S 221/Cen 157). In *L'Etre et l'événement* Badiou expresses this relation in different terms: in the Hegelian concept of number, the infinite is the truth of the pure presence of the finite (see EE 181–90/BE 165).

Badiou uses this understanding of the finite and the infinite to shape his account of contemporary art in a way that breaks both with the paradigm of incarnation and with its nihilistic sacrifice. A 'good infinite' can be drawn from the finitude of the work of art if it is considered through the optic of the act of production, the very emphasis, notes Badiou, of many contemporary and ephemeral installations that critique the finitude, immobility and commercial commodification of the space of the canvas (S 214/Cen 152). The finite work of art itself, taken as an act and not a product, is the 'good infinite' of which art is capable.

In contrast to the paradigm of incarnation (as spirit-infused materiality), the infinite here is no longer housed in finite materiality, rather it passes through the work. The work is numbed or paralysed (*transi*) by being, an immanent overflowing of its own finitude and not merely an abstract virtuality into which the Ideal can descend (*S* 219/*Cen* 155). The way to be rid of romanticism then is through a 'materialist formalisation' of the work of art, where the infinite does not descend from heaven but proceeds directly from the finite (*S* 221–2/*Cen* 156). The most radical instantiation of this vision are works as 'happenings' which exist only as long as they are being made, or improvisation, which frustrates the solidification of form (*S* 220/*Cen* 156). Given this new understanding, this new artistic articulation of the finite and the infinite takes a path between the Romanticism of incarnation and the nihilism of an art which does not think (*S* 218–19/*Cen* 155).

So ideally, Badiou argues, the work of art in the twentieth century is in fact nothing other than the visibility of this infinity as an act, for this is the way in which it overcomes the Romantic pathos of the incarnational descent of the infinite into the finite body of the work (*S* 223/*Cen* 155). The 'work' is no longer a work, much less a sacred object. A non-religious art – a post-theological art after the death of God – is an art where the infinite comes from nothing other than an empty repetition.

There is one further way in which the relation of the finite to the infinite in materialist art differs from the incarnational paradigm. The infinite is not itself contained within the finite; the work of art is not a truth per se but the local operation of an eternal truth, a finite fragment of a truth which does not exist outside its operations:

> on doit pouvoir penser comment une vérité vient à l'existence en tant que corps dans un monde déterminé. Comment, en somme, une vérité apparaît. [. . .] Je suis un platonicien sophistiqué, et non un platonicien vulgaire. Je ne soutiens pas que les vérités préexistent à leur devenir mondain dans un « lieu intelligible » séparé, et que leur naissance n'est qu'une descente du Ciel vers la Terre. (2*M* 35)[33]

If truths do not come from an 'intelligible place', then where do they come from? The answer is: right here. In the *Court Traité* Badiou stresses the importance, after the death of the gods of religions, metaphysics and the poets, of understanding that 'tout est ici, toujours ici [. . .] Ici est le lieu du devenir des vérités. Ici nous sommes infinis' (*CT* 23),[34] and the whole treatise is to be conceived 'comme une méditation, dans l'éclaircie de la mort de Dieu, de ce qu'il faut penser sous ce mot: « ici »' (*CT* 24).[35]

Badiou's 'sophisticated Platonism' translates the problem of incarnation into the language of appearing and compatibility, for the eternity of truths must be compatible with the singularity of their appearing as bodies (2M 36). Badiou's thought demands nothing less than a rational account of the appearance of eternity within time, a post-theological integration that adopts Descartes's theory of the creation of eternal truths, but without the equation of eternity with God (2M 144). It is in his determination to hold eternal truth together with uncompromising materialism that Badiou is moving beyond both imitative and residual atheisms to a post-theological integration. However, there is an equivocation on 'eternity' between Descartes and Badiou: Badiou's 'eternity' might better be rendered 'trans-temporality', for a truth can operate at different moments in history without having to reside in an otherworldly world of Ideas. Badiou is using the term to refer to that quality of truths by which they can be reactivated in different worlds very (geographically, temporally, culturally) removed from the world in which they were first instantiated (2M 144). So the emancipatory truth of Spartacus' slave revolt is resurrected in Haïti with Toussaint-Louverture as the 'black Spartacus' (LM 73/LW 64). For Descartes, however, eternal truths have been established by God, cannot exist without him, and are just as dependent on him as any of his creatures are.[36] The difference between the 'eternity' of truths operating trans-temporally and the 'eternity' of truths dependent on an eternal God is fundamental; Badiou cannot remove God and maintain the same understanding of eternity.

Turning now to incarnation in relation to the subject, once more we find that Badiou seeks to retain a notion of the infinite within the context of a rigorous materialism. A romantic, finite subject is a 'disguised form of the preservation of God, whatever name we use for him',[37] and once more, as in the case of art, a simple rejection of the paradigm of incarnation and its preservation of God will lead only to the destruction of the subject in its reduction to the animal, an ascetic path that Badiou determines not to take. The paradigm of the subject which Badiou elaborates rejects humanity merely as 'given' in favour of embracing possible changes in human life, to the very level of its animal substructure, made possible by twenty-first century science. It is the programme of man without God (S 238–9/Cen 169). Far from an ascetic acquiescence to a finite human condition with death as its horizon, the death of God leads to an infinite affirmation of human possibility, and death itself is redefined in *Logiques des mondes* as the passing of something that appears in a world from a positive value of existence to the minimal value, to inexistence (LM 612/LW 601), where inexistence is the 'null' value of being-there, the least possible intensity of existence in a world (LM 610/LW 587). Badiou's is an anthropology of truths, not of the physical body, and a body itself is defined as a multiple-being that makes the event appear in a world (*LM* 606/*LW* 580–1), a definition similar to Badiou's understanding of art as an impure presentation of the Idea. A body is 'ce type très singulier d'objet apte à servir de support au formalisme subjectif, et donc à constituer, dans un monde, l'agent d'une vérité possible' (*LM* 473),[38] or in other words the human species of animal can serve as the material for truths (*ASR* 234).

The notion of the work of art as a fragment of an infinite truth, though not that truth itself, finds an echo in Badiou's understanding of the subject, in which the subject is subordinated to the production of truth. Indeed, Badiou affirms that the 'real content of humanity' is the creation of truths (*OTP*), and the subject, like the artwork, is the local operation of the infinity of a truth. Badiou's anthropology of truths leads to an understanding of human life as having a dual potential: on the one hand mere biological life and on the other hand 'true life' (*2M* 214) or 'a life worthy of this name' (*2M* 21), where true life is a life under the sign of the Idea (*2M* 137). Whereas the 'imperative of the world' says merely 'live only for your satisfaction, and so live without an Idea' (*2M* 21), philosophy declares that to live is to act such that there is no longer any distinction between life and Idea, an indiscernability that Badiou calls 'ideation' (*2M* 20). So the 'human animal' lives without any idea, and is little different from any other animal, apart from in its ability to become the subject of a truth:

> l'animal humain doit être logé à la même enseigne que ses compagnons biologiques. Ce massacreur systématique poursuit dans les fourmilières géantes qu'il a édifiées des intérêts de suivre et de satisfaction ni plus ni moins estimables que ceux des taupes eu des cicindèles. (*E* 80–1)[39]

It is only through incorporation into a truth that the human animal can escape this miserable existence.[40]

Badiou seeks to develop a post-theological integration by affirming that this body-subject is an immortal subject. To live 'as an Immortal' (*vivre « en Immortel »*), as the Ancients desired, is within everyone's grasp (*2M* 20). This is an immortality that has no need of God or the divine, for it is here and now that we live as immortals (*LM* 536/*LW* 513), or receive the grace to be immortal (*LM* 98/*LW* 105). Badiou explains his proposition thus: in so far as the subject is only a form, in the Platonic sense, so far is it immortal (*LM* 57/*LW* 49). In other words, the subject is incorporated into an eternal truth and partakes, qua subject, of the eternity of that truth. A truth is the means by which we – the human race – can become engaged in a trans-specific procedure, and it is this trans-specificity that grants us the prospect of immortality (*LM*

80/*LW* 71). To this extent, a truth is an experience of the inhuman, of the excess of the inhuman in human beings (*LM* 533/*LW* 511), and an experience analogous to escaping from the shadows of Plato's cave (*E* 81/*Eth* 59). Immortality is not a denial of biological death, but a prize won in its teeth: 'Qu'à la fin nous mourrions tous et qu'il n'y ait que poussière ne change rien à l'identité de l'Homme comme immortel, dans l'instant où il affirme ce qu'il est au rebours du vouloir-être-un-animal auquel la circonstance l'expose' (*E* 28)[41]

Though every human being is capable of being immortal in this way, it is also true that not all human beings are immortal, and one must wonder in passing whether, on Badiou's understanding, some are more capable of it, for whatever reason, than others. Can those with a mental illness, for example, be immortal, or can they only be human animals? It is unclear from Badiou's notion of immortality what the answer to this question would be, given that the capacity for truth is 'the singularly human' and humanity is defined in terms of an 'ability' (PoP 128). Furthermore, Badiou's account of immortality as becoming engaged in a trans-specific procedure once more redefines the term, speaking about something radically different from the term's theological or religious usage. Badiou's approach to post-theological integration reveals itself as an asceticism: to 'be an immortal' means not not to live for ever but the rather more limited, residual horizon of being engaged in a trans-specific procedure.

In his thinking of both art and the body, Badiou stakes out the great antagonism between Romantic philosophies of finitude and his own post-theological philosophy of the infinite. On the one hand there is an ethical pathos of finitude that understands its most extreme gesture as death, introduces a temporalised (bad) infinite, leaves itself wide open to the religiosity of the 'open' and the 'promise', and thinks incarnation in terms of a hypostatic union. On the other hand there is an ontology of inconsistent multiplicity that wields an ahistorical, secularised, dispersed infinite and seeks to think the relation of the finite and the infinite in terms of a body-subject of immanent difference (see *C* 176/*Con* 110–11). In this way, Badiou seeks not only to have consummated the death of God but also to have recast the notions of truth, infinity and immortality in an post-theological mould, but it is a mould that cannot escape the charge of asceticism.

2.2 THE PRESENCE OF THE DEATH OF GOD

The twin motifs that characterise the Romantic God of the poets for Badiou are the open infinite and incarnation. Nancean thought also rejects these two motifs. In conversation with Jacques Derrida, Nancy confesses to finding the 'Open' a rather troubling word (*un mot vraiment embêtant*), insisting that he is not in the least at ease with the 'Heideggerian Hölderlinism' of the Open and its infinity (RSAV 191). As for the notion of incarnation as the descent of the infinite into the finite, Nancy argues, very much like Badiou, that it is a penetration of the principle into a materiality that obscures and offends it (*Cor* 59/ *Corp* 67), leaving the body as a shadowy sign pointing to the hidden light within (*Cor* 60/*Corp* 67).

It is crucial to Nancy to rewrite these two notions in the image of his own deconstruction of Christianity, but the way that he moves away from these Romantic notions is very different from Badiou's recourse to the Idea. The Open and incarnation are reworked by Nancy in a way that seeks to appropriate theological ideas for post-theological integration, not with the Idea but with spacing. What is at stake in this difference is whether there are two different ways of seeking to move beyond the atheistic impasse of parasitism and asceticism, or whether either or both of Nancy and Badiou fall back into parasitism or asceticism. In addition, their divergent responses to the Romantic God of the poets raises the question of whether their two approaches to post-theological thought are commensurable.

2.2.1 The Open, the Finite and the Art of Spacing

Nancy insists that, if we have to maintain that opening is always an opening onto the infinite (*à l'infini*), it is not itself infinite. The Open presents itself always in terms of a contour, the example given by Nancy being the contour of the open mouth (RSAV 191), the space opened by the parting of two lips. Nancy rewrites the infinite and receding 'open' horizon as a finite spacing, the spacing of being-with: 'être-avec est la même chose qu'être-l'ouvert [. . .] un avec qui n'est autre que l'effet d'un ouvert, et un ouvert qui n'est autre que l'effet d'un avec' (PD 7–8).[42]

For Badiou the Open is irreducibly religious and must be overcome by the regime of multiplicity for which nothing is inaccessible, but for Nancy the Open remains, though re-imagined post-theologically as a resistance to the idolatrous fixity of closure. In relation to his deconstruction of Christianity, Nancy develops and qualifies the notion of openness in terms of an un-closing (*déclosion*), usually translated 'dis-enclosure', 'l'ouverture d'un enclos, la levée d'une clôture' (DDC 16).[43] The Open is both the horizon of determinate sense and also the tearing (*la déchirure*) of that horizon (DDC 226/DisDC 156). Open-as-spacing and Open-as-disenclosure are related but not identical ideas. Open-as-spacing is a finite opening of singulars that rejects both self-enclosure and the Romantic open infinite; Open-as-disenclosure is the double movement of exhaustion discussed in the preceding chapter, that similarly frustrates both self-identicality and infinite dissipation alike. Both are gestures of the Nancean 'yet without':[44] the Nancean Open breaks with determinate sense yet without descending into nonsense, it breaks with the infinite horizon yet without closing in on itself in self-identicality.

Our civilisation with its scientific, juridical and moral rationality has led to a closing, a completing of reason and of the world that cuts athwart our impulse (*pulsion*) for contact with the 'open' (*ADC* 58). Where asceticism would renounce the impulse, Nancy re-inscribes it in the context of spacing; where parasitism would retain the open with the placeholder of Man in the place of God, Nancy forecloses the possibility of a substantialised open, recasting it as the mutual returns (*renvois*) of spacing:

> cet ouvert, nous le sommes nous-mêmes, le langage l'est, le monde lui-même l'est. (Dire « l'ouvert » est déjà un abus de langage. Il faudrait éviter ce substantif et ce qui pourrait le tirer soit vers le concept, soit vers le nom. Ça s'ouvre précisément à distance de l'un et de l'autre.) (*ADC* 58)[45]

As both the possibility and the 'tearing' (or disruption) of determinate sense, the Nancean Open breaks the enclosure and self-sufficiency of the divine, the presence and value of God, the meaning of salvation as escape from the world, and every heavenly value, along with heaven (*le ciel*) itself (*DDC* 120/*DisDC* 78). The Open therefore also breaks the self-sufficiency of any parasitic atheism that apes the divine, seeks to erect secular idols or reinscribe religious or theological notions in an atheistic frame:

> Un monde ouvert est un monde sans mythes et sans idoles, un monde sans religion s'il faut entendre par ce mot l'observance de conduites et de représentations qui répondent à une demande de sens comme demande d'assurance, de destination, d'accomplissement. (*ADC* 58)[46]

The danger of parasitism is the idolatrous closure or fixing of sense, but spacing opens an infinite returning (*renvoi*) of sense that alone can foreclose a relapse into parasitism. Furthermore, it is because of the Open that Nancy rejects Heidegger's last God, who comes after the 'calculating determinations' of monotheism, pantheism, atheism and theism, and who signals another (postmetaphysical) 'beginning of immeasurable possibilities for our history'.[47] This God, even as the name of the unnameable or the unnamed, can only for Nancy throw a veil over the opening of the sense of the world (*SM* 93 n.2/*SW* 184 n.54), a naming which, once more, opening-as-disenclosure disrupts. In Nancy's thinking, the open is in direct opposition to the sacred, for the open as spacing knows no qualitative distinctions between the singulars that are spaced, and so forecloses the possibility of sacred space with its enclosures, reserves and places set apart (see *DLD* 50/*ODP* 150).

Just as Nancy re-figures the open in terms of spacing, he also secularises the infinite according to his deconstruction of Christianity. Since the publication of *Une Pensée finie* in 1990, Nancy has written more extensively on the infinite, and the reading of Hegel's good and bad infinity that he elaborates in *Hegel: L'Inquiétude du négatif* and elsewhere marks an important development in his thinking. It is a reading that bears many similarities to Badiou's, but there are also important differences, both in the way in which Nancy understands the relation between the finite and the infinite, and in its implications for thinking after the death of God.

To understand what is at stake in Nancy's reading of the good and bad infinite, we need to begin by noting that he refuses to think finitude as the negation of the infinite, as it is for Badiou (see *Poids* 13/*GT* 78; *NN* 25/*NuN* 14).[48] He also disavows this finitude that seeks to portray itself as 'positive', affirming our all-too-human condition, comforting itself with the thought of a totalitarian completion of sense (*Poids* 16–17/*GT* 81). This is a negative finitude, Nancy insists in a Badiouian tone, a thought of incompletion, lack, relativity and weakness, and it throws the whole lexicon of finitude into doubt. This finite remains the name of the non-infinite, 'c'est-à-dire du mal-fini et du pas-fini au sens de l'inaccompli, de l'avorté, du raté, de la signification manquée ou tronquée' (*Poids* 17),[49] a finitude that always annuls itself because it is impossible to think privation at all without also thinking what there is privation *of* (*SM* 51/*SW* 29). In other words, Nancy like Badiou rejects the negative finitude of ascetic atheism, the limit beyond which all manner of gods may roam free.

So Nancy very much agrees with Badiou that there is a 'bad finite'. But a Hegelian 'good infinite' is not what is called for, because if the finite is rejected for being a negation, then the good infinite, the negation of the finite negation, compounds rather than alleviates the problem of negativity. Post-theological thinking requires a finitude that is infinite and complete, not an infinite which negates the finite in incorporating the finite into itself, nor an ascetic finitude of privation, unable to complete itself. The Hegelian good infinite – the negation of the negation – is closed, 'l'assomption et la résorption sans reste du sens en tant que rapport à soi' (*Poids* 13);[50] it is the negation of alterity, of the open, of the limit and of spacing (*l'écart*). The reason Nancy is resisting the Hegelian good infinite (and by extension Badiou's use of this Hegelian motif) is that it leaves no remainder of sense, no openness to disrupt parasitic atheism's idols.

Nancy proposes an alternative definition of finitude: as the *à*-structure of being (where *à* means 'towards' or 'at'), as absolute finitude, a finitude that is not negated by the dialectising movement of the good infinite. This is the concept of finitude, he insists, which we must make our own. This absolute finitude is no longer to be understood as the negation of the infinite, nor is it negated by the infinite. It is a completing that is never complete, 'qui ne finit pas, qui n'achève pas, qui ne totalise pas et qui, en ce sens précis, n'« infinitise » pas' (*Poids* 13).[51] It keeps itself in the availability (*disponibilité*) of the singular, the non-totalisable, the Open. It is finitude understood as dynamic, as movement towards, an opening that never becomes *the* Open.

That is why Nancy, instead of *infini actuel*, prefers to use the term *infini en acte* (meaning 'in actuality' as opposed to 'in potential', but also 'in action'). The infinite 'in action' is explicitly contrasted with the present, closed infinity of the Romantics (*AL* 69/*LA* 48). The infinite *en acte* is Romantic only in the sense of a 'romantisme en acte', as opposed to the presented infinite of Romantic rhetoric: 'c'est bien en n'étant pas là, jamais encore là, que le romantisme et le fragment sont, absolument. *Work in progress* énonce désormais l'infinie vérité de l'œuvre' (*AL* 69).[52]

Nancy is reading Hegel in the following way: the Hegelian actual infinite cannot be given; in other words it is unpresentable, because it is that by which the given is given (*HIN* 38/*HRN* 25). In this Nancy is identifying the infinite 'in action' with his own *sens*. Whereas *significations* are determinate meanings, *sens* (or occasionally *signifiance*) is the field in which such meanings appear and by which they are always exceeded: 'le « sens » est bien loin d'être identique à la « signification ». Car la signification, c'est le sens repéré – tandis que le sens ne réside peut-être que dans la venue d'une signification possible' (*OP* 14).[53]

Sense is the movement, the giving of significations, in the same way that, in *Hegel: L'Inquiétude du négatif*, the infinite 'in action' is the giving of the finite:

> Un procès infini ne va pas « à l'infini », comme au terme toujours reporté d'une progression (Hegel nomme cela « mauvais infini ») : il est l'instabilité de toute détermination finie, l'emportement de la présence et du donné dans le mouvement de la présentation et du don (*HIN* 18–19)[54]

What is infinite in the infinite process is the movement of giving, the excess of giving 'upstream' of the gift (*ADC* 23), the gesture of presentation; the movement of presenting and giving disrupt the finitude of presentation and gift. It is this disruption of the gift by giving that allows Nancy to avoid the ascetic atheism according to which the finite is understood negatively as a limit bordering onto, but deprived of, the infinite. Rather, for Nancy finitude/signification is *of* the infinite/sense:

> Il n'y aurait pas ce que nous nommons «finitude» – mortalité, natalité, fortuité – si, du fait même que nous le nommons, nous ne laissions pas transparaître que nous existons et que le monde existe ouvert sur l'infini, par l'infini. C'est-à-dire que le fait même de l'existence nie qu'elle soit «finie» au sens où elle manquerait d'une extension au-delà d'elle-même. (ADC 11)[55]

It is finitude itself that is infinite; there is an absolute, but it is resolutely located between birth and death, for it is the finite itself which is absolute. The infinite is in the finite, and the finite opens onto the infinite without opening onto the theological. These arguments are summarised powerfully in Nancy's post-face to Martin Crowley's *L'Homme sans*:

> La finitude [. . .] devrait ne désigner que le «fini» en tant que dans sa fin il atteint l'infinité. La fin devient ici non pas la marque d'une incomplétude essentielle, mais au contraire l'index de ceci que, aucune complétude n'étant possible, c'est au-delà de toute totalité achevée que le fini vient exposer l'infinité que proprement il est. (PHS 181)[56]

This reading of the in/finite also gives Nancy an understanding of the death of God. The death of God as it has slowly played itself out in the Western tradition is a movement from act to object, from *esse* to *essentia*, from the infinite *en acte* to the closure of the presented infinite (*SM* 55/*SW* 32). The divine is the opening of signification onto sense, the opening of finite existence to the infinite *en acte*, and the death of God is the collapse of the infinite *en acte* into an actual infinite closed within thought, presented as thought. Nancy is not a philosopher of the finite over the infinite; he is a philosopher of the infinite in the finite.

When it comes to a post-theological understanding of art, the accent for Nancy is once more on a resistance to substantialising the movement of the Open figured as spacing. Art is understood in terms of a dynamic to and fro of significations that resists reification:

> L'art, aujourd'hui, a la tâche de répondre à ce monde, ou de répondre de lui. Il ne s'agit pas de faire image de cette absence d'idée, car dans ce cas l'art reste pris sous le schème ontothéologique de l'image de l'invisible, de ce dieu qu'il fallait «imaginer inimaginable» selon Montaigne. (*Mu* 151)[57]

Though art is frequently given legitimation today only in ethical or political terms, for Nancy there can only be one legitimation of art: 'l'attestation et l'inscription sensibles du débordement du sens' (*DDC*

14/*DisDC* 176 n.3).⁵⁸ Art is a witness to the Open, to the dis-enclosure of significations, not in its content but in its movement-towards the excess of sense.

If for Badiou the arts are all about the Idea, then for Nancy they are all about the sharing of sense: whereas myth sought to give voice to the origin, literature captures the innumerable voices of our sharing (*ADC* 62). What we share is the withdrawal of the origin, and literature speaks as the interruption of myth. Literature is not the transcription of data but the opening and communication of possible, indeterminate and uncloseable (*inachevable*) sense (*ADC* 20). Language is signification, but it is also salutation and address, where salutation (*le salut*) is the term Nancy uses in *L'Adoration* to signify the address of language that exceeds any information the language conveys, or we might say the giving of the language in excess of the language as gift: 'nous savons, dès lors que nous parlons, que le langage s'adresse et nous adresse à ce dehors de la communication et de la signification homogènes' (*ADC* 10).⁵⁹

Language addresses and calls the unnameable, the reverse side of all nomination. Once more, Nancy refuses to allow this reverse to be an opening for theology. It is not a hidden side of the world, a thing in itself or a being, but it is rather *that there are* things, *that there is* a world.

As for the relation between art and philosophy, Nancy understands it neither in terms of the Romanticism Badiou rejects, nor in terms of Badiou's own premium on the Idea in inaesthetics, but once more in terms of opening-as-disenclosing and opening-as-spacing. In 'Un Jour, les dieux se retirent . . .', the flight of the gods coincides with the end of the regime of myth, in which what would later become literature and philosophy knew no separation. The creation of literature and philosophy as opposing genres with the flight of the gods creates an opening marked by their difference, like the opening or spacing of two lips:

> L'absence des dieux est la condition des deux, littérature et philosophie, l'entre-deux qui légitime l'une et l'autre, irréversiblement athéologiques. Mais à elles deux elles ont office de prendre soin de l'entre-deux : d'en garder le corps ouvert, de lui laisser la chance de cette ouverture. (*UJ* 12)⁶⁰

Though the 'sacred mingling' of literature and philosophy, or of narration and truth, is no longer, nevertheless there is something inextricable (*indémêlable*) between them. After the flight of the gods, truth can no longer simply be narrated, and narrative can no longer simply be true. The truth of narration will always from now on be suspect, and truth for its part will lack articulation, becoming a vanishing point that anamorphoses into a question mark: affirmative truth becomes 'what is truth?' (*UJ* 9/BST). The resultant relation between philosophy and literature is that they are both simultaneously mourning for, and desiring, the other, and yet rivalling with the other in framing and accomplishing this mourning and this desire. We see here once more the motif of spacing: there is a spacing between literature and philosophy, a mutual inextricability and a return (*renvoi*) from one to the other.

The opening between literature and philosophy is not an infinite absence but a division that joins, a spacing of inextricable incommensurables and a division as relation and as responsibility, the responsibility to guard the opening itself. Philosophy and literature share the dynamic of mourning and desire that also divides them. This insistence on both incommensurability and inextricability is in contrast to Badiouian inaesthetics and its privileging of the Idea in art, for it is the irreducible spacing between literature and philosophy, the opening that they both mutually – but neither individually – shape that is productive not of signification but of sense as passage, as the opening, the spacing, itself.

The predication of this division between literature and philosophy on the withdrawal of the gods should not fool us into thinking that Nancy is parasitising a religious register. Once more, he is careful to rethink the withdrawal of the gods in a way that goes beyond an ascetic atheism and seeks to occupy the territory previously guarded by theological concepts. From his earliest work, Nancy reinscribes the withdrawal of the gods within his paradigm of spacing.

Not content to abandon terms such as the Open, alterity and the divine because of their complicity with theology, Nancy seeks rather to re-situate them in a new, post-theological context. Neither renouncing nor perpetuating the Romantic Open and infinite, Nancy rethinks them in terms of spacing and action. This means, however, that there are no terms available with which to articulate this new understanding of 'elsewhere' (*ailleurs*) not now as theological transcendence but as spacing. All the existing terms – 'gods' or 'God', 'mystery', 'beyond', 'tao', 'nirvana', 'intoxication' 'ecstasy' 'clairvoyance' – are unusable (*ADC* 13–14). This is part of a larger crisis of sense that post-theological integration must address, in which whole chains of signification (including 'man', 'history', 'nature', 'law', 'science', 'love' and 'art') are becoming unusable. However, this is only experienced as a breakdown because we have grown to believe in a permanence of sense undergirding the expansion of Western reason, Nancy argues, whereas in fact sense is never unproblematically given, it is always on the brink of being lost, always an excess or a lack (*ADC* 14).

Nancy's own response to this crisis is to give the old words new meanings, to occupy the territory of theology and enjoy its fruit, yet without adopting its principles. Nancy's post-theological integration is a post-theological 'yet without': a rejection of imitative atheism's idolatry, yet without resolving to residual atheism's destitution. In *L'Adoration* Nancy wrestles with the notion of transcendence, seeking to rethink it in terms of the constitutive irreducibility of singular plurality to monadic identity, without returning to God or otherworldliness: 'il ne désigne pas l'état d'un « être » plus ou moins « suprême », mais le mouvement par lequel un existant sort de la simple égalité à soi-même' (*ADC* 30).[61] Once more, the theological term is de-substantialised and re-thought as a movement immanent to singular plural spacing: an existent is not closed upon itself in splendid isolation but always already with others. Nevertheless, in the end Nancy admits that 'transcendence', a term too heavily weighed down by centuries of being used in a static sense, must be renounced (*ADC* 31). Whether or not the term is retained, however, the impetus of Nancy's 'yet without' is the same: neither ascetically to renounce theological categories nor parasitically to adopt them wholesale, but rather to seek to occupy them with a radically post-theological thinking.

The most striking and daring example of this strategy of occupation is Nancy's re-working of 'God'. Nancy does use the language of God in relation to the Open, but it is to secularise the language of God, not to divinise that of the Open: 'Seule l'ouverture est divine, mais le divin n'est rien de plus que l'ouverture' (*CM* 93; cf *DDC* 74/*DisDC* 118).[62] In *L'Adoration* Nancy ventures an interpretation of the Qur'anic ayah that 'God created men to be adored by them' (*ADC* 31–2) that seeks to understand the verse wholly otherwise (*tout autrement*) than as an expression of divine narcissism. As with the deconstruction of Christianity, Nancy argues that God is only the 'front man' (*le prête-nom*) for the infinite relation to the infinite within the finite, a pure excess of the world and of existence beyond themselves and within themselves (*ADC* 31–2). 'God' no longer designates a being but a movement towards the incommensurable, a 'salutation' that plays on the double sense of *salut* as salvation and greeting (*ADC* 113): God as the movement-towards of the address. As for adoration (from *ad-oratio*, speak towards), it is the possibility of an unheard-of address that is no longer religious (*ADC* 31). Adoration for Nancy is a gesture of occupation that follows the pattern of the 'yet without'. We renounce the sacred, yet without abandoning ourselves to bad infinity:

> Notre souffrance: nous savoir démunis d'horizons et, avec eux, de justifications des malheurs (maladies, injustices) et de fondements pour la punition des crimes (pour la désignation des « méchants »). C'est là ce que veut dire

> l'autodissolution de l'Occident dans le déploiement de sa logique in-finie (dépourvue de fins), qui forme le revers de l'infini logique (la fin en soi à chaque instant présente [. . .]). Contre cette souffrance de l'in-fini (le capital, l'équivalence, mauvais infini), il faut une différenciation, une évaluation autre (Nietzsche), et donc une « adoration ». (*ADC* 108)[63]

The renunciation of theistic horizons and ends leads to the dissolution of the West, but adoration breaks with the regime of determinate signification, from the infinite circulation of equivalence, providing the 'yet without' of Nancy's approach to post-theological integration. Nevertheless, as we saw in our discussion of *Le Toucher* in the previous chapter, this gesture of moving beyond the 'front man' God to the infinite movement of which he provides one contingent instance risks being recuperated as a Christian hyperbole, a repetition of the move of seeking the truth behind the appearance, the heart behind the surface.

A similar strategy of seeking to occupy religious terms is in evidence in the earlier 'Calcul du poète', a reading of Hölderlin in which Nancy rewrites the withdrawal of the gods in a way that makes the withdrawal itself the 'divine'. For Nancy, the presence of the gods in Hölderlin is the tangential touch of passing contact; this is 'true presence': neither pleroma nor postponement, but passage. The presence of the gods *is* this passage: 'Le divin est le passage, et n'est que cela' (*DLD* 75).[64] It is not the gods which have withdrawn; it is the withdrawal which is the divine, but a resolutely post-theological divine, a divine which is here and now, which is the place of the coming and going of gods: 'Le dieu n'est que le lieu, le lieu est le lieu du départ et du retour' (*DLD* 76).[65] It is this withdrawal that 'makes sense', not as an infinite openness but as the tangent of passage touching the materiality of the poem. In short, Nancy understands poetry as 'calcul matériel du passage athée' (*DLD* 76).[66]

If we seek to compare this account with Badiou's way of dealing with the god of the poets, we are confronted with two radically different ways of seeking to avoid the theology latent in the Open and in the infinite. Nancy's infinite as giving and presentation bears a striking similarity to Badiou's understanding of the actual infinite as process, but we must not let this mask a deep division in their approaches. Nancy is foreclosing parasitism with movement towards (*à*), disrupting the closure of the infinite by making sure it remains 'work in progress', whereas Badiou is trying to overcome asceticism by denying the Open that allows for the withdrawal of the gods beyond its horizon. The difference is not in what Nancy and Badiou are trying to achieve but what they consider to be the constraints on any post-theological integration. Both want to move towards such an integration, but whereas for Nancy imitative atheism with its Christmas projection must be resisted with the 'yet without' that forecloses any gesture of completion, for Badiou residual atheism will always be a threat as long as Romantic inaccessibility is not done away with by axiomatics. In other words, Badiou sees residual atheism in Nancy's attempt to foreclose imitative atheism, and Nancy sees imitative atheism in Badiou's attempt to resist residual atheism. The problem is that there is no way to arbitrate between the two positions: each has a legitimate critique of the other within its own terms. What is at stake between Nancy's post-theological 'yet without' and Badiou's post-theological Idea is not just a difference but a differend within post-theological integration, and one to which we shall have occasion to return.

2.2.2 *Presence, Incarnation and Spacing*

Just as Nancy thinks openness and the infinite otherwise than according to the Romantic ontology that Badiou sets himself against and otherwise than Badiou's own art of the Idea, so also the Nancean thinking of incarnation is neither congruent with Badiou's understanding of Romanticism nor with his notion of the human animal becoming a body-subject through being incorporated into a truth. In 'La déconstruction du christianisme' Nancy identifies two prominent motifs of Christianity. The first, an interrogation of the origins of Christianity, was discussed in the previous chapter. The second element is incarnation. Of all the major Christian doctrines – creation, atonement, resurrection, judgment . . . – it is the incarnation that Nancy puts at the heart of Christology (*DDC* 219/*DisDC* 151), and at the heart of Western culture as a whole (*DDC* 125/*DisDC* 81). Nancy's reworking of the motif of incarnation follows the paradigm of spacing in terms of which he also refigures the open and the infinite. This section will see how Nancy re-thinks incarnation as 1) a dis-enclosed paralysis and 2) as a corporeal technicity.

In 'Dei paralysis progressiva' (*PF* 353–64/*BTP* 48–57) Nancy talks of the spacing of bodies, the presentation of presentation, as the 'nothing' (*rien*) that Romanticism strove to present but which is unpresentable. This 'nothing' of spacing, the condition of possibility of all bodies in the world, this giving of the gift of signification, cannot be presented in a Romantic incarnation, but it can be exposed in a movement of 'yet without'. In this essay Nancy rewrites the death of God in terms of the 'yet without' of dis-enclosure in a way that rewrites the Romantic attempt to present the 'nothing'. Nancy argues that Nietzsche dies *in persona dei*, as the successor to the dead God (*PF* 358/*BTP* 52), with the mask and in the pose of God (*PF* 353–4/*BTP* 48). The paralysis that gradually takes over Nietzsche's body figures the death of God not as a destruction, but as a presentation (*PF* 353/*BTP* 48), a laying open of the body here and now in a lepidoptery without death: *hoc est enim corpus meum*, this is my body. As the paralysis progresses it finally offers a death mask of eternity (*PF* 353/*BTP* 48). God presents himself as dead *in persona*, and rather than being the sign of an absence (as in the traditional paradigm of incarnation), this corporeal death-as-paralysis presents God with an absolute presence (*PF* 356/*BTP* 50).[67] But this is no Romantic theophany; the death of Nietzsche does not present the absolute presence of God, nor the absolute presence of God's absence, but the absolute presence of the incarnation of the dead God (*PF* 356/*BTP* 50). God presents himself dead, 'il s'incarne mort' (*PF* 356).[68] The death of God spells the end of this sort of presentation of death, the end of death in the horizon of its representation: tragic death or salvific death (*AFI* 88/*GOI* 44). God present(ed) as dead is God present as nothing (*rien*), not the reified Nothing of Romanticism but an immobile suspension in the 'nothing' 'qui ne peut même pas, en toute rigueur, être appelée « la mort », car elle n'a pas d'identité – mais elle emporte toute identité' (*PF* 356).[69] Incarnation is rewritten as a suspension, not a presentation, of the event, a rejection of the Romantic presentation of the nothing.

This first way in which Nancy re-thinks incarnation after the death of God follows the pattern of dis-enclosure. The second is in terms of spacing, what Derrida calls a deconstruction of Christian flesh[70] in the motifs of *techne* and *corpus*, brought together in Nancy's *techne du corps*. The *techne* of bodies provides Nancy with an alternative to the traditional (Platonic) notion of incarnation that resolves neither to a re-statement of a Christian position nor to Badiou's 'fragment of the infinite'. Nancy's starting point is that the death of God requires a re-thinking of the body. 'God is dead' means – according to the schema of the flight of the gods with which we are now familiar from *Un jour . . .* – that God no longer has a body, and it might very well be that with this body, all bodies have been lost, for according to the flesh/spirit dualism of the incarnational paradigm, 'en vérité, le corps de Dieu était le corps de l'homme même' (*Cor* 54).[71] The new thinking of the body which this demands is a rejection of all philosophies of the flesh, where flesh is always 1) 'nourished by sense', with meanings 'encrusted in its joints' in Merleau-Ponty's vivid phrase,[72] and 2) 'egological', in other words reliant upon an irreducible Cartesian self.

Crucially, the heart of incarnation itself for Nancy is not the distinction between flesh (*sarx*) and spirit (*psyche*), but rather their consubstantiality (*homoousia*). It is this identity or community of being and substance between Father and Son that is Christianity's true innovation, he argues, not that spirit entered matter but rather that the word *became* flesh[73] (*logos sarx egeneto*) (*ADC* 78), and it is this identity that he seeks to rework in his own notion of *corpus*.

Badiou replaces incarnation, it will be recalled, with two distinct categories: the human animal and the subject of a truth. There is no such distinction for Nancy; *corpus* is the universal human condition. *Corpus* disrupts the limit between spirit and flesh:

> Les corps n'ont lieu, ni dans le discours, ni dans la matière. Ils n'habitent ni « l'esprit », ni « le corps ». Ils ont lieu à la limite, *en tant que la limite:* limite – bord externe, fracture et intersection de l'étranger dans le continu du sens, dans le continu de la matière. Ouverture, *discrétion*. (*Cor* 18)[74]

This is a gesture with which we are now familiar. The body is an opening and a limit, not in the sense that it abuts a *nec plus ultra* beyond which spectres and gods can roam freely, but that it is a spacing, a circumscribed opening, between two incommensurables: discourse and matter. The dichotomy of matter and mind, like that of story and truth, is shown to be a posteriori, a dichotomous abstraction from a *corpus* that inhabits the opening of the two terms. This is also the point at which Nancy's thought questions Badiou's characterisation of 'democratic materialism' in *Logiques des mondes*, namely that there are only bodies and languages (*LM* 12/*LW* 1). For Nancy there are neither bodies nor languages in the way that Badiou means. For Nancy there is the opening of 'spirit' and 'body' of *corpus*, leaving discourse and matter only as a posteriori abstractions. So Ian James is right to say that Nancy rethinks Christian incarnation 'not as consubstantiality or *houmoousia*, but as a touch in separation of spirit and matter',[75] but only if we also understand this touch in separation not as the touch of two primordially separated elements, but as the touch of spacing, the touch of singular plurality. *Corpus* is not an animal struck by the lightening of truth and that retains a fragment of that truth to lift it above animality; it is always already the opening of an interval. This is figured most vividly in the mouth, the site of a *quasi permixtio* between soul and body, of the incommensurable common extension between them (*ES* 161). It is not the incarnation of the ideality of 'sense' but the end, in the opening of body to sense and sense to body, of an ideality which refers only to itself (*Cor* 24/*Corp* 23). In addition, incarnation is also rewritten in terms of opening as the spacing of finite beings: 'Incarnation: que l'infinité divine ait son effectivité dans le rapport des étants finis. Que le sens soit donc par essence fini : interrompu, suspendu sur la vérité vide afin d'éviter le remplissement étouffant d'une conclusion' (*ADC* 108).[76]

So as opposed to a notion of incarnation, previously the only way of thinking the relation of 'spirit' and 'flesh' in the West (*Cor* 77/*Corp* 87), Nancy proposes to re-think incarnation in terms of spacing and sharing:

> Les corps résistent, dures *partes extra partes*. [. . .] Les corps exigent encore, à nouveau, leur création. Non pas l'incarnation qui insuffle la vie spirituelle du signe, mais la mise au monde et le partage des corps. Non plus des corps employés à faire du sens, mais du sens qui donne et qui partage des corps. (*Cor* 73)[77]

Nancean *techne* is not to be confused with Heideggerian technics, a way of revealing the world in the age of instrumentalised industrial mechanisation.[78] *Techne* for Nancy is understood as 'art', 'craft' or 'creation' in the broad sense that blurs the distinction between the natural and the artificial, so the *techne* of the body is the medicinal, prosthetic and technological extensions of, modifications to and replacements for parts of the body that blur limits of the body (*Cor* 78/*Corp* 89). The *techne* of the neighbour is the sharing or 'compearing' of bodies that is neither purely natural nor wholly artificial (*Cor* 80/*Corp* 91). With the *techne* of the neighbour, the meaning of incarnation is no longer the descent of the idea into the flesh but rather an invitation to the sharing of sense: 'c'est à nous, humains, mortels, sans dieux et sans nature, techniciens engagés dans la production indéfinie d'un monde « notre », qu'il incombe de faire sens' (*ADC* 77).[79] However, this *partage* (sharing/dividing) simultaneously exposes Nancy to a danger of parasitism, as Derrida once more discerns in *Le Toucher*:[80]

> Voici donc encore une fois mon hypothèse, je l'avance timidement et non sans inquiétude: il y a partage, au sens de partition ou de séparation, de nouveau départ, dans cette prise en compte de la techné, là où, dans le même geste, elle se porte au-delà du corps chrétien.[81]

In other words, Nancy's *techne* may indeed be a sharing (*partage*) of bodies but it is also a partition (*partage*) between itself and the Christian body of incarnation, and this partition risks reinscribing Nancean *techne*, after all, back within the logic of the Christmas projection. As we saw in the case of the 'deconstruction of Christianity' itself, Nancy's approach to escaping parasitism, while successful in its explicit aim, cannot escape re-inscribing the parasitism it seeks to escape.

The explicit aim in this case is to have sharing as the rethinking of incarnation after the death of God in that the sharing of bodies produces no *signification* and yet opens up a bodily *sens*. In the paradigm of incarnation, bodies were signs that signified the intelligible, sepulchres of the soul that signified the light inside. But with Nancean spacing bodies once more signify, not in the production of significations, but in the opening of sense. Sharing and spacing mean that the body for Nancy is open and infinite, the open of closure itself (as we have seen in the dis-enclosure of Christianity), and the infinite of the finite itself (as we have seen in the infinite *en acte*) (*Cor* 107/*Corp* 122).

CONCLUSION

As we draw to the end of this discussion of the Open, the infinite and incarnation in Nancy and Badiou, we find them both closer and further apart than ever. The closeness can be most clearly seen in the articulation of the finite and the infinite in their reading of Hegel, a point recognised by Badiou in 'L'Offrande réservée': 'Je sais ce que Jean-Luc Nancy pense, et qu'il m'a souvent dit: que ce que j'appelle l'infini est en tout cas au point même de la pensée qu'il nomme « finitude »' (OR 20).[82] The way in which Nancy finds an infinite *en acte* in the finite itself and the way in which Badiou locates the infinite of art in its finite process do indeed allow us to say that, in this sense, finitude for Nancy stands 'at the same point' as the infinite for Badiou. We also, however, see Badiou and Nancy further apart than ever, inhabiting two sites of thought that can be brought into dialogue only with difficulty, if at all. For Badiou there is a primary dichotomy (bodies and truths, material art and idea) that needs to be bridged (by incorporating a fragment of truth in a body). For Nancy the dichotomy (matter and spirit, story and truth) is secondary, and the spacing of the two terms is what is important, in their inextricability and incommensurability.

Badiou's post-theological integration has two moves, that we could summarise with the shorthand 'being' and 'truth'. The existential axioms – of infinity and the empty set – do away with all finite limits in the infinite multiples of the equation of mathematics and ontology. This in itself, however, would amount to a residual atheism denied any notion of truth as Badiou conceives it. The second move in Badiou's atheism is the incorporation of the body-subject into the actual infinite of the Idea, a move that brings the notion of eternal (or at least transtemporal) truth back within atheism's purview. Nancy's post-theological integration also has two moves, but there the similarities end. Nancy's two moves are the 'yet without' of dis-enclosure – the break with determinate sense yet without being delivered over to nonsense, the opening of given significations onto the giving of sense, irreducible to what is given – and spacing, the spacing that is not an opening onto the infinite but the sharing and division of what was previously undivided (story and truth, body and soul).

Badiou's atheism must effect a definite break with the finite for the actual infinity of eternal truth, or else it is always possible that thinking will remain finite and therefore Romantic, an analysis which identifies Nancy's *sens* as unable to close the door on residual atheism. Nancy's post-theological 'yet without' seeks to avoid the 'Christmas projection' of a definite break, on pain of a gesture that imitates a quintessentially theological move; Badiou's account of the necessity of such breaks both in the birth of philosophy and in his account of truths is identified as a gesture that cannot escape imitative atheism. Whereas for Nancy the danger of the Christmas projection is that it violently reduces the complexity of becoming and ignores detail, Badiou makes a virtue of such simplifying 'points', and impugns in 'L'Offrande réservée' the sort of thinking that ascetically refuses to incorporate the Idea in the present:

> « Une pensée tout entière à venir! » Comme est irritant le style post-heideggérien de l'annonce perpétuelle, de l'à-venir interminable, cette sorte de prophétisme laïcisée ne cesse de déclarer que nous ne sommes pas encore en état de penser ce qu'il y a à penser, ce pathos de l'avoir-à-répondre de l'être, ce Dieu qui fait défaut, cette attente face à l'abîme, cette posture du regard qui porte loin dans la brume et dit qu'on voit venir l'indistinct! Comme on a envie de dire : « Écoutez, si cette pensée est encore tout entière a venir, revenez nous voir quand au moins un morceau en sera venu! » (OR 15–16)[83]

In other words, Nancy's thinking renounces the possibility of decisive action in the present. For Nancy in contrast, the danger of declaring that the Idea has arrived, for example that religion is *finished*, is that it constitutes the victory of the dialectical theology of the death of God, a return to imitative atheism.

We have come as far as the analysis to this point will allow us. Both Nancy and Badiou have grave concerns about the account of post-theological thought proposed by the other, and it is not clear how we might begin to arbitrate between their two accounts. In order to explore further to what extent these approaches to post-theological thinking seek to avoid parasitism and asceticism, we now need to sharpen our focus and examine more closely what we might call the characteristic moment of each one: the axiom for Badiou and the double movement of dis-enclosure for Nancy.

NOTES

1. Oscar Wilde, 'Epistola: In Carcere et Vinculis', in *The Complete Works of Oscar Wilde*, general eds Russell Jackson and Ian Small, vol. 2, ed. Ian Small (Oxford: Oxford University Press, 2005), p. 98.

2. 'like the trace of an afterlife in the movement that entrusts the overcoming of the religion-God and the metaphysics-God to the poem-God' (*BOE* 29).
3. The line is taken from stanza 8 of *Brot und Wein*, quoted from Hölderlin, *Selected Poems and Fragments*, p. 157.
4. This mediating role of poetry emerges in Hegel's later work, most acutely perhaps in the *Systemprogramm*: 'mythology must become philosophical, and the people reasonable, and philosophy must become mythological in order to make philosophers sensuous. . . . A higher spirit sent from heaven must found this new religion among us', quoted from Jochen Schulte-Sasse and Haynes Horne (eds), *Theory as Practice: A Critical Anthology of Early German Romantic Writings* (Minneapolis: University of Minnesota Press, 1997), p. 73.
5. See Martin Heidegger, *Identity and Difference*, trans. Joan Stambaugh (Chicago: University of Chicago Press, 2002), p. 72; Caputo, 'Atheism, a/theology, and the postmodern condition', p. 272.
6. See Marchart, *Post-Foundational Political Thought*, pp. 114–15.
7. 'So long as the finite remains the ultimate determination of being-there, God remains' (*Con* 99).
8.
> That our exposure to being is essentially finite and that we must forever return to our mortal-being, is that fact from which we endure the living God's death only to uphold, under multiple forms, the indistinct promise of a sense that has withdrawn, but whose 'come-back' has not been debarred. (*BOE* 29; translation altered)

9. In the *Petit Manuel* Badiou moves through speaking of poetry and theatre, Beckettian prose, cinema, and dance. The thinking that he elaborates largely in the book's early studies of poetry is selectively broadened, *mutatis mutandis*, to cover a number of other arts.
10. 'The poem only has to be devoted to the enchantment of what the world is capable of – as it is. It has only to discern the infinite "*surrection*" of invisible possibilities up to the impossible itself' (*BOE* 29).
11. 'this minimal consistency (a part, a conceptless immanence), which certifies in the situation the inconsistency from which its being is made' (*Man* 107).
12. 'Every poem seeks to uncover and to carry to the formal limits of language the latent void of sensible referents' (*NuN* 161).
13.
> By 'inaesthetics' I understand a relation of philosophy to art that, maintaining that art itself is a producer of truths, makes no claim to turn art into an object for philosophy. Against aesthetic speculation, inaesthetics describes the strictly intraphilosophical effects produced by the independent existence of some works of art. (*HOI* xiv)

14.
> Today the poem's imperative is to conquer its own atheism. From within, it destroys the powers of natural language, nostalgic phraseology, posturing of the promise, or prophetic destination to the Open. [...] it is poetry itself that will conduct, and has been conducting at least since the beginning of the last century, the task of putting its own God to death. (*BOE* 29–30; translation altered)

15. 'far from maintaining the appeal to the Open in distress, the power of the poem attempts instead to subtract thought from any returning of the gods and ascertain it in the steadfastness of the multiple' (*BOE* 35).
16. An 'Idea' for Badiou is that which proposes the horizon of a new possibility in relation to a determinate question (see *PE* 24).
17. Paul Valéry, *Œuvres*, ed. Jean Hytier, 2 vols (Paris, Gallimard: 1957–60), vol. I, p. 91. ' – No, says the tree. It says: No! By the sparking of its proud head, which the storm universally treats as it does a blade of grass' (Hartley, ed., *The Penguin Book of French Verse: 4*, p. 50).
18. 'Is it not this connection that Valéry is thinking of when the plane tree responds furiously to the one who wishes to reduce it to its particular appearance?' (author's translation).
19. 'Let us hear, in "storm" the eventual action, and in the "magnificent head" the incorporation of the plane tree into the universal consequences of the storm, into the coming to the world of a truth' (author's translation).
20. 'I think that literary events are indeed operative for philosophy, but when philosophy sets them as conditions for its own development, it none the less proceeds through operations of selection, change or transformation. These operations are not exactly falsifications but they are, after all, displacements' (*CCBT* 257).
21. See Meillassoux's lucid description of Badiouian worlds in HE.
22. Lecercle, *Badiou and Deleuze Read Literature*, p. 53.
23. Lecercle, *Badiou and Deleuze Read Literature*, p. 30.
24. Lecercle, *Badiou and Deleuze Read Literature*, p. 44.
25. Lecercle, *Badiou and Deleuze Read Literature*, p. 64.
26. Lecercle, *Badiou and Deleuze Read Literature*, pp. 69–70.
27. Lecercle, *Badiou and Deleuze Read Literature*, p. 103.
28. Lecercle, *Badiou and Deleuze Read Literature*, p. 198.
29. Lecercle, *Badiou and Deleuze Read Literature*, p. 200.
30.
> Philosophy's relation to art, like its relation to every other truth procedure, comes down to *showing* it as it is. Philosophy is the go-between in our encounters with truths, the procuress of truth. And just as beauty is to be found in the woman encountered, but is in no way required

of the procuress, so it is that truths are artistic, scientific, amorous, or political, and not philosophical. (*HOI* 9–10)

31. Hegel, *Hegel's Logic*, pp. 145–57.
32. See F. W. J. Schelling, 'Fernere Darstellungen aus dem *System der Philosophie*', in *Sämmtliche Werke* (Stuttgart: J. G. Cotta, 1859), vol. 4, p. 344.
33.
    we must be able to think how a truth comes to exist as a body in a particular world. How, in short, a truth appears. [...] I am a sophisticated Platonist, and not a vulgar Platonist. I do not hold that truths pre-exist their worldly becoming in an 'intelligible place' apart, and that their birth is only a descent from Heaven to the Earth. (Author's translation)
34. 'everything is here, always here [...] Here is the place where truths come to be. Here we are infinite' (*BOE* 31).
35. 'as in a meditation, in the clearing of God's death, of what must be thought in the word: "here"' (*BOE* 32).
36. See Descartes, letter to Mersenne, 15 April 1630, in *Œuvres de Descartes*, vol. 1, p. 145; *The Philosophical Writings of Descartes*, vol. 3, *The Correspondence*, p. 23.
37. Alain Badiou and N. Poirier, 'Entretien avec Alain Badiou', in *Le Philosophoire* vol. 9 (1999), p. 2, quoted in Peter Hallward, *Badiou: A Subject to Truth*, p. 6.
38. 'this very singular type of object suited to serve as a support or a subjective formalism, and therefore to constitute, in a world, the agent of a possible truth' (*LW* 451).
39. 'the human animal must be lumped in the same category as its biological companions. This systematic killer pursues, in the giant ant hills he constructs, interests of survival and satisfaction neither more nor less estimable than those of moles or tiger beetles' (*Eth* 58–9).
40. The reader will note that we are not attempting to provide here an exhaustive account of Badiouian truth and the subject, but our discussion is limited to dealing strictly only with those notions that have a direct bearing on our argument in relation to the God of the poets. Other crucial notions in the Badiouian account of truths – notably fidelity, the truth-event and the truth-process – are dealt with in subsequent chapters.
41.
    The fact that in the end we all die, that only dust remains, in no way alters Man's identity as immortal at the instant in which he affirms himself as someone who runs counter to the temptation of wanting-to-be-an-animal to which circumstances may expose him. (*Eth* 12)
42. 'being-with is the same thing as being-the-open [...] a with that is nothing other than the effect of an open, and an open that is nothing other than the effect of a with' (author's translation).

43. 'the opening of an enclosure, the raising of a barrier' (*DisDC* 6).
44. For an explanation of the motif of the 'yet without' in Nancy's thought, see Watkin, *Phenomenology or Deconstruction?*, p. 142.
45.

    this open, we ourselves are it, language is it, the world itself is it. (To pronounce 'the open' is already to abuse language. We should avoid this substantive and whatever could drag it either in the direction of the concept or towards the noun. It opens, precisely, at a distance from one as from the other). (Author's translation)

46.

    An open world is a world without myths and without idols, a world without religion, if we must understand by this word the observance of behaviours and representations that respond to a demand of/for sense as a demand for assurance, for a destination, for fulfilment. (Author's translation)

47. Heidegger, *Contributions to Philosophy*, p. 289.
48. The analysis of Nancy and Badiou on actual infinity here builds on Ian James, 'Incarnation and infinity'.
49. 'that is, of the *badly*-finished and the *not*-finished in the sense of the incomplete, the aborted, the failed, the missed or truncated signification' (*GT* 81).
50. 'the appropriation and the total resorption of meaning as relation-to-itself' (*GT* 78).
51. 'that does not complete or totalize and, in this sense, does not "infinitize"' (*GT* 78).
52. 'it is indeed in this not being there, this never yet being there, that romanticism and the fragment *are*, absolutely. *Work in progress* henceforth becomes the infinite truth of the work' (*LA* 48).
53. '"sense" is far from being identical to "signification." For signification is located meaning, while sense resides perhaps only in the coming of a possible signification' (*GT* 10; translation altered).
54.

    An infinite process does not go on 'to infinity,' as if to the always postponed term of a progression (Hegel calls this 'bad infinity'): it is the instability of every finite determination, the bearing away of presence and of the given in the movement of presentation and the gift. (*HRN* 12)

55.

    There would not be what we call 'finitude' – mortality, birth, fortuitousness – if, by the very fact of naming it, we didn't let it show through that we exist and that the world exists open onto the infinite, by the infinite. Which is to say that the very fact of existence denies that it is 'finite' in the sense of lacking an extension beyond itself. (Author's translation)

56.

Finitude [...] should indicate the 'finite' only in so far as in its end it attains infinity. The end becomes here not the mark of an essential incompleteness, but on the contrary the index – no completion being possible – of this: that it is beyond every completed totality that the finite comes to expose the infinity which it really is. (Author's translation)

57.

Art, today, has the task of answering to this world or of answering for it. It is not a matter of making this absence of Idea into an image, for art then remains caught in the ontotheological schema of the image of the invisible, of the god that, as Montaigne said, one had to 'imagine unimaginable'. (*Mus* 93)

58. 'the sensuous attestation to and inscription of the overflowing of sense' (*DisDC* 176).
59. 'we know, as soon as we speak, that language addresses itself and addresses us to this outside of homogeneous communication and signification' (author's translation).
60.

The absence of gods is the condition for both literature and philosophy to be in. It is the in-between which legitimates the one and the other, both of which are irreversibly atheological. But they both have the responsibility of taking care of the in-between: of guarding the open body, and of allowing it the possibility of this opening. (BST)

61. 'it does not designate the state of a "being" that is more or less "supreme", but the movement by which an existent departs from simple equality to itself' (author's translation).
62. 'Only the opening is divine, but the divine is nothing more than the opening' (*CWG* 114).
63.

Our suffering is this: to know that we are bereft of horizons and, along with them, of justifications for misfortune (illnesses, injustices) and of bases for the punishment of crimes (for singling out 'evil people'). That is what the self-dissolution of the West means, in the unfolding of its in-finite/un-ending logic (shorn of ends), which forms the reverse of the infinite logic (the end in itself, present at every instant [...]). Against this suffering of the in-finite (capital, equivalence, the bad infinite), we need another differentiation, another evaluation (Nietzsche), and thus an 'adoration'. (Author's translation)

64. 'the divine is passing and only that' (CalP 62).
65. 'the god is only the place, the place is the place of departure and return' (CalP 63).
66. 'the material calculation of this atheist passing' (CalP 63).
67. This paralysis is different from the Lacanian/Žižekian position that 'God is unconscious': 'La véritable formule de l'athéisme n'est pas que Dieu est mort; même en fondant l'origine de la fonction du père sur son meurtre, Freud protège le père. La véritable formule de l'athéisme est que Dieu est inconscient' (Jacques Lacan, *Le Séminaire, livre IX, Les Quatre concepts fondamentaux de la psychanalyse*, Paris: Éditions du Seuil, 1973, p. 58); 'the true formula of atheism is not *God is dead* – even by basing the origin of the function of the father upon his murder, Freud protects the father – the true formula of atheism is *God is unconscious*' (Lacan, *The Four Fundamental Concepts of Psychoanalysis*, p. 59). By asserting that God is unconscious, Lacan and Žižek mean that although we may think ourselves free of the prohibitions traditionally imposed by God, these prohibitions persist in our unconscious (See Slavoj Žižek, ' "God is dead, but he doesn't know it": Lacan plays with Bobok', at: http://www.lacan.com/zizbobok.html#_ftn1, last accessed: February 2010). This is different from Nancy's reading of Nietzsche's paralysis, which is not an appeal to the unconscious but to the presentation of death-in-life.
68. 'he is incarnated dead' (BTP 51).
69. 'that strictly speaking cannot even be called "death" since it has no identity. Rather, it takes away all identity. In the becoming-dead of God the identity of God is taken away' (BTP 51).
70. Derrida, *Le Toucher*, p. 248; *On Touching*, p. 219.
71. 'In truth, the body of God was the body of man himself' (Corp 61).
72. Merleau-Ponty, *Le Visible et l'invisible*, p. 152; *The Visible and the Invisible*, p. 114.
73. John 1: 14.
74.
> *Bodies don't take place in discourse or in matter.* They don't inhabit 'mind' or 'body.' They take place at the limit, *qua limit*: – external border, the fracture and intersection of anything foreign in the continuum of sense, the continuum of matter. An opening, discreteness.
> (Corp 17)

75. James, *The Fragmentary Demand*, p. 141.
76. 'Incarnation: that divine infinity has its effectiveness in the relation of finite beings. That sense is therefore essentially finite: interrupted, suspended on an empty truth in order to avoid the suffocating fulfilment of a conclusion' (author's translation).
77.
> Bodies resist, hard *partes extra partes*. The community of bodies resists. [...] Bodies demand, yet again, their creation. Not an incarnation

> inflating the spiritual life of the sign, but a birthing and a sharing of bodies. But also not bodies employed to make sense, but a sense that gives and divides bodies. (*Corp* 83)

78. See Martin Heidegger, 'The question concerning technology', in *The Question Concerning Technology and Other Essays*, p. 12.
79. 'it falls to us, humans, mortals, without gods and without nature, technicians engaged in the undefined production of a world that is "ours", to make sense' (author's translation).
80. I am grateful to Joeri Schrijvers for drawing my attention to this point.
81. Derrida, *Le Toucher*, p. 248.

> Here, then, is my hypothesis once again, and I proffer it shyly and a little uneasily: there is some sharing out as parting, in the sense of partition or separation, or a new departure, in this taking into account of *technē*, there where (in the same gesture) it reaches beyond any Christian body. (*On Touching*, p. 219)

82. 'I know what Jean-Luc Nancy thinks, and what he has often said to me: what I call the infinite is at any rate at the very point in thought that he calls "finitude"' (author's translation).
83.

> 'A thinking that is entirely to come!' How irritating is this post-Heideggerian style of the perpetual announcement, of the interminable to-come; this sort of secularised prophecy never ceases to declare that we are not yet in a position to think what is to be thought, this pathos of having-to-respond to being, this God who is lacking, this waiting before the abyss, this posture of gazing far into the mist and saying that we see the indistinct approaching! How we long to say: 'Listen, if this thinking is still entirely to come, come back and see us when at least a piece of it has arrived!' (Author's translation)

3. Difficult Atheism

> The constructive philosopher must have a religious faith, or some substitute for a religious faith; and generally he is only able to construct, because of his ability to blind himself to other points of view, or to remain unconscious of the emotive causes which attach him to his particular system.[1]

THINKING WITHOUT GOD?

So far we have charted and critiqued the very different ways in which Badiou and Nancy seek to respond to the death of God, Badiou in terms of the threefold affirmation that 'God is dead' and Nancy with a deconstruction of Christianity. They seek to avoid both the parasitism of imitative atheism (seeking to be rid of God in ways that assume or require God) and the asceticism of residual atheism (renouncing or retrenching, along with God, the notions of truth, goodness and beauty and so on that he underwrites) by searching for an post-theological integration that is neither parasitic nor ascetic. Now we come to the apex of our study: the question of atheism itself. In this chapter we seek to penetrate to the heart of Badiou's and Nancy's approaches to post-theological integration and to scrutinise their respective dominant motifs, asking whether either position succeeds in thinking without God. For Badiou post-theological integration hangs on his deployment of axioms. Both being and truths are axiomatic for Badiou, but because truths require the context of a mathematised ontology, we shall examine in the main the primary ontological axioms of the void and of infinity, upon which the rest of Badiou's thought rests. The dominant motif of Nancy's post-theological thought is the double movement either of dis-enclosure or of spacing, and in this chapter we shall examine how he deploys this double movement to disrupt the limit between theism and atheism itself. The main questions we shall seek to answer are these: to what extent are Nancy's and Badiou's approaches to finding a post-theological integration successful in avoiding the twin pitfalls of parasitism and asceticism? Is Nancy's deconstructive atheology commensurable with Badiou's axiomatic atheism?

3.1 BADIOU'S AXIOMATIC ATHEISM

3.1.1 Event and Miracle

Attempts to discern a latent parasitism in Badiou's atheism have more often than not focused on his notion of the truth and its relation to the event. Daniel Bensaïd argues that '[d]étaché de ses conditions historiques, pur diamant de vérité, l'événement, tout comme la rencontre absolument aléatoire du dernier Althusser, s'apparente au miracle'.[2] Slavoj Žižek argues in *The Ticklish Subject* that revelation must be the unnamed paradigm of what he calls Badiou's 'Truth-Event';[3] Peter Osborne talks about a 'religious dimension' in Badiou's thought, arguing that his absolute separation of truth (the event) from knowledge (being) 'is the path to mysticism'.[4] The charge is that a truth enters a situation from a transcendent beyond with the same instantaneous inexplicability as a religious miracle.

Badiou is not slow in replying to these critiques. Though he does use the language of miracle in his own discussion of Pascal in *L'Être et l'événement* (EE 235–45/BE 212–22), he refuses any implication of religiosity that it might harbour:

> as far as its material is concerned, the event is not a miracle. What I mean is that what composes an event is always extracted from a situation, always related back to a singular multiplicity, to its state, to the language connected to it, etc.[5]

In other words, Badiou can account in his own set-theoretical terms for a truth as subtracted from a particular situation, the indiscernible of its elements, and there is no need for anything like a miracle to account for its appearing. Novelty for Badiou does not drop from the sky or come out of nowhere, it comes from the situation itself, from what is not counted as one in the situation. An event names an unpresented *of the evental site*, an unpresented that is not brought forth from *the* void but from *a* (specific) void: the void of the situation (19R 258).[6] So for example the counting as one of the universal human subject in the French Revolution requires nothing in addition to the multiples that were counted as one in the three estates.

In addition to neglecting the import of Badiou's mathematisation for the origin of novelty, the miracle charge also misunderstands the nature of Badiouian truth, hastily reducing it to a truth-event, as Bruno Bosteels is at pains to point out.[7] The Badiouian event is not utterly divorced from being or from a situation, indeed:

> à mes yeux l'apport principal ce n'est pas d'opposer la situation à l'événement, ça en un certain sens tout le monde le fait aujourd'hui. L'apport principal c'est de poser la question: Qu'est-ce qui s'en déduit ou s'en infère du point de vue de la situation elle-même? (PLN 81)[8]

It is the *and* in 'being and event' that is crucial for Badiou's project. The miracle charge reduces Badiouian truth to an event *simpliciter*, a conflation which, Badiou warns, leads to a Christic vision of truth, reducing a truth to self-revelation (*PMI* 24/*HOI* 11). This conflation must be resisted, for truth is both an event and a process:

> je suis convaincu que le nouveau n'est pensable que comme processus. Il y a certainement une nouveauté du surgir mais cette nouveauté est toujours évanouissante, donc ce n'est pas elle qu'on peut fixer comme matérialité du nouveau. (PLN 82)[9]

Badiou's truth is not a pure miraculous beginning, but an interminable process of beginning over and over again.[10] For these reasons – namely that Badiou can adequately account for novelty in set-theoretical terms, and that truth does not conform to the paradigm of revelation – the miracle charge is misplaced.

Notwithstanding this rebuttal of the miracle charge, a further charge of parasitism is that, at the very point where Badiou affirms that he has no need of a 'miracle', he is but miming a common postmodern theological move, exemplified here by John Caputo: 'by the unconditional I do not mean some super-sensible being up above – that's what I share with death of god theology – but the event that stirs within the relative and contingent things around us'.[11] Badiou too speaks of the 'unconditioned' in relation to the event (*C* 221/*Con* 152), its truth (*LM* 12/*LW* 4) and its subject (*SP* 19/*SPe* 19), and he too rejects any 'up above' account of the event. This is enough for Caputo to proceed to co-opt Badiou as a theologian, arguing that Badiou's 'exceptional moment' of grace in the event contrasts with Badiou's own characterisation of Deleuzian thought for which 'grace is all', leaving Badiou and Deleuze as 'a couple of hoary theologians arguing about grace behind seminary walls.'[12]

The Badiouian subject's fidelity to a truth can, he continues, be refigured as covenant faithfulness in which 'the event constitutes a kind of covenant that has been cut with us', and it is a small step from this claim to the all-embracing conclusion that 'religion is the covenant that has been made – by whom we cannot quite say – between the event and us.'[13] Further to this, Caputo discerns a messianism in Badiou's reading of desire, aligning Badiou's 'ne pas céder sur ce que de soi-même on ne sait pas' (E 68)[14] with his own position that 'our desire is for the messiah who never shows up, which is what keeps desire going'.[15]

A similar charge has been laid that sees in Badiou's fidelity to an event an echo of religious faith. Rancière argues that the paradigm of the event proposed by Badiou suggests that there is only ever an event because of a prior decision about transcendence, a decision that, before being called fidelity, must be (religious) faith, and that the paradigm for Badiou's understanding of fidelity is the event of the cross.[16] Badiou for his part insists that the paradigm of his fidelity is not religious faith but deduction: unending faithfulness to a prescriptive nomination (19R 249).

Let us begin to respond with a point with which Caputo and Rancière would no doubt agree. Just because Badiou uses the term 'grace' or 'faith', it does not mean that his writing is theological. Imitative atheism is not a name-checking exercise. Badiou takes Jean-François Lyotard to task for a similar assumption, when challenged about his use of Pascal:[17]

> À propos de Pascal, il faudrait tout de même être raisonnable : peut-on, oui ou non, dégager, d'un texte et d'une conviction dont on ne partage aucun des paramètres explicites, la forme, ou la matrice, d'un philosophème qu'on a soi-même proposé et pensé, sans se voir retourner les paramètres en question comme votre inconscient enfin débusqué? (19R 291)[18]

There is to be sure a difference between drawing the matrix of a philosopheme from a text with which one shares no explicit parameters, and relying on structures which one's own thought disallows. Only the latter procedure is imitative in the sense that we are using the term in relation to atheism. In order to probe whether Badiou's atheism is imitative in this sense therefore, we need to look to the mathematic condition of Badiou's thought, and to ask whether it merely appropriates theological motifs within its own post-theological framework (a move of post-theological integration), or whether it implicitly relies on theological notions that it explicitly denies. Caputo and Rancière seem not to take into account the impressive and decisive armature of mathematisation that Badiou brings to his theory of the event. Caputo moves between his own theology and Badiou's event as if the laicisation of the infinite were no part of Badiou's thought at all, let alone a linchpin of his atheism. Attempts to theologise other aspects of the Badiouian event, such as the counting-as-one, fall foul of a similar objection: they are alighting on moments of Badiou's mathematised thought without paying any attention to its mathematised condition.

To take just one example, Badiou uses the term 'grace' in a post-theological way wholly detached from its Christian context. An event is a moment of grace because it is incalculable, and it is incalculable not because it is divine but because, in strict set-theoretical terms, it is a new universal subset indiscernible (that is to say, not counted as one) in a given situation. Grace for Badiou is that which subtracts itself from law, so a subject incorporated into a truth is 'no longer under the rule of law, but of grace' (*SP* 74/*SPe* 75), to be sure, but in a way that has nothing to do with divine favour.

In the *Second Manifeste pour la philosophie*, Badiou offers a brief account of why he draws on theological and religious concepts in a resolutely post-theological register:

> J'aime les grandes métaphores venues de la religion : Miracle, Grâce, Salut, Corps Glorieux, Conversion ... On a évidemment conclu de ce goût que ma philosophie était un christianisme déguisé. Le livre sur saint Paul que j'ai publié en 1997 aux PUF n'a pas arrangé les choses. À tout prendre, j'aime mieux être un athée révolutionnaire caché sous une langue religieuse qu'un « démocrate » occidental persécuteur de musulman(e)s déguisé en féministe laïque. (*2M* 149)[19]

Badiou is happy to admit that he could be taken for a religious person in disguise,[20] but this causes him little trouble because his aim is not ascetically to eschew every religious notion but to exploit the resources of religious thought in the service of his post-theological integration. It is the revolutionary stridency of the 'grand metaphors' of religion that appeals to Badiou, the desire to deploy their capitalised power in rejecting the West's disingenuous veneer of tolerance. Badiou may be rewiring theism's house with the current turned on, but thus far he has escaped unscathed. These religious terms do not in the least undermine Badiou's atheism, but nor is this the end of the story, for our investigation must not stop with the event. We must dig beyond these religious terms clustering around the event to inquire after the status of mathematics and the choice of ZFC set theory itself in order properly to address the question of Badiou's atheism.

The Badiouian account of being also relies on a number of axioms. Indeed, there are no less than three necessary decisions prior to the Badiouian event. They are, as Peter Hallward enumerates them: 1) the pre-ontological decision that opts for numbers over things, 2) the central decision that opts for the multiple over the one, and 3) the decision that the unending universe of mathematics is indeed actually infinite,[21] to which we will eventually need to add the decision that the empty set, or void, exists. Once these decisions have been taken, precisely because they are axiomatic, Badiou's system is robust in its own terms, as we saw with the test case of the miraculous. If we are to pursue the question of Badiou's theoretical and methodological atheism further, we must not dally with the event but turn our attention to the place of axioms in his account of being.

3.1.2 Being and Axioms

First, let us understand what is at stake in Badiou's axiomatisation of being. Badiou opposes axioms (which are decided) to definitions (which are empirically induced) (CT 106). Axiomatic decisions are, furthermore, unconditioned, 'un choix absolument pur, dégagé de toute autre présupposition que d'avoir à choisir, sans marque dans les termes proposés' (C 190).[22] Badiou's axioms are decisions taken in a state of undecidability, in the absence of sufficient reason or immediate evidential certainty. Axioms are not deduced or induced, but asserted. We do not conclude that the One is not or that the empty set exists; we decide it. Our purposes in this chapter will be served by focusing on the axiom of infinity and the axiom of the empty set, the two of the nine ZFC axioms that assert an existence (see EE 176/BE 157).

The axiom of infinity states simply that there exists an actually infinite set, or there exists a limit ordinal (NN 119/NuN 93), where 'limit' is understood as that which succeeds nothing, rather than as that which nothing succeeds (which would be Anselm's God). It is the axiom with which we are familiar from our discussion of the infinite in the first two chapters. The axiom of the empty set, or the axiom of the void, asserts that 'there is an empty set, one which contains no elements'.[23] Zero is not a construction of thought, but a fact of Being (NN 61/NuN 44), an axiomatic decision (see also NN 77/NuN 56). It is a first assertion, the very one that fixes an existence from which all others will proceed (NN 35/NuN 22). The two axioms of infinity and the empty set shape the whole of modern thinking about number: the pure void is that by nature of which there is number, and the infinite is that by which it is affirmed that number can think any and every situation (NN 76/NuN 57).

We can see why axiomatisation is necessary for Badiou's atheism by considering Jean-Luc Marion's objection to atheism in his essay 'De la "mort de Dieu" aux noms divins'.[24] Marion argues that simply pursuing the death of God from one divine name to the next – God of religions, God of metaphysics, God of the poets . . . – is a futile task, at least if one is seeking to argue a coherent case can be made for atheism:

l'athéisme d'un concept de Dieu [...] du fait de sa régionalité intrinsèque, loin de clore la question du Dieu, ouvre la question des autres concepts possibles pour Dieu. [...] La « mort de Dieu » implique directement la mort de la « mort de Dieu » puisqu'à chaque fois, en disqualifiant un concept défini de Dieu, elle ouvre de nouveau le lexique indéfini d'autres concepts possibles pour nommer un Dieu toujours autrement pensable, autrement dit.[25]

In fact, Marion goes on to argue, there is an infinite number of possible names for God, and for that reason God is by definition without finite definition:[26] the philosophical problematic of the death of God always leads to the theological theme of divine names. Indeed, in the *Court Traité* Badiou himself might seem to give a nod in this direction when he claims that the gods of religion, metaphysics and the poets are only the principle gods (*CT* 22/*BOE* 30), not an exhaustive list of all possible gods.

An atheism cannot claim to be both conceptual (or scientific) and dogmatic (or universal) at the same time warns Marion. If atheism is conceptual it cannot be dogmatic, because every concept or set of concepts is defined by its finitude, and thus its incompleteness.[27] Every concept has its limit and opens onto other concepts. Let us assume, Marion continues, that to every concept of God there corresponds an atheism. He refuses to allow that, from a finite number of such theisms, we could conclude anything other than that there is a finite number of regional atheisms, and that would certainly not yield a rigorous or conceptual atheism. By contrast, any atheism that is dogmatic cannot be conceptual, for in seeking to be total it must renounce the scientificity of the (constitutively finite) concept which will, as we have seen, always falls short of universality. Such a dogmatic atheism, without recourse to the concept, must for Marion rest on a moment of violence.[28]

The first of these arguments (that if atheism is conceptual it cannot be dogmatic) is easier to deal with from a Badiouian point of view, for rather than posing a challenge to Badiou's secularised infinite, this argument delineates elegantly Badiou's point that nothing short of an axiomatic rejection of finitude will do for securing an atheism that it truly post-theological. The second argument (that any atheism that is dogmatic cannot be conceptual and must rest on violence) requires a more developed answer, particularly in relation to the place and status of 'violence', which it is clear that Marion dismisses as an obviously undesirable feature, but which occupies a more nuanced position in Badiou's own thinking.

Badiou does not resile from acknowledging a certain violence in the axiomatic decision:

> Pour pratiquer dans la pensée la rupture décisive avec le romantisme [...] nous ne pouvons faire l'économie de ce recours, peut-être une fois encore aveugle, peut-être marqué d'une contrainte, ou d'une violence, aux injonctions de la mathématique (C 166–7)[29]

Rather than refuting the violence which Marion implicitly sees as a reason to reject dogmatic atheism, Badiou sees it as a necessary concomitant of having done with finitude and the shadow of the divine. In order to rupture with consensus and the status quo it is necessary to 'force' knowledge:

> On dira que la vérité force des savoirs. Le verbe forcer indique que la puissance d'une vérité étant celle d'une rupture, c'est en violentant les savoirs établis et circulants qu'une vérité fait retour vers l'immédiat de la situation, ou remanie cette sorte d'encyclopédie portative dans laquelle puisent les opinions, les communications et la socialité (E 62)[30]

Both Badiou's truths and the axioms of infinity and the empty set require such a violent forcing, and this violence is necessary because without axiomatisation there might remain an inaccessible region of being, a further divine name, that remains untouched by all existing regional atheisms. What Badiou achieves with the axiom of infinity is an ontology in which nothing is inaccessible.[31] The Romantic infinity of inaccessibility[32] will not do, Badiou insists (C 304/Con 227); infinity must be understood affirmatively, secured by an axiomatic decision. Badiou is most explicit on the importance of inaccessibility in a letter to Peter Hallward:

> Every atheist philosophy posits that nothing, in principle, is inaccessible. Hegel is decisive on this point: the whole of the real is rational. My own thesis is not that the Inaccessible is accessible. It is that there is nothing inaccessible. Neither the event, which has vanished, but remains as named and active as truth procedure, nor the unnameable (which is accessible to knowledge, and inaccessible only to truth), is inaccessible. As Mao used to declare: 'We will come to know everything that we did not know before.' It is, in any case, one of the implications of the laicisation of the infinite.[33]

By contrast, and quoting from the same letter, 'To pose the Inaccessible as Inaccessible, and so to open the way to an infinite hermeneutics, is the religious position *par excellence*' (*Eth* xliii n.38). It is in his discussion of inaccessibility that Badiou offers a convincing reply to Marion's argument about divine names. Badiou's mathematised axiomatisation of being, which also renders being infinite and univocal, does away with the regional deities and 'concepts' upon which Marion's argument relies. There is no room inside Badiou's system for Marion's divine names.

There is no room inside the system, but what about the system itself?

So far we have seen that, once Badiou's axioms are established, nothing is inaccessible for atheism. But what about the axioms themselves? Are they themselves accessible to the conditions that they lay down for Badiou's system? In other words, do the conditions of Badiou's thought obey themselves, and what are the consequences of our answer to this question? That is what we must now go on to consider.

3.1.3 Axioms, Conditionality and the Good

Lyotard discerns in Badiou's thinking what he calls a meta-axiom that equates ontology with mathematics: only mathematical meta-ontology can give an account of the multiple,[34] and the 'initial decision' to frame Badiou's philosophy in terms of mathematical ontology needs to be investigated further.[35] John Milbank argues that for Badiou 'the ultimate primacy of the Many over the One is a mere decision'. It follows from this, Milbank insists, that 'one might still decide, in divergence from Badiou's fundamental decision, to accord to unity a retroactive primacy (as indeed in the case of Trinitarian theology)'.[36] Both Badiou's fundamental axioms (the void and the infinite) are arbitrary, insists Milbank, and Justin Clemens similarly argues that 'Badiou understands the Platonist/constructivist debate as a polemic around a proposition that is undecidable in just this sense: the infinite exists. One must decide without criteria'.[37] Peter Hallward asserts that Badiou's axioms are 'expressions of a self-constituent authority'[38] and that 'Badiou *assumes* that there is no God',[39] while Bruno Bosteels argues that we must *assume*, upstream of the count, that being inconsists with no principle, no God and no origin.[40]

A variant of this argument is to identify Badiou's axioms with the arbitrariness of the wager. Jacques Rancière argues that Badiou's decision is an unfounded wager, the paradigm of which is Pascal's belief in miracles (even though, as he problematically continues, Pascal himself understood belief in miracles not as a wager at all, but as a certainty),[41] and Justin Clemens echoes this charge when he argues that 'given that there are no grounds for deciding one way or another, a decision must take place as a kind of gamble or, in the Pascalian terminology of which Badiou is fond, "a wager" '.[42]

So is the axiomatised ontology through which alone Badiou can be rid of God a blind wager? Badiou's own account of his axioms is substantially more subtle than these charges allow. Though axioms may be pure choices (in that they are not compelled or informed by any prior conditions), the axioms of infinity and the void nevertheless have for Badiou a certain historical necessity. In Badiou's account, the world of modern thought is itself brought forth by what would come to be known in the twentieth century as the axioms of infinity and of the empty set, and these two axioms are themselves decided 'sous la contrainte de l'injonction historiale de l'être' (NN 74).[43] The nature of that historical injunction is, according to Badiou, as follows: from the Renaissance onwards, with the rupture from the Greek (finite) cosmos, these axioms proved *necessary* in order to think anything at all in accordance with our pre-comprehension of the ontological demand (NN 74/NuN 56). Nevertheless, these decisions themselves are rigorously unverifiable. The infinite universe could not be deduced from observations using the newly invented telescope, and 'il y fallait un pur courage de la pensée, une incise volontaire dans le dispositif, éternellement défendable, du finitisme ontologique' (EE 167).[44] Though we had to wait until the beginning of the twentieth century for these decisions to be recognised as the axioms of infinity and the empty set, by that time they had already been operating in modern thinking for three centuries (NN 75/NuN 57). But this is also the source of their weakness, for 'dès lors qu'il s'agit là de purs constats, décidés comme tels, ils ont la faiblesse de leur historicité. Aucun argument ne peut les soutenir' (NN 75).[45]

Concluding his brief discussion of the two axioms in *Le Nombre et les nombres*, Badiou refers to them as ontological prescriptions: 'Qu'il s'agisse d'axiomes et non de théorèmes signifie que l'existence du zéro et de l'infini sont ce que l'être prescrit à la pensée pour qu'elle-même existe dans l'époque ontologique d'une telle existence' (NN 76).[46]

In other words, the axioms of the void and infinity are thought's way of catching up with, and responding to, the ontological realities of modernity. Far from arbitrary or unmotivated, they respond to the injunction of being. Indeed, unless the void and the infinite are entirely secularised, thinking could not (or could no longer) exist in the form, and with the force, that the age requires of it (NN 76/NuN 57).

This is not to say that Badiou's axioms are inevitable. Quite to the contrary, they are undecidable. Badiou insists that '[t]oute pensée – donc, la mathématique – engage des décisions (des intuitions) du point de l'indécidable (du non-déductible)' (CT 103),[47] and that the existence of an undecidable is never overcome but by an axiomatic assumption.[48] The mistake made by some readers of Badiou is to equate this undecidability too hastily with arbitrariness. The decision that the universe is actually infinite may not be the conclusion of a deductive argument; it may be rigorously undecidable from a finite universe, but nevertheless the injunction of being in modernity prescribes that such a decision be taken. It is not arbitrary, but rather the response to a demand.

Axioms, then, are for Badiou conditioned, but not inevitable. The nature of Badiou's axioms is captured in his agreement with Deleuze's account of thinking in the *Second Manifeste*:

> Deleuze soutient avec force – contre, à vrai dire, toutes les joyeuses interprétations spontanéistes et « anarcho-désirantes » de sa philosophie – qu'on ne pense jamais ni par décision volontaire, ni par mouvement naturel. On est toujours, dit-il, forcé de penser. La pensée est comme une poussée qui s'exerce dans notre dos. Elle n'est pas aimable ni désirée, la pensée. Elle est une violence qui nous est faite. Je suis parfaitement d'accord avec cette vision. (2M 124)[49]

Axioms are forced by a historical demand, to which they are thinking's response. This provides *en passant* sufficient refutation of the argument that Badiou's axioms are merely retroactively legitimated by the fruitfulness of their consequences. Axioms do not eventuate *ex nihilo*; they respond to an injunction of being. In a further nuance to the 'pure decision' account of Badiou's axioms, in conversation with Fabien Tarby he touches on the 'ultimate real point' that is discernible in many philosophical dispositions: Spinoza's intellectual intuition of God, or Plato's Good that he glosses in the *Republic* merely with the brief comment that he can offer no image of it: 'je suis d'accord avec Bergson sur le fait qu'il y a un point originaire de l'expérience, point que toute la didactique philosophique s'efforce de rejoindre et de transmettre' (*PE* 143).[50]

The third volume of *L'Etre et l'événement*, provisionally entitled *L'Immanence des vérités*, will in part attempt to circumscribe (*encercler*) this point as much as possible, with the hope of reducing its ineffability 'as much as possible'. Badiou admits 'Je ne sais pas pour autant, à l'heure actuelle, jusqu'où je dois aller dans cette direction' (*PE* 139),[51] though he does reveal that the equivalent point in his own philosophical disposition is incorporation, truth understood not in its objective logic but from the point of view of the subject, the intuition of which is accompanied by a 'singular affect' (*PE* 142). Asked what is the affect proper to philosophy, Badiou replies:

> Je pense que la philosophie doit inclure, à la fois dans sa conception et dans sa proposition, la conviction que la vraie vie peut être expérimentée en immanence. Quelque chose doit la signaler de l'intérieur d'elle-même, pas seulement comme un impératif extérieur, comme un impératif kantien. Cela relève d'un affect, lequel signale, indique, en immanence, que la vie vaut la peine d'être vécue. (*PE* 149)[52]

What Lyotard calls Badiou's meta-axiom is a response to the epoch – as the 'injunction of modernity' – and to an affect/conviction that true life is to be experienced in immanence. This is indeed, as he acknowledges, the point at which Badiou's thought needs to push further, not least because it is the point upon which the project of a post-theological integration hangs. If the encounter with the truth that enjoins a philosophical 'disposition' (such as idealism, empiricism, or indeed axiomatised mathematical ontology) is itself theological, then parasitism has re-entered and the project of post-theological integration is incomplete.

Plato is not much help here, Badiou conjectures, as he has said so little about the Good. A Galilean strand of interpretation has seen it as the very example of scientific rationality, while by the Neoplatonists it is taken as the very example of transcendent theology (*PE* 140–1). When Plato says that the Good greatly surpasses the Idea in prestige and power,[53] the negative theologians claim to have found the God about whom nothing can be said. The rationalist current of interpretation (within which Badiou places himself) seeks to understand the Good as 'un principe d'intelligibilité qui n'est pas réductible à l'Idée elle-même. Que l'Idée soit principe d'intelligibilité est naturellement au-delà de l'Idée' (*PE* 141).[54] Badiou does not provide reasons for his choice in this passage, and we shall return to this question of choosing a fundamental philosophical orientation in our conclusion to this volume.

Given that rationalism is what is at stake in Badiou's discussion of philosophical 'dispositions', it is a misunderstanding of Badiou's system to demand of him a rationalist proof or demonstration of his axioms. In 'Nouveauté et événement', Meillassoux takes Badiou to task for the circularity of his axioms. If there is a Cantor-event, as Badiou claims (*LM* 47/*LW* 38), then how can it be the condition of all events (NE 40)? How can axioms be truths, when they are the condition of an ontology of truths? Perhaps, like Plato's Good, they are an exception, not truths but conditions that do not conform to the ontological categories they themselves permit (NE 41), leading Meillassoux to dub them 'archi-vérités' (NE 41). The modern injunction of being and the affect of immanence, we suggest, provide the missing link that Meillassoux seeks.

Meillassoux also argues that, if there is a 'Cantor-event', then there is nothing to guarantee the perenniality of the category of 'event', and the ontology upon which it relies. Either one privileges the event above the essential historicity of ontology, or one privileges the historicity of ontology and its radical unpredictability above the event (NE 50). Meillassoux fixes on the moment in *L'Etre et l'événement* when Badiou argues that there is every reason to believe (*il y a tout lieu de croire*) that the event will always from now on be compatible with historical ontology (NE 52). This 'decision about the decision', Meillassoux argues, must remain for Badiou a hypothesis, a mathematically motivated belief: 'il y a tout lieu de *croire* – mais *il y a tout lieu* de croire' (NE

53).⁵⁵ This mathematical wager reveals the insufficiency of mathematics to connect us to the Eternal, for though we are accompanied the whole way by the impeccable machine of deductibility, we will always be left by ourselves to make the last step (NE 54). Meillassoux is right to identify this 'last step' as an exception from the axiomatic system it governs, and it returns us once more to Badiou's discussion of Plato's Good in *Philosophie et événement*: the 'mathematical faith' in the event is motivated by the injunction of being in modernity and by the affect of immanence. We see no reason in either of these motivations why Badiou's thought, as it has evolved since *L'Etre et l'événement*, requires the non-historicity of the event in order to support its system, unless the affect of immanence is claimed to be itself ahistorical.

The circle that *L'Immanence des vérités* must square is this: either 1) the affect of immanence and/or the injunction of modernity are necessary and unchanging, in which case Badiou's atheism falls at the last hurdle into a imitative atheism that unaccountably inscribes the moment of the choice of axioms as a parasitic *causa sui*, a self-grounding rationalism exempted from all rationality, or 2) the affect of immanence and the injunction of modernity are contingent and historically changeable, and just as the modern age and the move from the closed world to the infinite universe demanded the axioms of infinity and the void, so presumably another historical moment could equally demand other axioms that may contradict these two, and once again allow for a thinking of the divine. In which case any assertion of atheism along the lines that Badiou proposes is provisional, and irreducibly haunted by the spectre of future theism. Such a dilemma raises theological questions that Badiou is not be able to address by recourse to mathematisation and axiomatisation without begging the question.

Pending the third volume of *L'Etre et l'événement*, we shall argue that we can best make sense of Badiou's axioms as an axiology of the Good. Badiou's axioms are worthy (*axios*) because they promote the implicit Good in Badiou's own philosophy. Badiou evokes a contemporary 'ethics of thinking' (OPI 182) according to which it is 'better' to think all situations infinite (an adjective he uses three times in 'Ontology and politics'), and that this is 'more interesting' than declaring that we are finite. This adds a third conditionality to Badiou's choice of axioms. Axioms are not chosen simply under the injunction of being and the affect of immanence, but also because they are 'better' (or 'more interesting') than any alternative.

The question begged by this is: better *for what*? More interesting *for whom*? How do we decide that one axiom is better or more interesting than another? The Platonist will admit the axiom of choice,⁵⁶ Badiou argues, 'car l'univers avec axiome du choix est autrement plus large et dense en liaisons significatives que l'univers qui ne l'admet pas' (*CT* 104),⁵⁷ and his own explanation for choosing the axiom of infinity is that '[s]ans cette décision, il restera toujours possible que l'être soit essentiellement fini' (*EE* 167).⁵⁸ This is a reverse engineering from desired effect (infinite being) to its condition (axiom of infinity).

In view of this, it is not legitimate to conclude that axioms can themselves serve as premises in an argument to an ontological conclusion without begging the question. So for instance, when Peter Hallward asserts that the axiom of infinity gives the 'definitive proof of God's "nonexistence"',⁵⁹ he seems to be wanting to have his Badiouian cake and eat it. Axioms do not 'prove' anything, least of all God's non-existence. The secularisation of the infinite is the *decision* that will achieve the 'better' conclusion that God does not exist, not the proof or revelation of any such fact.

A number of attempts have been made to locate this hidden value supporting Badiou's axioms. John Mullarkey points to a 'transcendental vector in Badiou's thought', asking the question 'How can [Badiou] found a theory of error when any axiomatic approach can only claim more or less productivity for its set of axioms?'⁶⁰ Mullarkey notes that for Badiou, events are always for the good, 'because they concern emancipation and, as such, equality';⁶¹ in other words, the argument is that universal equality is Badiou's transcendental 'Good'. John Milbank levels a similar critique when he evokes what he calls the 'paraontological primacy of the good' in Badiou,⁶² not a good beyond being, but being as the supremely good and equally supremely true. Lyotard makes this same argument in his comment that 'pour décider de nommer, il faut avoir une affection particulière pour le vide'.⁶³ For Marc de Kesel, Badiou's mathematical ontology harbours 'a kind of belief in the truth and goodness of Being as such'.⁶⁴ If this is true, Badiou's axioms are covertly religious because they suppose a value that is not immanent to, and contained within, the axiomatised system but rather conditions the choice of axioms in the first place:

> While formally, the 'event' disrupts society's settled organization, at the level of content, disruption itself is presumed to be inherently good. [. . .] Being qua Being might be anarchic, impossible even to experience, but this impossible anarchy is surreptitiously considered an ontological 'archè'.⁶⁵

This is what Badiou prizes in the French Revolution: a casting off of the plurality of the three estates and their replacement with the proclamation of universal, generic human equality; it is also what he values in the universalism of Paul the apostle, the proclamation of a new universal humanity in which 'there is not Greek and Jew, circumcised and uncircumcised, barbarian, Scythian, slave, free; but Christ is all, and in all.'[66]

But once more there is a clear reply in Badiou's work to this argument. He insists that a commitment to universal equality can be generated immanently, purely from the necessity of choice itself:

> Cette situation est bien repérée par la philosophie, sous le nom de 'liberté d'indifférence'. Liberté qui n'est normée par aucune différence qu'on puisse remarquer, liberté qui fait face à l'indiscernable. Si nulle valeur ne discrimine ce que vous avez à choisir, c'est votre liberté comme telle qui est norme, au point où en fait elle se confond avec le hasard. L'indiscernable est la soustraction qui fonde un point de coïncidence entre le hasard et la liberté. (C 190–1)[67]

Nevertheless, to the extent that the principle of the 'freedom of indifference' is not immanent to Badiou's axioms, its introduction does not solve the problem. Furthermore, it is difficult to see how freedom alone can carry the weight Badiou wants and needs it to in this case. On the one hand, if we grant Badiou this immanent account of the motivation for the decision, and freedom becomes indistinguishable from chance, it would seem to issue in an ascetic atheism that betrays any political agenda as well as the injunction of being, and so to substantiate Jean-Jacques Lecercle's conclusion that 'Badiou's atheism undercuts Marxism as well as religion'.[68] On the other hand, if we say that freedom is the norm *in so far as it is universalising*, then we find ourselves right back at the question of the universal as the good which governs Badiou's seemingly unconditioned decision.

We would like to bring our discussion of Badiou's axioms to a close by arguing that the 'Good' for Badiou can be construed as atheism itself. In order to pursue further this question about what precisely is 'better' about the axioms of infinity and the void for Badiou, we turn our attention once more now to his treatment of atomism.[69] It is in his dialogues with Lucretius that the Good motivating Badiou's axioms becomes clear. In a discussion of the choice for the multiple over the one, Badiou seeks to clarify his intentions:

> Tout le point est de tenir aussi loin qu'il est possible, et sous les conditions les plus novatrices de la pensée, qu'en tout cas la vérité elle-même n'est qu'une multiplicité. [...] Ce qui exige un premier geste radical, à quoi se reconnaît la philosophie moderne: soustraire l'examen des vérités à la simple forme du jugement. Ce qui veut toujours dire: *décider* une ontologie des multiplicités. (CT 59)[70]

In this quotation Badiou makes it clear that the whole point of the decision for an ontology of multiplicities is to sustain as long as possible the equation of truth and multiplicity. It is this desire that demands (*exige*) the decision in favour of an ontology of multiplicities. The concern to secularise ontology positively demands the decision for the many over the one: 'Lucrèce voit bien que se soustraire à la crainte des dieux exige qu'en deçà du multiple il n'y ait rien. Et qu'au-delà du multiple il n'y ait encore que le multiple' (CT 30).[71]

The Epicurean's desire to escape the fear of the gods precedes and demands the ontology of multiplicity that Lucretius furnishes in his atomism and that Badiou secures with his axiomatised ZFC set theory. In order correctly to capture the way in which Badiou uses axioms in these quotations we need to return to the root *axios*, ('worthy', or 'fit'). Badiou's axioms are chosen to be worthy of the secularised, generic, universal notion of being that propels his thought. This is more than responding to the demand of being, however, for we can discern a therapeutic moment in Badiou's axiomatisation.

Lucretian atheism is not in fact the product of a deduction or a proof; its nature is therapeutic.[72] Holding the position that the gods, whatever gods there may be, are not going to interfere in any way with human beings, is a means to the end of *ataraxia*, the tranquillity of mind free from the fear of the gods prescribed by Pyrrho. Shades of this attitude can be seen in Badiou's articulations of his own post-theological position when he argues that '[i]l est donc impératif, pour s'établir *sereinement* dans l'élément irréversible de la mort de Dieu, d'en finir avec le motif de la finitude' (CT 19–20; author's emphasis).[73] In this instance, it appears that the death of God precedes the end of finitude, and it is necessary to have done with the finite in order not to be troubled by the reappearance of that which has been declared dead. Having been pronounced dead, God must now be killed, for the sake of the atheist's serenity. Further on, Badiou makes a similar move, arguing that:

> En effet, *il nous faut assumer*, comme Lucrèce, que le déploiement-multiple n'est pas contraint par l'immanence d'une limite. Car il n'est que trop évident qu'une telle contrainte avère la puissance de l'un comme fondement du multiple lui-même. (CT 28; author's emphasis)[74]

Once more, the necessity of the assumption that there are no limits to infinite multiplicities seems here to be the result of a desire to rest serene in the primacy of multiplicity over the one. Peter Hallward echoes this reasoning when he notes that 'axiomatic set theory is the only theory we have that *allows* us coherently to think inconsistent multiplicity as such'.[75] What is motivating Badiou's axioms, in addition to the injunction of modernity and the affect of immanence, is an atheistic ontological *ataraxia*.

We must not simply equate *ataraxia* with a reductive notion of happiness, however. Freedom from the fear of the gods for Badiou is not to be equated with what he castigates in *L'Ethique* as the nihilism of Man defined in terms of being-for-happiness, which amounts to just the same as being-for-death (*E* 54/*Eth* 35). Nor is it a renunciation; Badiou denies that there is any room in his philosophy for asceticism (*E* 75/*Eth* 53). We must not understand Badiou's desire for serenity as a shot of anaesthetic. Rather, it is a settled conviction, appropriate to the times, that in a manner never quite free from the charge of circularity and begging the question consummates the death of God.

So for both Badiou and Hallward here, axiomatic decisions are motivated decisions, decisions, indeed, that are *demanded*, and not simply demanded by the modern age. The desired end – that of a truly secularised philosophy – precedes and demands the means: the axioms of infinity and the empty set. The axiomatic decision is an instrument, indeed the only effective instrument, of secularisation. And this is the rub, because the agenda of secularisation itself comes at this point to occupy the place of the unspoken Good in Badiou's decision.

3.2 NANCY'S ATHEOLOGY

We have seen that, although Badiou can marshal robust responses to the charges that his event is a miracle and his truth is a quasi-religious revelation, his ontological atheism is begging the question when it comes to the status of his axioms. We now turn to Nancy, whose account of post-theological thought is very different to Badiou's but similarly unable finally to escape the shadow of the theological. The main target of Badiou's recourse to the axiom is finitude and ascetic atheism. Nancy's post-theological thinking is intended primarily to avoid parasitic atheism.

3.2.1 *A/théisme and Absenthéisme*

To begin with, Nancy does not see atheism as a decision that ruptures from theistic thought, but contemporaneous with, and the consummation of, monotheism: monotheism is an atheism (*DDC* 27/*DisDC* 14). The trajectory of atheistic thought for Nancy begins as far back as Xenophanes and his tirades against the anthropomorphic gods, a movement accelerated by the singular *theos* of Plato, replacing the paradigm of gods and mortals inhabiting the same space with the ontological distance that the name 'God' will henceforth measure (*DDC* 29/*DisDC* 16). The invention of atheism and the invention of theism are contemporaneous and correlative, because they both rely on what Nancy calls 'le paradigme principiel' (*DDC* 29/*DisDC* 16), the principial paradigm, which questions the principle or *archē* of the world, the axiological reason for what is given. Theism and atheism are bound by a complicity in this principial paradigm in a way that the assertion of atheism in the face of theism simply reinforces. An atheism that asserts the principial paradigm can only ever be parasitic.

The birth of monotheism is the birth of the *deus absconditus*; whereas the divinities of polytheism are 'presences of absence', the atheism of monotheism is the 'absencing' (*l'absentement*) of presence (*CM* 91/ *CWG* 69). What happens with the arrival of Christianity, when Jewish monotheism meets Greek atheism, is that the unicity of God is absorbed into the unicity of the principle. Christianity is then understood in terms of growing secularisation, echoing Marcel Gauchet's memorable phrase that Christianity is 'la religion de la sortie de la religion'.[76] Secularisation is not simply a by-product of Christianity for Nancy, but its essence as 'onto-(a)-theology' (*DDC* 34–5/*DisDC* 20).

To oppose the principle of monotheism with the principle of atheism does nothing to challenge the underlying a/theistic logic of onto-a-theology. The principle must be deconstructed, a move already begun in the Trinitarian God of Christianity that represents divinity as being-together, and so 'deconstructs' the logic of the principle, the divine 'One' of monotheism. The Trinitarian God is no longer 'God', Nancy argues, but an onto-theological species of being-together (*ESP* 81/*BSP* 200).

Nancy seems to be following a post-secular trajectory when he maintains that the Christian God is the God who 'self-atheises' (*s'athéise*), for Christ's incarnation is a kenosis, a self-emptying, by which the body becomes the name of no-god (*pas-de-dieu*), not as an affirmation of human self-sufficiency but of the lack of a founding presence (*DDC* 127/*DisDC* 82). But it would be a mistake to count Nancy among the postsecularists. The kenotic trajectory is one in which Christianity deconstructs itself, exposing a movement within itself deeper than itself, upon which its theistic trappings are merely contingent. Far from God being the truth of atheism, it is post-theological thought for Nancy that is the truth of Christianity.

To conclude this brief survey of Nancy's understanding of atheism, we can say that he rolls monotheism and atheism together (as *(a) théisme* or as *onto-a-théologie*), and argues that monotheism, in so far as it expels the principle of the world to an absent and inaccessible outside of the world, is atheism (*DDC* 51, 55/*DisDC* 32, 35). The history of 'God' in the West – Greek, Jew, Christian, humanist – is the history of atheism. Let us not miss this point: atheism for Nancy has a history; it is not the event of a rupture with the past, but a process (*DDC* 35/*DisDC* 20) as old as the West itself, and constitutive of the West itself, whether in its incorporation of the Jewish or Greek traditions. The Joycean conjunction greekjew/jewgreek conjoins nothing other than two formations of atheism (*DDC* 35/*DisDC* 20).

Conceived in this way, atheism is constituted as an ascetic lack of theism's divinities. We might venture to call this ascetic construal of atheism 'bad atheism', in a way that mirrors the 'bad infinity' discussed in the previous chapter:

> la pensée sans fin, la finitude sans fin, en somme l'infini – reste privative, soustractive et en somme défective – de même que l'est obstinément et sourdement, fût-ce à son corps défendant, la tonalité majeure de toute espèce d'athéisme. (*DDC* 31)[77]

Like Badiou, Nancy critiques this ascetic atheism that implicitly considers the world as incomplete without a creating deity (*SM* 236/*SW* 156). The problem with it is that it apes monotheism's logic of the principle while thinking that, in denying the existence of the gods, it is opposing monotheism, not realising that the telos of Western monotheism is this very denial. In its attempts to negate or escape monotheism, all it can do is repeat and consummate it.

Nancy critiques the logic of the principle (which he also calls the *principat*) as being either inconsistent, or incomplete. The great weakness of the logic of the principle is that the principle, whether it is affirmed or denied, can only ever collapse into its own affirmation or denial (*DDC* 37/*DisDC* 22). Either 1) a principle must make itself an exception to its own 'principiality' in an ever-repeated (bad infinite) gesture, or 2) it must confirm itself as an equally recurring bad infinite. It must except itself from its own 'principiality' in the sense that, while everything that follows it must be accounted for in its terms (in terms of 'In the beginning was the Word . . .' or 'All is matter . . .' or 'All is history . . .' etc.), no such constraint is demanded (or indeed possible) in the case of the principle itself. Or it must confirm itself infinitely in the sense of an infinite regress: it must account for its own principle, and the principle of that principle, and so on . . . If the principle is complete, it is not consistent, and if it is consistent, it is not complete. It is at this point that Nancy's critique of the principle crosses Badiou's atheistic recourse to axioms.

In order to name this asceticism, Nancy coins the term *absenthéisme* (see *CM* 54 n.1/*CWG* 120 n.23). In Nancy's earlier work, *absenthéisme* is a positive, or at least neutral, term. In *La Création du monde* (2002), *absenthéiste* describes the world without God to which monotheism inexorably leads, neither theistic nor atheistic (CM 54/CWG 50). Here, the triumvirate of myth, signification and sense are paralleled by the move from polytheism to monotheism to *absenthéisme* (CM 94/CWG 71). In his *Chroniques philosophiques* (broadcast between September 2002 and July 2003), *absenthéisme* is described as the anarchic (that is: rejecting the notion of an *archē*) positing of the singular existent, and a rejection of both theism and atheism (CP 28/PC 20). Similarly, *absenthéisme* is situated beyond both theism and atheism in 'Le nom de Dieu chez Blanchot' (DDC 129–34/DisDC 85–8, published in French in October 2003), but by the time of 'Athéisme et monothéisme' (written for publication in 2005), it seems that Nancy now employs the term to indicate an ascetic atheism that continues to respect the limit of the finite:

> L'horizon d'une soustraction, d'un retrait, d'une absence, voire l'horizon de ce que j'ai moi-même parfois nommé « absenthéisme » pour l'opposer à l'athéisme, continue à faire horizon – c'est-à-dire limite, impasse et fin du monde. (DDC 33)[78]

In other words, though *absenthéisme* rejects the logic of the principle, it is still inscribed within a horizon that sets it in opposition to an absent plenitude, a logic that makes common cause with the principle; it cannot think the world other than as finite and confined. It quite rightly acknowledges that there can no longer be any question of escaping from the world (as both theism and atheism seek to do, according to the logic of principle described above), but this does not therefore mean, Nancy now clarifies, that the world must be considered as a horizon. Finitude, as we saw in the previous chapter with Nancy's discussion of Hegel, does not limit the infinite, but must give infinity its expansion and its truth (DDC 33/DisDC 18). What Nancy is arguing here is that the finitude of the world does not, by virtue of imposing a horizon or a limit, provide the sort of inaccessible, sacred 'beyond' which Badiou is so eager to prevent. It is this 'bad' finitude-as-horizon that Nancy is now, in his later texts, calling *absenthéisme*.

3.2.2 Athéologie

The task Nancy sets himself is clear: to develop a new thinking that avoids the parasitic logic of the principle and the ascetic horizon, that escapes the dichotomy of a/theism otherwise than with an ascetic *absenthéisme* that inscribes the infinite within finite confines. What is called for is not an escape from monotheism, for such an 'escape' would parasitically repeat the necessity of a redemptive gesture that merely underlines the implied dichotomy of transcendence and immanence (*DDC* 34/*DisDC* 20), and it would be a repetition of the bootstrapping gesture of praying God to rid us of God (*DLD* 36–7/*ODP* 139).

As to what is necessary for this new thinking beyond a/theism, there are two main emphases that emerge in Nancy's writing. The first of these is faith, but not faith (*croyance*) as a weak, hypothetical or subjective form of knowledge that is unverifiable and requires an attitude of submission rather than the exercise of reason (*ADC* 128). The faith (*foi*) which Nancy's thinking beyond a/theism demands is 'l'acte de la raison se rapportant d'elle-même à ce qui d'elle se passe infiniment' (*DDC* 40).[79] This picks up the 'principle of intelligibility' that Badiou identifies in his reading of Plato's Good in *Philosophie et événement*: a principle that cannot be reduced to the Idea itself. In other words, for Nancy this faith (*foi*) is necessary in order to make post-theological thinking fully consistent, and a fully consistent thinking is one that has relinquished the belief (*croyance*) in the principle or the *principat*. Faith and belief are 'radically incompatible' (*DDC* 44 n.1/*DDC* 178 n.10), and the only complete, consistent post-theological thinking (as opposed to the inconsistency or incompleteness to which the logic of the principle always resolves) is to have done with belief in order to acknowledge and make room for faith. Indeed, it is in a Kantian idiom that Nancy argues for the necessity of such faith:

> C'est le point déjà formellement reconnu par Kant lorsqu'il parle, par exemple, de « l'incapacité où se trouve la raison, au regard de ses besoins, de se donner satisfaction par elle-même ». La raison ne se suffit pas à soi-même : pour soi elle n'est pas raison suffisante. Mais c'est dans la reconnaissance de cette insuffisance qu'elle se fait entièrement droit. (*DDC* 40)[80]

Foi is an embrace of insufficiency; *croyance* is a claim of sufficiency. This is not an evocation of faith intended to undermine reason or subordinate it to religious belief after all, but rather an appeal to faith to 'supplement' reason, in a Derridean sense. Faith is that which reason rejects, without which it cannot be fully itself, and with which it is not more than itself. It is only when reason recognises its need thus to be supplemented that it is fully reasonable, fully consistent. Furthermore, it is this appeal to faith that prevents Nancy's reason from being a violent rupture in thinking.

The stakes in this supplementing of reason by faith for Nancy could not be more important. Failure so to do leaves one with an irremediably parasitic atheism that fails to follow the death of God:

> La mort de ce Dieu – et c'est seulement ce Dieu-là qui est mort, Nietzsche lui-même le dit – n'est pas autre chose que la mort de toute Raison ainsi

> dotée des attributs de la nécessité et de la complétude de la fondation-production de l'étant en totalité. Cette raison ne voyait pas qu'elle se mettait elle-même à mort en érigeant cette idole d'elle-même qui n'était qu'un Dieu pour athées. (*ADC* 48)[81]

Atheism has essentially consisted in parasitically substituting a reason, cause, principle or finality for a God who was himself conceived as a higher Reason. The idolatry of self-sufficient reason can only be avoided by un-closing reason's self-sufficent closure: 'Déconstruire le christianisme veut dire : ouvrir la raison à sa raison même, voire à sa déraison' (*ADC* 39).[82] The un-closure of reason is what remains of a deconstructed Christianity, a reason freed from the will to do justice or to give a reason (*rendre raison*). It is a reason that knows that 'giving a reason' goes beyond any reason given, that one never ceases giving reasons (*ADC* 65).

Nancy develops his account of this faith in terms of Gérard Granel's 'faith that is nothing at all' (*foi de rien du tout*) (*DDC* 89–116/*DisDC* 61–74), a gesture that measures neither knowledge nor certainty, neither subjectivising nor objectivising, a faith that holds itself to a post-theological 'full atheism' (*athéisme sans réserve*) without flinching, a faith that is nothing other than the 'courage' called upon to speak the 'strange':

> cette foi de rien du tout: fidélité pensante, au-delà du concept, au « rien de ce Tout primitif », pensée confiée à ce qui lui vient d'ailleurs car de nulle part, de la part nulle du rien, et ainsi foi qui n'est en somme rien – que cette infime extrême touche de pensée posée sur ce rien. (*DDC* 104)[83]

In this faith one holds oneself to *not* asserting reason's self-sufficiency, and reason's completeness comes from this acknowledgement of its incompleteness. In this sense, faith is the truth of post-theological thought in the sense of 'true' preserved in the German *treu* and the English *troth*: a holding-oneself faithful to something or someone. Post-theological thought, in order to be true to itself, to its constitutive incompleteness, must have faith. A post-theological integration acknowledges it is supplemented by faith. In its refusal of all consolatory or redemptive assurance, post-theological thinkers have more faith (though not more belief) than the religious:

> Il n'y est pas question de « religion », mais bien d'une « foi » en tant que signe de fidélité de la raison à ce qui d'elle-même excède le fantasme de rendre raison de soi tout autant que du monde et de l'homme. (*DDC* 44)[84]

Reason cannot account for its own reason, and 'faith' is the faithfulness to that non-sufficiency, a resistance to pretending that it can perform such an accounting, and a fidelity to reason none the less. Nancy's reading of this making room for faith cannot therefore be co-opted for a 'post-secular' agenda where there would be some place off limits to reason, some post-modern critique of modernism, to reinstate the divine as a critique of reason, for faith holds itself precisely to refusing this move of supplementing reason. The point is this: there is something inaccessible to reason, but it is not reason's other. It is nothing other than reason itself. Reason does make room for faith, but it is not thereby denatured. In making room for faith reason makes room for nothing, and thereby becomes fully itself.

This faithful post-theological thought also overcomes ascetic atheism and its construction of atheism as a lack, in a move that Nancy characterises as the replacement of *insuffisance* with *non-suffisance*. Kant's 'moral faith', Nancy notes, has its essence not in an inadequacy of reason but, quite to the contrary, in the firmness with which reason confronts its own incompleteness. Moral faith does not see in reason an insufficiency, failing or lack that would condemn it to nihilism, but rather a non-sufficiency in the sense that it is no longer a question of 'sufficing' or 'satisfying', for there is no principle to which satisfaction or sufficiency would need to adequate. Faith is reason's own firm pledge to its own rejection of theological categories (*DDC* 41/*DisDC* 25), a pledge not to 'fill' reason's 'lack'. Nancy's faith is different to Badiou's fidelity therefore in this sense: while Badiou's subject holds itself axiomatically to the consequences of an event with a certain violence, Nancy's reason holds itself not to its effects but to its refusal violently to supplement its non-sufficiency. Nancy's faith is a refusal to force reason beyond itself; Badiou's fidelity is a predisposition to force the consequences of a truth.

Nancy is at pains to distinguish his own *non-suffisance* from Marion's principle of insufficient reason.[85] The latter, as Nancy presents it, names a necessary meeting of modernity and theology: modernity recognises insufficiency everywhere (in consciousness, in discourse . . .), and theology proposes a thinking of 'insufficient reason' as a gift of Charity, preserving the 'distinction' and 'distance' between beings as opposed to the plenitude of metaphysics (*DLD* 4/*ODP* 112). But this only confirms the opposite of what it claims, for God disappears all the more irrevocably as he splinters into all the names of generalised and multiplied difference. This sort of monotheism resolves to a 'polyatheism', and such a God infinitely removed from the supreme being of metaphysics can no longer be called 'God' or divine at all, and nothing can be said of this 'God' that cannot also immediately be said of the event, love, poetry and so on.

3.2.3 Athéologie and Athéisme

The second component of Nancy's bulwark against parasitic atheism is 'atheology'. Nancy takes the term from Georges Bataille's two published volumes of the *Somme athéologique*,[86] although he employs it in ways that differ from Bataille's. For Bataille, the atheological constitutes an assiduous pursuit of the consequences of the death of God, 'la science de la mort ou de la destruction de dieu',[87] and to this extent it is an anti-science, a science of the breakdown of science. Bataille is open about the extent to which his atheology constitutes a 'basically religious attitude':

> Si vous voulez, c'est une athéologie dont la considération fondamentale est donnée dans une proposition comme celle-ci: *Dieu est un effet du non-savoir*. Mais toujours est-il que, comme effet du non-savoir, il est connaissable, comme le rire, comme le sacré. Cela me permet de représenter ceci, c'est que cette expérience en somme se situe dans la ligne générale des religions. En parlant comme je fais, j'ai conscience non seulement de prendre une attitude religieuse au fond, mais encore de représenter une sorte de religion constituée.[88]

Atheology for Bataille is also a refusal dialectically to recuperate mystical experience, a refusal of the Christian economy of the redemption of suffering and loss into a productive dialectic, a thought according to which salvation and God intrude into the impossible, reducing spirituality to a platitudinous possible-without-loss.[89]

The aspect of Bataille's atheology that Nancy privileges is the refusal of a 'redemption' of atheism in a dialectical move that sees atheism bringing salvation from theism. The an-archic rejection of the logic of the principle is central to Nancy's understanding of atheology. A religious notion of creation is replaced not with an atheistic notion of rupture according to the 'Christmas projection', but with a spacing which, in *La Création du monde*, Nancy calls *le mondial*. Nancy's *mondial*, like Bataille's atheology, seeks to respond to the cosmic disorientation evoked in Nietzsche's account of the death of God, yet it does so not with an ascetic evocation of an inaccessible alterity but with an insistence on the becoming-world (*mondialisation*) of the world. This becoming-world has two components: 1) an acknowledgment that the world is thrown into the 'void' of a space-time whose finite measure (finite because there is no other measure) is the infinite, and 2) what Nancy calls a blurring within itself of territories and lands (*SM* 238–9/ *SW* 157–8), by which he means to evoke the dissolution of limits and borders that would themselves seek to 'sacralise' the world by setting apart – sanctifying – certain territories from others:

la mondialité de la terre – de l'homme – veut dire: remise en jeu de l'avoir-lieu en général. Le y n'est ni le ciel, ni l'humus, mais qu'il y a, et qu'il y a lieu de ressaisir le sens à partir de là. (SM 238)[90]

The spacing of 'the taking-place-there' (*l'y-avoir-lieu*) rejects the sub/superlunary dichotomy even in its mystical guise, refusing the notion of a radical alterity whose 'elsewhere' does duty for an absent deity. In this refusal, Nancy is seeking to achieve what Badiou claims for his assertion that 'nothing is inaccessible', and his claims for its necessity for post-theological thinking echo those of Badiou:

Aussi longtemps que nous ne prenons pas en compte, sans réserve, le mondial comme tel, nous ne sommes pas quittes des démiurges et des créateurs. Autrement dit, nous ne sommes pas athées. Être athée ne signifie plus nier un divin qui s'est de lui-même résorbé (et cela ne peut donc peut-être plus s'appeler «athéisme»). Cela signifie : ouvrir le sens du monde. (SM 238)[91]

Atheism, as Nancy is using the term here – in a way in which elsewhere he uses 'atheology' as opposed to traditional Western atheism and where for the sake of clarity we are using 'post-theological thought' – is an opening of the sense of the world according to spacing, without recourse to any notion of (divine) creation or the logic of the principle, whether that creation be theistic or atheistic. It is this nuance that Ben Hutchens flattens out when he calls this moment from *Le Sens du monde* 'one of [Nancy's] most explicitly atheistic claims',[92] for we must not miss the fact that Nancy is also re-defining the atheism that he affirms in contradistinction to the traditional understanding of the term.

Nancy has recourse to Lucretian atomism in order to develop this theme of *mondialisation*. Lucretius is, according to Nancy, far from elaborating a materialism in opposition to idealism, and is far from elaborating a notion of the privation of worldly sense in opposition to the thesis of a transcendent sense:

Ce que l'«atomisme» (bien ou mal nommé) représente est bien plutôt ce qu'il faudrait désigner comme l'autre archi-thèse de la philosophie (la première étant l'agathon de Platon), à savoir, l'espacement originaire en tant que matérialité, et cet espacement lui-même comme existential du rapport à l'agathon (SM 95)[93]

Spacing, then, is atomism's alternative to the Platonic Good that orders thinking and the world 'from above'; it is an order that emerges in the world from within, and comprehends no transcendent/immanent dichotomy, and therefore no mystically absolute alterity. What *le mondial* requires, Nancy argues, is a new thinking of sense. Our task is not to pave the way for a new divine kingdom, neither in this world nor in any other, nor is it to rediscover the immanent unity of the world of myth that was lost with the birth of Western monotheism, rather our task is to achieve a post-theological integration that avoids both the privation of asceticism and the latent theology parasitism; our task is 'penser un « sens-de-monde » dans un monde divisé de son propre être-monde, dans un monde acosmique et athéologique' (*DDC* 60),[94] yet a world which nevertheless remains the totality of beings and of possible sense.

Nancy's *athéologie* is therefore not to be confused with Mark C. Taylor's reworking of Thomas Altizer's 'death of God theology'[95] in terms of an 'a/theology' which seeks to position deconstruction as the 'hermeneutics of the death of God'.[96] Rather than a rejection of the categories which impose the binary choice between theism and atheism, Taylor's thought makes the less radical move of positioning itself on the slash between theism and atheism, where '[t]he / of a/theology [. . .] marks the *linamen* that signifies *both* proximity and distance, similarity and difference, interiority and exteriority. This strangely permeable membrane forms a border where fixed boundaries disintegrate. [. . .] Since it is forever *entre-deux*, a/theology is undeniably ambiguous'.[97] For Nancy, atheology is not between or before the decision for atheism or theism; it is otherwise than that decision. Nancean faith, as we have seen, has nothing to do with undecidability, and his *athéologie* is not a hesitation between theism and atheism but a refusal of the choice which such a hesitation presupposes.

Nancy's atheology is not without risk, however. As Badiou's atheistic axioms harbour a question-begging ontological *ataraxia*, so Nancy's refusal of the a/theism dichotomy also fails to banish the shades of the divine. Nancy attracts the accusation of maintaining a theology under the cover of atheology, a point probed by Jacques Derrida and Francis Guibal in 'Responsabilité, du sens à venir'.[98] In this exchange with Derrida and Guibal, Nancy comments that, if he were to have a motto, it might well be the Eckhartian dictum 'we beg God to rid us of God'.[99] He is cut short by Guibal, who reminds Nancy of the parasitism of this dictum and of his own warning from *Des Lieux divins*, that 'Si nous devons passer, un jour, par-delà notre athéisme, ce sera pour ne même plus prier Dieu de nous délivrer de Dieu' (*DLD* 36).[100] After acknowledging the well-foundedness of the intervention, Nancy turns to Blanchot's rejection of Feuerbach's replacement of God by Man in *L'Entretien infini*, noting that for Blanchot 'il s'agit de « tout autre chose », il s'agit de faire ou de mettre tout autre chose . . . « *à cet endroit-là* », quand même'.[101] 'Something else altogether' perhaps, but nevertheless 'in that place'. It sounds as if Blanchot is unable, after all, fully to wrest himself free from the parasitic thinking he identifies in

Feuerbach and others, and it looks as if Nancy joins him in that impasse too, for he continues

> Au fond, j'essaie peut-être de ne pas dire autre chose que ça: il y a là un certain endroit, une certaine place et un certain temps en tant que place et temps de . . . disons donc du divin, de la révélation, de l'ouvert.[102]

This point identified by Nancy crosses Badiou's truth as affect of immanence; both are instances of a moment necessary for their accounts of post-theological thought that nevertheless in the final instance escape the parameters established for and by that thought.

The divine, revelation and the Open have their place in Nancy's thought, not in terms of religious transcendence but in terms of spacing. Yet the flight from all positive revelation, and then the flight from that flight, which leads Nancy to think the relation of revealability (*Offenbarkeit*) to revelation (*Offenbarung*) in the same way that he thinks the relation of *sens* to *signification*, does not provide a radical alternative to theological thinking but a new means of thinking atheologically within and against the categories of theism and atheism. This does not mean that Nancy's spacing, his *mondialisation*, is irrevocably theological, or that it occupies exactly the place of the Christian God or Feuerbach's Man. This is clearly not the case, for with *le mondial* Nancy achieves a remarkable rethinking of transcendence and immanence in a *transimmanence* that is very different to the ascetic nihilism of immanence-without-transcendence into which imitative atheism falls. What it does mean is that Nancy's *mondial* does not free itself from the theism/atheism binary in one leap, or in one axiomatic decision. The status of the atheological is delicate; the double flight from signification and from revelation does not reject theological categories out of hand, but thinks *le mondial* from within them, transforming and frustrating them from the inside, seeking, as Nancy says, a resource buried deep within them that allows us to go beyond them (but not to leave them behind completely). Yet as we have seen already, this gesture is itself not free from Christian hyperbole. The project of post-theological thought, whether pursued in its 'finite' or 'infinite' guise, whether primarily as an avoidance of asceticism or an avoidance of parasitism, proves itself to be a difficult and as yet incomplete, possibly incompletable, task.

CONCLUSION

The fundamental difference between Badiou's and Nancy's approaches to post-theological thought can be seen in the difference between the necessity for Badiou of the 'nothing is inaccessible' and the tension in which this stands with Plato's principle of intelligibility, and Nancy's argument that reason is supplemented by a 'faith that is nothing at all'. Badiou (in his axiomatic mathematisation of ontology) and Nancy (in his *mondialisation* of spacing) agree that there is no sacred, no inaccessible domain. But for Nancy there is something inaccessible to reason: reason itself. In this, Nancy joins Badiou in recognising the importance of the choice of a 'philosophical disposition' on the basis of an ultimately unaccountable central term:

> Il y a, au cœur de chaque grande philosophie (et cela pourrait être la mesure de leur grandeur . . .), un mystère au sujet de Dieu ou des dieux. Cela ne veut surtout pas dire que ce mystère serait le cœur de la philosophie qui le porte. Assurément, il ne l'est pas; mais il est placé dans ce cœur, alors même qu'il n'y a pas sa place. (*DLD* 24)[103]

We must not too hastily conclude that the 'God of the philosophers' is an inane notion, cautions Nancy. Each philosophy experiences the approach and the flight of the divine. This claim from the early *Des Lieux divins* is echoed in *L'Oubli de la philosophie*, where Nancy both frames the argument in less religious language, and allows himself a longer elaboration. We quote the passage here in full:

> Platon, Descartes ou Kant ne proposent jamais une « vision du monde » sans faire en même temps le geste de toucher à la limite de toute vision du monde. Leurs discours prennent toujours en charge, d'une manière ou d'une autre, une clôture de la signification, le paiement d'une dette infinie au Sens, *et* l'ouverture d'une brèche ou d'un excès, l'abandon de la dette et de son économie. C'est même à cela, et à cela seul, que se reconnaissent les « grandes » philosophies: *elles ne sont jamais simplement des visions du monde,* elles ne sont jamais simplement des messages signifiants. Et c'est à cela aussi que nous devons leurs apories ou leurs énigmes, et avec elles *l'histoire* réelle, effective de la philosophie – le Bien ou l'Amour de Platon, l'évidence de Descartes, la joie de Spinoza, le schématisme de Kant, la logique de Hegel, la praxis de Marx, etc. (*OP* 75)[104]

Nancy is echoing here Edmund Husserl's contention in *The Crisis of European Sciences* that only 'secondary thinkers' remain ignorant of the regress ad infinitum, the assertion of an unjustified hypothesis, or the circularity of justification that must sooner or later assail every systematic philosophy.[105]

This is a condition of Badiou's philosophy as much as of Nancy's. There is no divine promise in Badiou's philosophy, no miracle, no revelation or smoking theistic gun, but his philosophy itself is nonsufficient without the promise of ontological *ataraxia* and the violence of the axiomatic decision that animate it. It is true that Badiou's disenchanted, mathematised universe contains no promise of a returning deity, but it is no less true that this same universe is itself chosen as 'better' according to the promise of ontological *ataraxia*. What is inaccessible to Badiou's philosophy is its own promise of atheism, a promise that has been exiled, or perhaps 'outsourced', outside Badiou's secularised mathematical ontology, as the faith by virtue of which his atheism consists. In short, the world is secularised for Badiou when and only when secularisation itself becomes the promise which decides the axioms of his mathematised universe in the first place. Does this mean that Badiou is thereby won for the post-secularists after all? That his thinking is, in the end, crypto-theological? Not a bit of it. It means only this: that Badiou's thought is an atheism after all. Not an atheism in the way he claims, though, for which 'nothing is inaccessible', but an atheism that must inevitably fall either into parasitism or into asceticism, an atheism that, like all great philosophies, is inaccessible to itself, and in that admission finally becomes consistent, as it makes room for fidelity to ontological *ataraxia*. Nancy's atheology is the truth of Badiou's atheism. Both Nancy and Badiou must finally acknowledge the impossibility of atheism's 'last step' to completion and consistency, and thereby come up short of a post-theological integration. It is the claim to have accomplished this final elusive step, and therefore to have consummated a post-theological integration, that draws us in the next chapter to the work of Quentin Meillassoux.

NOTES

1. Eliot, 'Leçon de Valéry', p. 77.
2. Daniel Bensaïd, 'Alain Badiou et le miracle de l'événement', p. 160; '[d]etached from its historical conditions, pure diamond of truth, the event, just like the notion of the absolutely aleatory encounter in the late Althusser, is akin to a miracle' (Bensaïd, 'Alain Badiou and the miracle of the event', p. 101).
3. Žižek *The Ticklish Subject*, p. 183.
4. Osborne, 'Alain Badiou's *Being and Event*', p. 26.
5. Badiou, 'The event as trans-being', *TW* 98. This passage on the miracle is added by Badiou in this English version, adapted from 'L'événement comme trans-être' (*CT* 55–9).
6. This is also why Badiou's atheism is not vulnerable at this point to the charge of negative theology: 1) the void is always the void *of* the situation and 2) in the language of *Logiques des mondes*, the inexistent is not an ineffable alterity but simply that in a world which exists to the least intensity possible.
7. Bosteels, *Alain Badiou*, p. 115.

8.

> in my eyes, the principal contribution of my work does not consist in opposing the situation to the event. In a certain sense, that is something that everybody does these days. The principal contribution consists in posing the following question: What can be deduced, or inferred, from there from the point of view of the situation itself? (CCBT 252)

9. 'I am convinced that the new can only be thought as process. There certainly is novelty in the event's upsurge, but this novelty is always evanescent. That is not where we can pinpoint the new in its materiality' (CCBT 253).
10. See Bosteels, *Alain Badiou*, p. 131.
11. Caputo, 'Spectral hermeneutics', p. 157.
12. Caputo, 'Spectral hermeneutics', p. 183 n.4. author's emphasis.
13. Caputo, 'Spectral hermeneutics', p. 52.
14. 'do not give up on that part of yourself that you do not know' (*Eth* 47).
15. Caputo, 'Spectral hermeneutics', p. 57.
16. Rancière, Untitled discussion of Alain Badiou's *L'Être et l'événement*, p. 220.
17. Simon Critchley makes a similar argument when he considers Badiou's moral theory to be structurally Christian, for the law (the encyclopaedia of a situation) is overcome by an act of love for the event, where 'le processus subjectif d'une vérité est une seule et même chose que l'amour de cette vérité' (*SP* 97); 'The subjective process of a truth is one and the same thing as the love of that truth' (*SPe* 92).
18.

> In relation to Pascal, we must show a little reason after all: is it possible, yes or no, to draw from a text and from a conviction whose explicit parameters you in no way share the form, or the matrix, of a philosopheme that you have proposed and thought out in your own right, without seeing the parameters in question turned back on you as your unconscious finally unmasked? (Author's translation)

19.

> I like the grand metaphors that come from religion: Miracle, Grace, Salvation, Glorious Body, Conversion . . . People have evidently concluded from this taste of mine that my philosophy is a Christianity in disguise. The book on Saint Paul that I published in 1997 with PUF didn't help things. All things considered, I prefer to be a revolutionary atheist veiled under a religious language than a western 'democrat' who persecutes Muslim men and women while disguised as a secular feminist. (Author's translation)

20. He admits as much in 'L'Investigation transcendantale': the relationship between multiplicity and generic procedure might appear somewhat

miraculous, from which '[i]l en résulte que, passant par mon essai sur Saint Paul, il n'est pas assez impossible, à mes propres yeux, de voir en « moi », comme le fait Nietzsche pour tout philosophe, du religieux camouflé' (IT 8); 'as a result, taking into account my essay on Saint Paul, it is not utterly impossible, in my own estimation, to see in "me", as Nietzsche does in every philosopher, a religious person in camouflage' (author's translation).

21. Hallward, *Badiou: A Subject to Truth*, p. 75.
22. 'an absolutely pure choice, one free from any presupposition other than that of a having to choose, in the absence of any distinguishing mark in the presented terms' (*Con* 124).
23. Tiles, *The Philosophy of Set Theory*, p. 121.
24. Marion, 'De la "mort de Dieu"'.
25. Marion, 'De la "mort de Dieu"', p. 27.

> the atheism of a concept of God [. . .] by virtue of its intrinsic regionality, far from closing down the question of God opens the question of other possible concepts for God. [. . .] The 'death of God' directly implies the death of the 'death of God' because each time, as it disqualifies one definite concept of God, it opens up once more the indefinite lexicon of other possible concepts to name a God that is always thinkable or speakable otherwise. (Author's translation)

26. Marion, 'De la "mort de Dieu"', p. 28.
27. Marion, 'De la "mort de Dieu"', p. 27.
28. Marion, 'De la "mort de Dieu"', p. 27.
29. 'To practice in thought the decisive rupture with romanticism [. . .] we cannot do without any recourse – which is perhaps once again blind, or stamped with constraint, or violence – to the injunctions of mathematics' (*Con* 111).
30.

> We shall say that truth forces knowledges. The verb to force indicates that since the power of a truth is that of a break, it is by violating established and circulating knowledges that a truth returns to the immediacy of the situation, or reworks that sort of portable encyclopedia from which opinions, communications and sociality draw their meaning. (*Eth* 70)

31. The introduction of 'inaccessible cardinals' in *Logiques des mondes* should not confuse us here. Badiou is not reverting to a finite thought of the limit. When Badiou insists that the cardinal of a world is an inaccessible cardinal (*LM* 316/*LW* 300), or that every world is measured by an infinite and inaccessible cardinal (*LM* 350/*LW* 332), what he means is that such a cardinal cannot be expressed as the sum of a number of smaller cardinals, and not by any means that it is inaccessible to thought.

32. Badiou groups under Romantic inaccessibility the Lacanian horror at the unsymbolisable Real, the Lyotardian *phrase*, and the end of Wittgenstein's *Tractatus*, according to which 'Whereof one cannot speak, thereof one must be silent' (*M* 76/*Man* 95).
33. Letter to Peter Hallward, 19 June 1996, quoted in Hallward, *Badiou: A Subject to Truth*, p. 320.
34. Lyotard, Untitled discussion of Alain Badiou's *L'Être et l'événement*, p. 236.
35. Lyotard, Untitled discussion of Alain Badiou's *L'Être et l'événement*, p. 228.
36. Milbank, 'The shares of being', p. 22.
37. Clemens, *The Romanticism of Contemporary Theory*, p. 209.
38. Hallward, 'Generic sovereignty', p. 99.
39. Hallward, 'Translator's introduction', in Alain Badiou, *Ethics*, p. xxxvii. Author's emphasis.
40. Bosteels, *Alain Badiou*, p. 108.
41. Rancière, Untitled discussion, p. 221.
42. Clemens, *The Romanticism of Contemporary Theory*, p. 208.
43. 'under the constraints of the historical injunction of being' (*NuN* 56).
44. 'What it took was a pure courage of thought, a voluntary incision into the – eternally defendable – mechanism of ontological finitism' (*BE* 148).
45. 'when we are dealing with pure declarations, decided as such, these declarations exhibit the fragility of their historicity. No argument can support them' (*NuN* 57; translation altered).
46.
> The fact that this is a matter of axioms and not of theorems means that the existence of zero and of the infinite are prescribed to thought by being, in order that thought might exist in the ontological epoch of such an existence. (*NuN* 57; translation altered)

47. 'Every thought – and, therefore, mathematics – sets off decisions (intuitions) from the standpoint of the undecidable (of nondeducible inference)' (*BOE* 95).
48. Hallward, 'Generic sovereignty', p. 97.
49.
> Deleuze forcefully maintains – actually against all the joyous spontaneist and 'anarcho-desiring' interpretations of his philosophy – that we never think either by voluntary decision or by natural movement. We are always forced to think, he says. Thinking is like a shove in our back. Thought is neither pleasant nor desired. It is a violence done to us. I completely agree with this vision. (Author's translation)

50. 'I agree with Bergson on the fact that there is an originary point that organises experience, a point that the whole of philosophical dialectics strains to catch up with and transmit' (author's translation).

51. 'For all that, I don't know at the present time how far I need to go in this direction' (author's translation).
52.
> I think that philosophy must include, both in its conception and in its proposition, the conviction that true life can be experienced in immanence. Something must signal it from inside itself, not simply as an exterior imperative, like a Kantian imperative. That comes as an affect which signals, indicates, in immanence that life is worth living. (Author's translation)

53.
> For the things which are known, say not that their being known comes from the good, but also that they get their existence and their being from it as well – though the good is not being, but something far surpassing being in rank and power. (Plato, *The Republic*, p. 216)

54. 'a principle of intelligibility that is not reducible to the Idea itself. It is naturally beyond the Idea that the Idea is a principle of intelligibility' (author's translation).
55. 'there is good reason to *believe* – but *there is good reason* to believe' (author's translation).
56. The axiom of choice states that 'If *a* is a set, all of whose elements are non-empty sets no two of which have any elements in common, then there is a set *c* which has precisely one element in common with each element of *a*' (Tiles, *The Philosophy of Set Theory*, p. 123), or in other words the axiom of choice assumes a function that allows one to 'choose' one element from each of an infinite number of sets, when those sets have no elements in common.
57. 'for the universe with Axiom of Choice is otherwise broader and denser in significant links than is one without the axiom' (*BOE* 96).
58. '[w]ithout such a decision it will remain for ever possible for being to be essentially finite' (*BE* 148)
59. Hallward, *Badiou: A Subject to Truth*, p. 149.
60. Mullarkey, *Post-Continental Philosophy*, p. 113.
61. Mullarkey, *Post-Continental Philosophy*, p. 104.
62. Milbank, 'The shares of being', p. 49.
63. Lyotard, Untitled discussion, p. 238; 'in order to decide to name, one must hold a particular affection for the void' (author's translation).
64. de Kesel, 'Truth as formal Catholicism', p. 13.
65. de Kesel, 'Truth as formal Catholicism', p. 14.
66. Colossians 3: 11.
67.
> In philosophy it is clearly identified under the name of 'freedom of indifference'. This freedom is a freedom that, confronting the

> indiscernible, is not governed by any identifiable norm of difference. If there is no value that discriminates things that you have to choose between, then your freedom as such constitutes the norm and merges with chance. The indiscernible is the subtraction that establishes a point of coincidence between chance and freedom. (*Con* 124)

68. Lecercle, 'Cantor, Lacan, Mao, Beckett, même combat', p. 12.
69. It is not our intention here to provide a detailed description of atomism, nor an exhaustive account of Badiou's relationship with it. The reader is referred to Bandres, 'Badiou et l'atomisme ancien', pp. 41–52.
70.

> The whole point is to contend, for as long as possible and under the most innovative conditions for philosophy, the notion that truth itself is but a multiplicity: [. . .] A radical gesture is precisely required here. Besides, this is how modern philosophy is recognized: by subtracting the examination of truths from the simple form of judgment. What this always means is to decide upon a single ontology of manifolds. (*BOE* 62; translation altered)

71. 'Lucretius clearly sees that subtraction from the fear of the gods requires that, short of the multiple, there is nothing. Beyond the multiple there is still only the multiple' (*BOE* 37).
72. Without referring explicitly to *ataraxia*, Martin Hägglund classes Lucretian atomism as therapeutic in his taxonomy of atheism in 'The challenge of radical atheism' (p. 229). See also Clay, *Lucretius and Epicurus*, and Nussbaum, *The Therapy of Desire*.
73. '[i]t is thus imperative, so as to be serenely established in the irreversibility of God's death, to finish up with the motif of finitude' (*BOE* 29).
74. 'In fact, we have to assume, as did Lucretius, that manifold-unfolding is not constrained by the immanence of a limit. For it is only too obvious that such a constraint proves the power of the One as grounding the multiple itself' (*BOE* 35).
75. Hallward, *Badiou: A Subject to Truth*, p. 90; author's emphasis.
76. Gauchet, *Le Désenchantement du monde*, p. ii; 'a religion for departing from religion' (Gauchet, *The Disenchantment of the World*, p. 4).
77.

> thinking without end, finitude without end, in sum, the infinite – remains privative, subtractive, and, in sum, defective – in much the way that the main tone of every species of atheism also remains obstinately and deafly defective, even against its own will. (*DisDC* 17–18)

78.

> The horizon of a subtraction, of a retreat, an absence, or even the horizon of what I once called 'absentheism,' to oppose it to atheism,

continues to form a horizon. That is to say, it forms a limit, a dead end, and an end of the world. (*DisDC* 18)

79. 'the act of reason that relates, itself, to that which, in it, exceeds it infinitely' (*DisDC* 25; translation altered).
80.

   Kant already recognized formally when he spoke, for example, of 'the incapacity in which reason finds itself, to satisfy by itself its own needs.' Reason does not suffice unto itself: *for itself* it is not a *sufficient reason*. But it is in the acknowledgment of this insufficiency that it fully justifies itself. (*DisDC* 25)

81.

   The death of God – and it is only this God that is dead, Nietzsche himself says so – is nothing other than the death of all Reason thus endowed with the attributes of the necessity and completeness of the foundation-production of beings as a whole. This reason did not realise that it put itself to death in erecting this idol of itself which is nothing but a God for atheists. (Author's translation)

82. 'To deconstruct Christianity means: to open reason to its own reason, indeed to its unreason' (author's translation).
83.

   this faith that is nothing at all: a fidelity thinking beyond the concept of the 'nothing of that primitive All', a thinking given over to that which comes to it from elsewhere because from nowhere, from *nulla partes*, from the null part of the nothing, and thus a faith that, in sum, is nothing – nothing but this tiny extreme touch of thought laid upon that nothing. (*DisDC* 73)

84. 'It is not a question of "religion," here, but rather of a "faith" as a sign of the fidelity of reason to that which *in and of itself* exceeds reason's phantasm of justifying itself as much as the world and man' (*DisDC* 28).
85. See Marion, *Étant donné*; *Being Given*.
86. Five volumes in all were projected, but only two were completed at Bataille's death, forming volumes V and VI of the *Œuvres complètes*.
87. Bataille, 'L'angoisse du temps présent et les devoirs de l'esprit', in *Œuvres complètes*, vol. VIII, p. 573; 'the science of the death or destruction of God' (Georges Bataille, *The Unfinished System of Nonknowledge*, ed. Stuart Kendall, Minneapolis: University of Minnesota Press, 2001, p. 166).
88. Bataille, *Œuvres complètes*, vol. VIII, p. 229.

   It is an atheology whose fundamental consideration, let us say, is present in the following proposition: God is an effect of un-knowing. He can nevertheless be known as an effect of un-knowing-like laughter,

> like the sacred. I can then say the following: that this experience is, on the whole, part of the general line of religions. In speaking as I do, I am aware not only of adopting a basically religious attitude, but further, of representing a kind of constituted religion. ('Un-knowing: laughter and tears', p. 99)

89. Bataille, *Œuvres complètes*, vol. VI, p. 310.
90.
> the worldliness of the earth – of the human being – means: the renewed putting into play of taking-place in general. The *there* is neither the heavens nor the humus, but that there is, and that there is a place for reconceiving sense on the basis of this point of departure. (*SW* 158)

91.
> As long as we do not take into account, without reserve, the worldly as such, we have not gotten rid of demiurges and creators. In other words, we are not yet atheists. Being an atheist is no longer a matter of denying a divine instance that has reabsorbed into itself (and this can perhaps no longer be called 'atheism'). It means: opening the sense of the world. (*SW* 158)

92. Hutchens, *Jean-Luc Nancy*, p. 87.
93. '"atomism" (whether well or poorly named) represents what one would have to call the other archi-thesis of philosophy (the first being Plato's *agathon*): originary spacing qua materiality, and this spacing itself as *existentiale* of the relation to the *agathon*' (*SW* 57).
94. 'to think a "sense-of-the-world" or a "world-sense" in a world divided in its own being-world, in an acosmic and atheological world' (*DisDC* 39).
95. See Altizer and Hamilton, *Radical Theology*.
96. Taylor, *Erring*, p. 6.
97. Taylor, *Erring*, pp. 12–13.
98. Derrida et al., 'Responsabilité – du sens à venir', pp. 165–200.
99. Schürmann, *Meister Eckhart*, p. 212.
100. 'If we are to pass beyond our atheism one day, it will be because we no longer pray to God to deliver us from God' (*ODP* 139).
101. Derrida et al., 'Responsabilité – du sens à venir', p. 94; 'it is a question of "something completely different", it is a question of making or putting something completely different "in that place", nevertheless' (author's translation).
102. Derrida et al., 'Responsabilité – du sens à venir', p. 94; 'Basically, perhaps I am trying to say nothing but that: there is a certain spot, a certain place and a certain time that are the place and time of . . . let us say, of the divine, of revelation, of the open' (author's translation).
103.
> There is at the heart of every great philosophy (and this could be the measure of its greatness), a mystery concerning God or the gods. This

is in no way to say that this mystery is the heart of the philosophy that bears it. It certainly is not; but it is placed in that heart, even though it has no place there. (ODP 129; translation altered)

104.
Neither Plato, nor Descartes, nor Kant ever proposed a 'worldview' without at the same time making the gesture of touching the limit of all worldviews. Their discourses in one way or another always take the responsibility for a closure of signification, for the payment of an infinite debt to Sense, *and* for the opening of a breach or an excess, the abandonment of the debt and its economy. For that matter, it is in this, and in this alone, that one recognizes 'great' philosophies: *they are never simply worldviews*, they are never simply signifying messages. And it is also to this that we owe their aporias and enigmas, and along with them, the real, effective *history* of philosophy: Plato's Good or Love, Descartes's evidence, Spinoza's joy, Kant's schematism, Hegel's logic, Marx's praxis, and so on. (*GT* 51–2; translation altered)

105. Husserl, *The Crisis of European Sciences*, p. 394.

4. Beyond A/theism? Quentin Meillassoux

De l'inexistence de Dieu s'infère un monde suffisamment insensé pour que Dieu même puisse s'y produire. (ID 3)¹

Dieu est pour l'athée une affaire de prêtre ; Dieu est pour le philosophe une affaire trop sérieuse pour être confiée aux prêtres. (ID 379)²

In the previous chapter we saw that, while Badiou maintains the dichotomy of theism and atheism in his axiomatic approach, Nancy moves beyond the dichotomy, exploring how the two positions share a common structure and how, to be 'without God', it is this structure that must be rejected, though we concluded that neither Nancy nor Badiou succeed in rejecting it. In this chapter we explore what such an atheological move might look like in an idiom closer to, but by no means identical with, Badiou's own, by turning to the thought of Quentin Meillassoux. Meillassoux's *Après la finitude* (2006) is an expanded treatment of part of his *thèse de doctorat* 'L'Inexistence divine: Essai sur le dieu virtuel', covering only the first 150 pages of a proposed 600 or 700 pages of work developing the whole of 'L'Inexistence divine'.³ This latter work is broader in its scope though less developed than *Après la finitude*, and we shall be moving between the two works in our discussion of Meillassoux in this chapter.

The 'finitude' to which Meillassoux is referring in *Après la finitude* is both the temporal boundedness of a human reason for which 'what is' correlates to 'what is thought', and the Pascalian wretchedness of a humanity incessantly humbled by the boundedness of its will and capacities. While Meillassoux's thought may seem to bear closer affinities to Badiou's than to Nancy's, we shall resist classing Meillassoux at the outset in terms of any particular philosophical clan.⁴ Badiou's preface to Meillassoux's *Après la finitude* indicates his own admiration for Meillassoux's thought:

> Il n'est pas exagéré de dire que Quentin Meillassoux ouvre dans l'histoire de la philosophie, conçue à ce stade comme histoire de ce que c'est que connaître, une nouvelle voie, étrangère à la distribution canonique de Kant entre « dogmatisme », « scepticisme » et « critique ». (PAF 11)⁵

Badiou sees strong parallels between Meillassoux's work and his own on the question of religion, commenting in the same preface that Meillassoux's critique of Kant's critique of reason 'autorise à nouveau que le destin de la pensée soit l'absolu, et non les fragments et relations partielles dans lesquelles nous nous complaisons, cependant que le « retour du religieux » sert de fictif supplément d'âme' (PAF 11).⁶ Meillassoux, as we shall see, is indebted to Badiou's ontological reading of set theory (AF 141/AfF 103), and he deploys this Badiouian borrowing in a central place in his own thinking. It would be very easy to over-stress the affinities between Badiou and Meillassoux, however, and Meillassoux himself is at pains to stress that he is not Badiou's disciple (HE). He critiques the place of the axiom in Badiou's thought, and in particular considers Badiou's employment of the empty set to be Heideggerian in so far as the void is 'enigmatic' (ID 125 n.41, quoting EE 72/BE 59).

As well as seeking a new position in relation to a Kantian understanding of dogmatism, scepticism and critique, Meillassoux also strikes out in a new way to accomplish what we are calling a post-theological integration. In this chapter we shall unfold and evaluate this approach, considering it alongside Badiou's atheism and Nancy's atheology and offering a critique of our own that casts doubt on Meillassoux's post-theological integration.

4.1 THEISM, ATHEISM AND PHILOSOPHY

Like Nancy, Meillassoux sees the dichotomy of theism and atheism as two routes to the same destination, though his reasons for rejecting the binary are for the most part divergent from Nancy's. Like Badiou, however, Meillassoux trains his sights primarily on the dangers of ascetic atheism. He argues that atheism as traditionally conceived accepts and works within the terms of reference of theistic thought, which in Meillassoux's case is the dichotomy between an immanence which can be known but which is fundamentally unsatisfying, and an unknowable, inaccessible yet ultimately satisfying transcendence (ID 369), where transcendence has been defined as exteriority in general, and exteriority to the concept in particular (ID 8). Religion posits a transcendence that alone can satisfy human desire, and the runt of immanence that remains once transcendence has taken this lion's share is limited, finite and incapable of sustaining happiness. Condemned to asceticism, atheism simply accepts the scraps of immanence that fall from religion's table (ID 379).

This sort of atheism must, for Meillassoux, lead to one of two possible outcomes, both of which are undesirable. The first is an ascetic renunciation of transcendence, stressing the courage and humility that will prove necessary to face up to our miserable state, and the second is revolt, an attitude of defiance that amounts to much the same as the negative making-do of renunciation. In both cases, the atheist regrets that she is right (ID 379). 'Atheology' is not spared Meillassoux's condemnation either, inasmuch as it still rests, along with theism and atheism, on a belief exterior to philosophy, making it the servant of theology (AF 63/AfF 47). This external belief is the faith or conviction that Nancy, for his part, seeks to distinguish from religious faith. For Meillassoux there is no such distinction and, as we shall see, his position relies on a claim to have done away with the need for faith of any sort.

As an altogether more satisfying alternative to inadmissible theism and miserable atheism, Meillassoux proposes a third term, 'philosophy', which distinguishes itself from both theism and atheism by refusing to accept religion's terms of engagement. What atheism fails to see is that its own limits, the frontiers of its own domain of immanence, are religious, and in order not to fall into the same trap, philosophy must speak of God and not remain silent; god(s) must not be construed as inaccessible to philosophy or beyond its limits, for the very good reason that, according to Meillassoux, philosophy has no limits. The philosopher refuses the atheist's limits because he does not sanction religion's division of immanence and transcendence, to which both the ascetic and parasitic atheist bow the knee (ID 377).

'Philosophy' does not reject God: that is atheism's great mistake. Philosophy devours him, taking away from religion all that religion holds as desirable (ID 377). The lexeme 'God' does not name one of the sides in the battle between theism and atheism, Meillassoux argues, but rather the territory on which the two camps fight. In reserving this name for the object of faith, atheism shows that it has ascetically sealed its own defeat. 'God' is what is at stake in the fight between immanence and transcendence, the revealed God of religion or the reviled God of the philosophers. The atheist, thinking himself outside the field of battle, confuses the priest and the philosopher from afar : 'Dieu est pour l'athée une affaire de prêtre ; Dieu est pour le philosophe une affaire trop sérieuse pour être confiée aux prêtres' (ID 379).[7] Meillassoux's philosophy is not a Ricœurean second naïveté, a post-religious faith chastened by passing through atheism's sieve or a 'returning to God after God',[8] but a pursuit of the battle against faith deep into theology's own territory.

From this initial rejection of a/theism, Meillassoux will make what may seem two rather unexpected moves: he will argue that philosophy is very close to religion, and that philosophy does in fact believe in God, though in an as yet unheard-of manner: philosophy believes in God *because* God does not exist. Together, these two positions comprise Meillassoux's approach to post-theological integration. To understand how he arrives at these arresting conclusions and what he means by them, we need to consider two important motifs in his thinking: 1) the treatment of metaphysics in relation to the motif of the 'nothing is inaccessible' that we encountered in relation to Badiou, and 2) what he calls 'the factial' (*le factual*) and the importance of a new conception of necessity for his move beyond a/theism. We begin with the question: how does philosophy speak of God without being theistic?

4.1.1 *Metaphysics, Necessity and Inaccessibility*

Like Badiou, Meillassoux diagnoses the current return of the religious as a symptom of the end of metaphysics, an end which has emptied reason of its pretensions to the absolute (*AF* 61–2/*AfF* 45). From this state of affairs, he is also clear on the direction that any philosophical challenge to religion must take. The challenge must come from metaphysics and not from relativism, because religious ontology is itself relativist. In fact, religion and relativism are, from an immanent standpoint, one and the same ontology (ID 242), because they both rely on a fundamental contingency. For relativism everything is contingent because there are no absolute laws to guarantee any intramundane necessity; for religion everything is contingent upon the sovereign will of an unconstrained God. Whereas relativism sees in logico-mathematical thought only a linguistic convention, religion sees only the divine will: 'eternal' truths are such only because, and only for so long as, God wills them as such.[9] This being the case, relativism represents no danger whatsoever for the religious thinking of transcendence; such thinking confines relativism within the finitude of ignorance left for it by religion, and leaves transcendence to the priests. For a serious challenge to religion therefore, we must look to metaphysics. In choosing this path, Meillassoux's construal of metaphysics elaborates in much greater detail on the throwaway comment of Badiou's in the *Court Traité* that the god of metaphysics is the enemy of the god of religion (*CT* 14/*BOE* 24), the personal God of relationship.

Meillassoux understands 'metaphysics' in terms of its project, namely to attain by reason alone the fundamental and eternal principle of everything that is (ID 265), and the way in which he constructs metaphysics' challenge to religion (in ID 268ff) parallels Badiou's insistence that, for a truly post-theological philosophy, there must be nothing inaccessible. His argument can be summarised in eleven points: 1) It is not metaphysics itself that is at bottom a discourse of transcendence, but anti-metaphysics, because this latter seeks to forbid any understanding of the eternal foundation (*fondement*) of being. In leaving this transcendent foundation inaccessible to reason, it allows religious transcendence to continue unchallenged. Furthermore, it is inevitable that anti-metaphysics should be transcendent in this way, because 2) any limit to reason always also legitimates a religious discourse which claims for itself those realms beyond reason (our notion of an ascetic 'residual atheism'). It is therefore inevitable that 3) any notion of a limit or boundary to reason will end up sacrificing reason to revelation (where reason and revelation are considered as dichotomised and irreconcilable), for in such a case it is only the irrational discourse of revelation that can grant access to the principle of or foundation of existence. If there can be no rational discourse of sense that deals with the eternal foundation of the world (which is precisely what there cannot be, in anti-metaphysics), then the door is left wide open for irrational revelation. This is for Meillassoux the definition of theology: the discourse which rests on the notion that revelation is essential for access to the divine, given that it is impossible for man to accede to the divine by the use of his reason alone (ID 278). As for the atheism that seeks to remain resolutely within the limits of finitude, it provides nothing but a legitimation of the religious in its most glorious irrationality (ID 274).

We now turn our attention away from anti-metaphysics to metaphysics itself. Metaphysics is the only thought that is not at bottom a thought of transcendence for Meillassoux, because it disallows in principle that there is anything inaccessible to reason. Therefore 4) metaphysics renders any religious discourse illegitimate because the terrain of revelation has always already been occupied by reason. Furthermore, 5) metaphysics alone can banish transcendence in this way, because metaphysics alone can occupy this 'enemy territory' otherwise left to revelation. According to Meillassoux, this is the fundamental trait of metaphysics: 'On ne comprend rien à la métaphysique si l'on ne saisit pas que sa particularité réside tout entière dans cette agressivité originaire envers toute forme de transcendance, *qu'aucune autre discursivité n'a possédée*' (ID 268–9; QM's emphasis).[10] In other words, metaphysics is the only discourse for which there is nothing inaccessible. 6)

Metaphysics therefore abolishes God precisely by speaking of God, by occupying with the discourse of reason the territory otherwise conceded to revelation. Meillassoux goes on to underline the necessity of metaphysics by insisting that 7) any discourse other than metaphysics – or, in other words, any limitation of reason – must produce a necessarily (as opposed to historically) fideistic argument, justifying religious belief in general as the only possible access to the absolute (AF 62–3/AfF 46).

Meillassoux is now able to argue that 8) fideism is identical to scepticism and radical relativism, for fideism, in demonstrating the inconsistency of all reasoning (inconsistent because reason must give way sooner or later to faith and revelation) and the inability of unaided reason to reach any eternal truth whatsoever, demolishes all certainty in just the same way as do scepticism and the most radical relativism (ID 269). Metaphysics itself, however, is not exempt from complicity in this humiliation of philosophy, for 9) contemporary metaphysics plays into fideism's hands, by showing religion to be irrational. This undertaking is profoundly misguided, however, for it simply secures the domain of revelation against any possible philosophical invasion. In contrast to this capitulation, philosophy must look to rationalise the domain of revelation, and therefore 10) the God of the philosophers is the great weapon of atheism, because it makes God rational. The God of the philosophers is no longer a God ('un Dieu qui n'en est plus un'), and yet it takes the place of the former God of revelation (ID 269). It is therefore in the God of Spinoza or of Hegel that true Western irreligion is to be found, not in Heidegger's anti-metaphysical declaration of atheism (ID 270). Meillassoux comes tantalisingly close here to implying that the only way to be rid of God is rationally to prove his existence, but we shall have to wait a little while longer for his conclusion on the existence of God. He completes his argument by asserting that 11) experimental science can never be the weapon of the atheist, because it relies on its own finitude in the order of knowledge (ID 281). The enlightenment project of science had an internal structure that was quintessentially religious, and there persists today an alliance between experimental science and theology, to the exclusion of the eternal truths of mathematics. To identify reason with science alone is to say that the most fundamental questions about the world cannot receive a rational answer, because they cannot be approached speculatively.

For all its pretension to enter and occupy religion's territory, Meillassoux nevertheless identifies a problem with metaphysics: though it rejects any limit to reason, it relies on a religious postulate, namely the possibility of a necessary existence (ID 380; PV 61). The dogma of revealed (and therefore rationally incomprehensible) truth requires a necessary being, but forbids intramundane necessity, for the principles and values of reason are temporary, liable to change according to the will of a sovereign God at any moment (ID 276). The fundamental thesis of metaphysics, by contrast, is that 'necessity is' (ID 277), in other words there are necessary laws governing nature and/or logic. This fundamental thesis of metaphysics is religious because only a God can guarantee or constitute such a necessity. It is in its reliance on the principle of sufficient reason (namely that for every entity, event, proposition, state of affairs and so on there must be a sufficient reason why it is as it is, and not otherwise, or more succinctly, 'nothing is without a reason' or, in Meillassoux's own terms, 'things are necessary') that metaphysics finds itself in the embarrassing position of being unable to demonstrate the necessity it nevertheless upholds and upon which it relies (SR 441). Relying as it does on such a self-undermining notion of necessity, metaphysics has been all but vanquished by relativism and religion. This is by virtue of the force of their critique of necessity: whereas relativism and religion maintain that there is no real necessity, metaphysics persists in the doomed enterprise of defending the notion of a real necessity (ID 242).

Necessity, Meillassoux argues, is also a hidden assumption in the binary oppositions that construct metaphysics. Both systems of metaphysics which privilege the one over the multiple, or identity over difference, as well as the contemporary critiques of metaphysics that privilege the multiple over the one or difference over identity, share the postulate according to which the primary and fundamental oppositions in terms of which thought takes place are precisely these (ID 136). But such affirmations or critiques of metaphysics are alike and equally incomprehensible, Meillassoux argues, because they suppose the *necessity* of these primary oppositions, a necessity which cannot be accounted for by the dichotomy itself. The antimetaphysician dethrones the One with a difference she cannot explain; the metaphysician says that the One is necessary because indivisible, but cannot account for the necessity of the indivisible One. To advance the primacy of the One over the many, or of the many over the One – or indeed to affirm that neither term is pre-eminent with relation to the other – is always already to have required the necessity of that pre-eminence, or lack of pre-eminence. This mirrors our own questioning of 'inconsistent multiplicity' in the first chapter: the weakness of Badiou's position is not in the first instance his privileging of the many over the one in inconsistency, but his adoption of the dichotomy of many and one as necessary. For Meillassoux these putatively originary oppositions – one/many, identity/difference – presuppose and require, therefore, a more fundamental opposition, that of necessity and contingency, and it is this latter dichotomy that Meillassoux advances as the primary opposition in all thought (ID 137).

Nevertheless, Meillassoux's own thought is not immune from similar questioning. The problem is that Meillassoux himself persists in occupying the space bequeathed to him by a certain contested religious tradition (we are thinking primarily of the fideistic reading of the first chapter of Paul's first letter to the Corinthians,[11] through Tertullian's division of sacred and secular learning in his oft-quoted and equally contested 'What indeed has Athens to do with Jerusalem?',[12] and Kierkegaard's 'qualitative leap' of faith[13]) in that he maintains a strict dichotomy of his own, this time not between the one and the multiple, but between faith and reason. The hidden premise at work in Meillassoux's reasoning here is that reason and revelation, like oil and water, can never mix, can never supplement each other or occupy the same space, and that the exercise of reason in a given area will in and of itself leave no room for a faith that, once again, Meillassoux assumes must be irrational. Why, simply because metaphysics can talk of something, must religion necessarily stop talking of that same thing? Can reason itself account for that mutual exclusivity? Can revelation? Or must we look outside reason for its justification? Meillassoux's dichotomising of faith and reason is not yet a refutation of the position taken by Nancy in his account of the 'faith that is nothing at all', where faith and reason are not dichotomised but faith is the 'nothing' that makes reason what it is. Nancy's faith is to Meillassoux's dichotomy of faith and reason as Meillassoux's necessity is to Badiou's dichotomy of the one and the multiple: it cuts across the binary and disrupts its terms.

In addition to faith and reason, we need to question Meillassoux's reliance on the dichotomy of necessity and contingency. After all, his critique of the dichotomies of identity and difference, of the one and the multiple, is not a critique of dichotomous thinking as such, merely a critique of the particular dichotomies which, he thinks, have been falsely considered to be primary. Nancy offers a critique of the dichotomy of necessity and contingency similar to his disruption of the dichotomy of the one and the many by singular plurality. 'Contingency' for Nancy is a philosophical term that dances to necessity's tune, measuring itself still by the contrast it draws with the religious notion of necessity. It is engaged in a dialectic where the totality of 'contingent things' (*contingents*) can form a general order of the world (ADC 20). In other words, contingency can easily become a placeholder or a 'front man' inhabiting the religious understanding of the world as cosmos (in Meillassoux's case we might evoke, in the spirit of the necessity of contingency, a 'cosmos of chaos'). Instead of this contingency parasitic on necessity's religiosity, Nancy proposes 'the fortuitous' (*le fortuit*). The fortuitous is less a nature or a state than a circumstance or movement, and it is not opposed in dichotomous relation to stasis or constancy:

> le fortuit, avec le fugace, le fuyant, l'inconsistant, l'éphémère, compose la rhapsodie mineure de notre système de références, dont le mode majeur veut le stable, le constant, le durable. [. . .] Rien à quoi se fixer, se tenir, rien où inscrire une profession de foi ni une assurance fondée. (*ADC* 21)[14]

As such, the fortuitous is an way to think, after the death of God, what in a parasitically religious frame would be called 'contingency' as the opposite of religious necessity. The fortuitous refuses to occupy the reason-giving place of religion.

The logic of assumed dichotomy is also at work in the way that Meillassoux talks about the relation between the God of religion and the God of the philosophers. The tenth step in Meillassoux's account of metaphysics relies on the God of the philosophers 'taking the place of' the God of religion (ID 269), but it is far from clear that this is what the God of the philosophers does, either for religious believers or for atheists. A principle does not necessarily dislodge or threaten a person, any more than reason need necessarily drive out (as opposed to sitting alongside) revelation, and the lack of any compelling reason from Badiou or Meillassoux why this should be the case is indicative of a confusion of categories.[15]

In order to overcome metaphysics' deficiency and elaborate a philosophy beyond a/theism that supposes no necessary existence (of a divine being, a set of natural or logical laws or anything else), Meillassoux rejects metaphysics in favour of speculation (SR 441), and introduces what he calls the factial (*le factual*),[16] according to which necessity is thought neither as the necessary indivisibility of the one, nor as the necessary dissemination of the multiple. In the same way that Badiou elaborates a notion of 'pure' difference in *L'Etre et l'événement*, Meillassoux seeks to unfold a pure thinking of necessity and contingency.

4.1.2 *Contingency and the Principle of Factiality*

The two errors that Meillassoux's *factial* must avoid in its thinking of necessity are exemplified by the 'correlationist' phenomenology of Husserl and Kant (ID 207–8). Correlationism, which Meillassoux elaborates at length in *Après la finitude*, is the position according to which there is no being, event or law that is not always-already correlated to a consciousness, as an action, perception, conception or affection (SR

409). For the correlationist, 'X is' means 'X is the correlate of thinking': to be is to be a correlate, which is why it is impossible to conceive anything in the absolute, separate from the thinking subject. With correlationism, philosophy has lost the geat outdoors (*le grand dehors*, AF 21/AfF 7), the pre-critical absolute Outside of thought. Kant's 'weak correlationism' holds the position that the in-itself, while not knowable, is nevertheless thinkable (as non-contradictory and existing, AF 48/AfF 35), whereas the 'strong correlationism' of Heidegger or Foucault argues that we cannot think the in-itself even to the extent of asserting that it is non-contradictory; strong correlationism denies that limits of the thinkable should be the limits of the possible? (AF 48/AfF 35).

So the challenge set for Meillassoux's factial is that necessity must be thinkable, but the necessity that is thinkable must not be a real necessity. In other words, the factial must 1) maintain some notion of eternal necessity, while 2) excluding any necessary being (ID 283); Meillassoux must refuse every metaphysical absolute, yet retain 'a little absolute' (*un peu d'absolu*, AF 68/AfF 49). This is why the factial, in carrying forward the project of metaphysics, can be neither metaphysical nor anti-metaphysical (ID 284). In order to establish the factial, Meillassoux disambiguates two notions of necessity which are confused, he claims, in Aristotle (ID 155): the eternal truths of logic and the constraining forces of nature. We shall deal first with Meillassoux's dismissal of the 'real necessity' of natural laws, before turning to the question of the eternal truths of logic.

The reason that a belief in perennial laws is religious is that it makes some transcendent action necessary to maintain the laws over time: 'Nous avons ôté les dieux, mais nous avons conservé la croyance en la divine solidité des lois' (ID 4).[17] For his part, Meillassoux insists that these constants can be abolished, for the simple reason that nothing sustains them from the outside (ID 4).[18] In other words, Meillassoux is identifying as parasitic that atheism which shares religion's assumption of the perennity of natural laws, namely (major premise) only the gods can break the natural laws. From this shared assumption, a belief in the perennity of natural laws proceeds to reason that (minor premise) there are no gods, so (conclusion) nothing can break the natural laws.

So in order to be truly free of God, the factial must think necessity otherwise than through the necessity of natural laws; natural laws must be contingent. There are three conceptions of contingency that have dominated in the Western tradition: 1) 'legal contingency' held by modern scientism, according to which the contingent is that which does not contravene the constants of experience, 2) 'representative contingency', exemplified by Hume's dissociation of logical and causal necessity according to which the contingent is all that I can imagine not existing, and 3) 'rational contingency', according to which the contingent is that for which a reason for its existing cannot be given, that for which one cannot say why it exists, rather than nothing (ID 223). The third, rationalist articulation of contingency comes from Judaeo-Christianity and is, according to Meillassoux, the only way to escape correlationism:

> Seule la religion monothéiste fonde l'idée d'une contingence de toute chose : le monde n'est pas éternel. Il est créé, sa contingence est admise, quoique sa non-existence (le pur néant) ne soit pas présentable. La thèse de l'existence d'un Dieu tout-puissant produit en retour, par un apparent paradoxe, une conception radicale de la contingence de tout étant fini, créé, – étant qui est le seul accessible à la pensée humaine. Le judéo-christianisme en posant que la nécessité de Dieu est inaccessible à la pensée humaine est entièrement contingent. (ID 236)[19]

It is this religious territory that Meillassoux's philosophy seeks to occupy, but whereas in a religious frame this rational conception of contingency leads to the necessity of transcendence, from an immanent point of view (that is to say a point of view accessible to human thought) it leads to the impossibility of thinking that any thing is necessary. Whereas Badiou puts all his effort into thinking change and novelty, Meillassoux's task is to account for relative stability.

There is now only one small – but important – step from this immanent side of rational contingency to Meillassoux's 'factial': whereas in the religious conception of rational contingency, necessity is incomprehensible, and whereas for the immanent side of rational contingency it is unthinkable, in the factial, necessity is accessible to reason. Meillassoux's argument is as follows. First, there can be no real necessity, on pain of fideism. Secondly it follows that the facticity of a thing is not itself a fact (AF 107/AfF 79), because if facticity were itself a fact (that is to say, contingent and not necessary) there could be a necessary being, and we would be back with religious fideism. So, the only necessity is contingency itself:

> ce qui est, est factuel, mais que ce qui est soit factuel, voilà qui ne peut être un fait. Seule la facticité de ce qui est ne peut pas être factuelle. Ou encore, dit autrement : ce ne peut être un fait que ce qui est soit un fait. ... La contingence de l'étant, et elle seule, n'est pas une propriété contingente de l'étant. (ID 44; QM's italics)[20]

Factiality, in other words, is the non-facticity of facticity (AF 107/ AfF 79). Contingency is itself necessary in order to avoid a necessary being which, after the death of God, we have no grounds to admit into our thinking. We may say that an object is de facto red, but not that it is de facto de facto (ID 46). And what is necessity? Necessity consists in the impossibility of qualifying contingency as contingent (ID 47). In order to avoid falling back into metaphysics, Meillassoux stresses that the principle of factiality does not maintain that contingency is necessary, but that *only* contingency is necessary (AF 108/AfF 80), as a direct correlate of the absence of any necessary being, event or law.

Meillassoux is at great pains to stress that the necessity of contingency does not replace the 'laws of nature' with a meta-law of contingency itself: 'il n'y a pas de loi du devenir, parce qu'il y a devenir des lois' (ID 5).[21] So although the necessity to which Meillassoux appeals is eternal, this eternity does not signify the eternity of the laws of becoming, but the eternity of the becoming of laws (ID 158). In 'Temps et surgissement ex nihilo' Meillassoux describes this state of affairs as an inverted Platonism: there is an illusory fixity of objects but a real contingency 'behind' that fixity; the intelligible is on the side of the most radical becoming, the sensible on the side of fixity.

Peter Hallward fails to take account of the difference between a law of becoming and the becoming of laws in his review of *Après la finitude*,[22] He argues that 'Meillassoux's rationalist critique of causality and necessity seems to depend on an equivocation between metaphysical and physical or natural necessity',[23] where metaphysical necessity is the principle of sufficient reason and natural necessity is a natural law giving a reason 'for anything to be the way it is'. But Meillassoux is not arguing that the physical world is perceptibly chaotic or impenetrable to reason, rather that the physical world is subject to an absolute contingency that itself can be discerned not through observation but through reason. Hallward himself seems to be confusing chaos and contingency when he insists that it is

> perfectly possible, of course, to reconstruct the locally effective reasons and causes that have shaped, for instance, the evolution of aerobic vertebrate organisms. There was nothing necessary or predictable about this evolution, but why should we doubt that it conformed to familiar 'laws' of cause and effect?[24]

This argument, which culminates in the conclusion that 'the only event that might qualify as contingent and without reason in [Meillassoux's] absolute sense of the term is the emergence of the universe itself',[25] misunderstands that for Meillassoux contingency does not mean that there must be no conceivable reason for such and such an event, but that there can be no *necessary* reason for it: whatever reason there may be is necessarily contingent. Apples can still fall to the ground in obedience to the law of gravity, and we can still explain their falling in terms of gravity;[26] Meillassoux's point is simply that we are not at liberty to take this gravity to be an eternal necessity. As Nathan Brown has it, 'he [Hallward] again addresses a *speculative* question concerning the possible contingency of the laws from within an *empirical* framework pertaining only to the laws as they currently are or have been'.[27]

Graham Harman makes the same mistake in his response to an oral presentation by Meillassoux when he suggests that 'for Meillassoux causation disappears' and 'in my view, since he is saying that everything is *absolutely* contingent, what he's really doubting is that there's any relationality at all'.[28] Harman classes Meillassoux as a hyper-occasionalist, where occasionalism is 'the idea that entities in the world exist only side by side, without any connection with one another'.[29] Meillassoux is not saying, however, that there is no causality or relationality, but that what causality there is, is contingent. Contingency is neither chaos nor non-existence, and for Meillassoux there are plenty of connections between things in the world (gravity being one); it is just that none of them are necessary.

This mistake of hypostatising Meillassoux's factiality and attributing to him some form of parasitic atheism is repeated when Hallward argues that

> it may be, however, that an argument regarding the existence or inexistence of God is secondary in relation to arguments for or against belief in this quintessentially 'divine' power – a supernatural power to interrupt the laws of nature and abruptly reorient the pattern of worldly affairs.[30]

Meillassoux's absolute contingency is not a power to interrupt the 'laws' of nature, nor is it a law itself. For Meillassoux there is no law of becoming, but a becoming of laws, no power of interruption, but the interruption of all power.

This notion of necessity brought by Meillassoux's principle of factiality is very different from the religious necessity called upon to regulate rational contingency. Both religious contingency and Meillassoux's contingency potentially issue in a radical *hyperchaos*, and have to try to make sense of the stability of the world. Whereas chaos is 'disorder, randomness, the eternal becoming of everything', hyperchaos (*surcontingence*) is a contingency 'so radical that even becoming, disorder, or randomness can be destroyed by it, and replaced by order, determinism, and fixity', or 'the equal contingency of order and disorder, of becoming and sempiternity' (TWB). The scholastic reconciliation with hyperchaos is to appeal to God's will, giving contingency an extrinsic norm. By contrast, the factial holds that it is contingency which, unlimited and absolute, becomes its own norm ('se norme elle-même', ID 239;

cf. *AF* 90/*AfF* 66). Metaphysics announces 'necessity is', and relativism counters 'there is no necessity', but the principle of factiality stakes out a fresh position: there is necessity because necessity cannot be (*'il y a de la nécessité parce que la nécessité ne peut être'*, ID 239; QM's italics).

Elsewhere, Meillassoux articulates the principle of factiality as an identification of ignorance with knowledge. The ignorance in question is the conclusion that, if everything is contingent, then it is without sufficient reason, and I therefore cannot know the sufficient reason of any thing. But this ignorance becomes itself the basis of a pure knowledge by a 'transmutation' of the concept of contingency: I do not know the necessity of any contingent thing, but I do know the necessity of contingency (ID 56), in what Meillassoux calls the 'principle of insufficient reason' (a term he later chooses to replace with the less negative-sounding principle of factiality, *AF* 69/*AfF* 50). This is not a Socratic ignorance because the necessity of contingency has non-negligible consequences for the understanding of being.

Meillassoux's invocation of the principle of insufficient reason is not to be confused with Nancy's *non-suffisance*, which is a break with the notion of contingency in so far as contingency (as opposed to fortuity) is still parasitic upon the regime of sufficient reason (*ADC* 33). Reason for Nancy is not insufficient but rather overflows all sufficiency, exceeds all satisfaction if sufficiency and satisfaction are considered as the significations of which sense is the giving, the information of which adoration is the address. Indeed, Meillassoux's principle of factiality would, by the yardstick of Nancy's *non-suffisance*, be parasitically theological, still a question of closure and *accomplissement*, of 'sufficing' or 'satisfying' the theological principle of (self-) sufficiency. In turn, Meillassoux would no doubt consider Nancy's *non-suffisance* as both ascetic in its renunciation of completion and parasitic in its recourse to faith (*foi*).

The necessity of contingency has two important and immediate consequences: it forecloses the possibilities both of self-contradiction and of the All, understood as a Hegelian Absolute, the being that negates its identity and becomes its own opposite (ID 48, 139–40). First, the All. If a thing is both itself and its opposite, then it cannot change, and by that token it is necessary and not contingent. And, given that contingency is necessary (because there is no necessary being or law to guarantee necessity), such a being cannot exist. Meillassoux records his debt to Badiou for breaking the link between the infinite and the All (ID 19, 22 n.6). Set theory for Meillassoux is the science of becoming that eternally breaks every particular or empirical structure, and its object is becoming as such (ID 41). This Badiouian borrowing allows Meillassoux to dismiss the divinity of Anselm's *Proslogion*: 'that than which nothing greater can be thought'[31] (ID 149). Indeed, according to the principle of factiality the God of Anselm is the *only* being whose non-existence it is possible to ascertain a priori (ID 150). This relies, of course, on adhering to the version of set theory according to which 'the transfinite of Cantor in mathematics and set theory demonstrated that there is no quantity of all quantities' (SR 442), in other words it depends on excluding the Cantorian absolute infinite, which we showed in Chapter 1 to be a contingent and not a necessary exclusion. It also depends, we should note, on the set theoretical dichotomy of the multiple and the one which, Meillassoux maintains, is contingent (because *only* contingency is necessary). As well as being able to dismiss a priori the Anselmian All, Meillassoux also forecloses any parasitic usurpation of its place by another being: 'Dieu, comme Tout ce qui est, ne pouvant exister, l'homme ne peut être Dieu' (ID 154).[32]

The second consequence of factiality is that it grounds the principle of non-contradiction by similar reasoning. If a being were contradictory it would be its own negation and therefore it could not be otherwise than it is. It would be necessary, and no being is necessary (ID 49). The principle of non-contradiction for Meillassoux is therefore not merely required for a consistent discourse, but it has ontological reach (ID 96): contradiction cannot exist, for it would violate the principle of factiality. These two 'figures' – of the impossibility of the All and the necessity of non-contradiction – show according to Meillassoux that the necessity of contingency does not mean that anything whatsoever can happen. Quite to the contrary, the derivation of non-contradiction from factiality means that 'the very expression "rational chaos" from that moment on becoming a pleonasm' (PV 61). Meillassoux has not unleashed the anarchy of chaos but discovered a *logos* of contingency (AF 104/AfF 77).

When he then comes to apply this reasoning to the question of God, Meillassoux uses the principle of factiality to argue that our incapacity to know God is in fact a great achievement (ID 138–9). Man, unlike the animals, can reason his way to the invisible property of all that exists, namely the absence of sufficient reason. But this opens up a reasoning ad infinitum: one thing is explained in terms of another, which in turn is explained in terms of a third . . . There is no regress to a point of no contingency. Nevertheless, thought can produce universal statements because it provides access to this infinite, unarrestable regress. If the questioning could come to a halt, there would exist a being impossible to question, a necessary being, or God. That is why we cannot understand God: as a necessary being we could not question him. At this point, Meillassoux turns this incapacity into an achievement: whereas religions would paint ignorance of God as evidence of incapacity due to our finitude, Meillassoux sees rather a capacity to understand that an end to the questioning is impossible, and this latter understanding is exactly what gives us access to the eternal truths of this world: 'Point remarquable: c'est parce qu'il est capable de ne pas comprendre Dieu que l'homme accède à l'éternel' (ID 139).[33] The absence of final reason is not a limit to our thinking, but the ultimate property of being itself (*AF* 72–3/*AfF* 53). Our inability to understand an ultimate reason is not a subjective incapacity but a capacity to grasp the objective impossibility of such a reason. This is not an index of man's wretchedness, but of his grasping grandeur (*grandeur saisissante* (ID 139)).

Meillassoux's rejection of any limitation to reason may in his own terms secure the status of his philosophy as distinct from a/theism, but it is not without potential problems, at least from Nancy's point of view. For Nancy, the desire exhaustively to give a reason for the world is already a religious move. Religious myth or a religious idol responds to the demand that reason should have no limits, or in other words it explains or comes to terms with existence (*rend raison de l'existence*) (*ADC* 58–9). This is the closure of religion on itself; 'c'est dans un désir de « rendre raison » que la religion peut s'épuiser en mythologie et en idolâtrie' (*ADC* 59).[34]

The desire to drive out all idols with the whip of reason, more specifically to do so self-sufficiently and without remainder, leads to reason itself becoming an idol in the sense that it exempts itself from the necessity of providing a reason. Myths and idols explain, or give a reason for, the sort of questions for the answer to which Meillassoux turns to his principle of factiality. For Nancy, such Reason is parasitic on religion's principle of giving sufficient reason, a new move in religion's old game, rather than a rupture with the logic that underlies religious myth or idolatry. In *L'Adoration* the argument runs as follows: Kant circumscribed 'understanding' in putting down (*mettre à bas*) any rational 'proof of God' or determination of the first principle (*Raison première*) of the world:

> Une place désormais était vide. Elle fut occupée par beaucoup d'instances suppléantes, par exemple la Raison hégélienne comme déploiement de l'Esprit. Mais dès Hegel lui-même, et plus encore de lui jusqu'à nous, ce qui devenait manifeste, c'est que *la place vide ne devait pas être occupée*. (*ADC* 49; J-LN's italics)[35]

'The empty place was not to be occupied'. There, in a nutshell, is Nancy's rejection of parasitic atheism. Nevertheless, there has been a series of attempts, all duly atheistic and more or less pitiful or frightening (ADC 49) to occupy this empty space while pretending not to do so: materialisms, positivisms, scientisms, irrationalisms, fascisms, collectivisms, utilitarianisms, individualisms, historicisms, democratisms and even juridicisms, relativisms, scepticisms and logicisms. Viewed in these terms, Meillassoux's principle of factiality shares this same parasitic drive. The difference is that Nancy sees a parasitism in this sharing, whereas Meillassoux sees an occupation of religion's territory, and the question around which the difference turns is: is the attempt to provide an exhaustive first principle of the world itself a religious move? Furthermore, Meillassoux sees an asceticism in ceding the territory of providing reasons to religion alone, rather than occupying it with a post-theological integration.

So which is it? Is Meillassoux parasitic here, or is Nancy ascetic, or both? We shall search for the answer by exploring further Meillassoux's appeal to reason to find out whether it is in fact self-grounding, as he requires it to be. What Meillassoux does with theism and atheism, namely shows that they share a set of common assumptions which means we must break with both, Nancy does with religion and reason considered as self-sufficient. For Nancy we must follow Christianity's self-deconstruction in order to break equally with the spirit of Christianity and the spirit of the rational West (ADC 42). So is Nancy more consistently post-theological because he discerns and distances himself from more of the assumptions that religion and parasitic atheism share (including the dichotomy of reason and faith), or is Meillassoux more consistently post-theological because he goes further in breaking from religion's compromise of reason with faith? In order to answer that question we need to press further into the status of reason in Meillassoux's thought.

4.2 BELIEVING IN GOD BECAUSE HE DOES NOT EXIST

Where then does the principle of factiality leave the question of God? In a position that can be adequately described neither as theistic nor as atheistic. There are four, and only four, possible ways that man can relate to God, Meillassoux argues, only three of which have hitherto been exploited (ID 388). In these four options, it is clear that Meillassoux is using 'belief in' not in the sense of 'assent to the existence of' but 'hope in'. First option: one can not believe in God because he doesn't exist. Meillassoux lets his attitude to this atheistic option be known by summing it up as a position that leads to sadness, lukewarmness, cynicism and *ressentiment*. It is, he concludes, the immanent form of despair, a form of what we are calling ascetic atheism. Secondly, one can believe in God because he exists, but this according to Meillassoux leads to the deadlocks of fanaticism, a flight from this world, and the confusions of holiness with mysticism and of God as love with God as power. It is the religious form of hope. Thirdly, one can not believe in God because he exists. This is the Luciferian posture of revolt, maintaining a haughty indifference which in effect is a mixture of animosity towards God (in which the displayed indifference is only hatred expressed in the most hurtful way) and classical atheism, whose deadlocks (namely cynicism, sarcasm towards every aspiration, and self-hatred) it exacerbates. It is the religious form of despair. The fourth way of relating man and God, and the option which has until now remained unexploited, is to believe in God because he does not exist: the immanent form of hope. This is the option with which Meillassoux identifies his philosophy: 'Le divin philosophique n'est ni une religion – a-t-on déjà vu un croyant nier l'existence de Dieu ? – ni un athéisme – a-t-on déjà vu un athée croire en Dieu?' (ID 384).[36]

But what does it mean to 'believe in God because he does not exist'? The response is found in examining Meillassoux's notion of divine inexistence, and the hope which he invests in it. If, as Meillassoux fiercely defends, there is no law of becoming, then becoming is capable even of God (ID 6), and every 'miracle' adds to the experimental proof of the inexistence of God (ID 5), because miracles demonstrate the contingency of the world, and show thereby that no divine will underwrites the 'perennial laws' of nature. God 'inexists', which is to say that he happens not to exist, but – in accordance with the principle of factiality – his possible existence is necessary. Just as everything that exists, exists de facto, so also everything that does not exist does not exist de facto (ID 75). Inexistence, Meillassoux insists, is not more negative than existence, because the essence of an thing's existence is that it can not exist, and the essence of a thing's inexistence is that it can exist (ID 87). Both contingencies (existence and inexistence) are designated by 'being'.[37]

Meillassoux's bold rejection of both theism and atheism in favour of a 'philosophy' for which nothing, not even God, is inaccessible, and for which everything, including God, can exist, has attracted a number of sceptical responses. Given Meillassoux's incorporation of the putatively 'miraculous' as evidence of his absolute contingency, Peter Hallward is off track in his review of *Après la finitude* when he evokes the miraculous as a critique of Meillassoux's hyperchaos:

> Rather than any sort of articulation of past, present and future, Meillassoux's time is a matter of spontaneous and immediate irruption *ex nihilo*. Time is

reduced here to a succession of 'gratuitous sequences'. The paradigm for such gratuitous irruption, obviously, is the miracle.[38]

This critique would only be persuasive if we had already abandoned Meillassoux's absolute contingency. Hyperchaos is not miraculous, for the notion of the miracle relies on a stable benchmark of predictable, non-miraculous normativity. For Meillassoux there is no such benchmark: contingency is the only absolute and it is not the least deviation from absolute contingency that a 'miracle' should occur.

Notwithstanding the failure of the critique that Meillassoux's hyperchaos is miraculous, it will be our argument here that hyperchaos is the undoing of the principle of factiality, and the exposure of Meillassoux's philosophy as parasitic after all. What Meillassoux is trying to prove is his principle of factiality and the law of non-contradiction that he derives from it. In *Après la finitude*, Meillassoux makes it clear in a way that remained obscure in 'L'Inexistence divine' that the laws of logic are just as contingent as the laws of nature: 'Tout peut très réellement s'effondrer – les arbres comme les astres, les astres comme les lois, les lois physiques comme les lois logiques' (AF 73).[39] Nevertheless, non-contradiction is derived from the principle of factiality and so stands, or so Meillassoux claims, as absolute, because it must be assumed in any attempt to contradict it. There are five reasons why it is problematic to hold this position.

The first reason is what we shall call the 'split rationality critique' of Meillassoux's proof, namely that he acknowledges that what is thought about (trees, stars, laws) is absolutely contingent, but he exempts from contingency the thinking itself. The problem for Meillassoux is that, in order to be consistent, his own thinking must be up for grabs in the contingency of logical laws. In other words, the processes by which he arrives at the notions of 'necessity', 'contingency' and 'factiality' must themselves be able to be replaced by other, currently unimaginable, ways of thinking.

In order to walk through this argument in more detail, let us consider Meillassoux's reconstruction of facticity. In this reconstruction, Meillassoux draws a necessity out of the strong correlationist model itself, where the strong model of correlationism is summarised as 'it is unthinkable that the unthinkable is impossible'. In this correlationist model, the 'logicity' of the world does not conform to the structures of logical reason, and the givenness of the world in a representation does not conform to the structures of representative reason (AF 55/ AfF 40). We cannot be sure that things are not Wholly Other to how they are represented to us. This uncertainty, the canonical limit of the rational, also legitimates faith in a God who transcends the limits of the thinkable (ID 49).

This reasoning yields a 'precise and remarkable' consequence: 'il devient *rationnellement illégitime* de disqualifier un discours *non rationnel* sur l'absolu sous prétexte de son irrationalité' (*AF* 56; QM's emphasis).[40] Let us try to reconstruct in our turn what is at stake here. There are two instances of rationality in play in this quotation. First, the 'non-rational discourse on the absolute' which cannot be disqualified, and secondly the 'rational illegitimacy' of such a disqualification. It is the second of these two instances that shall detain us, because it is this second instance that Meillassoux fails to take into account in his argument for absolute contingency. In order to know whether or not it is rationally legitimate or illegitimate to suppose p, I must have some notion of rational legitimacy. But this notion of legitimacy, just as much as the 'non rational discourse' that is its object, must be contingent. Like gravity, it may be clear enough for the moment, but it is not necessary that it remain for ever as necessary. So, to rephrase Meillassoux's reconstruction of strong correlationism with this proviso inserted: it is rationally illegitimate, *according to the contingent norms of rationality that prevail at the moment*, to disqualify a non-rational discourse on the absolute on pretext of its irrationality. A modest proviso, perhaps, but one with the deepest consequences for Meillassoux's principle of factiality. The very decision as to what may or may not be 'rationally legitimate' must not be unaccountably exempted from a possible future contingent rationality that in the present remains radically unforeseeable, on pain once more of fideism in the enduring necessity of rationality *as it is currently understood and practised*. We cannot bootstrap rationality out of contingency.

It might be objected here that we are just assuming Meillassoux's contingency in order to argue against it. We readily concede that we are, but that is no objection to our argument because we are suggesting something more radical: that even though contingency must be assumed now, it cannot be posited *now* as absolutely, or eternally, necessary, unless we also assume that the way in which we think about logic *now* (in terms of contingency and so on), is itself eternal, whereas all we can be sure about is that it is only eternal according to the way we think about it now (in terms of 'necessity', 'contingency', 'factiality' and so on). As soon as the laws of logic are part of the picture of contingency, notions such as 'necessity' and 'contingency' themselves become unstable and prone to hyperchaotic change.

It would indeed be self-defeating to argue that contingency always triumphs over every law of logic, for then contingency would, as

Meillassoux quite rightly argues, remain as absolute. But that is not what we are arguing, and such a refutation of our position would only work if we were to assume that the dichotomy of necessity and contingency is eternal. What we are suggesting here is not simply that the laws of logic are contingent, even less that contingency is contingent, but that contingency along with all the laws and principles of logic might well be unthinkably meaningless after any hyperchaotic change, along with the notions of 'hyperchaos' and 'change' themselves.

Building on this first argument about split rationality, our second reason for rejecting the claim that factiality and non-contradiction are absolute is the self-defeating nature of hyperchaos. Meillassoux tries to catch the objector with the following argument:

> si vous affirmez que votre scepticisme envers toute connaissance de l'absolu repose sur un *argument*, et non sur une simple croyance ou opinion – alors vous devez admettre que le nerf d'un tel argument est *pensable*. Or le nerf de votre argumentation c'est que nous *pouvons* accéder au pouvoir-ne-pas-être/pouvoir-être-autre de toute chose, y compris de nous-mêmes et du monde. Mais dire qu'on peut penser cela, encore une fois, c'est dire qu'on *peut* penser l'absoluité du possible de toute chose. (AF 80)[41]

Our scepticism with regard to knowledge of the absolute does rest on an argument, and it has three parts: 1) that the meaning of each one of the concepts in this argument from *Après la finitude* is (what for the time being we call) 'contingent', 2) that each one of these concepts (including 'hyperchaos') can hyperchaotically become not just different but incommensurable with current logic, and that 3) there is no hyperchaos that would itself escape this meaninglessness. According to Meillassoux, we must now admit that the nerve of such an argument is thinkable. But it is thinkable only for the time being, only as long as 'thinking' and 'argument' remain untouched by hyperchaos.

So when Meillassoux tells us that 'the core of your argument is that we can access everything's capacity-not-to-be, or capacity-to-be-other', this is only true for a domesticated other, an other recognisable as other, in truth no hyperchaotic 'other' at all but an other that remains identifiable as other within our current constellation of concepts and laws of logic, an other that remains commensurable with the binary of being/non-being. No doubt, to claim that we *can* think such an other would indeed, as Meillassoux concludes, be to say that we can think the necessary contingency of all things, but that would not be hyperchaos. Meillassoux evokes 'un hyper-Chaos, auquel rien n'est, ou ne paraît être, impossible, *pas même l'impensable*' (AF 87; author's emphasis),[42] but when he says 'unthinkable' here, he means 'thinkable as unthinkable' (in another instance of split rationality); we are arguing that there is an important difference between something which is unthinkable and something which is thinkable as unthinkable, between something which is either contingent or necessary and something which (in a way currently unthinkable) renders the binary of contingency and necessity meaningless or defunct.

If it should be objected that 'whatever change hyperchaotically takes place, hyperchaos cannot negate itself, on pain of introducing a necessary being', then we must reply: by virtue of what does our current understanding of 'impossible', 'unthinkable' and 'hyperchaos' authorise us to pronounce on what would or would not be 'thinkable' and 'possible' in any hyperchaotically incommensurable 'situation', as if those concepts would *necessarily* have any 'sense' at all 'there'? In other words, Meillassoux underestimates the radicality of his own notion of hyperchaos, assuming that our current conceptual armature ('hyperchaos' included) can be wielded in whatever situation might eventuate. The concepts of possibility and impossibility do not begin to account for hyperchaos (such that we can say: in hyperchaos, anything is possible). The least we can say about hyperchaos (which is also all we can say, and in truth nothing at all) is that it will have been incommensurable with the concepts of possibility and impossibility ... and incommensurability.

Our third – and much briefer – objection to Meillassoux's arguments for factiality and non-contradiction being absolute, and the second way in which Meillassoux's hyperchaos is not chaotic enough, is that it exempts temporality. Truly radical contingency cannot simply mean that 'anything can not be', but it must also entail that 'anything can have not been'. In other words, contingency is emasculated if it is confined to the present. Why should we exempt 'past' events from radical contingency, and why should we exempt temporal flow and the necessary progression of one instant after another in orderly fashion from radical contingency? Surely such a temporally strait-laced contingency would be no longer radical, but rather would be itself contingent on time.[43]

4.2.1 *Hume's Problem*

We can go further, however, than this denial to Meillassoux of the eternity of the principle of non-contradiction, because the critique we are in the process of unfolding has implications for Meillassoux's treatment of Hume's problem. We are happy to grant Meillassoux his solution to his reformulation of Hume's problem: how to explain the manifest stability of physical laws if these are supposed to be contingent

(AF 125/AfF 92), and we are happy to grant him his refutation of the Kantian 'necessitarian inference', according to which the stability of laws presupposes, as its imperative condition, the necessity of laws (AF 128/AfF 94). Nevertheless – and this is our fourth objection to facticity and contingency being absolute – because of the radicality of his principle of facticity, Meillassoux cannot allow himself the principle of non-contradiction in the same way that Hume can: 'Quant au principe de non-contradiction, il nous permet d'établir *a priori*, sans le recours à l'expérience, qu'un événement contradictoire est impossible, qu'il ne peut exister *ni aujourd'hui ni demain*' (AF 119; author's emphasis).[44]

Hume may well indeed be able to make this claim, but Meillassoux cannot, for two reasons. The first reason is the critique of the split instances of rationality that we do not want to risk the reader's patience by rehearsing again. The second reason is this: suppose that the laws of logic were to change radically. Would we *necessarily* know that such a change had taken place? Might it not *possibly* be the case that we would only discern such a change if our cognitive faculties and the laws of logic in terms of which they function were to remain untouched by such a change, able to observe a sequential 'before' and 'after'? Even if we could apprehend the change, it cannot be *necessary* that we should retain a knowledge of the former laws (unless our memories are now the object of a non-contingent idolatry), as long as the only necessity is contingency.

This objection does not directly undermine the principle of facticity or non-contradiction, but it radicalises the foregoing three arguments. Now it is not simply the case that facticity cannot be known to be 'absolute' because the truths about the universe necessary to make the notion of the 'absolute' meaningful are themselves up for grabs in hyperchaos, but in addition those laws may have changed without us necessarily apprehending it. It also follows from this argument that we are not at liberty to accept of necessity the empirical truth that Meillassoux refers to as the 'fait incontestable de la stabilité des lois de la nature' (AF 128).[45]

Graham Harman's critique of Meillassoux, briefly discussed above, returns in the context of our present argument with greater force: 'in my view, since he is saying that everything is *absolutely* contingent, what he's really doubting is that there's any relationality at all'.[46] We previously dismissed this argument with Meillassoux's example of gravity, but if we cannot be sure whether or not the laws have changed in a given period of time (because we cannot be assured that we would *necessarily* notice such a change, unless 1) our faculties are exempt from such a change and 2) we know that they are), then we cannot be sure of the relations of which either our logic or our senses inform us. Meillassoux's answer to Harman, namely that 'my conception is not to deny the existence of relations but just to affirm their factual existence' (where 'factual' means not factial but empirical),[47] is no longer sufficient to meet the critique, because it is the empirical itself that is being questioned. Meillassoux is caught between a rock and a hard place here. He has two options: if he affirms that our understanding and the laws of logic *cannot* have changed in this way, he is making an idol of one, or the other, or both; if he is more circumspectly reckoning that they will not have changed, then he is supplementing his principle of factiality with a faith that, like Nancy's faith, irreducibly makes reason what it is. Meillassoux's factiality is either an idol, or an article of faith. What it cannot be is neither.

4.2.2 Faith, Axiom, Demonstration and Intuition

Having sought to establish the necessity of contingency *eo ipso* in the principle of factiality (which Meillassoux gives as: it is necessary that there be a contingent world (ID 110)), and having sought to do so without any recourse to a divine will or necessary being, Meillassoux claims to have left no territory to which the theologian or mystic can flee. But we have shown that, in order to arrive at this point, he has either to make an idol of reason or supplement it with a moment of faith. We now propose to develop this critique by tracking a specific claim that Meillassoux makes about the principle of factiality: namely that it can be demonstrated. It is an important claim for our purposes because it is what distances Meillassoux from both Nancy and Badiou on the question of post-theological thought. Contra Nancy, Meillassoux claims to have abolished the need for the sort of reason-supplementing faith that we discussed in the previous chapter. Contra Badiou, he argues that the principle of factiality is not the subject of an axiomatic decision, but of a logical demonstration. We shall deal with these two claims in turn.

In relation to the Nancean argument that reason requires a moment of faith in order to be what it is, Meillassoux claims that the factial obviates the need for such a faith that holds reason to its incompleteness. The principle of factiality does rely on an eternal constant, but this constant is not transcendent; it is not given by revelation, and it does not rely on an act of faith. The necessity of facticity itself is an eternal 'there is' outside the existence and inexistence that it regulates (ID 77). For Meillassoux, this brings about a new possibility of grounding reason. Up until now, he explains, shadowing closely the contours of

Nancy's argument for the necessity of faith, reason demanded completion because its first principles, whatever they happened to be, were ultimately contingent, and 'la raison en quête d'un premier principe nécessaire, appelait donc d'elle-même à son propre dépassement et la foi pouvait légitimement se poser comme l'accomplissement du rationnel' (ID 51).[48] For Nancy, the difference is that faith does not complete reason but precisely resists such a self-closure. If the demonstration of the principle of factiality succeeds, Meillassoux continues, we will no longer have any need for such an articulation of faith and reason; it will no longer be possible to evince the facticity (that is, the necessary contingency) of reason's first principles as a means of introducing a supplement of faith, because these principles will now be grounded on the very necessity of facticity, with the glorious result that 'la raison apparaîtra capable à elle seule de rendre raison des vérités dernières du monde réel' (ID 51).[49]

Reason is excepted from having to ground itself for Meillassoux not by an appeal to faith as its supplement, but by appeal to the impossibility of contingency being contingent. Meillassoux inscribes this in the line of philosophical justifications beginning with Plato that follows the formula 'only X cannot be X' (ID 175). In a list that resonates with Badiou's discussion of Plato's *agathon* in *Philosophie et événement*, as well as with Nancy's assertions in *L'Oubli de la philosophie* and *Des Lieux divins* that every great philosophy must have 'un mystère au sujet de Dieu ou des dieux' (DLD 24) or 'le geste de toucher à la limite de toute vision du monde' (OP 75),[50] Meillassoux discerns this formula of non-duplication (*non-redoublement*) in Platonic ideas (because what makes a phenomenon such and such a phenomenon cannot be a phenomenon), in the Cartesian cogito (because I doubt everything apart from doubt), in Leibniz' logical truths (because nothing is in the mind that was not in experience . . . apart from the mind) and in a priori forms of perception in Kant (because the form of phenomenal data in experience cannot itself be given as a phenomenon in experience). Generally speaking, he concludes, the conditions of possibility of experience cannot themselves be given in experience, but far from limiting the exercise of reason in those philosophers who brush up against it, this paradox is used to found the exercise of reason and, what is more, to found it in terms of something that is immanent and necessary (ID 176). In other words, at the very point where Nancy sees the need for reason-supplementing faith, Meillassoux locates his moment of necessity. But as Badiou notes in his treatment of the Platonic principle of intelligibility (PE 141), the choice between the 'rationalist' and 'apophatic' deployment of Plato's *agathon*, or in this instance between faith and necessity, cannot be exhaustively determined; the choice contains an ineradicable unconditionality. If Meillassoux's proof of self-grounding reason works in its own terms – and we have yet to explore this point, to which we shall turn our attention below – it does not necessarily follow that for this reason alone it is to be preferred to, say, Nancy's 'faith that is nothing at all' (nor that faith is to be preferred to Meillassoux's necessity). If such a decision is made on exclusively rational grounds (assuming a mutually exclusive dichotomy of the rational and the irrational) then the commitment to rationality that precedes the choice of a philosophical orientation remains to be explained. In other words, demonstrating a self-grounding rationality will not in itself lead to the conclusion that a self-grounding principle is to be preferred over Badiou's axioms or Nancy's 'faith that is nothing at all'. The problem encountered in trying to 'choose between' the three accounts offered by Badiou, Nancy and Meillassoux, and more broadly in choosing a fundamental philosophical orientation, is more complicated than that.

Does Meillassoux succeed in showing that the principle of factiality is the object of a demonstration? We cannot say that he does, because his demonstration contains a confusion between two sorts of necessity. While non-duplication does indeed ground the necessity of contingency, it does not ground the necessity of mathematico-logical truths, because it is itself a mathematico-logical truth that would need to be grounded and that is, as we have seen, hyperchaotically subject to the two riders 'for the time being' and 'as far as we know'. Meillassoux is once again bootstrapping his argument, and there lies at the heart of his demonstration of necessity an aporia of origin. Meillassoux grounds necessity by having recourse to an ungrounded necessity (namely non-duplication itself). In the absence of any sufficient grounding of non-duplication outside our two riders, we must conclude that the 'demonstration' of necessity once more finally comes to rest either 1) on an idolatry or 2) on an act of reasonable faith, the very sort of faith that Meillassoux's dichotomy of faith and reason forecloses, and for which he therefore has no category (ID 310).

Turning now to Meillassoux's relation to Badiouian axiomantics, we see that the denial of any need for a reason-supplementing faith contributes to Meillassoux's argument that his principle of factiality is subject to demonstration and can have done with what he calls 'hypothetical reason'.[51] Meillassoux begins his argument by pointing to what he considers to be the weak spot of Platonic philosophy, namely that its axioms simply have to be accepted. The truths of mathematics for Plato to be sure do not rely on any poetic, inspired, arbitrary narrative,

Meillassoux notes approvingly, but rather on a constraining succession of deductions. The failing of such philosophy, however, is found at the origin of its reasoning, which itself is not a demonstration but simply assumed to be true because it is self-evident (ID 165). The problem here is with what Meillassoux calls 'hypothetical reason' (*la raison hypothétique*), which he defines as the position according to which the origin of reason can only be posited (as an axiom, postulate, thesis, hypothesis or whatever else), not demonstrated. It is a reasoning shared by mathematical logic (in its 'hypothetical-deductive' strand) and the natural sciences (in their inductive variety) (ID 53).

By contrast, factiality provides a first principle that is demonstrated, and thereby seems to re-connect with what Meillassoux, now with some irony, calls the deepest 'illusion' of philosophy since its Platonic inauguration, namely an *anhypothetical* principle: a principle to found rational thought that does not itself have to be posited irrationally and in a contingent manner, but which would itself be founded in reason. The necessity of an anhypothetical demonstration refers us back to the refutation of correlationism we encountered above. Meillassoux rejects recourse to a hypothetical axiom as insufficient both to refute correlationism and to found factiality:

> I'm looking for a creative refutation. That is, a refutation which discovers a truth, an absolute truth, inside the circle [of correlationism: author] itself. That's why I propose an access to the Real not grounded on an *axiom*, but on a *demonstrated principle* – the principle of factiality. (SR 426; translation altered)

Meillassoux's anhypothetical principle cannot be demonstrated directly, by deducing it from another proposition (in which case it would not be a principle at all), but only indirectly, by showing that anyone who would contest the principle must presuppose its truth in their very attempt to refute it (*AF* 83/*AfF* 61). Such is the principle of non-contradiction for Aristotle: to refute it (and therefore perforce to contradict it) is already to have respected it. Factiality is assumed, so Meillassoux argues, by strong correlationism itself: it must assume the necessity of thinking that everything could be radically otherwise than it appears.

In relation to the question of God, anhypothetical factiality achieves for Meillassoux what Badiou seeks to accomplish with his recourse to ZFC set theory: the death of the god of the poets. For Meillassoux, the language of being is not given by poetry, and it is not by that same token a language-to-come, but a discourse that is thoroughly demonstrative ('de part en part démonstratif' (ID 162)). Meillassoux does not abandon axiomatics, however. He seeks to marry Badiou's axiomatic approach to philosophy with his own elaboration of an anhypothetical principle in an attempt demonstratively and ontologically to ground the axiom of the empty set (ID 111).

For Meillassoux, the empty set is the sign of contingency itself: there is only one empty set,[52] hence the *unicity* of contingency. The sign of the empty set is also the sign of the unicity of *contingency* because its written form – Ø – is contingent, the shape of the mark designating the empty set could be anything at all. Like contingency, the empty set is the only necessity, the one, pure mathematical sign that refers to being qua being (where being qua being is contingency as such), thus anchoring mathematics to ontology (ID 123–4). It is therefore overdetermined, for by its unity it makes reference not only to its own contingency as a signifier, but to contingency in general. All signs have a common and unique referent: the unique and eternal contingency of being.

Acknowledging Badiou to be the first to have held that the empty set refers to being qua being, Meillassoux critiques Badiou as standing in the shadow of Heidegger when he conceives being as the impresentation of presentation (in other words as inconsistent multiplicity before counting-as-one), which Badiou qualifies as 'enigmatic' (*EE* 72/*BE* 59). We share Meillassoux's critique of Badiou at this point and it is this enigmatic nature of being, the retroactive inaccessibility that we discussed in Chapter 1, that Meillassoux seeks to rid himself of by identifying the referent of the void set with the non-contingent contingency of the sign, and not with an enigmatic withdrawal (ID 125 n.41). Meillassoux is here imputing to Badiou the same sort of Romanticism for which Badiou himself chastises post-Heideggerian philosophy.

Meillassoux seeks to refute the axiomatic approach with the help of another dichotomy. If we claim that reason must begin with a principle that is (axiomatically) posited, is that assertion itself posited? If yes, then it is in no way necessary and it must admit that the assertion 'reason begins with a principle that is demonstrated' is equally possible. If the assertion itself is not posited (that is: if it is necessary), then Meillassoux wants to see the demonstration of that necessity that does not itself rely on a posited principle (ID 60). Either way, the demonstration must come first, which is precisely the route taken by Meillassoux's own principle of factiality. But it appears that this argument once more harbours a false dichotomy, similar to the dichotomy between faith and reason that could conceive of no faith which is not exhaustively irrational. Are Badiou's axioms posited in the way that Meillassoux is suggesting all axioms must be? We saw in the previous chapter that they are chosen 'under the injunction of being' in modernity; as such, they fit neither of Meillassoux's two categories: they are not *merely* posited, and neither are they necessary.

Furthermore, Meillassoux's own demonstration is supplemented by what in 'L'Inexistence divine' he calls an intellectual intuition and in later texts a dianoetic intuition, which he defines as 'the intellectual access to factiality' (SR 432). There is an 'essential intertwining of a simple intuition and of a discursivity, a demonstration – both being entailed by the access to factiality' (SR 433). Meillassoux explains:

> The simple intuition of facticity is transmuted by a dianoia, by a demonstration, into an intuition of a radical exteriority. I thought that facticity was the sign of the finitude and ignorance of thought. I thought I had, in facticity, a relation to my own deficient subjectivity. I discover now that what I took for human idiocy was truly an intuition, a radical intuition – that is, a relation to the Great Outside. We have a *nous* unveiled by a *dianoia*, an intuition unveiled by a demonstration. This is why I called it an intellectual intuition: not, of course, because it is an intuition which creates its object, as Kant defined it, but because it is an intuition discovered by reasoning. (SR 433–4)

So it is intuition qua *nous* (an act of mind or thought, a sense or meaning) that is unveiled by a *dianoia* (intelligence, understanding, intellectual capacity), and we would do well not to traduce or polarise the semantic range of these two nouns by ascribing to Meillassoux's 'intuition' any of the mysticism that the term can elsewhere connote. It is an intuition because we discover absolute contingency in (*à même*) things themselves (AF 111/AfF 82). Nevertheless, there is a choice to be made in intuition, and it is not a choice guided solely by reason. It is the choice to project unreason into things themselves (AF 111/AfF 82), the decision that our ignorance of the reason of things is not a deficiency of our reasoning but the truth about things. It is at this point that Meillassoux finds him in the same place as the Badiou of *Philosophie et événement* who faces the undecidability of the apophatic and rationalist orientations, for it is here that Meillassoux's appeal to rationality faces a question-begging circularity that must be resolved by the violence of an (axiomatic) decision:

> I'm a rationalist, and reason clearly demonstrates that you can't demonstrate the necessity of laws: so we should just believe reason and accept this point: laws are not necessary – they are facts, and facts are contingent – they can change without reason. (TWB)

We should 'just believe reason'. Why is that necessary, rather than merely possible? Why not 'believe' the empirical constancy of phenomena, rather than the rational proof of their radical contingency? Meillassoux makes a similar appeal when he argues that:

since Hume has convinced us that we could *a priori* (that is to say without contradiction) conceive a chaotic modification of natural laws, why not have confidence in the power of thought, which invites us to posit the *contingency* of the laws of nature, rather than in experience, in which alone the presentation of the apparent fixity of observable constants finds its source? (SD 273; QM's italics)

The answer to this rhetorical question is, of course, that if we just believe reason then we are right back to the Nancean position that Meillassoux is seeking to avoid, whereby reason is supplemented by a faith, itself nothing at all, that makes reason what it is. In other words, Meillassoux does demonstrate his anhypothetical principle, but only on the condition that we 'just believe reason' and not 'observable constants'. Meillassoux has not demonstrated why rational demonstration *must* be the way of proceeding through this dilemma of the rational and the empirical. His 'demonstration' still stands or falls on an unaccountable act of faith, the faith inherent in the proclamation that 'I'm a rationalist . . .'.

Ray Brassier also identifies problems in Meillassoux's account of intuition, but for significantly different reasons. Brassier argues that

> if the only way to ensure the separation between the (contingently existing) ideality of meaning and the (necessarily existing) reality of the referent is by making conceptuality constitutive of objectivity, then the absolutization of the non-correlational referent is won at the price of an absolutization of conceptual sense which violates the materialist requirement that being not be reducible to thought. Far from reconciling rationalism with materialism, the principle of factuality, at least in this version, continues to subordinate extra-conceptual reality to a concept of absolute contingency.[53]

Conceptuality is 'constitutive of objectivity' in the sense that the 'concept' of factiality is the truth of everything that (in)exists, but this only issues in an 'absolutization of correlational sense' if the principle of factiality is indeed a concept. The principle does not reduce being to thought but intuits in (*à même*) being an unreason that the principle of factiality is then brought in to explain. Without this initial extra-theoretical butting up against the unreason of things, there would be no principle of factiality, and so the problem with Meillassoux's intuition is not that it 'threatens to re-invoke some sort of pre-established harmony between thinking and being',[54] but that it begs the question of rationality.

On the basis of this interweaving of demonstration and intuition, Meillassoux calls his reader to a 'conversion of the gaze' (*conversion du regard*) (ID 55; AF 72/AfF 53[55]), to intuit the contingency of all beings by cultivating the habit of perceiving, with a properly intellectual intuition, the real absence of reason of empirical beings, such that we make facticity a positive, a priori and indispensible point of access to being itself, 'en sorte de faire de la pensée une puissance sans limite de vérité' (ID 55).[56] This intuition does not add to the demonstration, rather it is a holding of oneself to the demonstration, and a determination not to traduce it through recourse to a necessary being. In this, it is remarkably similar to Nancy's notion of faith, which similarly does not add to reason but is precisely a holding of oneself to reason, a determination not to go beyond it.

CONCLUSION

As we draw our first consideration of Meillassoux to a close, what are we to conclude? First, that the exemplary clarity, force and ambition of his arguments draw forth passionate engagement. But does he succeed in going beyond the dichotomy of theism and atheism? The position of believing in God because he doesn't exist is certainly creative and audacious, but Meillassoux only goes beyond a/theism by introducing other dichotomies on the basis of which he undermines the a/theism binary, namely the split between the knowing-rationality and known-rationality, and reason and irrational faith. Does Meillassoux's own thought achieve a position that eluded both Badiou and Nancy? While he succeeds in occupying a position distinct from both Nancean and Badiouian thought, he does not close the deal on a/atheism, for his own thought either idolises reason in the same way that he criticises metaphysics for idolising necessity, or his thought is fideistic in the same way that, once again, he denounces in the case of metaphysics. With Meillassoux we are still not beyond a/theism.

In the final two chapters we shall approach the question of post-theological integration from a different angle. Taking our lead from the language of hope in which Meillassoux frames his own belief in the God who inexists, we shall adopt a more pragmatic approach, considering how the three different philosophies we have thus far discussed engender, translate into, or call for (the precise way to articulate the relation will prove to be large part of what is at stake) political justice, asking whether the positions taken up in relation to justice are occupied in a way that is rigorously 'without God'. This will open onto a further discussion of a possible criteriology for arbitrating between the three different approaches to post-theological thought.

NOTES

1. 'From the inexistence of God we infer a world sufficiently devoid of sense that even God can occur in it' (author's translation).
2. 'For the atheist, God is a matter for the priest; for the philosopher God is too serious a matter to be entrusted to priests' (author's translation).
3. So indicated Graham Harman in a mock objection to Meillassoux at the one day *Speculative Realism* conference at Goldsmiths College, London, on 8 December 2007:

   > And finally, my real objection to him is that he hasn't published his system yet, because I'd love to stay up the next three nights and read it! That would be great reading. He says he's got multiple volumes coming, six or seven hundred pages. I would be delighted to read this right now, so please hurry!' (Harman, 'Speculative realism', p. 338)

   Meillassoux himself refers to the future volume in a footnote in *Après la finitude*:

   > Nous ne pouvons ici qu'être très allusif sur le rôle prédominant du fidéisme dans la constitution de la pensée moderne. Nous en traitons de façon plus approfondie dans un ouvrage à paraître, où doivent être développés l'ensemble des positions théoriques esquissées dans ce livre, ainsi que leurs conséquences éthiques: *L'Inexistence divine. Essai sur le dieu virtuel.* (AF 67)

   > We can only allude here to the predominant role played by fideism in the constitution of modern thought. This issue will be treated in greater depth in a forthcoming work in which we hope to develop theoretical positions that we are merely sketching here, as well as their ethical consequences: *Divine Inexistence: An Essay on the Virtual God.* (AfF 132)

4. The term 'speculative realism' has been applied to Meillassoux's thought in a way that groups it somewhat awkwardly together with Graham Harman, Ian Hamilton Grant and Ray Brassier. His own characterisation of his thought is as a speculative materialism: 'speculative' inasmuch as his thought claims to accede to an absolute in general (AF 47/AfF 34; SD 275), and 'materialism' inasmuch as the in-itself (qua contingent) is independent of any correlation with thought. This speculative materialism is opposed to speculative idealism, where the noumenon is nothing but its correlation with thought. See Brassier, *Nihil Unbound*, p. 67.

5.
   > It would be no exaggeration to say that Quentin Meillassoux has opened up a new path in the history of philosophy, hitherto conceived as the history of what it is to know; a path that circumvents Kant's canonical distinction between 'dogmatism', 'skepticism' and 'critique'. (*AfF* vii)

6. 'allows thought to be destined towards the absolute once more, rather than towards those partial fragments and relations in which we complacently luxuriate while the "return of the religious" provides us with a fictitious supplement of spirituality' (*AfF* viii).
7. 'For the atheist, God is a matter for the priest; for the philosopher God is too serious a matter to be entrusted to priests' (author's translation).
8. See Kearney, *Anatheism*.
9. In his reconstruction of religion, Meillassoux chooses to elide the theological lack of consensus on the relation of truths and the divine will.
10. 'We understand nothing about metaphysics if we fail to grasp that its particularity resides in this originary aggression towards every form of transcendence, *that no other discursivity has possessed*' (author's translation).
11.
> For the word of the cross is folly to those who are perishing, but to us who are being saved it is the power of God. For it is written, 'I will destroy the wisdom of the wise, and the discernment of the discerning I will thwart.' Where is the one who is wise? Where is the scribe? Where is the debater of this age? Has not God made foolish the wisdom of the world? For since, in the wisdom of God, the world did not know God through wisdom, it pleased God through the folly of what we preach to save those who believe. For Jews demand signs and Greeks seek wisdom, but we preach Christ crucified, a stumbling block to Jews and folly to Gentiles, but to those who are called, both Jews and Greeks, Christ the power of God and the wisdom of God. For the foolishness of God is wiser than men, and the weakness of God is stronger than men. (1 Corinthians 1: 18–25, English Standard Version)

12. Tertullian, 'On prescription against Heretics' and 'On the flesh of Christ', trans. Peter Holmes, in *The Ante-Nicene Fathers*, vol. III, ed. Alexander Roberts and James Donaldson (Grand Rapids, MI: Wm. B. Eerdmans Publishing Company, 1951), p. 246. For the argument in favour of a non-fideistic reading of Tertullian, now the majority reading, see Osborn, *Tertullian*, pp. 28–9.
13.
> If I am able to apprehend God objectively, I do not have faith; but because I cannot do this, I must have faith. If I want to keep myself in faith, I must continually see to it that I hold fast the objective uncertainty, see to it that in the objective uncertainty I am 'out on 70,000 fathoms of water' and still have faith. (Kierkegaard, *Concluding Unscientific Postscript*, p. 204)

14.
> the fortuitous, along with the fleeting, the inconsistent, the ephemeral, forms the minor rhapsody of our system of references, whose major

mode would be the stable, the consistent, the enduring. [...] Nothing upon which to fix, to hold, nowhere to inscribe a profession of faith or a grounded assurance. (Author's translation)

15. Given the crucial importance of dichotomous thinking – or the principle of non-contradiction – to Meillassoux's thought at a number of points, it is notable that Badiou signals that *L'Immanence des vérités*, the third volume of *L'Etre et l'événement*, will introduce the notion of paraconsistent negation, allowing that contradictory perceptions of a truth can coexist without interrupting the unity of the truth (*PE* 138).
16. We are following Ray Brassier's translations in *After Finitude*, rendering *factualité* with 'factiality' and *facticité* by 'facticity'. 'Factual' will be used to refer to contingency, and 'factial' to the necessary.
17. 'We have removed the gods, but we have kept the belief in the divine solidity of laws' (author's translation).
18. Meillassoux deals at length with the obvious objections that could be raised to this adherance to the contingency of natural laws, foremost among which is the observation that natural laws have remained constant over a long period: the notion that natural laws could change at any instant is surely belied by the fact that they do not change. The argument is not directly relevant to our argument here, and so we are not at liberty to examine it at length, but it hinges on the difference between chance (defined as one of a finite number of possibilities, like a dice throw) and contingency (for which there is no known number of possible outcomes). Whereas chance presupposes a prior structure within which it operates (for example the structure of the faces of a die), contingency obeys no law and works within no such structure (ID 13) and argues that we cannot use probabilistic reasoning about the set of all possible worlds, because there is no set of all possible worlds (ID 36–8). Contingency is the appearance of a new universe of cases, not the appearance of any given universe (ID 16). Chance therefore cannot be a good precept upon which to base the variation of physical laws, because chance itself is only thinkable under a regime of the stability of physical laws. If I throw a die a given number of times, I can only establish a probability of the result providing that physical laws continue to assure the fall and the coherence of the die.
19.
    Only monotheistic religion grounds the idea that everything is contingent: the world is not eternal. It is created, its contingency is accepted, even though its non-existence (pure nothingness) cannot be presented. The thesis that an omnipotent God exists produces in return, by an apparent paradox, a radical conception of the contingency of every finite and created being – the only being that is accessible to human thinking. Judaeo-Christianity, in asserting that the necessity of God is inaccessible to human thought, is entirely contingent. (Author's translation)

20. *what is, is factical, but that what is is factical, this itself cannot be a fact. Only the facticity of what is cannot be factical. Or again, in other words: it cannot be a fact that what is is a fact ... The contingency of beings, and it alone, cannot be a contingent property of that being.* (Author's translation)
21. 'there is no law of becoming because there is a becoming of laws' (author's translation).
22. Hallward, 'Anything is possible'.
23. Hallward, 'Anything is possible', p. 57.
24. Hallward, 'Anything is possible', p. 57.
25. Hallward, 'Anything is possible', p. 57.
26. Meillassoux uses the example of gravity to argue this point in SR 393.
27. Brown, 'On *After Finitude*', p. 2.
28. Harman, 'Speculative realism', pp. 385, 386.
29. Harman, 'Quentin Meillassoux', p. 114.
30. Hallward, 'Anything is possible', p. 56.
31. Anselm, *Monologion and Proslogion*, p. 28.
32. 'Given that God, as All of what is, cannot exist, man cannot be God' (author's translation).
33. 'A remarkable point: it is because he is capable of not understanding God that man accedes to the eternal' (author's translation).
34. 'it is in a desire to "explain" that religion can exhaust itself in mythology and in idolatry' (author's translation).
35. 'From now on, a place was empty. It was occupied by many deputies, for example Hegelian Reason as an unfolding of Spirit. But since Hegel himself, and more so from him to us, what became clear is that *the empty place was not to be occupied*' (author's translation).
36. 'The philosophical divine is neither a religion – have you ever seen a believer deny the existence of God? – nor an atheism – have you ever seen an atheist believe in God?' (author's translation).
37. Meillassoux's understanding of inexistence differs from Badiou's use of the term in that, for the Badiou of *Logiques des mondes*, the inexistent of a situation is precisely defined as that one element of an object in the world that attests to the contingency of that object's being-there (*LM* 341/*LW* 324), whereas for Meillassoux inexistence, while still the index of contingency, is not framed in terms of a specific element of an object but in the untrammelled virtualities of hyperchaos.
38. Hallward, 'Anything is possible', p. 56.
39. 'Everything could actually collapse: from trees to stars, from stars to laws, from physical laws to logical laws' (*AfF* 53).
40. 'it becomes rationally illegitimate to disqualify irrational discourses about the absolute on the pretext of their irrationality' (*AfF* 41).

41.
    So long as you maintain that your skepticism towards all knowledge of the absolute is based upon an argument, rather than upon mere belief or opinion, then you have to grant that the core of any such argument must be thinkable. But the core of your argument is that we can access everything's capacity-not-to-be, or capacity-to-be-other; our own as well as the world's. But once again, to say that one can think this is to say we can think the absoluteness of the possibility of every thing. (*AfF* 58)
42. 'a hyperchaos, for which nothing is or would seem to be impossible, not even the unthinkable' (*AfF* 64).
43. This argument is made by Ray Brassier, who concludes that 'the only hope for securing the unequivocal independence of the *'an sich'* must lie in prizing it free from chronology as well as phenomenology' (Brassier, *Nihil Unbound*, p. 59).
44. 'As for the principle of non-contradiction, it allows us to establish a priori, and independently of any recourse to experience, that a contradictory event is impossible, that it cannot occur *either today or tomorrow*' (*AfF* 87).
45. 'incontestable fact of the stability of the laws of nature' (*AfF* 94).
46. Harman, 'Speculative realism', p. 386.
47. Harman, 'Speculative realism', p. 392.
48. 'reason, in search of a first necessary principle, thus itself called for its own surpassing, and faith could legitimately put itself forward as the fulfilment of the rational' (author's translation).
49. 'reason will show itself capable of accounting for the ultimate truths of the real world by itself' (author's translation).
50. 'a mystery concerning God or the gods' (ODP 129); 'the gesture of touching the limit of all worldviews' (*GT* 51; translation altered).
51. The other major contributory factor is his argument that thought gives access to the in-itself. Though we do not have space to rehearse this argument in these pages, its essential contours will be clear in the discussion of demonstration that follows.
52. This is a common and uncontroversial set theoretical principle. According to the principle of extensionality, two sets are equal if they contain the same elements. Any set with no elements is the one and unique empty set, not simply *an* empty set. By heuristic analogy, 'no pigs' is the same as 'no cows' or 'no people'.
53. Brassier, *Nihil Unbound*, p. 93.
54. Brassier, *Nihil Unbound*, p. 139.
55. In *AfF* 53 Brassier tones down the religious connotations of the phrase by translating 'une « conversion du regard »' as 'a "change in outlook"'.
56. 'so as to make thought a limitless power of truth' (author's translation).

5. The Politics of the Post-Theological I: Justifying the Political

> Si j'ai supprimé Dieu le père, il faut bien quelqu'un pour inventer les valeurs.[1]

We now turn to consider the ethical and political implications of the three different approaches to post-theological thinking under discussion,[2] namely Nancy's 'atheology', Badiou's 'atheism' and Meillassoux's 'philosophy'. In pursuing its aims, this chapter and the next will be asking two broad questions. In the present chapter, we shall seek the criteriology of any possible relation between atheism/atheology/philosophy and any ethics or politics whatsoever, opening the question of justice. In the final chapter we shall return to the question of justice in order to investigate how each position seeks to secure a notion of universal justice. The question of justice will allow us to explore to what extent each position is a post-theological integration that neither ascetically renounces the notion of universal justice nor parasitically strives for it on the basis of theological assumptions. The decision to treat 'ethics' and 'politics' side by side in these chapters is neither innocent nor unproblematic. It is a decision necessitated by the desire to do full justice to each position, for an exclusion or sequestration of the ethical would prohibit reference to material in all three authors that is germane to our two questions. Notwithstanding, care will be taken not to conflate the ethical and the political, and to allow each thinker to reconstruct his own understanding of what is meant by these terms, as well as their relation to each other.

The possibility of a post-theological ethics and politics has to contend with threats both of parasitism and asceticism. On the side of asceticism, Simon Critchley evokes a 'moral deficit' at the heart of democratic life 'bound up with the felt inadequacy of official secular conceptions of morality', wondering along with Jay Bernstein whether

The Politics of the Post-Theological I: Justifying the Political 169

'modernity itself has had the effect of generating a motivational deficit in morality that undermines the possibility of ethical secularism'.³ Part of this deficit can be ascribed to what has come to be known as Hume's is-ought problem, the difficulty of drawing a moral or political imperative form a constative statement:

> In every system of morality, which I have hitherto met with, I have always remark'd, that the author proceeds for some time in the ordinary ways of reasoning, and establishes the being of a God, or makes observations concerning human affairs; when all of a sudden I am surpriz'd to find, that instead of the usual copulations of propositions, is, and is not, I meet with no proposition that is not connected with an ought, or an ought not.⁴

It is our aim in the pages that follow to address in relation to the three thinkers under consideration the relation between what is and what ought to be.

A second ascetic problem for a post-theological politics is found in the twin propositions that, 'if God is dead then everything is permitted', and, conversely, 'if God is dead then nothing is permitted'. The first proposition is a misquotation of Dostoyevsky's Ivan Fyodorovitch. The original passage speaks of faith in God and immortality, and draws its conclusion not in terms of permission but of morality:

> Ivan Fyodorovitch added in parenthesis that the whole natural law lies in that faith, and that if you were to destroy in mankind the belief in immortality, not only love but every living force maintaining the life of the world would at once be dried up. Moreover, nothing then would be immoral, everything would be lawful, even cannibalism.⁵

The second proposition comes from the seventeenth volume of Lacan's *Seminar*, where Lacan points out that the ethical mandate of 'permission' disappears along with the death of God (or of the father) who can permit, forbid or indeed forgive certain actions:

> Il y a longtemps que j'ai fait remarquer qu'à la phrase du vieux père Karamazov, *si Dieu est mort*, alors tout est permis, la conclusion qui s'impose dans le texte de notre expérience, c'est qu'à *Dieu est mort* répond plus rien n'est permis.⁶

This second proposition exposes the first as a parasitism, seeking to retain the category of divine permission while denying the divine. Both propositions equally raise the problem of the ethical or political mandate upon which post-theological thought can draw: by virtue of what can a philosophical position lay claim to sanction, normativity or imperative without parasitising the concepts of divine permission or divine mandate?

A further challenge to a post-theological politics comes as an accusation of parasitism. At least since Carl Schmitt's influential elaboration of the 'theo-political' in *Political Theology*, there is the question of the extent to which modern politics per se parasitises religious/theological ideas. Schmitt's famous claim is that:

> All significant concepts of the modern theory of the state are secularized theological concepts not only because of their historical development – in which they were transferred from theology to the theory of the state, whereby, for example, the omnipotent God became the omnipotent lawgiver – but also because of their systematic structure, the recognition of which is necessary for a sociological consideration of these concepts. The exception in jurisprudence is analogous to the miracle in theology. Only by being aware of this analogy can we appreciate the manner in which the philosophical ideas of the state developed in the last centuries.[7]

Whether Schmitt's thesis is homological (some political concepts resemble some religious concepts) or genealogical (modern political concepts are conditioned by and reliant upon religious concepts),[8] by 'imitative atheism' we mean something stronger than either of these theses. It is not enough to show that political notions 'owe their contours to the very theological traditions and practices, the systems of thought and sensibilities, whose authority they seek to curb or hold in check'.[9] Our concern will rather be with the extent to which post-theological conceptions of politics implicitly require the persistence, in the theological notions they appropriate, of theological assumptions they explicitly reject; in other words we are concerned not with analogy or genealogy but dependency, with the extent to which post-theological politics might not simply parallel the theological, but parasitise it.

5.1 MEILLASSOUX: FAITH, VALUE AND HYPERCHAOS

It is notable that, in 'L'Inexistence divine', Meillassoux moves the axis of discussion from the (in)existence of God to a register of hope and justice: 'croire, désormais, ce n'est plus avoir la foi, ce n'est plus croire en la loi, c'est espérer une justice *digne de ce nom*' (ID 384).[10] What is most keenly at stake for Meillassoux in the four ways of relating man and God seems to be the ethical import of each position. In 'L'Éthique divine', the third part of 'L'Inexistence divine', Meillassoux sketches how being and value have drifted asunder in the history of Western thought. Plato seeks the unification of being and value in the Ideas: justice is written into the harmony of the elements; cosmos and sky become the images of the Good itself (ID 305), and this 'cosmological symbol' is the first of three 'symbols' (from *sym-ballein*, to cast or thrust together, in this case the grouping together of value and being) that, in the history of Western thought, have provided an ontological link between being and value (ID 303). This attempted reconciliation of being and value ends, however, with Newton, after whom justice seems like a convenient convention (ID 306). Two rearguard actions, two further symbols, seek to re-establish the link between value and being.

The second symbol is naturalist or Romantic, and it tries to compensate for the Newtonian split by inscribing value not within the natural but the social world: man is born good, and there is an inscription of the good in the living, no longer in the matter of the cosmos (ID 306). The third, 'historical', symbol looks to History as the inhuman and non-natural entity that finally assures the objectivity of value for human beings. Today, Meillassoux argues, we are experiencing the death of this Symbolism of modernity. We have lost the certainty that history is on our side (ID 308). This failure to reconcile being and value leaves both belief and atheism wanting, Meillassoux argues, for whereas belief cannot be rational, atheism cannot be virtuous (ID 310). Nevertheless, the task of any philosophy worthy of that name remains, in Meillassoux's account, to unite being and value (ID 302), and in so doing to avoid both atheistic despair and religious obscurantism by providing a rational account of the ontological harmony between our measureless demand for justice and the absurdity of a world without God (ID 300).

Philosophy has hitherto provided three solutions to the problem of determining the relationship between the Good and the true (ID 295): 1) the Good is true because it harkens back to a primordial and necessary reality, although this reality is beyond thought; 2) the Good is true because it refers to some ideal, although the ideal is inaccessible; 3) the Good is a real and manageable (*maîtrisable*) possibility. This third option, Meillassoux stresses, is of a revolutionary bent: justice can be fully realised by human action alone. But this, like the other options, is inadequate, because it cannot repair injustice, simply hope for future justice. All three solutions proposed hitherto suffer from requiring that the Good be real or that there be a real prospect of achieving it (ID 308), which is why Meillassoux proposes a fourth solution: 'la vérité du Bien, comme Quatrième Monde, ne désigne ni une réalité, ni une impossibilité, ni une possibilité maîtrisable: *le Bien désigne la vérité d'une possibilité non maîtrisable*' (ID 296; QM's italics).[11]

For Meillassoux's factial account of justice the Good is not an ideal but an unreal (*un irréel*), that is to say a real possibility, but one which escapes all prediction. It is the truth of becoming itself that teaches us this demand for justice (ID 311–12), for it affirms that something which has no relation to the real (in this case: perfect justice) can hyperchaotically come to be.

Only hyperchaos can deliver a justice that maintains the demand of its original excess, namely that justice must be universal in the sense of being for all, which would include justice for those now dead. Whereas universal justice is absurd for the atheist, who has no hope of justice for the dead, the only position that has thus far been able to promise such an excessive justice as to include the dead is the religious premise of the resurrection of the dead (ID 338). However, the theistic position also undermines justice because the existence of any God who would have allowed the atrocities of the twentieth century to unfold would itself, Meillassoux argues, be a great injustice (ID 286). There is no religion or morality, he asserts, that must not bow to one or other of these two conditions. So the circle that Meillassoux gives himself to square '*comes down to making thinkable the statement conjugating the possible resurrection of the dead [...] and the inexistence of God*' (SD 267–8; QM's italics). This is accomplished by the principle of factiality, for which everything that is logically possible is really possible, including resurrection (ID 290).

In Meillassoux's fourth symbol, value is re-inscribed into being in terms of the real and ineliminable possibility of 'illegal' change (that is: change not conforming to pre-existing laws) (ID 312). Thus the absurdity of hyperchaos itself, far from being the rock upon which the desire for justice runs aground, provides the very pledge of possible justice (ID 299).

Meillassoux freely acknowledges that this link between value and truth is unfounded:

> la philosophie part toujours d'un postulat qui peut fort bien être impossible à démontrer, qui peut fort bien être faux, ou idéologique, à savoir: la valeur n'est pas une simple invention humaine, la valeur est la découverte d'une vérité concernant le monde, le réel extra-humain, et cette vérité doit être dégagée par la seule raison, sans l'intervention de la révélation transcendante. (ID 300)[12]

So with value we are back in the realm of postulates, not demonstrations. Meillassoux makes explicit that there is no discourse that can lead the reader by degrees to accept his hope for universal justice; 'il se fera ou non du biais de l'acceptation ou du refus du temps tel que nous l'avons pensé' (ID 288).[13] He cannot build a cumulative argument for it, and must simply immerse the reader in the postulate *in medias res*.

The certainty that value is not a social construction, that it bespeaks a truth about the world, rests in Meillassoux's reconstruction of philosophy on a wager. Indeed, he seeks to re-write Pascal's religious wager in his own philosophical terms. Whereas the man who believes in transcendence sees in earthly events signs to be deciphered (ID 373), Meillassoux's gamer is the one who has the power (*puissance*) not to make a given event into a sign, even in the case of the most striking coincidence (ID 374). What this gamer seeks is an encounter not with destiny, but with chance (ID 375).[14] Pascal's mistake is that he assumes the gamer wants to win, Meillassoux argues, but in fact the gamer wants to come face to face with chance, inaccessible to probabilistic calculations (ID 376). Meillassoux re-frames the wager along these lines, addressing the gamer in the second person: the great dice thrower is the one who hopes for justice, and continues hoping as he plays and plays again. We need dice-throwers who will approach justice like they approach the gaming table (ID 376). So the gamer throws, and hopes. She hopes for the appearance (*surgissement*) of a new justice, and her hope is founded on the ontological truth of necessary contingency (ID 33). We shall return below to the question of what precisely we are to understand by throwing the die; for now we shall continue to pursue the question of justice.

Meillassoux distinguishes the dice-thrower's hope for justice from illusion, as well as from a religious or abstract principle; it is the rational anticipation of what he calls the fourth World of justice. The three worlds which this fourth World succeeds are matter, life and thought (ID 293), all of which appeared *ex nihilo* within the world that preceded them. Meillassoux uses the term *ex nihilo* as a cognate for 'contingent' when he is describing certain appearances that cannot be explained by a theory of chance (ID 38). As opposed to an idea of chance which understands change in terms of a pre-ordained, finite repertoire of potential outcomes (like throwing a six-sided die), contingency exceeds every pre-existing totality of cases, even an infinite one, and claims that cases themselves can be created (ID 22). *Surgissement ex nihilo* is without any reason, and by that token limitless (ID 12). Meillassoux's privileged example of such appearing from nothing is the emergence of life on earth, the coming to being of a qualitatively new set of circumstances not contained within that which preceded them (ID 16).

A similar argument can be made for a number of different cases of emergence: sensation cannot be reduced to a material structure, and conceptual thought cannot be reduced to sensation (ID 33–4). Life (including the sensation of pain) is not a latent property of matter, as if pain was asleep in matter beforehand (ID 31), and to the objection that the *ex nihilo* is simply too unconstrained to be taken seriously (why would it be life that emerges from matter, not any of an infinite number of other virtualities?), Meillassoux replies 'avant de contester ce surgissement *ex nihilo* pour son caractère fantastique, il faudrait se demander s'il n'est pas plus fabuleux de confondre la matière avec un dormeur' (ID 32).[15]

Crucially, Meillassoux argues that the World of justice, also called the truth of the Good (*la vérité du Bien*, ID 296) is the *only* world that can succeed the third World of thought: 'si un monde surgit encore, ce ne peut être que le Monde de justice. Car tout autre surgissement ne constituerait qu'une variation « monstrueuse » des trois Mondes antérieurs' (ID 296).[16] The reasoning is opaque here, but it appears that Meillassoux is arguing that any change other than the appearing of the World of justice will simply be a change *within* the existing world (ID 290–1). It follows that, if the only necessity is contingency, the only necessity for the present world is the possible appearing of the world of justice. The inevitability of a further hyperchaotic change bringing about the World of justice must also be understood in terms of Meillassoux's assertion that 'rien ne peut surpasser l'homme' (ID 293)[17] (where man is distinguished from other animals by his reason, more specifically by his capacity to intuit the principle of factiality (ID 138)), a move that seems to be the logical extension of his exemption of his own reasoning from hyperchaotic change. Despite his best protestations, it remains unclear, at least to this reader, how holding the position that the World of universal justice is the only world that can succeed the present one can possibly avoid flying in the face of hyperchaos otherwise than by idolising human reason.

A further critique of Meillassoux's position could take the following form: what if hyperchaotic change were to bring about a situation not in which the world suddenly conformed to our sense of justice (through the resurrection of the dead or whatever other means), but in which our sense of justice suddenly conformed to the world as it is? What if the surprising chance is that we suddenly consider our world to have been perfectly 'just' all along? This is unthinkable (both logically and ethically) perhaps, but surely not hyperchaotically impossible, unless our sense of justice is idolatrously exempted from hyperchaotic change. This critique echoes the argument we mounted against Meillassoux in the previous chapter. Brown is quite right to suggest that 'a speculative demonstration that whatever situation is contingent rather than necessary (despite its manifest stability) does not undermine the political urgency of working toward the contingent stability of *another* situation – toward new and different ways of structuring or distributing relations among the given',[18] but his intervention, like Meillassoux's argument, does beg the question of justice: our understanding of what is just must in some way (once again) be exempt from hyperchaos (or we must at least wager that it will not change – or we will not recognise it to have changed – for the foreseeable future) whereas the principle of factiality insists that contingency alone, and not our current understanding of justice, is necessary. This poses a significant problem for any criteriology of ethics or politics in relation to Meillassoux's philosophy.

A final set of questions that Meillassoux needs to face concerns the analogy of throwing the die itself. What does it mean to throw the die in the 'real world'? How, in other words, might we influence a hyperchaotic change? Can the die be 'loaded'? And, if it cannot, does this not expose Meillassouxian hope as a distraction from practical steps to bring about meaningful political change? Peter Hallward voices this latter concern in relation to *Après la finitude* when he critiques Meillassoux for not being able to think concrete political situations:

> Rather like his mentor Badiou, to the degree that Meillassoux insists on the *absolute* disjunction of an event from existing situations he deprives himself of any concretely mediated means of thinking, with and after Marx, the possible ways of changing such situations [. . .] the abstract logical possibility of change (given the absence of any ultimately sufficient reason) has strictly nothing to do with any concrete process of actual change.[19]

Hallward's argument is answered with reference to *Après la finitude* by Nathan Brown, who responds that 'Meillassoux's book has nothing whatsoever to do with an empirical analysis of political or social situations or possible ways of transforming them',[20] but from 'L'Inexistence divine' we can go further, and see that Hallward's reading of Meillassoux is only at best partially correct.

Meillassoux addresses the question of quietism directly, arguing that the constant possibility of the appearing of justice does not lead to passive waiting, but on the contrary to the awareness of human possibility (ID 347). Far from being a mere waiting game (*attentisme*), it is in hoping for a justice worthy of the name that the individual is moved to act in conformity with that hope. Meillassoux also deals with the question of the 'real world equivalent' of the dice throw, in a section of 'L'Inexistence divine' entitled 'Le Fatalisme' (ID 326–7). There is no fatalism in factiality, passively waiting for the appearing of justice, Meillassoux insists, but rather '*la condition pour que l'universel advienne, c'est donc qu'il soit désiré en acte*' (ID 327; QM's emphasis).[21] Each time I act in accord with justice I renew this waiting: 'On peut ainsi comparer l'acte libre à un coup de dé – coup de dé qui ne garantit pas la chance, mais qui seul la rend possible' (ID 327).[22] So it seems that, by dint of throwing the dice (that is: by actively desiring the universal) enough, I provide the condition for its coming. And by dint of acting in accordance with universal justice here and now, I avoid a passive waiting. But this seems completely out of line with the justice for the dead that Meillassoux insists is the only universal justice. How do I 'actively will' the resurrection of the dead? What differentiates Meillassoux's desiring from sacrifices offered to the gods of rain or victory, in the hope that such actions might influence the future course of events? And why should human desire make any difference at all to hyperchaotic change? Meillassoux seems to argue that it does, but remains as yet opaque on the mechanism of any such influence.

Nathan Brown's counterargument to the quietism charge is illuminating here:

> precisely *because* any given or constructed situation is absolutely contingent rather than necessary, it has to be upheld by conviction and by force, even if we cannot assure its protection against the perpetual threat of disintegration.[23]

Maybe, but this is a very different conception of 'hope' for a future justice. What role, then, do 'conviction and force' have? Only that we throw the die until we get what we want, and then we stop throwing, hoping *against* the 'perpetual threat of disintegration'. It seems that necessary contingency is now the enemy of our convictions, not their only hope, and our real hope is in our ability to produce *just that* change we want, before closing down the possibility of change once more.

5.2 NANCY: ETHOS AND CALL

Like Meillassoux, Nancy rejects the notion of any 'move' from ontology to certain ethical or political principles. Such a move is dangerous:

> on devrait savoir que, d'une pensée, disons de l'être, ou de l'essence, ou des principes – peu importe ici – , à une politique et à une éthique, la conséquence n'est jamais bonne (pourquoi oublie-t-on systématiquement l'adhésion massive et durable au régime nazi de tant de théoriciens de la « philosophie des valeurs »?) (*EL* 214–15)[24]

The error in such a move is to pass unproblematically from the interrogation of 'the principle' as such, to the fixing of certain determinate principles. 'Principles' cannot be deduced from 'the principle', understood as the originary sharing of being, the principle of freedom. To fix any such determinate principles would be to parasitise religion, to erect in the place of a 'proof of God' an originary Reason of the world, which is exactly what Nancy's atheology seeks to avoid (*ADC* 49). The rejection of any Reason or End for the world does not result, however, in ignoring the question of ethics altogether, rather 'notre question est de part en part la question du Bien dans un monde sans fin ou à fins singulières' (CM 77–8).[25]

Furthermore, to distinguish physics and ethics is already to be functioning within the history of philosophy governed by closure of metaphysics (the closure of meaning into signification). It is to stop asking where something like 'ethics' comes from, and what, prior to any 'domain of ethics', could authorise any ethical law in general (IC 116/RP 29). It is not that ontology and politics are bridged, more that it is denied that their separation was originary. It is only a parasitic metaphysics that divided ontology and ethics in the first place, that the supposed gulf between them should need to be bridged.

5.2.1 Ethos

The discourses of ontology and ethics are for Nancy post facto reductions of a *sense* which is both ontological and ethical. It is a mistake to suppose that we need to make a 'move' from ontology to ethics, because being for Nancy is not a brute fact, an *il y a*, in the first place (PD 90, 93/FT 176, 178). Being is not the 'there is' of a brute given, but rather *that* there is giving ('qu'il y a don'), in other words no signification can be ascribed to the fact *that* being is, in the same way that we might ascribe signification to *what* there is. It is Nancy's distinction between *signification* and *sens* that is doing the work here. There can be no signification of sense, because sense is the condition of possibility of signification. Nancy summarises this situation helpfully when he says that ethics is 'phatic' rather than 'semantic', that sense-making exscribes itself rather than inscribing itself in maxims or works (*œuvres*) (PD 112/FT 195). Ethics is not the discipline concerned with moral signification, as opposed to cognitive or physical significations, but the touching of being. It follows that all disciplines – the cognitive, the logical, the physical, aesthetic, moral – are 'originally ethical' (PD 105/FT 188); in fact, only ontology can be ethical (ESP 39/BSP 21), and ethics is the ontology of ontology itself (PD 103/FT 187). To understand these latter two claims we need to examine first Nancy's plural singularity and then the notion of ethics as *ethos*.

The elision of the difference between ontology and ethics is part of Nancy's elaboration of the spacing of singular plural being. Singular plural being not only requires a rethinking of being such that the question of social being becomes the primary ontological question (ESP 78/BSP 57), but being also needs to be rethought so that it is no longer a first philosophy upon which ethics supervenes. When Nancy insists that singular plurality (or plural singularity, as *singulier pluriel* can equally be translated[26]) is not only another signification but also another syntax (*ESP* 57–8/*BSP* 37), he means that we must not simply think of filling the categories 'ontology' and 'ethics' with new content, but we must rethink the categories themselves, casting singular plural ontology as an *ethos* and a *praxis*.[27] Just as it situates itself before the distinction between the singular and the plural, being singular plural situates itself before the distinction between ontology and ethics, or between being, acting, sense and behaviour (*ESP* 87/*BSP* 65). Pure reason is in itself practical reason Nancy insists, adopting a Kantian idiom, because it is, irreducibly, common reason (*raison commune*), with the *avec* at its groundless ground: 'Il n'y a de différence entre l'éthique et l'ontologique : l'« éthique » expose ce que l'« ontologie » dispose' (*ESP* 123).[28]

This re-definition of ontology is necessary in order to overcome a parasitic political theology of self-sufficiency. Any ontology that does not touch the limit where all ontology gets tied up with something other than itself resolves to just such a theologico-political self sufficiency (*SM* 175/*SW* 112). The insistence that the distinction between ontology and ethics is derivative forms an important element of Nancy's attempt to leave 'theologico-politics' to elaborate an atheological space of politics (*SM* 181/*SW* 118).

In order to elaborate a thinking which does not recognise as primary the disjunction of being and value, Nancy employs the term *ethos*, an a priori synthesis of concept and affect (*PD* 108/*FT* 191). *Ethos*, Nancy explains, has two distinct meanings: on the one hand presence and disposition, on the other hand stay (*séjour*) and behaviour. The two meanings blend in the motif of 'holding oneself' (*la tenue*), and it is such a 'holding' that is at the bottom of every ethics (*CM* 36/*CWG* 42). This is no 'moral philosophy' derived from a 'first philosophy', but rather a 'thinking of being' that is neither ethical nor ontological, neither theoretical nor practical (*PD* 105/*FT* 189).

This is an idea of Heideggerian inspiration, for in terms of Heidegger's fundamental ontology, Nancy argues, it is not simply that the thinking of being implies an ethics but, more radically, that the thinking of being presents itself as an ethics: Heidegger's 'fundamental ontology' is justly called an 'original ethics' (*PD* 105/*FT* 189). Nancy is at pains to stress that *ethos* is not superimposed on being from the outside, nor does it imbue being with any values alien to being itself. *Ethos* for Nancy is a behaviour, and the thought of this behaviour is 'original ethics': *ethos* as conducting oneself (*la conduite*) according to the truth (*PD* 105/*FT* 189) that is prior to any 'ethics' or 'politics' (*VD* 62/*TD* 33), namely the truth of singular plural being.

So what does it mean to conduct oneself according to the truth of singular plural being? It means to preserve that freedom by virtue of which there can be any relation to values or to law in the first place (*EL* 200/*EF* 163). The importance of freedom is paramount in understanding Nancy's *ethos*. *Ethos* is not the Good, however that may be conceived in a given philosophy (Plato's *agathon*, Kant's good will, Spinozan joy, Marxian revolution, Aristotle's *zoon politikon*), but the archi-originary ethicity without which there would be no such determinations of the good (*EL* 200/*EF* 163), namely the free decision to 'receive oneself' (*se recevoir*), to hold oneself as a decision (*de se tenir elle-même comme décision*). The Good for Nancy relies on this freedom of decision, a decision which is the 'empty' moment of any ethics. We have to decide about ethical content and ethical norms, laws, exceptions, cases and negotiations, but there is no law or exception for the decision, unless it is the law that withdraws from (and stands behind) all laws, namely freedom itself (*EL* 200/*EF* 163).

Nancy is not, for all that, propounding an 'ethics of freedom', because freedom is *ethos* itself as the opening of space (*EL* 187–8/*EF* 146), *ethos* as the space of ethics (and of ontology), rather than an ethics of *ethos*. Once more, this resonates with the relation between sense and signification:[29] there can be no gift of sense (*sens*) because sense is the giving of the gift of signification, and similarly there can be no ethics of *ethos* because *ethos* is the possibility, the space, of ethics. Freedom is not the property of such and such a being (any more than a given signification 'has' *sens*), rather being itself is opened by freedom. Ethics is rethought *as ethos*, where the freedom of the free choice – rather than the choice of the free choice – is paramount.

An ethical imperative only makes sense if it is addressed to a freedom of speech which its address both confirms and conceals (*IC* 123/*RP* 36). Furthermore, the command only makes sense if it addresses a *finite* freedom. The imperative is part of the structure of finitude, Nancy affirms from his reading of Heidegger's *Kantbuch*, where Heidegger affirms that a being which, in its very ground, is subject to a duty or imperative, knows itself to be in a state of non-completion, and knowing itself in this state at its very ground, such a being knows itself to be finite (*IC* 124/*RP* 37). In other words *ethos*, inscribed in the warp and woof of being itself, bears an irreducible relation to finitude. But it is not an ethics *of* finitude (which would leave us once more with an ethical domain supervening upon a prior, finite, ontological situation), but finitude as ethics and as the opening of ethics (*IC* 124/*RP* 37). The difference between the two is this: whereas the ethical imperative has always been construed as the properly infinite teleonomy[30] of a being which, though itself only provisionally finite, nevertheless is promised the appropriation of its end, Nancy is arguing that we understand finitude-ethics as the expropriation, or opening-as-disenclosure, of any end, in other words we must understand ethics in terms of freedom and *ethos*.

The insistence on freedom means that *ethos* yields a thought which, says Nancy quoting Heidegger, has no result (PD 106/FT 189 n.62),[31] not in the sense that it is impotent, but in the sense that it yields no fixed norms or sets of values. Nevertheless, it is its own result: it is possible as a thought only to the extent that it is already a behaviour (*une conduite*). It does not guide behaviour, rather it itself guides, and it guides itself (the two senses of *elle conduit elle-même*) to thinking behaviour in general. As such, *ethos* avoids two equal and opposite errors. On the one hand, it is incommensurable with the 'philosophy of values' which would attempt to fix signification by projecting it into some 'beyond' or other, circumscribing the ethical to any determinate idea, concept or discourse. In this sense, again, it has no result. On the other hand, neither does *ethos* yield a subjective, autonomous ethical free choice, which in fact amounts to the same fixing of sense as the philosophy of values itself. It avoids this pitfall because, although it has no result, it is its own result: it is possible as a thought only to the extent that it is a behaviour (*conduite*). In an admirably short formulation from 'Une exemption de sens', Nancy sums up the twin dangers, 'Garder, préserver le sens d'être rempli aussi bien que d'être vide, voilà l'éthos' (*DCD* 180).[32] There *is* a way of holding oneself that accords with with singular plural being, and it is to preserve the freedom of decision. Neither a philosophy of value nor autonomous choice can assure human dignity (PD 106/FT 189), where dignity is understood as having, in one's being, to make sense of being. It follows that dignity, like ethics, must be seen in relation to finitude, where finitude signifies the condition in which *sens* is the ground and its truth is sense-making (*faire-sens*). Infinitude, by contrast, Nancy continues, would be the condition of a being whose meaning would be its finished product, self-possessed and self-sufficient.

Our contemporary moral disarray, insists Nancy, stems from not having found a way to think values and free choice together (PD 106/FT 189). It is this negotiation of values and free choice that is provided by Nancy's *ethos*, in the same way that *sens* provides for significations, without being reduced to any signification in particular. The move from a system of values to *ethos* as ethics is a distinctly atheological move for Nancy, in a world which is essentially not the representation of a universe or of a 'here below', but the excess of *ethos* beyond any representation in a world which holds itself, configures itself, without any relation to a given principle or fixed end (CM 46–7/CWG 47). Furthermore, it follows in such a world for Nancy that atheism (in the sense of the post-theological) is the only *ethos* possible, the only dignity of the subject (DDC 30/DisDC 17).

5.2.2 The Call

There remains, nevertheless, an unanswered question for Nancy's *ethos*. Even if ontology and ethics are a posteriori reductions of a more originary *ethos*, by virtue of what does or can that *ethos* exert a normative purchase on behaviour? In other words: why act in accordance with freedom, or with being singular plural? Can *ethos* command, or prescribe, acting in accord with the marriage of freedom and values? It is for a response to these sorts of questions that we need to consider Nancy's notion of the call or appeal (*appel*).

Let us be clear: Nancy certainly does use the language of obligation in relation to singular plural being. The *ethos* of thinking 'us' in singular plurality is an obligation, but it is an imperative without a command:

> On pourrait dire qu'il y a dans la liberté l'impératif ontologique, ou l'être comme intimation – mais à la condition d'ajouter que c'est sans commandement [...] ou que le commandement se confond avec l'abandon de la liberté à elle-même, jusque dans le caprice et jusque dans la chance. (EL 198–9)[33]

This imperative that does not become a commandment, Nancy argues in *La Pensée dérobée*, is also an address, and the call or the address is itself nothing other than sense (PD 172/AfS 88), sense as address, as the opening of the possibility of return or response (*renvoi*).

In *L'Adoration*, Nancy develops the idea of a response to this call as 'adoration'. Taking his cue from the etymology of 'adoration' – *oratio* as solemn speech or, more precisely, speech held (*tenue*), a tension of the voice, and *ad*-oratio as speech addressed to something or someone – Nancy uses the term to signify speech the content of which is inseparable or indiscernible from its address (ADC 28), whether it be invocation, call, adjuration, imploring, celebration, dedication, salutation, or address itself. Adoration is the 'salut!' of an address which contains almost nothing other than itself, that bears a recognition, an affirmation of the existence of the other (ADC 29), and is not sublimated into a higher order of speech.

But does this imperative, call, or address that elicits adoration have any ethical weight, so to speak? Is there any obligation to heed it, to adore? The most persuasive way to find such a force is explored by Martin Crowley in his *L'Homme sans*.[34] Crowley rejects the task of deriving a politics of equality from an ontology, but nevertheless employs the notion of a call to suggest a relation other than that of derivation: 'si celle-ci [une politique égalitaire] n'est assurément *donnée* par aucune ontologie, il se peut bien qu'elle soit néanmoins *appelée* par toute ontologie qui pose, comme on aime à le dire aujourd'hui, l'égalité de chaque un avec chaque un.'[35]

In a very carefully chosen phrase, Crowley evokes 'this exposition which, in common, we do not have' (*'cette exposition qu'en commun nous n'avons pas'*)[36] as the ontological situation which demands to be taken into account in our politics. Crowley follows Robert Antelme's argument in *L'Espèce humaine* that the revelation of the indivisible unity of the human race definitively disqualifies all discrimination, rendering actually existing differences intolerable.[37] It would be hasty to discern here an ethics of victimhood of the sort that Badiou dismisses as reducing the human to the animal datum of its tortured body (*S* 246–7/*Cen* 175), for the notion of equality cannot be reduced to the corporeal, and an appeal to ontological equality is not an oppressive metaphysics of pity (*S* 248–9/*Cen* 176) because the call is not addressed to empathy but to *ethos*, to the ethico-ontological condition of existence. Nevertheless, the position is still open to the charge of being reactionary, for the resistance against inequality relies on there being inequalities to resist, and beyond this resistance struggles to provide a constructive political vision.

The ground of equality for Crowley is human finitude: there is no human being who is not finite. This 'proposition of finitude' establishes an irreducible ontological equality and, at the same time, demands (*exige*) its political realisation.[38] For Crowley, the ethical imperative of finitude demands variously that we verify and realise,[39] honour[40] and translate into action[41] its ontological equality. Nevertheless, the question remains: why should we heed this call? Simply because it is ontological? But why should ontology be normative? This Everest ethics (we obey the demand 'because it's there') lacks persuasiveness. If things were ontologically otherwise, for example in the logically possible and ethically repugnant situation where there would indeed be a fundamental ontological difference between different groups of 'human beings', would such an ontology also issue a demand it would be intolerable to disobey, or would there be certain possible ontologies that it would be our duty to 'resist' and not to 'verify'? Why should what is ontologically most fundamental necessarily be normative, to use Crowley's language 'by this very token' (*par là même*)?[42] We might conclude that it is because Crowley's ontology is one of *equality*, not because this equality is *ontological*, that it is considered normative here, and if this is so then it begs the question of why equality should be normative.

In relation to the call/demand and response, there is the additional complicating factor of the theological connotations of any such call. Critchley derives his notion of 'the unfulfillability of the ethical demand' in part from Lévinas,[43] and when he tries to secularise the call in his ethics of finitude in *Very Little, Almost Nothing*, its interpolative power crumbles into a 'minimal, fragile, *refusable*' ethics of 'the experience of what I call atheist transcendence',[44] in an unappealing choice between a theological call and a 'moral recommendation, even exhortation, an appeal to the individual reader from an individual writer'.[45] This is neither how Nancy or Crowley understands the demand.

By the time of publishing *Infinitely Demanding* Critchley has modified his stance to that of an methodological ethical agnosticism:

> The ultimate metaphysical source of ethical obligation, should there be such a thing, is simply not cognizable. In my more extreme view, the question of the metaphysical ground or basis of ethical obligation should simply be disregarded as a philosophical wheel spinning with neither friction nor forward motion. Instead, the focus should be on the radicality of the human demand that faces us, a demand that requires phenomenology and not metaphysics.[46]

But the question is: precisely *what* human demand faces us? Short-circuiting the metaphysics of resistance or commitment by an answer with the structure of 'we all know . . .' does not yet address the question of what makes the 'good' good, but rather opens the structure of demand and response to being hijacked by 'undesirable' demands emanating from 'undesirable' ontologies.

It seems that, one way or another, the notion of a demand, call or appeal cannot provide – or at least has not yet provided – the link between ontology and ethics that Critchley and Crowley need it to: Critchley ends up supplementing his demand with a Badiouian ethics of decision, and Crowley cannot give an account for why ontological equality should be normative. Nancy's own notion of *ethos*, according to which the distinction between ontology and ethics is itself derivative, masking a more primitive *tenue* or *habitus*, begs the same question: it may be *original*, but that does not in itself make it *good*.

Nevertheless, this meditation on the call has not been in vain, because it allows us to respond to a number of critiques that have been made of Nancy's sense and singular plural *ethos*. Bruno Bosteels charges Nancy's notion of withdrawal/retracing (*retrait*) – whereby Nancy critiques the withdrawal of the field of political possibilities (*le politique*) such that a determinate form of politics (*la politique*) fills the whole political horizon – with abandoning the possibility of real political change that can abolish the current state of politics in favour of seeking to anticipate a truly unheard-of event, a true encounter with the real.[47] In other words, Nancy's politics of the *retrait*, and, by extension, his ethics as *ethos* and call/address as adoration, is ascetic, politically emasculated, anaemically unable to engineer radical change.

In *L'Adoration* Nancy recognises a similar danger himself, meditating on the importance of 'enthusiasm' (etymologically 'passage into God' or 'sharing of the divine') for a secular politics: 'comment ne pas emporter l'enthousiasme dans la mort de Dieu?' (*ADC* 113).[48] Nancy responds to his own question: we must begin by not confusing the fervour of enthusiasm with the fury of fascism, which always refers to a closed and determined figure (the people, the party, the leader, the idea, the vision . . .). That is not adoration, but adulation. The fervour of adoration, by contrast comes in the dilection that accords or recognises the unique and incalculable value of the other, both for the lovers in the throes of passion and desiring that passion for all beings:

> Elle est ferveur pour l'existence multiple et singulière : pour chacune, donc, tour à tour, pour chacune à l'exclusion des autres, et cependant pour toutes, en droit, et en fait au moins pour plusieurs qui répondent à plusieurs modes de cet « amour » unique et polymorphe (*ADC* 113)[49]

So Nancy's response to the charge of political quietism is not to search after all for an idea or a party as a focus for political fervour, but to seek the enthusiasm of that which precisely transcends every idea. Nancy's is not the fury of signification, of ethics or of *la politique*, but enthusiasm, after the death of God, for *sens*, *ethos* and *le politique*. It is a false dichotomy, Nancy argues, to assume that this has nothing to do with determinate political situations: 'Parler de "sens" et de "vérité" au milieu de l'agitation militaire, des calculs géopolitiques, des souffrances, des grimaces de bêtise ou de mensonge n'est pas "idéaliste", c'est toucher à la chose même' (*CA* 16).[50] The 'thing itself' here is the ontological equality to which alone appeal can be made for concrete political action in political situations. In Crowley's terms,

> Ces êtres sans qualités, sans part, sans phrase, exilés des processus de subjectivation politique, récusent *par là même* le formalisme des droits humains existants, en exigeant *par là même* que soit incessamment vérifiée et réalisée l'égalité ontologique que déclare la finitude.[51]

For his part, Simon Critchley departs most decisively from Nancy in his dislocation of politics from any ontological presuppositions:

> We are on our own and what we do we have to do for ourselves. Politics requires subjective invention, imagination and endurance, not to mention

tenacity and cunning. No ontology or eschatological philosophy of history is going to do it for us.⁵²

In an analysis which is more Badiouian than Nancean, Critchley affirms that 'politics is a disruption of the ontological domain and separate categories are required for its analysis and practice. There is no transitivity between ontology and politics.'⁵³ But when Critchley sketches what ontologising politics would mean, it is 'seeing politics as the expression of some common substance'.⁵⁴ Nancy's *ethos* is not the expression of some common substance, as – once more – Crowley succinctly captures with his 'exposition which, in common, we do not have'. Critchley fails to see the difference between *sens* and *signification*, between *ethos* and ethics.

Furthermore, in rejecting the ontologico-ethical imperative of *ethos* and seeking to meld a Lévinasian theory of demand and subjectivity with a Badiouian decision and commitment, Critchley opens himself to a pointed Badiouian critique. In his response to *Infinitely Demanding*, Badiou questions Critchley's contention that at the core of his (Critchley's) neo-anarchism lies not an ontology but an infinitely demanding ethics of commitment. Badiou agrees with Nancy against Critchley when he points out that 'you stay within the opposition of ontology and ethics. And that is the great idea of Lévinas. But after all it is not certain that there is an opposition between ontology and ethics'.⁵⁵ Indeed, Badiou continues, there is no such opposition in his own thinking, for

> the becoming-subject of an individual under the condition of the process of the truth, and finally under the commitment to an event, is of an ontological nature in one sense: because it is something, an event, which is a rupture in the order of being as such.⁵⁶

It is to Badiou's own disruption of the dichotomy of ontology and ethics that we now turn.

5.3 BADIOU: SUBTRACTION AND WAGER

Badiou's rethinking of ethics and politics is motivated by a determination to expel from them any vestiges of theological or religious influence, to inscribe the re-founding of politics in a philosophical horizon disengaged from latent theology. To this end, ethics and politics must extricate themselves from two legacies: Lévinas's ethics of absolute Alterity, and Kant's ethics of judgment. In this section we will deal with each of these legacies in turn, beginning with Badiou's reading of, and response to, Lévinas. What Badiou objects to above all in Lévinasian ethics is that the Other is only ever the immediate phenomenon of a transcendent principle of absolute Alterity, the *Tout-Autre*, which is 'bien évidemment le nom éthique de Dieu' (*E* 39).[57]

This ethics is nothing more than a child of theology, guaranteed at every point by the ineffable God. Badiou's critique of Lévinas at this point is radical: there is no separating alterity from the *Tout-Autre* upon which it relies at every point, and as such Lévinas has no philosophy, properly speaking, at all, nor even a theology (which assumes that divinity can be predicated and identified), but rather an ethics, an ethics that has now become the ultimate name of relating to others and to the Altogether-Other, of relating as *re-ligio*. The conclusion: every attempt to make ethics into the principle of thought and action is religious in essence (*E* 40/*Eth* 23).

Badiou also defines his own ethical and political position in contradistinction to Kant's ethics of judgment. What Badiou objects to most is Kant's ethical finitude, his perpetual examination of limits, his obsession with critique, 'car une seule pensée est bien plus vaste que n'importe quel jugement' (*Circ1* 71–2),[58] and the lack of 'thought' in such an ethics – where thought is the sort of decisive rupture we encountered in Chapter 1 with the birth of philosophy – amounts to nihilism: 'Où l'homme puisera-t-il la force d'être l'immortel qu'il est? Quel sera le destin de la pensée, dont on sait bien qu'elle est invention affirmative, ou qu'elle n'est pas?' (*E* 30).[59] The ethics of judgment relies on the notion of a general human subject, the subject of human rights for whom ethics is reduced to humanitarianism, defining the human subject as a victim (*E* 26/*Eth* 10) and as the white-Man as the good-Man behind the victim-Man (*E* 28/*Eth* 13). In contrast to Lévinas's ethics of the Altogether-Other, Badiou offers an ethics and politics of the event, and in contradistinction to Kant's ethics of judgment, he elaborates an ethics and politics of the decision.[60]

5.3.1 Politics of the Event, Politics of the Real

In a footnote on Rimbaud's *Une Saison en enfer* in *Conditions*, Badiou defines his own thinking in contrast to what he sees as the identification of ontology and politics in Nancy (*C* 140 n.22/*Con* 229 n.15). This false identification, Badiou argues, comes from having excluded science (specifically mathematics) from thinking. For Nancy there is only one thinking, the thinking of sense, and this allows Nancy no means qualitatively to distinguish the ontological from the ethical or political, whereas in contrast to Badiou's own thought allows multiple places of thought (namely politics, science, art, love). Further on in *Conditions*,

Badiou marks his disagreement from Nancy over what he sees as the latter's 'ontologisation' of the event, which leads inevitably to the 'doctrine of sense' (*C* 249 n.22/*Con* 307 n.17). For his part, Badiou's is a politics not of being but of the event, where a political event is understood as the appearing of a possibility (such as the Republic, or the power of the workers) which was previously unnoticed, a local opening of political possibilities (*PE* 19–20). An event is political (as opposed to amatory, scientific or artistic) if its 'material' (that which is incorporated into its subjective) is collective, or if the event cannot be attributed to anything other than the multiplicity of a collective (*AMP* 155/*MetP* 141). The political event furthermore, like all events, is both situated (in that it is always the event *of* a given situation) and supplementary (in that it is never part of, nor counted in, the situation: in set theoretical terms it is included, but does not belong) (*E* 92/*Eth* 68). The supplementary, situated event is crucial for understanding Badiou's post-theological politics.

For Nancy in *Une Pensée finie*, the event may be 'la venue à la présence de la chose' (*PF* 203),[61] but the essence of the event in Badiou's own account is pure disappearance, and the 'thing' (as truth) comes not as sense, within the encyclopedia of a situation, but as non-sense. In other words, it is basic for Badiou that ethics and true politics must rupture with ontology, not be a simple extension of how things already are; they are susceptible of no proof, derivable from no theory, and provable by no argument. The event 'demonstrates what is impossible for the count' (*PP* 129), and what is at stake for any truly political thought is counting as one what is uncounted (*AMP* 165/*MetP* 150). The Badiouian 'ought' is not founded on the ontology of a situation, but on a world's inexistent; it is a choice for things that are not over things that are (*SP* 59/*SPe* 46–7, quoting Romans 4: 17), such that the essence of the political is not a plurality of opinions but the prescription of a rupture with what there is (*AMP* 34/*MetP* 24). This ethical and political rupture with ontology is indispensible if Badiou's thinking is to be post-theological.

Emblematic of politics as rupture is Rousseau who, with the social contract, establishes the modern concept of politics (*EE* 380/*BE* 345; see also *PP* 13). The social contract is an event in Badiou's sense in so far as it is the announcement of the law without law, an illegitimate intervention (*EE* 254/*BE* 230), the possibility of the impossible and the ground of politics (*PLP* 78). The exemplarity of Rousseau is broader than this, however, for 'la politique commence par le même geste par lequel Rousseau dégage le fondement de l'inégalité : laisser de côté tous les faits' (*PLP* 78).[62] The political event, like Rousseau's contract, is not guided or circumscribed by the facts of the situation within which it is proclaimed.[63]

If Badiou's ethic of truths-as-events stresses the importance of rupture, his ethic of truths-as-processes emphasises the significance of faithfulness. If the Rousseauian contract is a political event, then the Jacobin 'constant effort of virtue' (*AMP* 148/*MetP* 133) is a faithful holding-oneself to the self-attesting sovereignty of the general will. This fidelity is not commanded or impelled by any fact of the situation, not deduced or observed, and the event itself is the product not of a fact, but of an interpretation (*PLP* 77), a poem (*PLP* 63), and therefore politics is much more of an art than a science (*PLP* 90), an art of the interpretative intervention. Under these conditions, an ethics of fidelity is not an ethics of alterity as that which is, but of the same as that which comes to be (*E* 46/*Eth* 27). Difference is what there is; the discourse of what ought to be is sameness.

For Badiou there is no single discourse of ethics, but as many situated ethics as there are situated truths:

> L'éthique n'existe pas. Il n'y a que l'éthique-*de* (de la politique, de l'amour, de la science, de l'art). [. . .] Une philosophie se propose de construire un *lieu de pensée* où les différents types subjectifs, données dans les vérités singulières de son temps, coexistent. Mais cette coexistence n'est pas une unification, et c'est pourquoi il est impossible de parler d'*une* éthique. (*E* 47)[64]

It would also be impossible to speak of there being only one ethical imperative, if that imperative were to enjoin any particular conduct. Nevertheless, there are indeed ethical imperatives in Badiou, but they do not mandate any particular truth, rather the courage and consistency with which a subject remains faithful to a truth: '*Aimez ce que jamais vous ne croirez deux fois*' (*E* 75),[65] 'Continuer!' (*E* 74),[66] and his own re-working of Lacan's 'ne pas céder sur son désir' (*E* 68),[67] where desire is the unknown par excellence, the unknown of the inexistent (*E* 68/*Eth* 47), or the void, or the impossible (PP 121). The import of the imperative translated more transparently into Badiou's own idiom is 'ne pas céder sur ce que de soi-même on ne sait pas' (*E* 68).[68] What is called for is a 'discipline of the real' (*Circ2* 48/*Pol* 57). We see a homology here between Nancy's and Badiou's ethics, for whereas Nancy's *ethos* does not dictate particular determinate ethics but addresses rather the way in which one is to hold oneself in relation to all ethics, so here Badiou's maxims concern not the quality of one truth in contrast to another, but the faithfulness with which any truth is to be followed.

5.3.2 The Decision

We have seen that Badiou rejects Lévinas's ethics of Absolute Alterity before ontology in favour of an ethics of the situated same that ruptures from within ontology. What remains to be investigated is the precise nature of that rupture, and this brings us to Kant. Badiou rejects Kant's ethics of judgment for an ethics of hypothesis and decision. In the opening pages of *L'Ethique*, Badiou opposes Kant's ethics of judgment to Hegel's ethics of the decision. For Kant's practical reason, 'l'éthique est principe de jugement des pratiques d'un Sujet, que ce sujet soit individuel ou collectif' (*E* 16).[69] For Hegel on the other hand, ethics (*Sittlichkeit*, as opposed to morality, *Moralität*) is an immediate, not a reflexive action, and ethics essentially consists in the immediate firmness of decision.

Badiou rejects the determinant judgment of Kant's second critique (*AMP* 26/*MetP* 16), with its fixing of maxims of action, and he rejects it not simply as bad politics, but as apolitical, for 'la discussion n'est politique qu'autant qu'elle se cristallise dans une décision' (*AMP* 24–5).[70] The sort of judgment required in politics is not the determinant judgment of the *Critique of Practical Reason* but the reflective judgment of taste in the *Critique of Judgment*:

> l'engagement politique a la même universalité réfléchissante que le jugement de goût pour Kant. L'engagement politique n'est inférable d'aucune preuve, et il n'est pas non plus l'effet d'un impératif. Il n'est ni déduit ni prescrit. L'engagement est *axiomatique*. (*PLP* 75–6)[71]

Badiou does not shy away from the way in which reflective judgment would seem to reorient politics as a matter of like or dislike: 'La politique se donne dans un jugement public où s'énonce si *ceci* – qui n'est pas un objet, mais un apparaître, un avoir-lieu – me plaît ou me déplaît' (*AMP* 26).[72] Furthermore, the function of the reflective judgment is not to proclaim whether a particular event is 'good' or 'bad', but to give consistency to the event that it interprets by proclaiming its name, and thereby to organise fidelity to the event (see *PLP* 78). This judgment is ethical in Badiou's sense, where ethics is the courage and persistence of holding to a truth.

The name for a political engagement that bears no causal or direct relation with any ontological situation is axiomatic (*PLP* 76). Such an engagement is heterogeneous to opinions and also to (existing) knowledge; it is militant and combative as it fights against every attempt to interrupt or corrupt it, to reduce it to the immediate interests of the human animal, to repress it or meet it with sarcasm (*Circ3* 40–1/*Pol* 133). Its reaction to all these attempts is to name them as enemies. Axiomatic political engagement rests not upon a proof or a deduction, but upon a hypothesis (*PLP* 75). This is its point both of maximal difference and of greatest proximity to the Nancean call. The difference is that, whereas the Nancean call issues an injunction that demands to be obeyed, there is no such call issued by the Badiouian event. That Badiou the atheist should choose the example of Christ's resurrection in *Saint Paul* illustrates how the event is not an event because it compels adherence, but by virtue of a subject's pure decision to be faithful to it. Thus when Badiou says that a truth addresses all, he means only that it is universalising, not that it issues a compelling demand. This is also the point of greatest proximity, however, because Nancy's call requires something like the Badiouian decision to ford the gap of compulsion that we identified above, whereas the Badiouian decision, we shall argue below, requires something like the Nancean demand if his atheism is not to undermine his Marxism.

The political tense for Badiou is the future anterior; it is a tense of organisation, as its double dimension suggests (*PLP* 105–6):

> Le pari politique présume que de l'interruption, de l'inadmissible, l'organisation va se déduire, selon des paris successifs actualisables, déployant ainsi au futur antérieur un radicalisme jamais barré par le roc de la loi. [...] Il s'agit d'organiser ceci, que d'un événement réel, donc absurde du point de la loi, peut procéder l'infini. (*PLP* 113)[73]

Badiou's political future anterior is not without a certain violence. Nothing that overcomes the finitude of the human animal by incorporating it into a subject and subordinating it to the eternity of Truth has ever arrived without anxiety, courage and justice, nor as a general rule without terror (*LM* 99/*LW* 88). It is democratic materialism which, assuming that there are no eternal truths but only bodies and languages, and that the only absolutes on the horizon of existence are life, suffering and finitude, can make no distinction between political terror (which attacks living bodies) and the 'terror of the matheme' (which attacks customary ways of thinking) (*LM* 98/*LW* 88).

The future anterior violence of political intervention is, in Badiou's way of thinking, the object of a wager:

> C'est ce type d'intervention que seul son effet qualifie, et qui est sous le péril de la nullité, que j'appelle intervention en pari. La politique est pascalienne de prétendre qu'il vaut mieux en tout cas parier, lorsqu'on est parvenu à l'extrême limite de ce que la sécurité d'analyse autorise, et que prolonge, comme je l'ai dit, l'intervention discriminante. (*PLP* 104; see also *PLP* 90)[74]

Politics is Pascalian not only in that it claims that, having arrived at the limit of all demonstration and proof, it is better to wager, but also in that the arrival at the limit of all demonstration and proof is inevitable:

> Le monde n'est pas plus transitif à Dieu pour Pascal que pour moi le social ne l'est à la politique. De même que les ensembles sociaux sont inconsist-

ants en politique, de même – pour Pascal – le «double infini» du Monde ne dessine nul tout d'où inférer Dieu. Le rapport subjectif à Dieu est dans l'aléatoire d'un pari (il faut aussi parier la politique communiste : vous ne la déduirez jamais du Capital). (*PLP* 86–7)[75]

The parallel with Pascal is, however, inexact, but not for the reason elicited by Jacques Rancière,[76] who critiques Badiou for confusing Pascal's wager and his understanding of miracles. The miracle, Rancière points out, is not for Pascal the object of a wager, but a certainty. But contra Rancière, it is not the 'miracle' – truth as event – that is at stake at this moment in Badiou's thought, but rather the future anterior of truth as process. Belief in God cannot be deduced from the facts and opinions of a situation, but that does not make it a miracle. What is wagered, if we follow Badiou's reconstruction, is that God, or communism, *will have been* and not, precisely not, that they *are*. The parallel with Pascal is inexact because Pascal's account of the relation between proof and faith is more nuanced than Badiou's. While Pascal considers metaphysical proofs of God as of little account,[77] he admits of other categories of proof that he does take to be convincing:

> Tous ceux qui ont prétendu connaître Dieu et le prouver sans J.-C. n'avaient que des preuves impuissantes. Mais pour prouver J.-C. nous avons les prophéties qui sont des preuves solides et palpables. Et ces prophéties étant accomplies et prouvées véritables par l'événement marquent la certitude de ces vérités et partant la preuve de la divinité de J.-C. En lui et par lui nous connaissons donc Dieu.[78]

Prophecies, which themselves come not from exterior proofs but through an inner and immediate feeling,[79] are none the less 'solid and palpable' when they are fulfilled and proved truthful. If, at a push, we can refer to prophecy itself as a future anterior wager in Pascal, then what Pascal refers to as its proof can no longer be spoken of as a 'to have been'. Neither metaphysical proof nor proof by prophecy can be spoken of as a wager for Pascal; the former is next to useless and the latter is solid and palpable.

Furthermore, just as Badiou's mathematical axiomatisation is motivated by the injunction of modernity, so also this political axiomatisation is itself the response to an experience. In *Théorie de la contradiction* Badiou describes the events of May 1968 as his Damascus road experience (*TC* 9), and in the course of an extemporaised debate in English with Simon Critchley in New York, Badiou explains the relation between this experience and his political thought:

> The great question for me is not really what being is. Ok, mathematics. I know all that and I can make subtle remarks about being qua being but my

fundamental question is a very simple one, quite small. This question is: What exactly is something new? What is novelty? What is creation? This is biographical because it is for me fundamentally the consequence of my experience in France of May '68, and its consequences. It's not an abstract question as I really underwent the experience of a complete change of life and experienced the conditions of an event. So I have to justify this experiment [author: experience?] philosophically. It's not a hard academic problem. My beginning was not: ok, I know what knowledge is, I have to know what truth is. This was not my way. My way was: I have had a living experience of what is something absolutely new and a vivid experience of when something happens, the very nature of which is novelty, something like the birth of a new subject. And I first experienced this point in my life and only after had to create the concepts to justify and clarify this point. (ONTS 361–2)

It would be incorrect to assume that the axioms governing Badiou's politics are chosen *ex nihilo*; they are considered responses to a powerful political experience, reverse engineered to facilitate and account for the sort of political event that the young Badiou experienced. Badiou's politics of the decision and event are his own 'adoration', responding to, and seeking to create the conditions for, the political event. The difference is the central role that language plays in Nancean adoration, contrasted with Badiou's premium on fidelity to the subtractive event.

There are further questions that need to be raised in relation to Badiou's position. It does not necessarily follow, from a critique of Lévinas's reliance on the *Tout-Autre*, that we need to dispense with an ethics of alterity. Simon Critchley draws his reader's attention to 'Blanchot's discreet critique of Lévinas' in which 'the absolute relation can *only* be understood socially', not in ethical terms as the trace of an Absolute Alterity or a Good beyond being, but as the alterity of the neutral, anonymous being of the *il y a* (there is).[80] Blanchot's otherness is shorn of the ethical and theological connotations it retains for Lévinas. Critchley himself follows Blanchot's lead and elaborates what he calls an 'atheist transcendence' based on 'the other's claim on me and how that claim changes and challenges my self-conception'.[81] But for Badiou this is robbing Peter to pay Paul. For Badiou, Kant drives the One from his ontology only to let it re-enter via his ethics. Here, Blanchot and Critchley seek to expel the divine from their ethics of finitude, but in that insistence on finitude they deny the 'nothing is inaccessible' that alone can guarantee the expulsion of the divine. Even if an ethics of finitude succeeds in not relying on God as its ultimate referent, such secularisation is in vain for it can never rid itself of the inaccessible God beyond its limits. There is no such thing as 'atheist transcendence'.

One further critique of Badiou's politics comes once more from Rancière, who claims to discern in it a latent Christianity. The model of Badiouian faithfulness, Rancière argues, must be the Christ event: 'La fidélité dont la nécessité se déduit de l'indécidable du geste mallarméen vient en effet trouver son modèle dans la mise en circulation d'un événement bien particulier, l'événement de la croix'.[82] The Christ event, Rancière argues, enters the lists against a God of the philosophers which allows no move from philosophy to politics, no re-founding of philosophy after a political impetus. Rancière reverses Pascal's dictum: instead of Plato preparing us for Christianity,[83] for Badiou it is Pascal, with his rejection of the God of the philosophers in favour of the 'God of Abraham, Isaac and Jacob' who prepares us for Badiou's Platonism.[84] The folly of the cross marks out the place of this new Platonism, lifting politics' submission to 'ordinary' democratic means. Rancière concludes:

> Le prix de l'opération, il me semble, est que cette politique mathématisée ne puisse être qu'ecclésiale dans sa forme et suspendue à une événementialité autoréférentielle, soit celle du miracle autour duquel l'Eglise s'organise, soit l'exercice de la récusation interminable de tous les noms sous lesquels la politique dans son ordinaire se présente.[85]

This charge, in so far as it evokes the supposed miraculous nature of the Badiouian event, falls in with similar critiques of Badiou in neglecting the dual nature of Badiouian truth as event and process, with which we dealt in Chapter 3. In so far as it claims that the unstated paradigm for Badiouian truth – both its event and the process of faithfulness – is the Christ event, then Badiou's elaboration of his four truth conditions coupled with his insistence on being able to use religious terms in his own secular context leave Rancière's reading vulnerable to the charge that it is reasoning *post hoc ergo propter hoc*: if Badiouian truth resembles a certain reading of the Christian tradition, as Badiou in his book on Saint Paul is all too ready to acknowledge it does, we cannot from this conclude that truth adopts or assumes all the features of that tradition, most saliently its theism. It does not *necessarily* follow, but might it still none the less be the case? Badiou's own account of the event in set theoretical terms in *L'Etre et l'événement* and his further elaboration in terms of the inexistent and points in *Logiques des mondes* provide a robust non-theistic reading of politics that leaves Rancière's charge speculative at best. As we shall see in the following chapter, it is not at this point that Badiou's politics is vulnerable to the charge of a latent theology, but in its faith in the goodness of equality.

The question of whether Badiou's future anterior construction of the truth-process is in fact a latent eschatology is raised by, among others, Quentin Meillassoux.[86] Noting that the vast majority of Marxists have renounced eschatology as a religious residue, Meillassoux singles Badiou out as isolating Marxism's eschatological moment and disseminating it among the four truth conditions: 'Au lieu que la critique dissolve chez Badiou l'illusion religieuse de l'eschatologie, l'eschatologie devenue irréligieuse de l'événement déploie sa puissance critique sur le présent terne de nos renoncements ordinaires' (TES 10–11).[87] Meillassoux's characterisation of Badiou's eschatology as 'irreligious' (rather than, say, atheist or secular) is not to be taken here as suggesting a compromise with the theological.[88]

Meillassoux is, however, following in the footsteps of the many who underestimate the importance of incremental effort and process in Badiou's notion of the event. In *Saint Paul* Badiou is careful to distinguish his reading of Paul from judicial eschatology: 'Paul semble plutôt caractériser l'espérance comme simple impératif de la continuation, principe de ténacité, d'obstination' (SP 99).[89] Nevertheless, as we shall explore more in the final chapter Badiou's politics does share the inevitability of the eschatological vision (PE 21), and if historical inevitability is in and of itself eschatological, then Badiou's thought does have an eschatological dimension. If Badiou's thought is eschatological on this score then so is Meillassoux's own, however, for as we have seen he insists that the world of justice is the only world that can succeed the third world of thought (ID 296). We see no warrant to count every inevitability as an eschatology, and so we do not see in Badiou's politics (or in Meillassoux's) either a religious eschatology or what Meillassoux calls the irreligious eschatology of the event.

A further critique of a politics of the interpretative event is that it makes political events too rare, especially when compared with a politics of the ontological demand, or call, and that Badiou's politics struggles to escape the charge of quietism or, in the terms of our investigation in this book, asceticism. Whereas for Badiou the sequences that lead to political events are rare (AMP 115/MetP 101; EE 379/BE 344) for Critchley:

> I see politics as everywhere, as being a really quite banal, or rather mundane, call to forms of mobilization that begin from the place where you are, where you are working (or where you are not working), the place where you are active and where you are thinking[90]

Similarly, Slavoj Žižek identifies in Badiou's thought the 'quietist patience' of 'awaiting the unpredictable arrival of a not-to-be-actively-precipitated "x" sparking genuine change',[91] and Andrew Gibson discerns a 'pathos of intermittency' in the all-too-rare events that punctuate periods in which we are captive to the idea that nothing begins or is going to begin (*S* 113/*Cen* 140). For Badiou's part, however, simply defining politics into being by widening the scope of what we call 'political' is hardly a solution to the rarity of politics. However rare it is, politics has existed, exists and will exist (*AMP* 167/*MetP* 152). As for the charge that the infrequency of an event may lead to a political quietism as we wait for the event to arrive, Badiou once more stresses the importance of process as well as event:

> Cette vision de ma philosophie qui tend à identifier purement et simplement vérité et événement n'est qu'un court-circuit. Dans toute situation il existe des processus fidèles à un événement antérieur. On n'a pas affaire à l'attente désespérée d'un événement miraculeux. Il s'agit plutôt de tenir jusqu'au bout, jusqu'à saturation, ce que l'on a pu tirer de l'événement antérieur et d'être ainsi préparé autant que faire se peut à la réception subjective de ce qui se produira inévitablement. (*PE* 21)[92]

But what does it mean to be 'prepared', if we are not to wait for the event as a grace (*PE* 22)? Badiou's response to this question, like Meillassoux's account of the relation between the dice throw and hyperchaotic change, leaves itself open to the charge of being too weak:

> « Être préparé à un événement » cela veut dire être dans une disposition subjective de reconnaissance de la nouvelle possibilité. Puisque l'événement est nécessairement imprévisible, n'étant pas dans la loi des possibilités dominantes, préparer l'événement, c'est être disposé à l'accueillir. [. . .] Être préparé à un événement, c'est être dans un état d'esprit où l'ordre du monde, les puissances dominantes n'ont pas le contrôle absolu des possibilités. [. . .] L'autre façon d'être préparé, connexe à la première, c'est la critique de l'ordre établi. (*PE* 22–3)[93]

Preparedness, then, equates to being disposed to recognising and welcoming necessarily unforeseeable, unheard-of possibilities, to cultivating a state of mind where the way things are is not the way they need to be, and to critiquing the way things are. In Badiou's case it is important that we understand this preparedness, however, in the context of eternal truths: the universalising event (for example: Spartacus) has already happened and there is always already a process of fidelity to the event underway.

In addition the rarity of the event, Critchley also argues for a more circumspect understanding of the political in the face of what elsewhere he calls Badiou's 'heroism of the decision':[94]

> what I suspect in Badiou is the *seduction of a great politics*, the event that would, in Nietzsche's words, break history in two. But perhaps the epoch of great politics, like the epoch of great art for Heidegger and Hegel, is over. Perhaps. And perhaps that is a good thing. Perhaps we have had enough

of the virile, Promethean politics of the will, the empty longing for total revolution.[95]

Over against this 'great politics', Critchley himself concludes that 'perhaps we have to content ourselves with smaller actions and smaller victories, an everyday and heroically anti-heroic militancy'.[96] However, this seems to be not an alternative to Badiou's politics, but a subset of it. We have seen that Badiou is quite happy to accommodate modest gestures of fidelity to the event, and once more it seems that Critchley is joining those who focus on Badiou's understanding of truth as event and neglect truth as process. Furthermore, the charge of a heroism of the decision is one that Badiou, for his part, welcomes:

> On me dit quelquefois que je ne vois dans la philosophie qu'un moyen de rétablir, contre l'apologie contemporaine de l'ordinaire et du futile, les droits de l'héroïsme. Pourquoi pas? Cependant, l'héroïsme ancien prétend justifier la vie par le sacrifice. Mon vœu est de le faire exister par la joie affirmative que procure universellement le suivi des conséquences. Disons qu'à l'héroïsme épique de qui donne sa vie, succède l'héroïsme mathématique de qui la crée point par point. (LM 536)[97]

This justification of heroism from *Logiques des mondes* provides us with a fitting summary of Badiou's politics, with its ineradicable heroism, but nevertheless a heroism not exclusively of the grand gesture, but of the 'point by point' creation of the 'life' of truths.

It might be thought that the way to a post-theological integration is through a syncretism of call and decision, for it would seem that what Badiou's atheism is lacking is the imperative of a Nancean demand, and what Nancy's atheology is lacking is the trenchancy of a Badiouian decision. Such is the approach of Simon Critchley in *Infinitely Demanding*. Critchley tries to bring together Badiouian fidelity with an understanding of demand and response closer to Nancy's. This eclecticism leads him to some philosophical shoehorning, trying to marry aspects of systems of thought which, if not utterly incompatible, are not shown to cohere. He claims that 'the logic of the event in Badiou is that an event is that which makes a demand on a subject, *of* which the subject approves and *to* which it decides to bind itself, to be faithful'.[98] But in Badiou's axiomatic politics it is far from clear that the event makes a demand; it is addressed to all, but not as an imperative. The Badiouian event does not interpellate me in the same way as singular plural being. To be fit for Critchley's purpose, an already-event would have to interpellate a not-yet-subject, but this would undermine Badiou's future anterior, truth as process, and the heterogeneity of the event to the situation. There is no easy way of fusing Nancean demand with the Badiouian decision. Furthermore, such a fusion would not be the last word on post-theological integration. The decision does not make the call compelling (that would violate the axiomatic cornerstone of Badiou's thought), and the call does not make the decision inevitable (that would violate the principle of freedom by which Nancy seeks to avoid parasitising religion). Bringing together call and decision in these terms, even if that were possible, would not bring about a post-theological integration.

CONCLUSION

The aim of this chapter has been to probe how our three thinkers seek to draw criteria for thinking the political from their respective approaches to the post-theological, and to evaluate to what extent they can integrate the political positions that they testify to holding into those reworkings. In Meillassoux's case the claim that universal justice is the only World that can follow the current world of thought is ultimately unconvincing, and the injunction to act in accordance with that becoming therefore lacks force. Hyperchaos, the condition of Meillassouxian faith in the God who inexists, seems to pose insurmountable problems for his desire to develop the consequences of a desire for universal justice in the direction of concrete action in the present.

For Nancy, while *ethos* obviates the need for a reconciliation of ontology and ethics, the call, based as it is on an appeal to (or on the appeal of) singular plural being, fails ultimately to provide a compelling justification for regarding equality as politically normative. It is difficult to see how the call could have normative value without it becoming parasitic on the structure of divine injunction, and without such force it risks atheistic asceticism. Furthermore, the struggle against inequality perversely relies on the continuing existence of what it seeks to eradicate; it is unable to see beyond the horizon of resistance.

In Badiou's case, it is far from convincing to claim that his politics is parasitic on the Christ event, on the Pascalian wager, or on Christian eschatology, but his understanding of the political in relation to the event is ascetic measured by the yardstick of the political change he seeks to bring about. As in our discussion of the principle of intelligibility in the previous chapter, we are returned to an inaugural experience, compelling for the one whose experience it is (in this case, Badiou's own experience of May 1968) but lacking universal compulsion. Part of our task in the final chapter will be to trace this motif of an original experience or desire more thoroughly through all of our three thinkers, and reflect on its implications for their post-theological thinking.

Though the question of the criteriology of the political is partially addressed by each position, there is in each case a weakness that leaves the respective political commitments ultimately undernourished by the post-theological thinking in whose soil they grow. In the final chapter we shall continue this investigation by focusing more closely on the question of universal justice, probing what measures our three thinkers can bring to bear in their approaches to fashioning a notion of the universal as they seek to develop their various post-theological integrations.

NOTES

1. Jean-Paul Sartre, *L'Existentialisme est un humanisme* (Paris: Gallimard, 1970), pp. 36–7; 'if I have excluded God the Father, there must be somebody to invent values' (Sartre, 'Existentialism and humanism', p. 44).
2. In these final two chapters we continue to use 'atheism' in two related senses, a narrow sense in which atheism is parasitic upon theism and both are rejected in favour of atheology or philosophy, and a broader, looser sense in which 'atheism' covers the three positions under discussion inasfar as they each seek to think 'without God'. The context will sufficiently determine in which sense the term is being used in each instance.
3. Critchley, *Infinitely Demanding*, p. 8.
4. Hume, *A Treatise of Human Nature*, p. 521.
5. Fyodor Dostoyevsky, *The Brothers Karamazov* (Oxford: Oxford University Press, 1998), p. 87.
6. Jacques Lacan, *Le Séminaire, livre XVII*, p. 139; 'I have long remarked that to the phrase of old father Karamozov, if God is dead, everything is permitted, then the conclusion imposing itself within the text of our experience is that the response to God is dead, is nothing is any longer permitted' (Lacan, 'A theoretical introduction', p. 15).
7. Schmitt, *Political Theology*, p. 36.
8. The nature of Schmitt's claim is unclear. For a discussion of what is at stake in the different interpretations, see de Vries, *Religion and Violence*, pp. 218–19.
9. Hent de Vries, 'Introduction: before, around and beyond the theologico-political', in de Vries and Sullivan (eds), *Political Theologies*, p. 1.
10. 'to believe from now on, is no longer to have faith, is no longer to believe in the law, it is to hope for a justice *worthy of this name*' (author's translation).
11. 'the truth of the Good, as the Fourth World, does not designate a reality or an impossibility or a controllable possibility: *the Good designates the truth of a possibility that is not controllable*' (author's translation).

12.
> philosophy always begins with a postulate that may very well be impossible to demonstrate, that may very well be false, or ideological, namely: value is not simply a human invention, value is the discovery of a truth concerning the world, the extra-human real, and this truth must be found uniquely by reason, without the intervention of a transcendent revelation. (Author's translation)

13. 'it will happen, or not, through accepting or refusing time as we have thought it' (author's translation).
14. It is hard not to conclude that Meillassoux's gamer does indeed see coincidence as a sign, precisely as a sign of chance, ascribing to it an aleatory explanation in the same way that a religious believer might ascribe it a providential explanation. Meillassoux's argument from miracles relies on just such an ascription, seeing the 'miraculous' as a sign of hyperchaos.
15. 'before contesting this appearing *ex nihilo* because of its fantastical character, you should wonder if it is not even more marvellous to confuse matter with someone asleep' (author's translation).
16. 'if another world appears, it can only be the World of justice. Because every other appearing would only constitute a "Monstrous" variation on the three previous Worlds' (author's translation).
17. 'nothing can surpass man' (author's translation).
18. Brown, 'On *After Finitude*'.
19. Peter Hallward, 'Anything is possible', p. 55.
20. Brown, 'On *After Finitude*'.
21. '*the condition for the arrival of the universal is thus that it be actively desired*' (author's translation).
22. 'We can thus compare the free act to a dice throw – a dice throw that does not guarantee luck, but which alone makes it possible' (author's translation).
23. Brown, 'On *After Finitude*'.
24.
> we should know that in the move from a thinking, let us say of being, of essence, or of principles – it matters little here – to a politics and an ethics, the consequence is never good (why do we systematically forget the massive and enduring adherence of so many theorists of the 'philosophy of values' to the Nazi regime?). (*EF* 171)

25. 'our question is through and through the question of the Good in a world without end or without singular ends' (*CWG* 64).
26. This point is made by Philip Armstrong in *Jean-Luc Nancy* (p. 125).
27. Nancy intriguingly informs his readers (*ESP* 87 n.1/*BSP* 201 n.56) of his intention to publish a volume with the title *L'Ethique originaire*.
28. 'There is no difference between the ethical and the ontological: the "ethical" exposes what the "ontological" disposes' (*BSP* 99).

29. The equivalence is not foreign to Nancy's thought, as we see from a discussion of art in *Les Muses*:

> C'est un devoir pour l'art de mettre fin à l'« art ». Mais ce devoir ne dresse pas, sur un mode puritain, une « éthique » contre une « esthétique ». Il ne relève pas non plus de ce qu'on serait tenté d'appeler une « éthique de l'esthétique ». Ce devoir énonce le sens comme ethos. (*Mu* 68)
>
> It is a duty for art to put an end to 'art.' But this duty does not, in some puritan mode, erect an 'ethics' against an 'aesthetics.' Nor does it stem from what one would be tempted to call an 'ethics of the aesthetic.' This duty utters *sense* as *ethos*. (*Mus* 38)

30. The word 'teleonomy' was first coined by Colin S. Pittendrigh 'in order to emphasize that recognition and description of end-directedness does not carry a commitment to Aristotelian teleology as an efficient causal principle' (C. S. Pittendrigh, 'Adaptation, natural selection and behavior', in A. Roe and George Gaylord Simpson, eds, *Behavior and Evolution*, New Haven, CT: Yale University Press, 1958, pp. 390–416). It is notably taken up by Jacques Monod in *Le Hasard et la nécessité* (Paris: Éditions du Seuil, 1970).
31. The comment comes in the context of a close reading of Heidegger's *Lettre sur l'humanisme*, trans. Roger Munier (Paris: Aubier, 1963), p. 155.
32. 'To keep, to protect sense from being filled, as well as from being emptied – that is *ethos*' (*DisDC* 122).
33.
> One could say that in freedom there is the ontological imperative, or being as intimation – but under the condition of adding that this is without commandment [. . .] or that the commandment is lost in freedom's abandonment to itself, all the way to caprice and chance. (*EF* 155)

34. Crowley, *L'Homme sans*. Simon Critchley's exploration of these themes in *Infinitely Demanding* leads to the circumspect conclusion that 'we have to accept that the universality of the moral law should interest us without being able to explain the cause of that interest' (p. 33). Critchley eventually argues, along with Badiou, for the necessity of an intervention, a decision, to motivate ethics (Critchley, *Infinitely Demanding*, pp. 49, 128).
35. Crowley, *L'Homme sans*, p. 19; author's emphasis; 'if the latter [an egalitarian politics] is definitely not *given* by any ontology, it can none the less very well be *called* by every ontology that posits, as we like to put it these days, the equality of each one with each one' (author's translation).
36. Crowley, *L'Homme sans*, p. 95.
37. Crowley, *L'Homme sans*, pp. 66–7.
38. Crowley, *L'Homme sans*, p. 19.
39. Crowley, *L'Homme sans*, p. 171.

40. Crowley, *L'Homme sans*, pp. 71–2.
41. Crowley, *L'Homme sans*, p. 116.
42. Crowley, *L'Homme sans*, p. 171.
43. Critchley, *Infinitely Demanding*, pp. 10–11.
44. Critchley, *Very Little*, p. 28.
45. Critchley, *Infinitely Demanding*, p. 9.
46. Critchley, *Infinitely Demanding*, p. 55.
47. Bosteels, *Alain Badiou*, pp. 192–3.
48. 'how can we avoid enthusiasm being carried off with the death of God?' (author's translation).
49.
    It is a fervour for multiple and singular existence: for each one, therefore, each in turn, for each one to the exclusion of the others, and yet for all, *de jure*, and *de facto* at least for several who respond to several modes of this unique and polymorphous 'love'. (Author's translation)
50. 'To speak of "sense" and "truth" in the midst of military agitation, geopolitical calculations, suffering, and the grimaces of stupidity or of lying, is not "idealistic", it is to border on the thing itself' (author's translation; the translation of *CA* in *CC* begins on page 25 of the French original).
51. Crowley, *L'Homme sans*, p. 171.
    These beings without qualities, without parts, without qualifications, exiled from the process of political subjectivisation, challenge *by that very token*, the formalism of existing human rights, as they demand *by that very token*, that the ontological equality declared by finitude be unceasingly verified and realised. (Author's translation)
52. Critchley, *Infinitely Demanding*, p. 132.
53. Critchley, *Infinitely Demanding*, p. 147.
54. Critchley, *Infinitely Demanding*, p. 147.
55. Badiou, 'On Simon Critchley's *Infinitely Demanding*', p. 161.
56. Badiou, 'On Simon Critchley's *Infinitely Demanding*', p. 161.
57. 'quite obviously the ethical name for God' (*Eth* 22).
58. 'For a single thought is far greater than any judgment' (*Pol* 35).
59. 'From what source will man draw the strength to be the immortal that he is? What shall be the destiny of thought, which we know very well to be affirmative invention or nothing at all?' (*Eth* 14; translation altered).
60. In a way that echoes Jean-Jacques Lecercle's reading of Badiou on literature, Simon Critchley reads Badiou's accounts of Kant and Lévinas as 'necessary caricatures' necessitated by the fact that 'philosophy works through the leverage of straw men and women' (Baldwin and Haeffner, '"Fault Lines"', p. 304). In a more Badiouian idiom, we discern in these readings an example of the politics of the decision itself, the forcing of a 'point', a violent reduction of detail in order to present a binary choice: either Lévinas/Kant or Badiou.

61. 'the coming into presence of the thing' (*BTP* 171).
62. 'politics begins with the same gesture by which Rousseau uncovers the foundation of inequality: leaving aside all the facts' (author's translation).
63. In 'Philosophie sans conditions' Nancy gestures at a proximity between *ethos* as receiving-oneself and holding-oneself and Badiou's fidelity. Expounding on *ethos* as 'the art of holding to that which, in general, allows us to keep going with composure (*de tenir et d'avoir de la tenue*)' (*CM* 134/*CWG* 90; translation altered), Nancy juxtaposes this definition with Badiou's Ahmed the philosopher in his determination to 'Tenir ce point! Le trouver et le tenir! La philosophie n'a pas d'autre but! Que chacun trouve son point et le tienne!' (*PSC* 79/*PWC* 49, quoting *AP* 101). The difference between Badiou's fidelity and Nancy's holding-oneself as *ethos* is that Badiouian fidelity is faithful not to an ontological condition but precisely to that which inexists within a situation, and it is a decision that breaks with the ontological, not a recognition of our ontological condition.
64.
    Ethics does not exist. There is only the *ethic-of* (of politics, of love, of science, of art). [...] A philosophy sets out to construct a *space of thought* in which the different subjective types, expressed by the singular truths of its time, coexist. But this coexistence is not a unification – that is why it is impossible to speak of *one* Ethics. (*Eth* 28)

65. 'love what you will never believe twice' (*Eth* 52).
66. 'Keep going!' (*Eth* 52).
67. 'do not give up on your desire' (*Eth* 47)
68. 'do not give up on that part of yourself that you do not know' (*Eth* 47).
69. 'Ethics is the principle that judges the practice of a Subject, be it individual or collective' (*Eth* 2).
70. 'debate is political only to the extent that it crystallizes in a decision' (*MetP* 15).
71. 'political engagement has the same reflexive universality as Kant's judgment of taste. Political engagement cannot be inferred from any proof, and neither is it the effect of an imperative. It is neither deduced nor prescribed. Engagement is *axiomatic*' (author's translation).
72. 'Politics can be found in a public judgment which states whether *this* – which is not an object, but an appearing, a taking-place – pleases me or displeases me' (*MetP* 16).
73.
    The political wager presumes that organisation will be deduced from interruption, from the inadmissible, according to successive actualisable wagers, thus unfolding in the future anterior a radicalism that is never blocked by the rock of the law. [...] This is what must be organised: that the infinite can proceed from an event that is real, and thus absurd from the point of view of the law. (Author's translation)

74.
> It is this type of intervention, qualified only by its effect and imperilled by nullity, that I call a wager-intervention. Politics is Pascalian when it claims that it is always better to wager when you have arrived at the farthest limit of what is allowed by the security of analysis, and of what is extended by the intervention that discriminates, as I have said. (Author's translation)

75.
> The world is no more transitive to God for Pascal than the social is to politics for me. In the same way that social sets are inconsistent in politics, for Pascal the 'double infinite' of the World does not plot any whole form which God can be inferred. The subjective relation to God is in the unpredictability of a wager (Communist politics must also be wagered: you will never deduce it from Capital). (Author's translation)

76. Jacques Rancière, Untitled discussion', pp. 220–1.
77. Blaise Pascal, *Pensées* [Lafuma] 190/[Brunschvicg] 503.
78. Pascal, *Pensées*, 189/547; see also 355/706.

> All those who have claimed to know God and prove his existence without Jesus Christ have only had futile proofs to offer. But to prove Christ we have the prophecies which are solid and palpable proofs. By being fulfilled and proved true by the event, these prophecies show that these truths are certain and ths proves Jesus is divine. In him and through him, therefore, we know God. (*Pensées*, trans. Krailsheimer, p. 56)

Krailsheimer follows Lafuma's numbering.

79. Pascal, *Pensées*, 328/732.
80. Critchley, *Very Little*, p. 82.
81. Critchley, *Very Little*, p. 82.
82. Rancière, Untitled discussion, p. 220. 'The faithfulness whose necessity is deduced from the undecidable of the Mallarméan gesture in fact finds its model in the circulating of a very particular event, the event of the cross' (author's translation).
83. Pascal, *Pensées*, 612/219.
84. Rancière, Untitled discussion, p. 223.
85. Rancière, Untitled discussion, p. 223.

> The price of the operation, it appears to me, is that the form of this mathematised politics can be nothing other than ecclesial in its form and suspended on a self-referential eventuality, either that of the miracle around which the Church organises itself, or the exercise of the never-ending challenging of all the names by which ordinary politics presents itself. (Author's translation)

86. The question is also pursued by Liam A. O'Donnell in 'Saint Paul: apostle, militant, communist'. O'Donnell identifies Badiou's 'persistence of the revolutionary demand' as a secular eschatology (p. 349). We reject this eschatological misreading of the demand for the same reasons that we distance ourselves from Rancière.
87. 'Instead of critique dissolving the religious illusion of eschatology for Badiou, the now irreligious eschatology of the event unfolds its critical power in the drab present of our usual renunciations' (author's translation).
88. In 'L'Inexistence divine', Meillassoux uses the term *irréligieux* to suggest a true metaphysical atheism, not a position parasitic on religious categories. For example:

> Ainsi, les philosophies « héritières » qui se veulent aujourd'hui des pensées de l'athéisme le plus intransigeant de la finitude assumée, sont en vérité des reprises radicalisées de ces thèses dont la fin effective n'est qu'une légitimation du religieux dans sa pleine irrationalité. C'est donc la métaphysique, et non l'antimétaphysique, qui est en son fond une entreprise résolument irréligieuse. (ID 274)

> Thus the philosophies styled as 'descendants', that want to be the most intransigent opponents of assumed finitude in contemporary atheistic thought, are in truth a radicalised return of these ideas issuing in effect only in a legitimation of religion in all its irrationality. Thus it is metaphysics, and not anti-metaphysics, that is at bottom a resolutely irreligious enterprise. (Author's translation)

89. 'Paul seems instead to characterize hope as a simple imperative of continuation, a principle of tenacity, of obstinacy' (*SPe* 93).
90. Baldwin and Haeffner, ' "Fault Lines" ', p. 296.
91. Žižek, *In Defense of Lost Causes*, p. 391.
92.

> This vision of my philosophy which tends purely and simply to identify truth with event is nothing but a short circuit. In every situation there are processes faithful to a preceding event. It has nothing to do with the hopeless wait for a miraculous event. Rather it has to do with holding on to the end, to the point of saturation, what we have been able to draw from the preceding event, and in this way to be prepared as much as possible for the subjective reception of what will inevitably occur. (Author's translation)

93.

> 'To be prepared for an event' means to be in a subjective disposition of recognising the new possibility. Since the event is of necessity unforeseeable as it is not in the law of dominant possibilities, to prepare for the event is to be disposed to welcome it. [. . .] To be prepared for an event

is to be in a state of mind where the order of the world, the dominant powers, do not have absolute control over what is possible. [...] The other way of being prepared, connected to the first, is the critique of the established order. (Author's translation)

94. Critchley, *Infinitely Demanding*, pp. 47–8.
95. Critchley, 'Demanding approval', p. 27.
96. Critchley, 'Demanding approval', p. 27.
97.
I am sometimes told that I see in philosophy only a means to re-establish, against the contemporary apologia of the futile and the everyday, the rights of heroism. Why not? Having said that, ancient heroism claimed to justify life through sacrifice. My wish is to make heroism exist through the affirmative joy which is universally generated by following consequences through. We could say that the epic heroism of the one who gives his life is supplanted by the mathematical heroism of the one who creates life, point by point. (*LW* 514)

98. Critchley, *Infinitely Demanding*, p. 48; see also Critchley, 'Comment ne pas céder sur son désir', p. 223.

6. The Politics of the Post-Theological II: Justice

> Plaisante justice qu'une rivière borne.[1]

Having considered in general terms how Badiou, Nancy and Meillassoux understand the relation of their post-theological ontologies to matters ethical and political, in this final chapter we take one political idea, namely justice, to serve as a case study of post-theological integration. In interrogating how our three thinkers understand and deploy the notion of justice we shall be asking whether their respective treatments succeed in avoiding both parasitism (seeking to be rid of God in ways that assume or require God) and asceticism (renouncing or retrenching, along with God, the scope of the theological notion of justice). Furthermore, can post-theological thought appropriate the notion of justice in a way that adequately addresses what Simon Critchley identifies as 'the felt inadequacy of official secular conceptions of morality'?[2] In particular, the question we shall pursue is whether post-theological integrations can secure a notion of universal justice.

6.1 MEILLASSOUX: UNIVERSAL JUSTICE AND RESURRECTION

Meillassoux's discussion of the question of justice in 'L'éthique divine', the third section of 'L'Inexistence divine', begins with a denial: justice is inaccessible both to theism and to atheism. Universal justice is absurd for the atheist, who has no hope of justice for those now dead, but it is also absurd for the believer, who can only hope for justice from a God whose reign is manifestly not one of justice (ID 286). There is no religion or system of morality, Meillassoux insists, that is not prey either to the atheist's problem, or to the theist's. The believer desires justice, but he must sacrifice his reason on the altar of that desire; the virtuous atheist, while keeping his lucidity, has to sacrifice the demand for universal justice. He may try to mask his mutilation of justice, but if the Good is not, there is only pleasure and pain (ID 353). The problem common to both positions is 'cette absurdité bâtarde, mi-religieuse, mi-athée, de la désespérante pérennité des lois de la nature, indifférentes à notre soif de justice' (ID 6).³

6.1.1 The Philosophical Divine

Unwilling to sacrifice the hope for universal justice, even for the dead, Meillassoux splits the horns of a/theism's unsatisfying dilemma by introducing the position he calls 'the philosophical divine' (ID 371). Like the religious believer, the philosopher believes in God, and can therefore claim as her own the religious hope for universal justice; like the atheist, the philosopher denies the existence of God, and so is not saddled with having to charge current injustice to God's account (ID 384). The philosopher is not caught in the 'spectral dilemma' of having 'either to despair of another life for the dead, or to despair of a God who has let such deaths take place' (SD 265). The difference between the atheist and the philosopher is this: whereas the atheist accepts that regret is on his side of the argument (regret that there will be no justice for the dead, and therefore no universal justice), the philosopher admits no such thing. More than this, the philosopher moves the burden of regret to the religious position, for no-one, Meillassoux conjectures, can wish to be saved by an actually existing God charged with all the horrors of history.

Meillassoux's philosophy, as we have seen, embraces a messianic hope for justice. Unlike the nihilist, who hopes for justice in another life, the philosopher hopes for immortality in this life (immortality, this time, in the sense of living for ever) and does not seek any alibi to defer or lift that hope, not even the alibi of engaging in the struggle for it (such that, implicitly, the struggle becomes more important than the goal, as is the risk for positions that simply resist injustice). Religion and atheism alike rely on the identification of this life with Pascalian wretchedness, but the philosopher affirms that the fight for justice – with its necessary condition of injustice and wretchedness – is not an essential condition of existence (ID 358).

But in what sense does the philosopher hope for immortality in this life? To begin with, the principle of factiality allows immortality to be thought as an immediate virtuality among the hyperchaotic, non-totalisable infinity of other virtualities, and as a real – that is to say, non-contradictory – possibility (ID 290). Everything that is logically possible is really possible, including the rebirth of bodies (ID 290). Furthermore, if the hope for justice is out of all proportion with the current state of the world, that simply reflects the disproportionality (*démesure*) of hyperchaotic becoming (ID 339).

Meillassoux couches this hope in his teleological narrative of four Worlds that we began to explore in the previous chapter. The fourth World, the World of Justice and the world of the rebirth of man, is the world in which humanity acquires immortality, which Meillassoux argues is the only life worthy of the human condition. Foreclosing any poetic reading of this desire, he insists that rebirth is not a metaphor; the actual rebirth of bodies is the only condition that makes justice thinkable (ID 297). If there is to be universal justice we must be born again, because only the rebirth of man makes possible universal justice, up to and including the injustice of a life snatched away (ID 292).

But we must question this conclusion. Does rebirth efface any injustice done in this present life? If I am raped (for example), no prolongation of life will efface the injustice of that violation. If I live for an eternity in bliss I was still raped, and that rape was still unjust. Justice requires more, in remedying an injustice, than the subsequent absence of wrong. Surely an equally possible solution, on Meillassoux's absolute contingency, and one that satisfies the condition of universal justice more fully, would be for my understanding of what is just and unjust to be hyperchaotically transformed such that the rape would not, after all, be unjust. Only by such means could the rape be effaced as an injustice. Otherwise, injustice remains, regardless of what does or does not succeed it in a span of time however long. Such a solution would only be thought repulsive if we were to retain our current understanding of justice which, in the nature of the case, we would not.

When it comes to how such a justice will arrive, Meillassoux's occupation of religion's territory is even more pronounced. He begins from the position that religion's desire for justice is a desire for the wholly other, and as such is unthinkable; any inability to take man as the end of action is religious (ID 328). Meillassoux's hope for universal justice is therefore human: there is a human mediator between our current situation and universal justice. This mediator is called variously by Meillassoux the Child of Man, or God, and s/he receives the power (from where?) to produce the rebirth necessary for justice by the same appearing (*surgissement*) *ex nihilo* that brought life from matter (World two) and rational intelligence from life (World three). It is this progression to which Meillassoux appeals in justifying why this particular *ex nihilo* appearing should be desired. What humanity aspires to is 'enfanter Dieu, comme la matière a enfanté la vie et la vie la pensée' (ID

380),[4] a desire that expresses itself in terms of the ill-defined dice-throw discussed in the previous chapter. We are God's ancestors, and not his creatures: 'Dieu est précisément le surgissement de l'étant factuel par qui advient la renaissance en vue de la justice' (ID 381).[5] God will be the 'last-born' (*le dernier-né*) of humanity. This Christic aspect of the universal is in no way a rational religion, Meillassoux stresses, but an immanent ethic radically stripped of religiosity; it is not parasitic, but an appropriation of religious motifs within a frame rigorously without God. The Child of Man assures the impossibility of a religious vision of appearing; s/he teaches that her or his power is not the manifestation of a transcendence, but a contingency.

The Child of Man has, according to Meillassoux, five qualities: 1) goodness: its action is guided by the universal; 2) omniscience: it possesses knowledge of the singular becoming of the living and the dead (in other words, it knows the truth of absolute contingency); 3) omnipotence: it possesses the power to achieve the rebirth of the dead by an act of the will (*volontairement*); 4) it possesses the power once and for all to abolish its own omniscience and omnipotence; and 5) the mediator in fact does divest itself of these powers once and for all, after the rebirth has been brought about, thereby submitting the power of contingency that it has received to the will to become a man among men, equal to all others.

These five stages trace for Meillassoux an inverted Christic Hegelianism. In Hegel's notion of God in the *Science of Logic*, the infinity of God requires that He pass into finitude, becoming contingent, limited and incarnate, in order that finitude itself be overcome as the limit of the infinite. But the inclusion of the finite in the infinite cannot be definitive, because then the infinite would be finite. The finite must be a *moment* of the infinite. The Christ must die, in order to assure the dialectic movement infinite – finite – infinite, or God – man – God (see ID 133). In this Hegelian conception, contingency is subordinated to the real necessity of the All (ID 333). With Meillassoux's Child of Man we see this process reversed. Contingency itself is an expression of necessity, and rather than finitude being dialectically overcome in the One-All of divine infinity, divinity itself is brought under the one universal condition of contingency in the dialectic finite – infinite – finite, or man – God – man (ID 334). While Meillassoux shares with Hegel the intuition of the Christic character of the rational (ID 382), the terms are reversed.

Meillassoux argues that with this inverted Christic Hegelianism Man is no longer denigrated, as in religion and atheism alike, but neither is he elevated to a dangerous Promethean pedestal. Promethean humanism is nothing but the religious vision that man makes of and for himself (promé-*théisme*/'Prome-*theism*'), an instance of what we are calling imitative atheism that makes an idolatry of the power of man instead of the power of God; such a 'man-made God' can commit all God's atrocities in God's stead (ID 123). Factial ethics gives humanity no such warrant to be exalted as a messianic saviour; humanity merely gives birth to the Child of Man.

It is the possible appearing of the Child of Man that provides the normative moment in Meillassoux's ethics:

> être digne de l'enfant de l'homme devient le paradigme de ma relation à l'autre: rappeler par un geste l'autre homme à sa propre humanité, ce qui revient à être attentif à la singularité possible de l'autre; savoir répondre par ses actes propres à l'appel attentif de l'autre homme, ce qui revient à être digne de celui qui a su exemplairement se faire homme parmi les hommes. (ID 382)[6]

In this, Meillassoux's ethics structurally bears much in common with a Christianity that looks to Jesus the Son of Man for its ethical paradigm. To make this comparison is not to threaten Meillassoux's thought with parasitism, however, for this is precisely his aim. In fact, Meillassoux's philosophy has everything in common with religion in general (and, most often, with Christianity in particular) apart from belief in an actually existing God. Nevertheless, 'God' remains, now understood in terms of the principle of factiality and the Child of man: 'Dieu, désormais, peut désigner la possibilité d'une vie philosophique, éveillée et espérante, au-delà de la croyance religieuse et des lois naturelles. Une vie enfin sans foi ni loi' (ID 335).[7]

For Meillassoux's philosophy, everything desirable about religion can be incorporated into immanence, 'en sorte que la philosophie ne se distingue ultimement de la religion que par la permanence en cette dernière d'un Dieu actuellement existant qui ne peut plus alors être véritablement désiré' (ID 371).[8] Meillassoux has no qualms about branding himself a believer. The philosophical divine believes not in the existence of God but in God, as opposed to the priest who, because he believes in the existence of God, does not believe in God (ID 386).

In this move, which is nothing if not bold, Meillassoux claims to have united Jewish religion and Greek reason. Hitherto the synthesis has either been religious (Augustine, Aquinas), or rational (Hegel). But finally, with the factial, Judaic messianism no longer runs athwart the eternity of mathematical truths, because the principle of factiality, and not mathematical truths, now describes the real eternity of this world. So in a strong claim for what we are calling post-theological integration, the hope for justice offered by the Judaeo-Christian understanding

6.1.2 The Ethical Jolt

One piece remains to be added to this jigsaw of Meillassoux's account of universal justice: the jolt (*la saccade*). There are two 'jolts' in 'L'Inexistence divine'. We have already met the first as the moment of intuition by which a human being becomes aware that the illusory nature of sense experience veils the eternal inconstancy of the intelligible. This ontological intuition is the 'essential jolt' (*saccade essentielle*), the jolt by which one comes to 'see' the eternal. The second jolt follows the first. Convinced, by the essential jolt, of the possibility of immortality (because, like everything else, it is a virtuality), the individual breaks through his religious disgust for humanity to arrive at an active *desire* for immanent universality (ID 386). This second shift is to hope for and desire the justice that is revealed to be possible by the first jolt; it is to 'feel' the universal (ID 345, 369). To understand Meillassoux's account of justice, the two jolts must be taken together: '*Le cœur de l'éthique factuale réside ainsi dans le nouage immanent de l'étonnement philosophique et de l'espoir messianique*' (ID 294; QM's italics).[9]

The desired justice is, Meillassoux freely admits, far from the current state of the world. But factial ethics focuses not on the difference between desire and reality but rather on the real possibility of desire. It is not possible to desire absolutely a conceivable object; in trying to conceive an image of Paradise we succeed only in obtaining an adequate representation of Hell (ID 356). Meillassoux's ethics then does not prescribe to humanity a determinate end, but simply promises a happiness beyond the range of any anticipatory representation, yet not beyond this world and not beyond humanity. This does not render the factial useless, however, because this hope is superior to nihilism's renunciation of hope and the desirability of what is hoped for. Rather than counteracting the excess of desire by hoping for some religious, otherworldly satisfaction, I unveil the real possibility of the most extreme desire, rejecting all religious hope in the name of this desire (ID 356). With the jolt, the hope for justice is liberated from the transcendence of a God-master, as well as from the rationalism of a real necessity; both religion and relativism are exposed as a deficit of thinking (ID 354).

Seeking a common trait that ethically unites all people, Meillassoux finds it in the capacity for the two jolts and the desire for justice. Desired justice is indifferent to what de facto distinguishes and divides humanity, including death, and in this it makes a bid for universality, like Nancy's spacing or Crowley's exposure 'which, in common, we do not have'.[10] It is less clear in Meillassoux's case, however, how to include within this universality the ethical status of humans who have lost, or who never had the capacity to participate in the ontological and divine 'jolts', or who for whatever reason act less 'rationally' than others. Are those with congenital mental disabilities or geriatric mental deterioration, having lost irrevocably the capacity to think the eternal, still human? Are some humans more human than others? Any universality that rests on a capacity or on a desire risks undermining itself as universal.

There is another problem with grounding humanity in the capacity for rational thought and the desire for justice. Meillassoux writes about the possibility of justice with a puzzling teleological certainty: '*Rien ne peut donc advenir au-delà de l'homme [. . .] la seule nouveauté possible succédant à l'homme est le recommencement de l'homme*' (ID 293).[11] But surely it is not logically impossible that some other being (electronic, organic or an amalgam of both perhaps) should be able to think eternity, either as the result of a gradual process or all of a sudden. We know that nothing can surpass man (ID 293), Meillassoux affirms, but it remains unclear by virtue of what we can make that claim.

There are at least two further questions raised by Meillassoux's divine philosophy and the ethical jolt. The first is this: how do we move from a logical-real possibility of immortality to its desirability? Why should everyone at all times want to achieve immortality in this life? Unless Meillassoux is proposing a hell to accompany his beatific vision of justice, why not politely decline the second jolt? Furthermore, the desire for justice is not sufficient to ground a desire for immortality, for either 1) the righting of all wrongs may take a very long time but it would not of necessity take an eternity, in which case we would desire to live just as long as it takes for justice to be done, or 2) justice takes an eternity to accomplish, in which case the desire for justice is never achieved, contra Meillassoux's insistence that it can be achieved. Immortality cannot be desired on account of a desire for justice alone.

Secondly, these reflections compound the need for Meillassoux to address the question we raised in the previous chapter and that rests on our analysis in Chapter 4 of the place of logical laws in Meillassoux's system. If everything is contingent, why is my desire for justice not contingent? Why can it not either 1) discontinue as a desire or 2) radically change, so that what I consider just and unjust shifts, either partially or entirely? We have seen that Meillassoux is careful not to prescribe the detail of a future happiness because any image of Paradise would be an adequate representation of Hell, but this analogy requires the capacity to distinguish Paradise from Hell and for that distinction itself to be non-contingent. On Meillassoux's account, *why not* hope that the problem of evil will be solved by a change in my understanding of what is just, rather than by a rebirth of humanity? I cannot reply that it is ethically repulsive to hope for the former, for that simply misunderstands the radical nature of contingency; of course I cannot conceive how I could ever be content to view the current state of things as just, precisely in the same way that I cannot conceive what a just situation will resemble, but neither hope is logically impossible.

6.2 NANCY: UNIVERSAL DEMAND FOR JUSTICE

Nancy's account of justice, like Meillassoux's, deploys a range of theological and religious terms. We shall trace Nancy's understanding of justice through the notions of capitalism, democracy, and communism, arguing that what Nancy calls his ontological communism is with respect to politics what his atheology is with respect to religion. In seeking to address the problems of capitalism Nancy rejects both theistic and atheistic solutions, and moves towards a position that bears many similarities to Meillassoux's approach to occupying the ethico-political territory of the religious believer non-parasitically.

6.2.1 *Capital*

In *L'Adoration* Nancy argues that there have been three great mutations in the way in which human beings have organised themselves in the world. The first two he identifies as the Neolithic revolution and the age of empires, and the third mutation replaced the 'scheme of reproduction' with the 'scheme of production'. In the scheme of reproduction power is exerted to maintain the glory of the observances and hierarchies of the established order, whereas in the scheme of production efforts are directed instead to the fruitfulness of production (*ADC* 117). With this third great transition, the sumptuous opulence of sacred riches gave rise to another sort of wealth, a wealth of accumulation, growth and investment, a wealth of that which returns to the wealth holder as *surplus value* (*PD* 152).

This new regime of wealth was later called 'capitalism', the substitution of productive and invested wealth for unproductive and glorious wealth (*ADC* 30). The growth of value for its own sake circulated in the autonomous and purified sealed bubble of the financial markets (*PD* 152). Capitalism brings about what Nancy after Marx[12] calls a 'general equivalence', a notion as old as Plato who, in his *Laws*, argues for the beneficence of the retailer who 'reduces the inequalities and incommensurabilities of goods to equality and common measure'.[13] Capitalism is first and foremost the choice of a mode of evaluation, namely evaluation by equivalence. When a society takes the decision that value *is* in equivalence, that society is capitalist (*VD* 45/*TD* 23). Ends, means, values, meaning (*sens*), actions, works and persons are all exchangeable and circulable, for all are substitutable according to the universal equivalence of capital.

Capital's universal is the indefinite (*l'indéfini*), a bad infinity that merely perpetuates indifference, rather than the true infinite which inscribes affirmative difference; it is tolerance rather than confrontation, and grey rather than colour (*VD* 57/*TD* 31). Nancy calls this bad infinite a world without sky, dissipating the world in a 'globalisation' that, while infinitely expansible, is always closed in upon itself in its one universal value that destroys all other value (*CM* 45–6/*CWG* 46). Capital reduces spacing to banal general equivalence.

With capital it is not simply a question of value, however; it is also a question of ontology. Capital is an ontology in so far as being becomes a symbol of production itself; co-existence follows the technical and economic pattern of networks of exchange (*ESP* 71/*BSP* 50), an ontology alien to any notion of value beyond exchange. In so doing it also lays bare the *with* as the fundamental trait of being and sense (*ESP* 86/*BSP* 64), an ambivalence that gives capital a certain necessity in Nancy's thought, though not a sufficiency. Capital even unfolds the simultaneity of the singular and the plural, but its singular is the indifferent and interchangeable particularity of the unit of production, and its plural is the network of market exchange (*ESP* 97/*BSP* 73).

Atheism is powerless to resist capitalism. In fact, it is intricated in capitalism's historical moment: 'Le commun est orphelin de toute religion, religieuse ou civile – et cela même, cette conjonction de l'athéisme et de l'individualisme, par conséquent aussi, de toute évidence, du capitalisme, cela doit donner à penser' (*DDC* 30).[14] In *L'Adoration*, Nancy sketches a response to this issue raised in *La Déclosion*. It cannot be denied, he argues, that we must find some way of regulating capitalism's accumulation, that such accumulation needs to be 'moralised' (*ADC* 119). Any such morality cannot be that of individual interests, however, because either such a morality is driven by 'man' as individual, producer and subject, which is the very same model upon which capitalism thrives, or else, in its more revolutionary guise, it is cast according to the presuppositions of a particular individual (*ADC* 119). In seeking a way to check capitalism from the inside, Nancy looks to

John Maynard Keynes, quoting an affirmation that he (Nancy) qualifies as strong, courageous and still up to date:

> I see us free, therefore, to return to some of the most sure and certain principles of religion and traditional virtue – that avarice is a vice, that the exaction of usury is a misdemeanour, and the love of money is detestable, that those walk most truly in the paths of virtue and sane wisdom who take least thought for the morrow. We shall once more value ends above means and prefer the good to the useful. We shall honour those who can teach us how to pluck the hour and the day virtuously and well, the delightful people who are capable of taking direct enjoyment in things, the lilies of the field who toil not, neither do they spin.[15]

The question for Nancy, however, is how to determine the ends that are to be valued above means, the good that is to be preferred to the useful. The answer is not to be found in the economy itself, nor indeed in beginning with the idea of regulation, but it must be sought by beginning with 'ends', with metaphysics or, if we prefer, with the mystical or the poetic, all ways of evoking our relation to infinite sense (*ADC* 120–1). We must seek a *sense* that is beyond distributive and calculative justice, the excellence or hyperbolic virtue of justice, that can disrupt the regime of power (*force*) and capital as we know them (*ADC* 90). It is the search for this sense that will take us through Nancy's understanding of democracy and communism.

6.2.2 Ontological Communism

The possibility of striking up a new relation to capital is what Nancy explores in his treatment of democracy and communism. Democracy for Nancy is a detotalising politics, and in line with Nancy's atheology that rejects a/theistic dogmas, democracy resists both theocratic and secular versions of political theology. Perhaps the only meaning (*sens*) that can be given to democracy is that it is a-figural: it provides no figurable destiny, no truth of the common, rather it configures the space of the common so that we can open out in that space the abundance of forms that the infinite can take (*VD* 50/*TD* 27). In this, democracy plays for Nancy in his political thought a role equivalent to sense in relation to signification: it is the giving of a gift, opening of a field in which meanings or values can circulate. As such, 'democracy' for Nancy is 1) the name of a regime of sense whose truth engages man as such, and cannot be subsumed under any ordering instance, be it religious, political, scientific or aesthetic, and 2) the duty to invent the politics not of ends but of means to open, and keep open, the spaces in which those ends are set to work (*mises en œuvre*) (*VD* 60–1/*TD* 33).[16]

Politics thus configured must be thought as distinct from the order of ends, just as sense must not be collapsed into the significations the space for which it opens. Nancy's democracy is first a metaphysics – a metaphysics of spacing and opening – and only thereafter a politics (*VD* 62/*TD* 34). Nancy takes care though to stress that metaphysical democracy does not found political democracy. Indeed, that would confuse a distinction that is consubstantial with democracy itself: the order of the State does not decide on the ends of man, either communal or singular (*VD* 62/*TD* 34).

The way in which Nancy understands democracy to loosen the grip of capitalism's general equivalence can be seen in considering his claim that democracy exceeds the political order, that it reconfigures ontology as an-archic, in the sense that it has no principle (or end), no precondition and no model. In other words, democracy takes seriously the 'nothing' in Bataille's understanding of sovereignty as nothing (*VD* 57/*TD* 31), not giving the final word to religion or to nihilism, both of which hypostatise nothing (*rien*) into Nothingness (*le Néant*). An atheological politics is a politics without the 'Christmas projection' (*DDC* 121/*DisDC* 145) of a principial moment, be it the tablets of Sinai or the social contract. Instead of a final word, democracy takes the *rien* seriously in the infinity that it opens within finitude.

This anarchy is not subsumed under any principle or end, and if it does have a meaning it is that it has no identifiable authority other than from a desire which expresses a real possibility of being 'tous ensemble, tous et chaque un de tous' (*VD* 29).[17] Anarchic democracy provides the basis of a challenge to capital's general equivalence in what Nancy calls 'creating the world', and the name of this challenge is 'justice':

> Créer le monde veut dire: immédiatement, sans délai, rouvrir chaque lutte possible pour un monde, c'est-à-dire pour ce qui doit former le contraire d'une globalité d'injustice sur fond d'équivalence générale. Mais mener cette lutte précisément au nom de ceci que ce *monde* sort de rien, qu'il est sans préalable et sans modèle, sans principe et sans fin donnés, et que c'est exactement *cela* qui forme la justice et le sens d'un monde (*CM* 63; J-LN's emphasis).[18]

Anarchic democracy incites to (*engage à*) actions, operations, even struggles that allow the absence of *archē* to be rigorously preserved (*VD* 57/*TD* 31). The demo-cratic 'power of the people' is the power to bring to ruin the *archē* and then to take in hand the infinite opening thereby disclosed. This is a fundamental choice made by a whole civilisation, just like the choice of a whole civilisation for capitalism, but the choice for anarchic democracy results in the annulment of the general equivalence that perpetuates the indefinite rather than inscribing the infinite. Furthermore, this is no notional or theoretical choice: 'Entrer dans cette pensée, c'est agir déjà. C'est être dans la praxis par laquelle se produit un sujet transformé plutôt qu'un produit conformé, un sujet infini plutôt qu'un objet fini' (VD 58).[19]

The choice for anarchic democracy is not merely a position of dissent or revolt, but it works loose the very basis of general equivalence and questions its bad infinity. Nancean democracy deconstructs the *archē* of general equivalence and opens a space for the inscription of the actually infinite – that is to say, the giving of value, the *sens* of equivalence's *signification* – in its indefinite bad infinite.

Democracy opens general equivalence, but in itself it does nothing to offer another understanding of value. An initial indication of what form 'another understanding' of value might take is given by capitalism itself, however, in its awkward attempts to gesture toward a value that escapes equivalence, an absolute value that it cannot incorporate. Nancy explores this uneasy relation in his discussion of the art market in *La Pensée dérobée*, where he sees in the inflated prices commanded by works of art as capitalism's impotent indication of a value foreign to capital:

> Le très grand prix est comme la manifestation – impuissante, gesticulatoire – de l'absence absolue de prix: une toile de Vinci est *sans prix* ([this parenthesis is not closed: author] et dans un cas pareil, en fait, le sens propre et le sens figuré de cette expression tendent l'un vers l'autre. On ne peut chiffrer le prix de la *Joconde*, bien qu'on le puisse pourtant, comme à la limite, dans une logique d'assurance par exemple. (PD 151–2)[20]

In his own thought, Nancy elaborates this incommensurable value in terms of a communism which is the truth of democracy. If democracy is the un-principle – or an-arche – of politics as sense, then communism is its *ethos*. The stakes are these: democratic capitalism tries to make a world with simple atoms, but that world dissipates in general equivalence. Something more, something else, something other than capital's general equivalence is necessary for a world: some 'clinamen' (CD 17/ InC 3).

What the atomised individuals of democratic capitalism have 'in common' is articulated by Nancy in terms of ontological communism. When Nancy says that communism (like democracy) is an ontological, not a political proposition (Com 65/Comp 378), we are to understand this ontology as the being-in-common that is incommensurable with what exists, the giving which cannot be reduced to anything that is given. Communism is the truth of democracy as sense is the truth of signification: it is the *with* of being-with that replaces capitalism's exchangeability of equivalent generalities with the spacing of incommensurable singularities. Nancy's *Vérité de la démocratie* is a plea not for the preservation of existing democracy, but for the reinvention of democracy, with communism as its truth (*VD* 55/*TD* 30) and with 1968 as the first murmurings of its demand. Unless democracy becomes communist it will remain a system of managing necessities and least worst options, shorn of any desire or spirit, of any breath or sense (*VD* 30/*TD* 15).

Ontological communism precedes and exceeds every 'given' and is that by which anything in general can take place (*avoir lieu*). As such, communism is not an ontology of 'Being' or 'what is', but of being inasmuch as it is nothing of what is, '*l'être* en tant qu'il n'est rien de ce qui est' (*Com* 65).[21] But the ontology of being-in-common must also be a radical political programme:

> Non pas au sens des thèses et des projets d'un parti, mais bien plutôt au sens où le politique lui-même et en totalité doit s'y « re-programmer », doit inscrire un à-venir que ne recèlent nul concept ni programme de la « politique » consubstantielle à une autre ontologie, à toutes nos ontologies. (*Com* 87–8)[22]

The political programme of communism is a political re-programming, a civilisational decision *not* to install equivalence as the only value, *not* to establish a politics that apes our capitalo-democratic ontology, to take account of the exposure of plural singularities, not simply of capital flows. It is not a return to the sacred values and hierarchies of the pre-capitalist world, but neither is it a reconciliation to the general equivalence of a secularising capitalism. Neither theistic nor atheistic, it is political atheology.[23]

In *La Comparution* Nancy insists that, to begin with, 'communism' was simply the injunction to think after God, but (according to what in these pages we are calling imitative atheism) it became confused with any number of theological or onto-theological interpretations of the 'death of God' in terms of Man, History or Science. These interpretations are now coming to an end, however, and the thinking and praxis of sharing (*partage*) indicates what arrives with this end (*Com* 57/ *Comp* 374). In other words, ontological communism refuses to replace God with any idol of humanity or human progress; it takes the death of God seriously by refusing any parasitic pretenders to the divine throne.

Just as it is threatened by such idolatry, communism is also threatened by dissolution into capital's general equivalence. It is a discordant paradox of atheism, Nancy argues, that although it may be the only possible contemporary *ethos*, the only dignity of the subject, nevertheless its historical conjunction with individualism and capitalism means that the disappearance of religion leaves the orders of the common and of culture orphaned, renewing the still unsatisfied desire for communism (*DDC* 30/*DisDC* 17). Only an ontological communism can resist dissolving into capitalism's general equivalence; only an ontological communism can challenge the atomised ontology of general equivalence that sustains political capitalism:

> Si « politique » doit à nouveau dire quelque chose, et dire quelque chose de nouveau, ce ne peut être qu'en touchant à cette « essentialité » de l'existence qui est à elle-même sa propre essence, c'est-à-dire qui n'en a pas, qui est « archi-essentiellement » exposée à cela même – et d'une exposition qui comporte à la fois, dans sa structure et dans sa nature, la finitude de toute singularité et l'en-commun de son partage. (Com 92–3)[24]

The communist ontology of 'being inasmuch as it is nothing of what is' forms the basis of a political demand: 'Tout d'abord, nous sommes en commun. Ensuite, nous devons devenir ce que nous sommes : la donnée est celle d'une exigence, et celle-ci est infinie' (*VD* 24–5).[25] This demand cannot be determined or defined; there is no pre-vision, no fore-sight, and the demand is open because it is incalculable, defying capital's general culture of calculation and its anticipation of outputs and yields (*VD* 31/*TD* 16). More than that, this incalculability is ontological (because the communist demand is issued in singular plural being itself), and by that token it cannot be subsumed by capitalism as an internal critique, remaining as an anarchic subversion of capital's closed loop of general equivalence.

In addition to eschewing the atheism intricated with individualism and capitalism, Nancy's appeal to the incommensurable also occupies religious terminology in *L'Adoration*. The name Nancy gives to our relation to sense beyond justice is adoration, from *ad-oratio*: speaking towards, speech whose content is inseparable from its address (*ADC* 29). Nancy's privileged example of adoration is the simple greeting 'salut!' We cannot salute that which is produced, because it enters into general equivalence and into the circulation of all 'products' which can multiply and be invested, but which cannot salute (*ADC* 30). The relation here entertained between the informative sense of language and its absolute affirmative sense is the enigma that plays out in the relation in the art market between exchange value and absolute value (*PD* 152).

In singular plural being, singular existences are not related by a universal exchange value but only by the incommensurability of their 'dignity', 'value' and 'price', a price without price that Nancy equates with sense. It is to this inestimable value that adoration is addressed, making adoration itself the evaluation of that which cannot be valued, of that which is of absolute value (*ADC* 88–9). In Nancy's ontological communism, the incommensurable has replaced capitalism's universal exchangeability. Adoration speaks not of universal exchange but of an infinite and mutual referral (*renvoi mutuel infini*) that first addresses itself to adoration. Adoration is not the production of unending wealth but the praise of infinite sense (*ADC* 22). Nancy gives this address to the incommensurable the name 'God' (*ADC* 113), God not as a determinate being but only as the 'salut' of address. It is a mistake to interpret these theological terms as so many concessions to, or the unmasking of, a latent religious framework in Nancy's political thinking, that is to say as a simple religious parasitism. Like Meillassoux's evocation of the Child of Man, Nancy's use of religious terms is the point at which his post-theological integration is at its most aggressive. Adoration and the inestimable value of communism are not a manifestation of the theologico-political any more than singular plural being is divine. This point is perhaps best made by clarifying what Nancy does and does not mean by incommensurability.

Nancy identifies two measures of incommensurability in the Western tradition: incommensurability according to the Other and incommensurability according to the with (*l'avec*). The Other, with its intimacy and proximity, is other than the social, where the social is an expression of the common as shared being. It is also, of course, one of Janicaud's main objections to the theological turn in French phenomenology and the focus of Badiou's dismissal of Lévinas's politics as a crypto-theology in *L'Ethique*. By contrast, the other of being-with is an other that cannot be inscribed within the dichotomy of immanence and transcendence that residual atheism perpetuates; it must be understood within the context of Nancy's own *transimmanence*, as the 'just measure of the *with*' or the 'just measure of the incommensurable'. The 'just measure of the *with*' is a subjective genitive: the *with* is the just measure of the gap (*écart*) of one singular origin to another (*ESP* 105/*BSP* 81). It is in this way that Nancy draws from his communism a justice (which in this context means a universality and an equality) which does not dissolve either into capital's general equivalence or into the antisocial intimacy of incommensurability according to the Other. In other words, Nancy's notion of justice is neither parasitically theo-political nor atomistically atheistic.

This is not just a politics of distributive justice, however. Nancy's politics demands more than simply the equal distribution of rights and freedoms. Distributive justice will always come second, after existence in common (*ADC* 12). What is demanded is an effective equality (*égalité effective*) of the 'surgissement unique et incommensurable d'une singularité [...] mesurable à aucune signification.' This 'more than justice' could be called fraternity, understood as 'l'acte de nouage [...] l'acte de partage et du tissage qui comme tel n'a pas de sens mais donne lieu à tout événement de sens' (*SM* 179).[26] This can be neither, on one hand, an exclusive fraternity of communal essences nor, on the other hand, a fraternity of general equivalence. It is the fraternity of the in-common, not of the Other or of capital. What ontological communism demands is the fraternal equality of the in-common. It is therefore a misguided conflation of the two forms of incommensurability to read this evocation of fraternity in Nancy as a concession to community as communion or shared essences.

Nancy's ontological communism might be thought to be weak in its potential for bringing about political change or unduly pessimistic in the finitude of the singular plural being it assumes. In his treatment of Nancy's communism in *Alain Badiou, une trajectoire polémique*, Bruno Bosteels reads Nancy too much like Derrida, stressing that Nancy understands communism to be unforeseeable, still entirely to-come, failing to draw attention to Nancy's ontological communism that drives the demand for this communism to come.[27] For Bosteels, Nancy's communism is separated from all the dreams or nightmares of immanence and transcendence, possessing no common measure with substances or subjects,[28] but for Nancy himself this 'ontological detachment' (though Nancy would prefer to call it an *ethos*) is the means by which his communism can mount anything but a superficial resistance to the unrestricted circulation of capital. It is *because* communism is ontological that it exerts an immediate and ineradicable demand. As for communism possessing 'no common measure' with substances or subjects, Nancy stresses that ontological communism simply is the just measure of the *with*: it does not *possess* common measure because it *is* common measure.

In relation to the objection we saw formulated by Meillassoux above, that thinking the human according to finitude will conjure up the Christian model of man as a poor fallen creature condemned to an ailing wretchedness with no way out other than divine salvation, Martin Crowley provides us with a Nancean response. Recognising the hostility to all finite thinking on the part of those who can see in it nothing but the limits of this christianising vision that reduces the human to the pathos of a victim-existence from which only a God can save us,[29] Crowley points out that there is no inevitable move from affirming human finitude to seeing every contestation of 'the way things are' perishing in the indifference of a metaphysical destiny.[30] Ontological communism provides precisely such an affirmation of the finite human that still leaves open the possibility of radical change. In one final move, Crowley seeks to secure the universality of this politics: 'Ne puisant ainsi aucune valeur dans quelque paradis perdu ni dans quelque terre promise, l'articulation politique de l'inachèvement humain se fondera par impossible dans la seule universalité admissible: c'est-à-dire, dans le *besoin*'.[31] As a marker of universal humanity, need has an advantage over Meillassoux's capacity to think the eternal, namely that all humans all the time are subject to some level of material need. Moreover, since material need is not a value, it cannot be negated. Thirdly, though not all humans are equally needy all the time, this universal is negatively manifested in the bodies of the abused, so the human universal lines up politically (*s'aligne politiquement*) with those in most need.[32] This alignment of humanity with need does, however, reproduce the awkward position of locating universal humanity in terms of lack and orientating politics to a reactive mitigation of that lack.

6.3 BADIOU: JUSTICE OPEN TO ALL

'From Plato until today, there is one word which can sum up the concern of the philosopher with respect to politics. This word is "justice"' (PP 29). Justice is the central concern of Badiou's politics, but unlike Nancy's communism, the notion is for Badiou emphatically not ontological: justice is an axiom. Justice stands in relation to the State as inconsistency stands in relation to the count; it is 'the philosophical name of the inconsistency, for the state, of any equalitarian political orientation' (PP 32). The effect of such an orientation is 'to undo the ties, to desocialize thought, to affirm the rights of the infinite and the immortal against finitude, against Being-for-death' (PP 32). In the terms of *Théorie du sujet*, justice demands the dialectic precariousness of law, that law be open to being shaken, being split (*TS* 176/*ThS* 159). As such, justice must not be defined, because 'any definitional and programmatic approach to justice makes of it a dimension of the action of the state' (PP 30). Justice is not to be found in any positive definition; it can 'only name the most extreme moments of inconsistency'.[33] 'Justice' itself, however, is not a political term; it is a generic category 'by which a philosophy attempts to seize the equalitarian axiom inherent in a veritable political sequence' (PP 30). The 'equalitarian axiom' is a political term, and is given by singular statements, in other words statements within a particular situation or world.

The term Badiou uses to describe how philosophical justice relates to the political equalitarian axiom is seizure or grasping (*saisie*): justice 'seizes the latent axiom of a political subject' (PP 30). Justice therefore is not an aspiration or the blueprint for a political programme, for 'the equalitarian axiom is present in political statements, or it is not present. And by consequence, we are within justice, or we are not' (PP 30). Justice here is simply a judgment on the collective being – in other words the subject – of a political truth, and therefore '[p]olitical equality is not what we want or plan, it is what we declare under fire of the event, here and now, as what is, and not what should be' (PP 30). On a number of occasions Badiou returns to a phrase from Beckett's *How it is* to sum up this axiomatic understanding of justice: 'En tout cas on est dans la justice je n'ai jamais entendu dire le contraire.'[34] There is no finality in Beckett's account of justice, Badiou notes; it refers purely to the equality of the figures (or members) of a collective subject of a political truth.

Justice is a term used to describe the universal subject of political truths. The 'justice' or 'equality' evoked is not universal in the Nancean sense – in the sense that each singularity is ontologically equal in its incommensurability with all others – but in the same sense in which Badiou employs universality in relation to truths: *de jure* universal because open to all without exception, but de facto limited to those incorporated as the subject of the truth. Justice and equality are no more and no less than the justice and equality enjoyed by the subject of a political truth, and 'a political orientation worthy of being submitted to philosophy under the idea of justice is an orientation whose unique general axiom is: people think, people are capable of truth' (PP 29). By extension, people are also capable of justice. There is, however, no guarantee that all necessarily are indeed capable of truth (or justice), as Badiou fully acknowledges: 'There is no political orientation linked to truth without the affirmation – affirmation which has neither a guarantee nor a proof – of a universal capacity for political truth' (PP 29). This leaves Badiou exposed to the same problems we identified with Meillassoux's account of justice resting on the capacity to think the eternal. If there is no guarantee that there is indeed a universal capacity for political truth, it follows that there is no guarantee that there can ever be universal justice.

6.3.1 Capital

It is clear, in this context, why capitalism for Badiou can never be just. The free circulation of wealth and the rule of majority opinion in what Badiou calls capitalo-parliamentarianism is the antithesis of the subject seized by the truth of an equalitarian maxim:

> Le monde du capitalisme généralisé et arrogant où nous vivons nous ramène aux années 1840, au capitalisme naissant, dont l'impératif, formulé par Guizot, est: « Enrichissez-vous! ». Ce que nous traduirons par: « Vivez sans idée ». Nous devons dire qu'on ne vit pas sans idée. (Circ5 56)[35]

The result of this absence of idea is that 'what is fuses miserably with what can be' (PP 31) and capitalism facilitates no possibility of radical change. Nevertheless, just as the role played by capitalism was not wholly negative for Nancy, so also for Badiou capital has an important function.

In his first *Manifeste*, Badiou closely ties his understanding of capital to the disenchantment of the West. The enchanted cosmos was governed by a notion of presence with which we are familiar from our discussion of the God of the poets in the second chapter. It is this presence, Badiou argues, that underwrites the sacred hierarchy and sacred bonds of the enchanted cosmos. So in order to move from this enchanted cosmos to a disenchanted universe, it is necessary to break these sacred bonds and overcome the incarnational notion of presence that underpins the sacred cosmos. What makes this a real possibility for our epoch, Badiou argues, is capital: 'A qui devons-nous d'être délivrés du mythe de la Présence, de la garantie qu'elle accorde à la substantialité des liens et à la pérennité des rapports essentiels, sinon à l'automaticité errante du capital?' (M 37).[36]

It is capital, then, which provides the historical vehicle for a disenchanted cosmos; the working of capital and the working of disenchantment here run in parallel.

Just as, for Nancy, capital exposes the simultaneity of the singular and the plural, so also for Badiou it plays here an important role in preparing the way for communism. Capital exposes the pure multiple as the foundation of presentation because it is universal, dissolving all particular values into one universal exchange value. To be clear: capital is to justice as axiomatised set theory is to truth. Neither capital nor set theory are timeless; they are both historical articulations which privilege the quantitative over the qualitative, in other words that privilege counting, and one way of counting, to the rigorous exclusion of other measures of quantity/value.

In so far as the flow of capital knows no bounds or restrictions, it exposes sacred resistance to free exchangeability as contingent and constructed, and so performs on the social level what mathematics achieves for Badiou's ontology: purging it of any bonds or ties. In so doing capital violently creates a new basis (*assise*) for generic humanity (BF 126), in the same way that mathematised ontology clears the ground, so to speak, for truth. Any philosophy worthy of the name must be able to measure up to capital (*M* 39/*Man* 58).

In this Badiou is following Marx, as he acknowledges in 'Politics and Philosophy':

> Emancipatory politics, as I say somewhere in my *Manifesto for Philosophy*, must be at least equal to the challenge of capital. That is Marx's idea. When Marx says that capital destroys all the old ties, all the ancient sacred figures, that it dissolves everything in the frozen waters of selfish calculation, he says it with a certain admiration. (PoP 113)

This leaves us with a tension: if capital is to be overcome, then should it not follow, by Badiou's own logic, and by the shape of Badiou's own thought, that disenchantment too, that parallel of capital, is to be overcome? If capitalism is not an end in itself for Badiou, then neither is disenchantment And, if this is the case, what would the overcoming of disenchantment – as a parallel to the overcoming of capitalism – look like? The answer: it looks like an post-theological integration.

If disenchantment and the atheism of 'nothing is inaccessible' were ends in themselves for Badiou then he would be quite satisfied with universal and unrestricted capitalism having brought about precisely the dissolution of sacred bonds that disenchantment demands. But this alone is insufficient for a post-theological integration, because having secured a disenchanted universe Badiou moves in on the territory previously occupied by religion and argues that the overcoming of presence and a cosmos of sacred bonds opens the way for truth:

> la désacralisation n'est nullement nihiliste, pour autant que « nihilisme » doit signifier ce qui prononce que l'accès à l'être et à la vérité est impossible. Tout au contraire, la désacralisation est une condition nécessaire pour qu'un tel accès s'ouvre à la pensée. (M 37)[37]

So the role that capital plays for Badiou is necessary and irreducible, but not final, because he is not simply seeking to resist theism but to occupy its territory: the objective Marxist analysis is indispensible, but it cannot of itself give rise to a politics of emancipation because any such resistance will always already have stoked the fires of totality and dominant power (BF 121).

In a figure that neatly captures his rejection both of asceticism and parasitism, Badiou renounces Romanticism's imitative hypostatisation of Life and an ascetic capitulation to the general equivalence of the market that forecloses any Truth:

> comment sortir [. . .] du romantisme, sans consentir à la sophistique nihiliste dont le pur présent est le marché mondial, l'économie, et l'automatisme consensuel du capital? Comment n'être pas pris dans l'alternative: la Vie (mythème) ou la Bourse (celle du Capital)? (19R 268)[38]

The way to avoid these two unappetising alternatives is to recognise that the false universal of capitalism (false because it is indefinite, not actually infinite) prepares the way for the universal of truth.

Despite, or even because of its place in preparing the way for his post-theological integration, capital occupies a problematic place in Badiou's thought. The parallel between capital as the untying of social bonds and ZFC set theory as the undoing of all substantial relations relegates capitalism, as Žižek is quick to point out in *In Defense of Lost Causes*, to 'the naturalized "background" of our historical constellation', depriving Badiou of the ability to mount a critique of *political* economy:

> if not the immediate goal of the emancipatory politics, anti-capitalism should be its ultimate aim, the horizon of all its activity. Is this not the lesson of Marx's notion of the 'critique of political economy' (totally absent in Badiou)? Although the sphere of the economy appears 'apolitical,' it is the secret point of reference and structuring principle of political struggles.[39]

Nancy's critique of capitalism is more robust than Badiou's on this point. An ontological communism can challenge the atomised ontology of general equivalence that sustains political capitalism in a way that a communism subtracted from ontology as a truth cannot. Ontological communism cannot be subsumed by capitalism as an internal critique, for it remains as an anarchic subversion of capital's closed loop of general equivalence, with the same force as that general equivalence. For Nancy, communism is the truth of democracy, not the truth of capitalism, and this allows him to reject capital while still drawing communism from a democratic general equivalence. It is Badiou's conflation of capital and democracy in his capitalo-parliamentarianism that makes it difficult for him to articulate communism in a way that does not either presuppose or neutralise capitalism.

6.3.2 Communism

The difficulties multiply when we see that communism stands in relation to capitalism in the same way that truths stand in relation to the privilege of the count (over qualitative measurements) brought about by ZFC set theory. Communism for Badiou is an Idea, a truth that can be incorporated by different subjects at different historical moments. As an Idea, 'communism' should not be rendered as an adjectival adjunct to a particular politics, and this short-circuit between the idea of communism and actually existing politics has led to 'communisms' that spawned oxymorons like 'Communist party' or 'Socialist state' (*Circ5*

189/CH 240). Badiou rejects the socialisms of the twentieth century as abject failures, having adopted a capitalist dogma of inequality (*Circ5* 10/CH 5), and he rejects the adjectival uses of 'Communist' and 'Socialist' as no longer able to uphold the idea of communism (*Circ5* 202/CH 257). Instead, he favours a recovery of the generic sense of 'communism' found in the young Marx (2M 153), an understanding of communism as 'une hypothèse régulatrice qui enveloppe les champs variables et les organisations nouvelles de la politique d'émancipation' (2M 153–4).[40] 'Communism' as a philosophical concept can be equated with justice; it is the ground (*fond*) of every emancipatory orientation (*Circ4* 151/*MOS* 113–14), inasmuch as it names forms of political organisation not modelled on a hierarchy of places (*Circ5* 52/CH 60). In other words, communism operates under the equalitarian maxim.

When Badiou refers to communism as an 'Idea' he is adumbrating the third volume of *L'Etre et l'événement*, provisionally entitled *L'Immanence des vérités* (the immanence of truths) (*PE* 105). An Idea offers the horizon of a new possibility; neither political practice nor a political programme, it is the possibility in the name of which we act, transform, or have a programme (*PE* 24). It is the subjectivation (in other words the incorporation of a truth in a body that makes that body – be it an individual, a group or a work of art – into a faithful, reactive or obscure subject) of a relation between the singularity of a truth procedure and a representation of History (*Circ5* 185/CH 235). For example, the French Revolution had three great ideas – liberty, equality, fraternity. However, notes Badiou, the French Revolution subordinated equality to the freedom to own property, whereas the great idea of communism is that equality norms liberty and fraternity (*PE* 25, 26).

It is important to be clear that the Idea of communism is not understood by Badiou as an abstract notion. It comprises three components: political, historical and subjective. The political component is a political truth, an eternal truth subtracted from the bodies and languages of democratic materialism; the historical component is the local inscription of a political truth-procedure in a particular situation; the subject is the collective and in-principal universal group of those faithful to the political truth. For this reason, it is better to understand the Idea of communism as an operation, rather than as a notion (*Circ5* 187/CH 237): '[l]'Idée communiste est l'opération imaginaire par laquelle une subjectivation individuelle projette un fragment de réel politique dans la narration symbolique d'une Histoire' (*Circ5* 189).[41] So the 'Idea of communism' means that a subject holds itself to a truth in a given situation, and it cannot be equated with the animating notion behind all actually existing or previously existing communist states; it is not a purely political name, nor purely historical, nor purely ideological (*Circ5* 187/*CH* 237). Badiou coins the term 'ideation' to describe the indiscernability of life and Idea in the subject of a truth (*2M* 20), a 'true life' (*2M* 124).

This tripartite understanding also helps us to avoid the error of thinking that Badiou's communism is an idealistic and impotent waiting for the never-to-come Revolution. To say that an Idea is a horizon does not mean that it is solely to-come. An Idea presents a truth as if it were a fact (*comme si elle était un fait*), or it presents certain facts as symbols of the real of a truth. Through the Idea of communism we can articulate the process of a truth in the impure language of the State (*Circ5* 200/*CH* 254), with the understanding that the post-revolutionary State will be the State of the withering away of the State, the State that organises the transition to the non-State (*Circ5* 195–6/*CH* 238–9).

Though the Idea is always affirmed in the present, it will not always succeed in its eventual realisation. Badiou sees this as in no way detrimental to the hypothesis itself. Taking the analogy of Fermat's last theorem (*Circ5* 11/*CH* 6) Badiou notes that from Fermat's formulation of the hypothesis to Wiles's demonstration there elapsed a number of years (358 in fact) and countless attempts at its justification. What was imperative during the three centuries that intervened was not to abandon the hypothesis despite the ongoing impossibility of proving it. More than that, the failures themselves were productive and drove forward the life of mathematics: 'En ce sens, l'échec, pourvu qu'il n'entraîne pas qu'on cède sur l'hypothèse, n'est jamais que l'histoire de la justification de cette dernière' (*Circ5* 11).[42] Badiou traces the same process through the events of May 1968, the Cultural Revolution and the Commune of Paris: in each case, apparent and sometimes bloody failures were and remain stages in the proof of the communist hypothesis. The 'propagandist use' of the notion of the failure of communism is therefore to be resisted (*Circ5* 12/*CH* 7). Every failure can be localised to a *point*, to a binary choice in the development of an Idea, and so every failure is a lesson that can finally be incorporated into the positive universality of the construction of a truth (*Circ5* 33/*CH* 39). In other words, political difficulties are never global but contained within a 'space of possible failures', a space where we must search, after a failure, for the *point* at which, from now on, we will not permit ourselves to fail (*Circ5* 34/*CH* 39–40). Some may not like the legitimation of political violence implicit in this position, but it is hard to criticise it as a quietism that refuses to engage in the 'real world'.

It is also important to understand that for Badiou communism does not refer to one subset of political events, but to political events in general. All political truths are communist because all political truths are universalising and equalitarian (OR 16). In so far as 1) only a politics with an Idea (or a politics of truths) deserves to be called a real politics, 2) the Idea of communism is the ground of every emancipatory orientation, and 3) political truths for Badiou are always emancipatory in that they break down hierarchies and declare a universal subject, communism is the only Idea with which to confront the 'Get rich!' mantra of capitalo-parlemantarianism.

One final nuance. In comparing Badiou's axiomatic and Nancy's ontological justice, we need to recognise that Badiou does evoke ontological equality in his gloss on Beckett's 'En tout cas on est dans la justice je n'ai jamais entendu dire le contraire',[43] albeit as the ontological equality of the subject: 'La justice ici évoquée, qui est un jugement sur l'être collectif, ne se rapporte évidemment à aucune espèce de finalité. Elle concerne uniquement l'égalité ontologique intrinsèque des figures du sujet' (C 356).[44]

The difference between Nancy and Badiou is not that Nancy's justice is ontological whereas Badiou's is not, but that Nancy's ontological justice is universal *in esse*, the ontological condition of each singular without exception, whereas Badiou's ontological justice is universal *in posse*, for though no human animals are in principle excluded from the collectivity bound to an equalitarian truth (save perhaps those incapable of understanding the truth), in practice not all human animals are incorporated in any such truth.

So what of the difference between Nancy's ontological communism and Badiou's communism of the Idea? For his part, Nancy's critique of Badiou's justice is couched in terms that we would now recognise as suggesting that it is an imitative atheism, an idolatry of the Idea. For Nancy the communist hypothesis generates forms which model a historical given that is itself pre-formed by the general motif of 'progress' and the possibility of spicing up (*arraisonner*) the course of events with a ready Idea. He contrasts these objectives of such a hypothetical thinking (in addition to 'communism' these could include 'man' or 'humanism', 'community', 'sense' or 'realisation') to the in-principle excess (*un outrepassement de principe*) of his own understanding of communism, *ethos* and sense (VD 24/TD 11). As a pre-vision of a desired *telos*, the Idea is theologically abstracted from history. It is this difference between Badiou's anticipatory pre-vision and his own exposure that crystallises Nancy's difference from Badiou:

> C'est pourquoi le « communisme » doit être moins avancé comme une « hypothèse », ainsi que le fait Alain Badiou – et par conséquent moins comme une hypothèse politique à vérifier par une action politique elle-même prise dans le schème d'une lutte classique – que posé comme une donnée, comme un fait: notre donnée première. (VD 24–5)[45]

A hypothesis or Idea will always prescribe and pre-judge what it posits as its final goal, but ontological exposure presents not a vision but a demand: 'Tout d'abord, nous sommes en commun. Ensuite, nous devons devenir ce que nous sommes : la donnée est celle d'une exigence, et celle-ci est infinie' (VD 25).[46] But this is a deficient reading of Badiou. Badiou's Idea is more nuanced than Nancy's account gives us to believe, in its tripartite structure of the political, historical and subjective. The political Idea of communism is no more pre-established than the 'given demand' of Nancy's own ontological communism. Furthermore, the historical and subjective aspects of the Idea allow for just the sort of creative improvisations and compromises which Nancy seems to be suggesting Badiou's Idea precludes. The charge that Badiou's justice harbours an imitative atheism is not to be made at this point, but at the point of his equation of ontology with the Good (see Chapter 3).

In his comments on Nancy's account of communism, Badiou strikes a more conciliatory tone. Communism means that each one of us is in common, together (*communément*), and given that Nancy's ontological communism is an ontology not of what is but of being in so far as it is 'nothing of what is', Badiou concludes '[l]à, nous sommes si proches que je ne nous distingue plus' (OR 16).[47] Though Nancy reports that Badiou expresses reservations at Nancy's language of 'community', preferring his own 'equality' (see CA 42 n.1/CC 25), he recognises that Nancy's community is not a substantialised homogeneity. Furthermore, Badiou is very happy to call the coming of being 'in so far as it is nothing of what is' an event, and the generic truth of an event might also be called 'in-common': 'Alors, qu'en définitive tout événement soit « communiste », c'est ce que Jean-Luc Nancy affirme, et qui est si vrai pour moi que j'y perds jusqu'au lexique de la malfaisance' (OR 16).[48] Nevertheless, the difference between Idea and singular plural being, between *eidos* and *ethos*, does trace a fundamental fault line between Nancy's and Badiou's communism, not to mention that it seems impossible to evoke the 'event' in both cases without equivocation. Exposure is not inexistence, and a fortiori the universal of the exposure which, in common, we do not have (which is ontological, and always-already) is not the universal of the event (which is a rupture with ontology, and contingent).

CONCLUSION: JUSTICE BEYOND ATHEISM

At the end of our case study we are in a position to make a number of comparative conclusions about the capacity of the three approaches to post-theological thinking under discussion to integrate a notion of universal justice. Meillassoux's is certainly the most ambitious integration. His bold recognition of the scope of a justice which is universal in the sense of applying to all without exception, including justice for the dead, cedes nothing in extent to the theologian's Final Judgment, but his justice predicated on belief in a God who does not exist comes at a price, namely a hyperchaotic virtuality which is light on justification and which relies on the argument that it can be brought about by human desire, an argument that, pending more detailed elaboration, as yet fails to convince. Meillassoux's position requires the ontological and the ethical jolts, or what we might call a 'leap' of integration, which remains far from straightforward or compelling. More than this though, Meillassoux's justice does fail to integrate the redemption of past wrong: past injustice remains an offence. All Meillassoux offers is the consolation that injustice will not be continued, but he does not suggest that past injustice will be repaired. This would require the one hyperchaotic change he seems unwilling to contemplate, namely an (from the present point of view) unthinkable change in our understanding of what is just and what is unjust. In this sense, his justice lacks universality. Meillassoux also has to sacrifice the notion of justice itself on the altar of post-theological thinking, for he cannot guarantee that our notion of what is 'just' will not change. Both Meillassoux and Badiou make justice contingent on a particular human faculty (for Badiou it is the capacity for truth and for Meillassoux the capacity to think the eternal and desire justice), which further renders problematic the universality of justice. Can justice truly be for everybody if it requires a certain capacity in the individual?

Meillassoux's ambition to have everything in common with religion apart from the belief in an actually existing God labours under its own weight. The principle of universality itself may be beautifully simple – though by no means simplistic – but the evocation of the Child of Man and the desire for justice is baroque by comparison. 'L'Inexistence divine' presents the least ascetic of the three positions we are considering, but its two 'jolts' require more good faith than many readers will be able to give. If we are not persuaded by the two jolts, however, let us not allow that to distract our attention from the crucial importance of his treatment of divine inexistence for the future course of post-theological integration. 'L'Inexistence divine' is important in the way that Meillassoux seeks aggressively to occupy religion's territory, to have everything in common with religion apart from belief in an actually existing God. It opens new possibilities for post-theological integration that will no doubt be refined and developed as Meillassoux continues to publish and as others follow his lead.

Nancy's justice is universal in its application: the demand for justice issues from everyone, whoever they are and however they are suffering. This universality is the least conditional of the three positions, in that it does not require any capacity to be present in those for whom justice is demanded (though even here it could be argued that it is contingent on a capacity to suffer, to feel or to be judged to be undergong physical or emotional pain in a way that is not, it might be argued, the case for all human beings at every moment), but it lacks the scope and ambition of Meillassoux's justice even for the dead. All it promises is a greater demand for justice when humanity is denied, not the hope that such justice will in fact be done. Whereas Meillassoux's justice (if we accept the jolts on which it relies) is universal in its application, Nancy's is only universal in its demand. Nancy's primary concern is to avoid parasitism, and his anarchic democracy repeats the move with which we are now familiar, whereby he resists the 'Christmas projection' of foundations and ends. Furthermore, ontological communism refuses to replace God with any idol of humanity, reason or human progress. His notion of justice without precondition and without model does open him to the criticism that his idea of justice is ascetic, in other words that the demand for justice lacks a compelling universalising of the *passage à l'acte*. This critique is in part mitigated by Nancy's disruption of the dichotomy of theory and action in *ethos*, but his understanding of justice still does not sufficiently explain the conflation of ontology and normativity.

Badiou's notion of justice is the most de facto restricted of the three. It is universal only *in posse*: all those incorporated in the subject of a political truth are equal, and the equalitarian maxim is on Badiou's own admission rarely seized (*AMP* 115/*MetP* 101; *EE* 379/*BE* 344). The problematic nature of letting universality rest on a human capacity, the capacity for truth, further nuances his account of universal justice. Badiou's justice shares with Meillassoux's a future anterior focus, but Badiou's 'continuer!' allows for an incremental series of steps towards justice which seem precluded by Meillassoux's dice throw. Through coming to understand the 'point' at which a particular historical communism failed, Badiou has a mechanism whereby the subject of a truth can learn from the mistakes of the past, whereas Meillassoux's injunction to live now in the light of coming justice does not, it seems, have such a heuristic dimension. Badiou's understanding of justice leaves him in relation to capital in the same position as what he calls the 'ethics of victimhood' occupies in relation to human suffering: the parallel between capitalism and mathematised ontology leaves him unable to reject capitalism consistently or, as Žižek suggests, to mount a critique of *political* economy.[49] If Nancy is most preoccupied to avoid atheistic parasitism, then Badiou's axiomatic account of justice sets itself against the asceticism that he perceives in the previous generation of 'linguistic philosophers'. His recourse to axioms, however, leaves him once more with the problem of the 'principle of intelligibility' that we discussed in the previous chapter.

The notion of universal justice for each of our three thinkers encounters the problem of a latent or unexplained conflation of goodness and equality, or goodness and justice. For Nancy, justice and communism may be ontological, but it still remains to be shown why we *should* prefer an *ethos* that reflects or honours this ontological communism to one that does not. Blurring the boundary between ontology and ethics/politics in *ethos* does not yet show why one particular ethos should be preferred over another. In other words, there is no reason to obey the demand issued by singular plural ontology if it is not a good demand, and there are no non-circular means to verify its goodness.

For Badiou, the problem can be expressed as follows: truths are necessarily universalising and equalitarian, and this universal equality can only be justified in terms of the inconsistent multiplicity that is retrojected from the counting-as-one of any situation, countings-as-one that introduce hierarchies, relations and divisions foreign to the void. A truth destroys such hierarchical divisions (for example: the three estates of pre-revolutionary France) and brings into being a new universal category (for example: the universal human subject), that counts as one in a way more faithful to the retroactively apprehended non-hierarchised inconsistent multiplicity. There is no justification for privileging the stripping away of inequalities other than through an implicit appeal to privileging the equality of inconsistent multiplicity. For Badiou it is not ontology per se that justifies the equalitarian maxim, but inconsistent multiplicity. There can only be one reason for preferring truth and subjecthood over animality and the 'get rich!' maxim: inconsistent multiplicity is *eo ipso* Good.

For Meillassoux, the difficulty comes down once more to trusting that our current understanding of justice is non-contingently 'Good', when there seems to be no basis in Meillassoux's own thought for such a supposition, on pain of parasitic idolatry. For each of Badiou, Nancy and Meillassoux there is an unaccountable moment of 'goodness' (Why is inconsistent multiplicity good? Why obey the demand of the singular plural? Why is our current, contingent understanding of justice good?) that exposes each notion of justice to the charge of idolatry, of excepting one concept or moment of thinking from the need to be thought about. For each there is a necessary moment of circumspection (justice is universal only *in posse*; justice is universal only in its demand; justice for the dead is not redemptive) which exposes their notions of justice to the charge of asceticism. Finally, each notion of justice relies on a problematic moment that remains unjustified: (axiom, demand, intuition/jolt), and upon which the three notions of justice, as well as the three approaches to elaborating an post-theological integration, rely. It is to these problematic moments that we will turn as we draw our final conclusions.

NOTES

1. Pascal, *Pensées* [Lafuma] 60/[Brunschvicg] 294; 'It is a funny kind of justice whose limits are marked by a river', Pascal, *Pensées*, trans. A. J. Krailsheimer, p. 16.
2. Critchley, *Infinitely Demanding*, p. 8.
3. 'this bastard absurdity, half religious and half atheist, of the hopeless perdurance of natural laws that are indifferent to our thirst for justice' (author's translation).
4. 'to give birth to God, like matter gave birth to life and life to thought' (author's translation).
5. 'God is precisely the appearing of the factical being through whom rebirth with a view to justice takes place' (author's translation).
6.
   > being worthy of the child of man becomes the paradigm of my relation to the other: calling the other man back to his own humanity with a gesture, which comes down to being attentive to the possible singularity of the other; knowing how to respond with one's own acts to the attentive call of the other man, which comes down to being worthy of the one who knew how to make himself a man among men in an exemplary way. (Author's translation)
7. 'Henceforth, God can designate the possibility of a philosophical life that is awakened and full of hope, beyond the religious belief in natural laws. A life, in short, with neither faith nor law' (author's translation).
8. 'so that, ultimately, philosophy is only distinguished from religion by the permanence in the latter of a currently existing God who can no longer be truly desired' (author's translation).
9. '*Thus the heart of factial ethics rests in the immanent knotting of philosophical astonishment and messianic hope*' (author's translation).

10. Crowley, *L'Homme sans*, p. 95.
11. '*Nothing therefore can happen beyond man* [. . .] *the only possible novelty to succeed man is the renewal of man*' (author's translation).
12. Whereas the term 'general equivalence' itself is borrowed from Marx to designate money and market in so far as they operate the levelling of distinctions and the reduction of excellence to mediocrity (*VD* 44/*TD* 23).
13. Plato, *Laws*, 918b.
14. 'The in-common finds itself orphaned of all religion, whether religious or civil. And, as a conjunction of atheism and individualism, it is even orphaned, consequently and obviously, in regard to capitalism – which ought to make us reflect' (*DisDC* 17).
15. Keynes, 'Economic possibilities for our grandchildren', *The Collected Writings*, vol. 9, p. 331. Quoted in French in *ADC* 120.
16. The discussion of ends and means here is not to be confused with the same terms in the passage from Keynes quoted above. Keynes's 'ends' are the particular significations that appear in the field of the political, and his 'means' are the instrumental measures deployed to achieve those ends. Nancy's 'means' in *Vérité de la démocratie* by contrast is the disruption of such significations.
17. 'all together, all and each one among all' (*TD* 14).
18.
>   To create the world means: immediately, without delay, reopen each possible struggle for a world, that is, for what must form the contrary of a global injustice against the background of general equivalence. But this means to conduct this struggle precisely in the name of the fact that this world is coming out of nothing, that there is nothing before it and that it is without models, without principle and without given end, and that is precisely what forms the justice and the meaning of the world. (*CWG* 22)

19. 'To enter into this thought is already to act. It is to be engaged in the praxis whereby what is produced is a transformed subject rather than a formed product, in infinite subject rather than a finite object' (*TD* 31; translation altered).
20.
>   The very high price is like the manifestation – impotent, gestural – of the absolute absence of a price: a da Vinci canvass is *priceless* (and in such a case, in fact, the literal and figurative senses of this expression converge towards each other). We cannot say how much the *Mona Lisa* is worth, and yet we can, just, in the logic of insurance for example. (Author's translation)

21. Tracy Strong translates the phrase incorrectly as 'being insofar as it is a matter of that which is' (*Comp* 378).

22.
> not in the sense of theses and partisan projects, but rather in the sense that the political itself must completely 're-program' itself, must inscribe a to-come that can be hidden by no concept or 'political' programme consubstantial with another ontology, with all our ontologies. (Comp 87–8; translation altered)

23. In the discussion that follows we will be alternating the terms 'atheology' and 'atheism'. Nancy equivocates on the term atheism, sometimes using it to refer to the sort of metaphysical rejection of God that his atheology avoids, and at other times employing it in a way synonymous with his own atheology.

24.
> If politics is again to mean something, and mean something new, it can only be in touching this 'essentiality' of existence – which is itself its own 'essence,' that is to say, which has no essence, which is 'arch-essentially' exposed to that very thing – and of an exposure that in its structure and nature contains at the same time the finitude of all singularity and the in-common of its sharing. (Comp 390, translation altered)

25. 'Before all else, we are in common. Then we must become what we are: the given is an exigency, and this exigency is infinite' (*TD* 54).

26.
> unique and incommensurable emergence of a singularity [...] that is not measurable in terms of any signification' fraternity understood as 'the act of tying [...] the act of apportioning and interweaving that, as such, has no sense but gives place to every event of sense. (*SW* 114–15)

27. See Bosteels, *Alain Badiou*, pp. 175–7.
28. Bosteels, *Alain Badiou*, p. 175.
29. Crowley includes the Badiou of *L'Ethique* among those who dismiss finite thinking for this reason, along with Jacques Rancière in *La Mésentente* (Paris: Galilée, 1995) [*Disagreement: Politics and Philosophy*, trans. Julie Rose (Minneapolis: University of Minnesota Press, 1999)], *Aux Bords du politique* (Paris: La Fabrique, 1998) [*On the Shores of Politics*, trans. Liz Heron (London: Verso, 2007)], and 'Who is the subject of the Rights of Man?', *South Atlantic Quarterly*, 103: 2/3 (Spring/Summer 2004), pp. 297–310.
30. Crowley, *L'Homme sans*, p. 18.
31. Crowley, *L'Homme sans*, p. 89. 'Drawing no value from some lost paradise or some promised land, the political articulation of human incompleteness will ground itself against all odds in the only admissible universality: namely, in *need*' (author's translation).
32. Crowley, *L'Homme sans*, pp. 90–1.

33. Marchart, 'Nothing but a truth', p. 113 n.32.
34. Beckett, *Comment c'est*, p. 150; 'in any case we have our being in justice I have never heard anything to the contrary' (Beckett, *How it is*, p. 135).
35.
>The world of global and arrogant capitalism in which we live is taking us back to the 1840s and the birth of capitalism. Its imperative, as formulated by Guizot, was: 'Get rich!' We can translate that as 'Live without an idea!' We have to say that we cannot live without an idea. (CH 66–7)

36. 'To whom must we be grateful to be delivered from the myth of Presence, the guarantee which it grants to the substantiality of the bonds and to the durability of essential relations, if not to the errant automaticity of capital?' (*Man* 57; translation altered).
37. 'desacralization is not in the least nihilistic, insofar as "nihilism" must signify that which declares that access to being and truth is impossible. On the contrary, desacralisation is a *necessary condition* for the disclosing of such an approach to thought' (*Man* 56).
38. 'how can we leave [...] romanticism without bowing to the nihilistic sophism whose pure present is the world market, the economy and the consensual automatism of capital? How do we avoid being caught in the alternative: Life (mytheme) or Stock Exchange (capital)' (author's translation).
39. Žižek, *In Defense of Lost Causes*, pp. 403–4.
40. 'a regulatory hypothesis that envelops the variable fields and novel organisations of emancipatory politics' (author's translation).
41. 'the communist Idea is the imaginary operation whereby an individual subjectivation projects a fragment of the political real into the symbolic narrative of a History' (CH 239).
42. 'In that sense, failure is nothing more that the history of the proof of the hypothesis, provided that the hypothesis is not abandoned' (CH 7).
43. Beckett, *Comment c'est*, p. 150; 'in any case we have our being in justice I have never heard anything to the contrary' (Beckett, *How it is*, p. 135).
44. 'The justice mentioned here, which is a judgment on collective being, obviously is not related to any sort of finality. It uniquely concerns the intrinsic ontological equality of the figures of the subject' (*Con* 275).
45.
>That is why 'communism' must not be put forward as a 'hypothesis,' as we see in Alain Badiou – and consequently less like a political hypothesis to be verified by a political action that is itself caught in the schema of a classic struggle – but must instead be posited as a given, as a fact: our first given. (TD 54; translation altered)

46. 'Before all else, we are in common. Then we must become what we are: the given is an exigency, and this exigency is infinite' (TD 54).

47. 'at that point, we are so close that I no longer distinguish between us' (author's translation).
48. 'So, the fact that all events are at bottom "communist", that is what Jean-Luc Nancy affirms, and that is so true of my own thinking that at this point I shed even the language of wrongdoing' (author's translation).
49. Žižek, *In Defense of Lost Causes*, p. 404.

General Conclusion: How to Follow an 'Atheism' That Never Was

> Was für eine Philosophie man wähle, hängt davon ab, was für ein Mensch man ist. Denn ein philosophisches System ist nicht ein toter Hausrat, den man ablegen könnte, wie es uns beliebt, sondern es ist beseelt durch die Seele des Menschen, der es hat.[1]

> Chaque penseur dogmatique, en vertu d'une fiction dont il est dupe, et dont le public a pris l'habitude, parle, enseigne et décrète en se targuant de l'autorité d'une raison impersonnelle et d'une indubitable aperception du vrai, comme si l'expérience ne nous avait point appris que cette prétendu raison se contredit d'un philosophe à l'autre, et que, tant vaut la direction morale et intellectuelle de la personne, tant vaut la pensée, ni plus ni moins.[2]

We began this investigation by arguing that both imitative and residual atheisms are new moves in an old game and that their failure rigorously to think 'after God' is indicated by their systematic colonisation by 'postsecular' theologians. The implicit complicity of imitative atheism with the theological notions it explicitly rejects has been exposed (by Blanchot and others), and the asceticism of residual atheism, its ceding to theology of truth and goodness along with its Romantic inability to consummate the death of God, is lamented by Badiou and Meillassoux. As a recognition of and reaction to the inadequacy of both imitative and residual atheisms, it is our argument that a consensus has emerged around a desire to move beyond both parasitism and asceticism to a post-theological integration that cuts the theological root of parasitism without renouncing its fruit.

The possibility of a post-theological integration is an important one for French thought more broadly, not least because it is, as we have shown, inextricable from the question of ethical and political action, justice and equality, but also because it takes us to the heart of what is at stake in the divergence of fundamental orientations in French thought today, the divergence between axiom and Idea, deconstruction and the 'yet without', demonstration and factiality. Furthermore, the possibility of a post-theological integration is an important question whose time, it appears, has come, as diverse philosophers today are each returning to the difficulty of thinking and acting after God.

Engaging with this important current requires a double focus. First, in order to make sense of the similarities between Meillassoux, Nancy and Badiou it is important to see that what is common between them, namely seeking a post-theological thinking after atheism, is indicative of a shared new determination to grapple with the legacy of the death of God in a deeper way than every before, re-making philosophy from the ground up as a thinking 'without God'. Secondly, in order to appreciate both what is at stake for, and what is sought in, thinking after the death of God today, it is important to give full weight to the very different ways in which Meillassoux, Nancy and Badiou seek (and fail) to elaborate a post-theological integration.

For Nancy, post-theological thinking demands an atheology of the 'yet without' that disengages from the logic of principles and ends, and from the dichotomies that perpetuate theological binaries, not least the dichotomy of theism and atheism itself. His singular plural spacing rejects the transcendent/immanent dichotomy that bedevils residual atheism, and the way he thinks sense and signification, faith and reason, allows him to resist an idolatrous self-sufficiency. However, he remains caught in the bind identified by Derrida in *Le Toucher*, namely the bind of the deconstruction of Christianity always threatening to reveal itself as a Christian hyperbole, a charge that his claim to be finding something in Christianity of which God is only the 'front man' does not dispel. In addition, his recourse to *ethos* and the call fall short of providing the justification of equality that he requires.

For Badiou an atheism of the Idea must overcome the parasitic One and ascetic finitude with an axiomatised mathematical ontology for which nothing is inaccessible, thereby avoiding an ascetic withdrawal behind the limit of finitude. Nevertheless, the 'Christmas projection' of his account of philosophy, the uncertain status of inconsistent multiplicity and the unspoken good that motivates the event reintroduce the spectre of parasitism, while by the side of Meillassoux's justice for the dead and the Christian Final Judgment, Badiou's justice looks ascetic.

For Meillassoux, the attempt to demonstrate the principle of factiality seeks to liberate him from imitative atheism, while the 'philosophical divine' seeks to found a radical hope for future justice on hyperchaos with an appeal to two 'jolts' in a way that cedes nothing to religious notions of justice. However, the hyperchaos which is so powerful in leveraging his integral move beyond atheism also poses his project severe difficulties that remain to be addressed: the principle of non-contradiction is not exempt from hyperchaotic change, and the necessity of the two jolts compromises his pure demonstration of self-sufficient reason. These problems and difficulties with each of the three approaches to thinking following the death of God indicate that, though a post-theological integration has been clearly defined as a goal for contemporary thought, there is further work to be done in elaborating a thinking that moves beyond both parasitism and asceticism.

There are two reasons that we can no longer use the term 'atheism' or even 'atheisms' to characterise this new direction in French philosophy. First, the term is explicitly rejected by Nancy and emphatically rejected by Meillassoux, and to use it to characterise their thought would be unnecessarily to cut against its grain. Secondly, it designates one of the three approaches, namely Badiou's, and to use it in both a local and global sense would risk causing unnecessary confusion. Nor will 'thinking after God' do (for Meillassoux's philosophical divine is before God, not after him), nor for that matter 'thinking without God' (for Nancy uses the term 'God' freely in his writing, and Meillassoux's philosophy not only concedes but requires the real possibility of God's existence). The best way to understand and articulate what is happening in French tought today is to talk about the post-theological in general, and the goal of post-theological integration in particular. If we are to avoid a reductive approach to the current re-assessment of the West's theological legacy we will henceforth need to circumscribe the term 'atheism' itself much more tightly and see it as but one possible response to the legacy of the death of God, alongside atheology and the philosophical divine.

Having acknowledged these differences, however, we must return to the question of to what extent we can in fact talk about 'post-theological integration' as a coherent direction of thinking in the first place. Are Meillassoux, Badiou and Nancy showing three paths up the same mountain? To approach this question we must return one last time to that point at which our three thinkers diverge, namely the decision that chooses one fundamental philosophical orientation over another in the first place (why decision? why dis-enclosure? why demonstration?). Further work on post-theological thought needs to engage with the question of fundamental philosophical orientation, for the failure to account adequately for the disparity between dis-enclosure, decision or demonstration as approaches to post-theological thinking will always beg the question of any philosophy, whatever position it occupies in relation to the theological. Until this question is more adequately addressed no-one claim that they are following the death of God without a certain uncomfortable circularity in which any philosophy without God can be unmasked as a self-fulfilling prophecy.[3]

This notion of a fundamental philosophical orientation appears under different guises in each of our three thinkers. Badiou argues that there is an 'originary point of experience' that the whole of didactic philosophy strives to reach and transmit (*PE* 143), which for Badiou's thought is an intuition of subjective incorporation into a truth accompanied by an affect (*PE* 140–1) or, more personally, the experience of May '68 (ONTS 361–2). In contrast to Nancy, however, this point is not an opening but must fit with the conviction that 'real life' can be experienced in immanence (*PE* 149). Evoking Plato's *agathon*, to which Nancy also refers in the passage on philosophical blindspots from *L'Oubli de la philosophie*, Badiou argues for a principle of intelligibility that cannot be reduced to the Idea itself (*PE* 141), a principle with Neoplatonist and Galilean interpretations that seem, pending *L'Immanence des vérités*, to be undecidable.

For his part, Meillassoux uses a similar form of reasoning to try to close this opening of the system to its outside, claiming to have found the anhypothetical principle searched for since Plato. He presents a list similar to Nancy's in *L'Oubli de la philosophie*,[4] this time with the accent on the formula of non-duplication – 'only X cannot be X' where X in Meillassoux's case is Reason – and argues that this formula founds the exercise of reason in the impossibility of facticity itself being a fact. Nevertheless, his intellectual or dianoetic intuition re-introduces a necessary moment in his thought that is neither demonstrated nor demonstrable, a moment that resonates with Nancy's opening of signification to sense and with Badiou's 'originary point of experience'. Subtending the fundamental disagreement whether to proceed by judgment, decision or demonstration, there is a shared recognition among all three thinkers that more is at stake in a fundamental philosophical orientation than a philosophical judgment, decision or demonstration alone.

There is an experience with which philosophy has to catch up and transmit, an intuition that it seeks to justify, a blind spot around which it turns or a god in its midst. Nancy, Badiou and Meillassoux provide three variations on this theme. But is the theme itself 'without God'? Badiou admits that the rationalistic interpretation of the *agathon* is, at this stage in his thinking, undecidable from the apophatic; Nancy calls it on one occasion a mystery about God or the gods and on another occasion the gesture of touching the limit of every worldview; Meillassoux's discomfort is signaled in his move from intellectual to dianoetic intuition in interventions that postdate *Après la finitude*. This inaugural moment of thought stands as a witness to the need for ongoing work in the development of thinking without God, and leaves a question mark over the possibility of moving beyond the parasitism and asceticism that still haunt Nancy, Badiou and Meillassoux. It is a moment that shows, despite Badiou's, Nancy's and Meillassoux's approaches to the post-theological, just how difficult atheism and its successors remain.

NOTES

1. Fichte, *Werke*, vol 1, p. 434.

    The kind of philosophy one chooses thus depends upon the kind of person one is. For a philosophical system is not a lifeless household item one can put aside or pick up as one wishes; instead, it is animated by the very soul of the person who adopts it. (Fichte, *Introductions*, p. 20)

2. Renouvier, *Esquisse*, p. 357.

    Every dogmatic thinker, by virtue of a fiction which deceives him and to which the public has grown used, speaks teaches and decrees while boasting of the authority of an impersonal reason and an indubitable apperception of the true, as if experience had never taught us that this so-called reason contradicts itself from one philosopher to the next and that, where the moral and intellectual direction of the person leads, their thinking will follow, nothing more and nothing less. (Author's translation)

3. This circularity is evident in Martin Hägglund's treatment of Derrida in *Radical Atheism*. Hägglund's arguments have force if Derrida's fundamental orientation is taken for granted, but beg the question of that choice of orientation. For example, Hägglund argues that 'For Derrida life is essentially mortal, which means that there can be no instance (such as God in Marion's account) that is immortal' (Hägglund, *Radical Atheism*, p. 8). It is the 'for Derrida' of this argument that needs interrogating, the criteriology of the choice for a philosophical orientation for which life is essentially mortal in the first place.

4. Meillassoux includes Platonic ideas, the Cartesian cogito, Leibniz' logical truths, Kant's a priori forms of perception and Schopenhauerian will, whereas Nancy has Plato's Good, Descartes' evidence, Spinoza's joy, Kant's schematism, Hegel's logic and Marx's praxis.

Bibliography

Abel, Olivier, 'Les temps de Dieu', *Critique*, LXII: 704–5 (2006), pp. 129–41.
Adamek, Philip M., 'The intimacy of Jean-Luc Nancy's *L'Intrus*', *CR: The New Centennial Review*, 2: 3 (2002), pp. 189–201.
Agamben, Giorgio, *Homo Sacer: Sovereign Power and Bare Life*, trans. D. Heller-Roazen (Stanford: Stanford University Press, 1998).
—, 'Note liminaire sur le concept de démocratie', in Giorgio Agamben et al., *Démocratie, dans quel état?* (Paris: La Fabrique, 2009), pp. 9–14.
—, *The Coming Community*, trans. M. Hardt (Minneapolis: University of Minnesota Press, 1993).
Agamben, Giorgio, Alain Badiou, Daniel Bensaïd, Wendy Brown, Jean-Luc Nancy, Jacques Rancière, Kristin Ross, and Slavoj Žižek, *Démocratie, dans quel état?* (Paris: La Fabrique, 2009).
Albert, Eliot, 'Deleuze's impersonal, hyzolic cosmology: the expulsion of theology', in Mary Bryden (ed.), *Deleuze and Religion* (London: Routledge, 2001), pp. 184–95.
Alliez, Eric, 'Badiou: the grace of the universal', *Polygraph*, 17 (2005), pp. 267–73.
Althusser, Louis, 'Ideology and ideological state apparatuses (notes towards an investigation)', in Slavoj Žižek (ed.), *Mapping Ideology* (London: Verso, 1994), pp. 100–40.
Altizer, Thomas J. J. and William Hamilton, *Radical Theology and the Death of God* (Harmondsworth: Penguin, 1968).
Ansell-Pearson, Keith, *Germinal Life: The Difference and Repetition of Deleuze* (London: Routledge, 1999).
—, 'The simple virtual: Bergsonism and a renewed thinking of the one', *Pli*, 11 (2001), pp. 230–52.
Anselm, Saint, *Monologion and Proslogion*, trans. Thomas Williams (Cambridge: Hackett, 1996).
Armstrong, Philip, *Jean-Luc Nancy and the Networks of the Political* (Minneapolis: University of Minnesota Press, 2009).
Aron, Raymond, *The Opium of the Intellectuals* (New Brunswick, NJ: Transaction Publishers, 2001).

Atchley, J. Heath, 'The silence of the secular', *Literature and Theology: An Interdisciplinary Journal of Theory and Criticism*, 21: 1 (2007), pp. 66–81.
Augustine, Saint, *The City of God*, ed. R. W. Dyson, Cambridge Texts in the History of Political Thought (Cambridge: Cambridge University Press, 1998).
Badiou, Alain, *Abrégé de métapolitique* (Paris: Éditions du Seuil, 1998).
—, *Ahmed le philosophe suivi de Ahmed se fâche* (Paris: Actes du Sud, 1995).
—, 'A propos du «et» entre être et événement', in *Écrits autour de la pensée d'Alain Badiou* (Paris: L'Harmattan, 2007), pp. 103–4.
—, 'Author's preface', in *Being and Event*, trans. Oliver Feltham (London: Continuum, 2007), pp. xi–xv.
—, 'Author's preface', in *Theoretical Writings*, ed. and trans. Ray Brassier and Alberto Toscano (London: Continuum, 2004), pp. xiii–xv.
—, *Beckett: l'increvable désir* (Paris: Hachette, 1995).
—, *Being and Event*, trans. Oliver Feltham (London: Continuum, 2007).
—, 'Being by numbers [Interview with Lauren Sedofsky]', *Artforum*, 33: 2 (1994), pp. 84–90.
—, *Briefings on Existence: A Short Treatise on Transitory Ontology*, trans. Norman Madarasz (Albany, NY: SUNY Press, 2006).
—, *Circonstances 1: Kosovo, 11 septembre, Chirac/Le Pen* (Paris: Éditions Léo Sheer, 2003).
—, *Circonstances 2: Irak, foulard, Allemagne/France* (Paris: Éditions Léo Sheer, 2004).
—, *Circonstances 3: Portées du mot «juif»* (Paris: Éditions Léo Sheer, 2008).
—, *Circonstances 4: De quoi Sarkozy est-il le nom?* (Paris: Nouvelles Éditions Lignes, 2007).
—, *Circonstances 5: L'hypothèse communiste* (Paris: Lignes, 2009).
—, *Conditions* (Paris: Éditions du Seuil, 1992).
—, *Conditions*, trans. Steven Corcoran (London: Continuum, 2008).
—, *Court Traité d'ontologie transitoire* (Paris: Éditions du Seuil, 1998).
—, *Deleuze: La Clameur de l'être* (Paris: Hachette, 1997).
—, *Deleuze: The Clamor of Being*, trans. Louise Burchill, Theory Out of Bounds (Minneapolis: University of Minnesota Press, 2000).
—, 'Dix-neuf réponses à beaucoup plus de questions', *Cahiers du Collège International de Philosophie*, 8 (1989), pp. 247–68.
—, 'Drawing', *Lacanian Ink*, 28 (2006), pp. 42–8.
—, 'Eight theses on the universal', in *Theoretical Writings*, ed. and trans. Ray Brassier and Alberto Toscano (London: Continuum, 2004), pp. 143–52.
—, *Ethics: An Essay on the Understanding of Evil (Wo es War)* (London and New York: Verso, 2001).
—, 'Fifteen theses on contemporary art', trans. Peter Hallward (2005). Retrieved from: http://www.lacan.com/frameXXIII7.htm. Last accessed: July 2010.
—, *Handbook of Inaesthetics*, trans. Alberto Toscano (Stanford: Stanford University Press, 2004).

—, 'Hegel and the whole', in *Theoretical Writings*, ed. and trans. Ray Brassier and Alberto Toscano (London: Continuum, 2004), pp. 221–32.

—, 'Homage to Jacques Derrida', in Costas Douzinas (ed.), *Adieu Derrida* (Basingstoke: Palgrave Macmillan, 2007), pp. 34–46.

—, *Infinite Thought: Truth and the Return to Philosophy*, trans. Oliver Feltham and Justin Clemens (London: Continuum, 2005).

—, 'Kant's subtractive ontology', in *Theoretical Writings*, ed. and trans. Ray Brassier and Alberto Toscano (London: Continuum, 2004), pp. 135–42.

—, *L'Antiphilosophie de Wittgenstein* (Paris: Nous, 2009).

—, *L'Éthique: Essai sur la conscience du mal* (Caen: Nous, 2003).

—, *L'Être et l'événement*, L'ordre philosophique (Paris: Éditions du Seuil, 1988).

—, 'L'Humiliation ordinaire', *Le Monde*, 15 November 2005.

—, *L'Hypothèse communiste* (Paris: Nouvelles Éditions Lignes, 2009).

—, 'L'Investigation transcendantale', in Charles Ramond (ed.), *Alain Badiou: Penser le multiple* (Paris: L'Harmattan, 2002), pp. 7–20.

—, 'L'Offrande réservée', in François Guibal and Jean-Clet Martin (eds), *Sens en tout sens: Autour des travaux de Jean-Luc Nancy* (Paris: Galilée, 2004), pp. 13–24.

—, 'La scène de deux', in *De L'amour* (Paris: Flammarion, 1999), pp. 177–90.

—, 'Language, thought, poetry', in *Theoretical Writings*, ed. and trans. Ray Brassier and Alberto Toscano (London: Continuum, 2004), pp. 233–41.

—, *Le Concept de modèle* (Paris: Fayard, 2007).

—, *Le Nombre et les nombres* (Paris: Éditions du Seuil, 1990).

—, *Le Siècle* (Paris: Éditions du Seuil, 2005).

—, *Logics of Worlds*, trans. Alberto Toscano (London: Continuum, 2009).

—, *Logiques des mondes* (Paris: Éditions du Seuil, 2006).

—, *Manifeste pour la philosophie* (Paris: Éditions du Seuil, 1989).

—, *Manifesto for Philosophy* (Albany, NY: SUNY Press, 1999).

—, 'Mathematics and philosophy: the grand style and the little style (translated from a previously unpublished manuscript)', in *Theoretical Writings*, ed. and trans. Ray Brassier and Alberto Toscano (London: Continuum, 2004), pp. 3–20.

—, *Metapolitics*, trans. Jason Barker (London: Verso, 2005).

—, *Monde contemporain et désir de philosophie* (Reims: Noira, 1992).

—, 'Notes sur *Les Séquestrés d'Altona*', *Revue Internationale de Philosophie*, 231 (2005), pp. 51–60.

—, 'Notes toward a thinking of appearance', in *Theoretical Writings*, ed. and trans. Ray Brassier and Alberto Toscano (London: Continuum, 2004), pp. 177–88.

—, *Number and Numbers*, trans. Robin Mackay (Cambridge: Polity Press, 2008).

—, *On the Truth Process* (2002) [cited February 2010]. Retrieved from: http://www.lacan.com/badeurope.htm. Last accessed: January 2010.

—, 'On Simon Critchley's *Infinitely Demanding: Ethics of Commitment, Politics of Resistance*', *Critical Horizons*, 10: 2 (2009), pp. 154–62.
—, 'On subtraction', in *Theoretical Writings*, ed. and trans. Ray Brassier and Alberto Toscano (London: Continuum, 2004), pp. 103–18.
—, 'One, multiple, multiplicities', in *Theoretical Writings*, ed. and trans. Ray Brassier and Alberto Toscano (London: Continuum, 2004), pp. 67–80.
—, 'Ontology and politics: an interview with Alain Badiou', in *Infinite Thought: Truth and the Return to Philosophy*, trans. Oliver Feltham and Justin Clemens (London: Continuum, 2005), pp. 127–45.
—, *Petit Manuel d'inesthétique* (Paris: Éditions du Seuil, 1998).
—, *Petit Panthéon portatif* (Paris: La Fabrique, 2008).
—, *Peut-on penser la politique?* (Paris: Seuil, 2008).
—, 'Philosophy and mathematics: infinity and the end of romanticism', in *Theoretical Writings*, ed. and trans. Ray Brassier and Alberto Toscano (London: Continuum, 2004), pp. 21–38.
—, 'Philosophy and politics', *Radical Philosophy* (1999), pp. 29–32.
—, 'Philosophy, sciences, mathematics (interview)', *Collapse I* (2006), pp. 11–26.
—, 'Platonism and mathematical ontology', in *Theoretical Writings*, ed. and trans. Ray Brassier and Alberto Toscano (London: Continuum, 2004), pp. 49–58.
—, *Pocket Pantheon: Figures of Postwar Philosophy*, trans. David Macey (London: Verso, 2009).
—, *Polemics*, trans. Cécile Winter (London: Verso, 2006).
—, 'Politics as truth procedure', in *Theoretical Writings*, ed. and trans. Ray Brassier and Alberto Toscano (London: Continuum, 2004), pp. 153–60.
—, 'Politics: a non-expressive dialectics', *Urbanomic* (2005), pp. 1–13. Retrieved from: http://blog.urbanomic.com/sphaleotas/archives/badiou-politics.pdf. Last accessed: July 2010.
—, 'Préface: destin des figures', in Danielle Eleb, *Figures du destin* (Ramonville Saint-Ange: Éditions Erès, 2004), pp. 9–11.
—, 'Preface', in Quentin Meillassoux, *Après la finitude* (Paris: Éditions du Seuil, 2006), pp. 9–11.
—, *Saint Paul: La Fondation de l'universalisme* (Paris: Presses Universitaires de France, 1997).
—, *Saint Paul: The Foundation of Universalism*, trans. Ray Brassier (Stanford: Stanford University Press, 2003).
—, *Second Manifeste pour la philosophie* (Paris: Fayard, 2009).
—, 'Some replies to a demanding friend', 'Afterword', in *Think Again*, ed. Peter Hallward (London: Continuum, 2004), pp. 232–7.
—, 'Spinoza's closed ontology', in *Theoretical Writings*, ed. and trans. Ray Brassier and Alberto Toscano (London: Continuum, 2004), pp. 81–93.
—, 'The being of number', in *Theoretical Writings*, ed. and trans. Ray Brassier and Alberto Toscano (London: Continuum, 2004), pp. 59–66.
—, *The Century*, trans. Alberto Toscano (Cambridge: Polity Press, 2007).

—, *The Communist Hypothesis*, trans. David Macey and Steve Corcoran (London: Verso, 2010).
—, 'The event as trans-being', in *Theoretical Writings*, ed. and trans. Ray Brassier and Alberto Toscano (London: Continuum, 2004), pp. 97–102.
—, 'The formulas of L'Étourdit', trans. Scott Sacaiano, *Lacanian Ink*, 27 (2006), pp. 80–95.
—, *The Meaning of Sarkozy*, trans. David Fernbach (London: Verso, 2008).
—, 'The question of being today', in *Theoretical Writings*, ed. and trans. Ray Brassier and Alberto Toscano (London: Continuum, 2004), pp. 39–48.
—, 'The subject of art', *The Symptom*, 6 (2005). Retrieved from: http://www.lacan.com/symptom6_articles/badiou.html. Last accessed: January 2010.
—, 'The transcendental', in *Theoretical Writings*, ed. and trans. Ray Brassier and Alberto Toscano (London: Continuum, 2004), pp. 189–220.
—, *Theoretical Writings*, ed. and trans. Ray Brassier and Alberto Toscano (London: Continuum, 2004), pp. xiii–xv.
—, *Théorie de la contradiction* (Paris: Maspero, 1975).
—, *Théorie du sujet* (Paris: Éditions du Seuil, 1982).
—, *Theory of the Subject*, trans. Bruno Bosteels (London: Continuum, 2009).
—, 'Truth: forcing the unnameable', in *Theoretical Writings*, ed. and trans. Ray Brassier and Alberto Toscano (London: Continuum, 2004), pp. 119–34.
—, 'Un, multiple, multiplicité(s)', *Multitudes* (2000). Retrieved from: http://multitudes.samizdat.net/Un-multiple-multiplicite-s. Last accessed: January 2010.
Badiou, Alain, and Bruno Bosteels, 'Can change be thought? A dialogue with Alain Badiou', in Gabriel Riera, *Alain Badiou: Philosophy and its Conditions* (New York: SUNY Press, 2005), pp. 237–62.
—, and Bruno Bosteels, 'Peut-on penser le nouveau en situation?', *Failles: Situations de la Philosophie*, 2 (2006), pp. 62–93.
—, and Simon Critchley, 'Ours is not a terrible situation', *Philosophy Today*, 51: 3 (2007), pp. 357–65.
—, and Peter Hallward, 'Politics and philosophy: an interview with Alain Badiou', *Angelaki*, 3: 3 (1998), pp. 113–36.
—, and Analía Hounie, 'The question of democracy', *Lacanian Ink*, 28 (2006), pp. 54–67.
—, and Fabien Tarby, *La Philosophie et l'événement* (Meaux: Germina, 2010).
—, and A. Toscano, 'Plato, our dear Plato!', *Angelaki*, 11 (2006), pp. 39–41.
—, and Tzuchien Tho, 'New horizons in mathematics as a philosophical condition: an interview with Alain Badiou', *Parrhesia*, 3 (2007), pp. 1–11.
—, Peter Hallward and Bruno Bosteels, 'Beyond formalisation: an interview with Peter Hallward and Bruno Bosteels', trans. Bruno Bosteels and Alberto Toscano, *Angelaki*, 8: 2 (2003), 111–36.
Baldwin, Jon, and Nick Haeffner, '"Fault Lines": Simon Critchley in discussion on Alain Badiou', *Polygraph*, 17 (2005), pp. 295–307.
Balibar, Étienne, '«Histoire de la vérité»: Alain Badiou dans la philosophie

française', in Charles Ramond (ed.), *Alain Badiou: Penser le multiple* (Paris: L'Harmattan, 2002), pp. 497–524.

Balibar, Étienne, '"The History of Truth"', *Radical Philosophy*, 115 (2002), pp. 16–28.

Bandres, Lenin, 'Badiou et l'atomisme ancien', in Bruno Bensana and Oliver Feltham (eds), *Ecrits autour de la pensée d'Alain Badiou* (Paris: L'Harmattan, 2007), pp. 41–52.

Barker, Jason, *Alain Badiou: A Critical Introduction* (London: Pluto Press, 2002).

—, 'Topography and structure', *Polygraph*, 17 (2005), pp. 93–104.

Bataille, Georges, *Écrits posthumes, 1922–1940. Œuvres complètes*, vol. 2 (Paris: Gallimard, 1970).

—, *Guilty*, trans. Bruce Boone (Venice, CA: Lapis Press, 1988).

—, *L'histoire de l'érotisme, Le surréalisme, Au jour le jour, Conférence 1951–1953, La souveraineté, Annexes. Œuvres complètes*, vol. 8 (Paris: Gallimard, 1976).

—, *La Somme athéologique I. L'Expérience intérieure, Méthode de médiation, Post-scriptum 1953, Le Coupable, l'Alleluiah. Œuvres complètes*, vol. 5 (Paris: Gallimard, 1973).

—, *La Somme athéologique II. Sur Nietzsche, Mémorandum, Annexes. Œuvres complètes*, vol. 6 (Paris: Gallimard, 1973).

—, 'Un-knowing: laughter and tears', trans. Annette Michelson, *October*, 36: *Georges Bataille: Writings on Laughter, Sacrifice, Nietzsche, Un-Knowing* (1986), pp. 89–102.

—, *Visions of Excess: Selected Writings, 1927–1939*, ed. Allan Stoekl, trans. Allan Stoekl with Carl R. Lovitt and Donald M. Leslie Jr (Minneapolis: University of Minnesota Press, 1985).

Baumbach, Nico, 'Something else is possible: thinking Badiou on philosophy and art', *Polygraph*, 17 (2005), pp. 157–73.

Beckett, Samuel, *Comment c'est* (Paris: Les Éditions de Minuit, 1961).

—, *How it is* (London: John Calder, 1964).

Bell, Daniel M., Jr, 'Badiou's faith and Paul's Gospel: the politics of indifference and the overcoming of capital', *Angelaki*, 12: 1 (2007), pp. 97–111.

Bensaïd, Daniel, 'Alain Badiou et le miracle de l'événement', in *Essai de taupologie générale* (Paris: Fayard, 2001), pp. 143–70.

—, 'Alain Badiou and the miracle of the event', in Peter Hallward (ed.), *Think Again: Alain Badiou and the Future of Philosophy* (London: Continuum, 2004), pp. 94–105.

Bensaïd, Daniel, 'L'emblème démocratique', in Giorgio Agamben et al., *Démocratie, dans quel état?* (Paris: La Fabrique, 2009), pp. 15–26.

Bergen, Véronique, 'Pensée et être chez Deleuze et Badiou (Badiou lecteur de Deleuze)', in Charles Ramond (ed.), *Alain Badiou: Penser le multiple* (Paris: L'Harmattan, 2002), pp. 437–56.

Berger, Peter L., *The Sacred Canopy: Elements of a Sociological Theory of Religion* (New York: Anchor Books, 1990).

Besana, Bruno, 'One or several events? The knot between event and subject in the work of Alain Badiou and Gilles Deleuze', *Polygraph*, 17 (2005), pp. 245–66.

—, 'Quel multiple? Les conditions ontologiques du concept d'événement chez Badiou et Deleuze', in Bruno Besana and Oliver Feltham (eds), *Écrits autour de la pensée d'Alain Badiou* (Paris: L'Harmattan, 2007), pp. 23–40.

Besana, Bruno, and Oliver Feltham (eds), *Écrits autour de la pensée d'Alain Badiou* (Paris: L'Harmattan, 2007).

Blanchot, Maurice, *Faux pas* (Paris: Gallimard, 1975).

—, *Faux Pas*, trans. Charlotte Mandell (Stanford: Stanford University Press, 2001).

—, *L'Entretien infini* (Paris: Gallimard, 1969).

Blanton, Ward, 'Apocalyptic materiality: return(s) of early Christian motifs in Slavoj Žižek's depiction of the materialist subject', *Journal for Cultural and Religious Theory*, 6: 1 (2004), pp. 10–27.

Bogue, Ronald, 'The betrayal of God', in Mary Bryden (ed.), *Deleuze and Religion* (London: Routledge, 2001), pp. 9–29.

Borgeaud, Philippe, 'Une rumeur bien entendue. Le retour de(s) Dieu(x)', *Critique*, LXII: 704–5 (2006), pp. 59–68.

Bosteels, Bruno, *Alain Badiou: Une trajectoire polémique* (Paris: La Fabrique, 2009).

—, 'Badiou without Žižek', *Polygraph*, 17 (2005), pp. 221–44.

—, 'Force of nonlaw: Alain Badiou's theory of justice', *Cardozo Law Review*, 29: 5 (2008), pp. 1905–26.

—, 'Logics of antagonism: in the margins of Alain Badiou's "The Flux and the Party"', *Polygraph*, 17 (2005), pp. 93–107.

—, 'On the subject of the dialectic', in Peter Hallward (ed.), *Think Again: Alain Badiou and the Future of Philosophy* (London: Continuum, 2004), pp. 150–64.

—, 'Vérité et forçage: Badiou avec Heidegger et Lacan', in Charles Ramond (ed.), *Alain Badiou: Penser le multiple* (Paris: L'Harmattan, 2002), pp. 259–94.

Boulnois, Olivier, 'Dieu, raison ou religion?', *Critique*, LXII: 704–5 (2006), pp. 69–78.

Bradley, Arthur, 'Thinking the outside: Foucault, Derrida and negative theology', *Textual Practice*, 16: 1 (2002), pp. 57–74.

Brassier, Ray, *Nihil Unbound: Enlightenment and Extinction* (Basingstoke: Palgrave Macmillan, 2007).

—, '*Nihil Unbound*: remarks on subtractive ontology and thinking capitalism', in Peter Hallward (ed.), *Think Again: Alain Badiou and the Future of Philosophy* (London: Continuum, 2004), pp. 50–8.

—, 'Speculative realism: presentation by Ray Brassier', *Collapse* III, Speculative Realism (Annex to Collapse II) (2007), pp. 308–33.

—, 'Stellar void or cosmic animal? Badiou and Deleuze on the dice-throw', *Pli*, 10 (2000), pp. 200–16.

—, 'The enigma of realism: on Quentin Meillassoux's *After Finitude*', *Collapse* II (2007), pp. 15–54.
Breger, Claudia, 'The leader's two bodies: Slavoj Žižek's postmodern political theology', *Diacritics*, 31: 1 (2001), pp. 73–90.
Brown, Nathan, 'On *After Finitude*: a response to Peter Hallward'. Retrieved from: http://nsrnicek.googlepages.com/Response_to_Hallward_on_Meillass oux.pdf. Last accessed: March 2010.
Brown, Wendy, 'Nous sommes tous démocrates, à présent', in Giorgio Agamben et al., *Démocratie, dans quel état?* (Paris: La Fabrique, 2009), pp. 59–76.
Bryant, Levi R., 'Symptomal knots and evental ruptures: Žižek, Badiou, and discerning the indiscernible', *International Journal of Žižek Studies*, 1: 2 (2007). Retrieved from http://www.zizekstudies.org/index.php/ijzs/article/view/30/89. Last accessed June 2010.
Bryden, Mary (ed.), *Deleuze and Religion* (London: Routledge, 2001).
Bryden, Mary, 'Introduction', in Mary Bryden (ed.), *Deleuze and Religion* (London: Routledge, 2001), pp. 1–6.
—, 'Nietzsche's arrow: Deleuze on D. H. Lawrence's *Apocalypse*', in Mary Bryden (ed.), *Deleuze and Religion* (London: Routledge, 2001), pp. 101–14.
Buckner, S. Clark, and Matthew Statler (eds), *Styles of Piety: Practicing Philosophy After the Death of God*, Perspectives in Continental Philosophy, ed. John D. Caputo (New York: Fordham University Press, 2006).
Calcagno, Antonio. 'Jacques Derrida and Alain Badiou', *Philosophy and Social Criticism*, 30: 7 (2004), pp. 799–815.
Camus, Albert, *Lettres à un ami allemand* (Paris: Gallimard, 1945).
—, *Resistance, Rebellion, and Death*, ed. and trans. Justin O'Brien (New York: Vintage, 1974).
—, *The Myth of Sisyphus*, trans. Justin O'Brien (London: Hamish Hamilton, 1955).
Caputo, John D., 'Atheism, a/theology, and the postmodern condition', in Kevin Vanhoozer (ed.), *The Cambridge Companion to Postmodern Theology* (Cambridge: Cambridge University Press, 2007), pp. 267–83.
—, 'On the power of the powerless: dialogue with Gianni Vattimo', in Jeffrey W. Robbins (ed.), *After the Death of God* (New York: Columbia University Press, 2007), pp. 114–62.
—, 'Spectral hermeneutics: on the weakness of God and the theology of the event', in Jeffrey W. Robbins (ed.), *After the Death of God* (New York: Columbia University Press, 2007), pp. 47–88.
—, *The Weakness of God: A Theology of the Event* (Bloomington: Indiana University Press, 2006).
Caputo, John D., and Gianni Vattimo, *After the Death of God* (New York: Columbia University Press, 2007).
Chiesa, Lorenzo, and Alberto Toscano, '*Agape* and the anonymous religion of atheism', *Angelaki*, 21: 1 (2007), pp. 113–25.
Classen, C. Joachim, 'Poetry and rhetoric in Lucretius', *Transactions*

and *Proceedings of the American Philological Association*, 99 (1968), pp. 77–118.

Clay, Diskin, *Lucretius and Epicurus* (Ithaca, NY: Cornell University Press, 1983).

Clemens, Justin, 'Had we but worlds enough, and time, this absolute, philosopher ...', *Cosmos and History: The Journal of Natural and Social Philosophy*, 2: 1–2 (2006), pp. 277–310.

—, 'Platonic meditations: the work of Alain Badiou', *Pli*, 11: 2 (2001), pp. 200–29.

—, *The Romanticism of Contemporary Theory: Institution, Aesthetics, Nihilism*, Studies in European Cultural Transition, gen. eds Martin Stannard and Greg Walker (Aldershot: Ashgate, 2003).

Clemens, Justin, and Jon Roffe, 'Philosophy as anti-religion in the work of Alain Badiou', *Sophia*, 47 (2008), pp. 345–58.

Comte, Auguste, *System of Positive Polity*, trans. Henry Bridges (Bristol: Thoemmes, 2001).

Cousineau, Thomas, 'The future of an illusion: Melville's deconstruction of Deleuze's a/theology', in Mary Bryden (ed.), *Deleuze and Religion* (London: Routledge, 2001), pp. 115–25.

Critchley, Simon, 'A heroism of the decision, a politics of the event', *London Review of Books*, 29: 18 (2 September 2007), pp. 33–4.

—, 'Comment ne pas céder sur son désir (sur l'éthique de Badiou)', in Charles Ramond (ed.), *Alain Badiou: Penser le multiple* (Paris: L'Harmattan, 2002), pp. 207–34.

—, 'Demanding approval: on the ethics of Alain Badiou', *Radical Philosophy*, 100 (2000), pp. 16–27.

—, *Infinitely Demanding: Ethics of Commitment, Politics of Resistance* (London: Verso, 2007).

—, 'Mystical anarchism', *Critical Horizons*, 10: 2 (2009), pp. 272–306.

—, 'On Alain Badiou', *Theory and Event*, 3: 4 (2000). Retrieved from: http://muse.jhu.edu/journals/theory_and_event/v003/3.4critchley2.html. Last accessed: July 2010.

—, 'Oscar Wilde's faithless Christianity', *The Guardian*, (15 January 2009). Retrieved from: http://www.guardian.co.uk/commentisfree/belief/2009/jan/14/religion-wilde. Last accessed: July 2010.

—, *Very Little ... Almost Nothing: Death, Philosophy, Literature* (London: Routledge, 1997).

Crockett, Clayton, 'St Paul and the event', *Journal for Cultural and Religious Theory*, 6: 2 (2005), pp. 84–8.

Crowley, Martin, *L'Homme sans: Politiques de la finitude* (Paris: Lignes, 2009).

Crownfield, David, 'Extraduction', in Edith Wyschogrod, David Crownfield and Carl A. Raschke (eds), *Lacan and Theological Discourse* (New York: SUNY Press, 1989), pp. 161–9.

Cunningham, Conor, *Genealogy of Nihilism: Philosophies of Nothing and the*

Difference of Theology, Routledge Radical Orthodoxy, ed. John Milbank, Catherine Pickstock and Graham Ward (London: Routledge, 2002).

Dale, Catherine, 'Knowing one's enemy: Deleuze, Artaud and the problem of judgment', in Mary Bryden (ed.), *Deleuze and Religion* (London: Routledge, 2001), pp. 126–37.

David-Ménard, Monique, 'Être et existence dans la pensée d'Alain Badiou', in Charles Ramond (ed.), *Alain Badiou: Penser le multiple* (Paris: L'Harmattan, 2002), pp. 21–38.

Davies, Oliver, 'Thinking difference: a comparative study of Gilles Deleuze, Plotinus and Meister Eckhart', in Mary Bryden (ed.), *Deleuze and Religion* (London: Routledge, 2001), pp. 76–86.

de Kesel, Marc, 'Truth as formal Catholicism – on Alain Badiou, Saint Paul: La Fondation de l'universalisme', *International Journal of Žižek Studies*, 1: 2 (2004). Retrieved from: http://žižekstudies.org/index.php/ijzs/article/view/25/86. Last accessed: July 2010.

de Vries, Hent, *Religion and Violence: Philosophical Perspectives from Kant to Derrida* (Baltimore: Johns Hopkins University Press, 2001).

de Vries, Hent, and Lawrence Eugene Sullivan (eds), *Political Theologies: Public Religions in a Post-secular World* (New York: Fordham University Press, 2006).

Deleuze, Gilles, 'Mathesis, science and philosophy', *Collapse* III (2007), pp. 141–55.

Deleuze, Gilles, and Félix Guattari, *Qu'est-ce que la philosophie?* (Paris: Éditions de Minuit, 1992).

Depoortere, Frederiek, *Badiou and Theology*, Philosophy and Theology (London: Continuum, 2009).

—, *Christ in Postmodern Philosophy: Gianni Vattimo, René Girard, and Slavoj Žižek* (London: T&T Clark, 2008).

—, *The Death of God: An Investigation into the History of the Western Concept of God* (London: Continuum, 2008).

Deranty, Jean-Philippe, 'Rancière and contemporary political ontology', *Theory And Event*, 6: 4 (2003). Retrieved from: http://muse.jhu.edu/journals/theory_and_event/v006/6.4deranty.html. Last accessed: July 2010.

Derrida, Jacques, *De la Grammatologie* (Paris: Éditions de Minuit, 1967).

—, *Force de loi. Le 'Fondement mystique de l'autorité'* (Paris: Galilée, 1994).

—, 'Force of Law: the mystical foundation of authority', in Drucilla Cornell, Michel Rosenfeld and David Carlson (eds), *Deconstruction and the Possibility of Justice* (New York: Routledge, 1992), pp. 3–67.

—, 'I have a taste for the secret', in Jaques Derrida and Maurizio Ferraris, *A Taste for the Secret*, ed. Giacomo Donis and David Webb, trans. Giacomo Donis (Malden, MA: Polity, 2001), pp. 3–18.

—, *Le Toucher, Jean-Luc Nancy* (Paris: Galilée, 2000).

—, *Negotiations: Interventions and Interviews, 1971–2001*, ed. and trans. Elizabeth Rottenberg (Stanford: Stanford University Press, 2002).

—, *Of Grammatology*, trans. Gayatri Chakravorty Spivak (Baltimore: Johns Hopkins University Press, 1997).

—, *On Touching – Jean-Luc Nancy*, trans. Christine Irizarry (Stanford: Stanford University Press, 2005).

Derrida, Jacques, and Jean-Luc Nancy. 'Responsabilité – du sens à venir', in François Guibal and Jean-Clet Martin (eds), *Sens en tout sens: Autour des travaux de Jean-Luc Nancy* (Paris: Galilée, 2004), pp. 165–200.

Desanti, Jean-Toussaint, 'Some remarks on the intrinsic ontology of Alain Badiou', in Peter Hallward (ed.), *Think Again: Alain Badiou and the Future of Philosophy* (London: Continuum, 2004), pp. 50–8.

Descartes, René, *Œuvres de Descartes*, vol. 1, ed. Charles Adam and Paul Tannery (Paris: Vrin, 1974).

—, *The Philosophical Writings of Descartes*: vol. 3, *The Correspondence*, ed. John Cottingham, Robert Stoothoff, Dugald Murdoch and Anthony Kenny (Cambridge: Cambridge University Press, 1991).

Descombes, Vincent, *Modern French Philosophy*, ed. and trans. L. Scott-Fox and J. M. Harding (Cambridge: Cambridge University Press, 1980).

Dews, Peter (ed.), *The Limits of Disenchantment: Essays on Contemporary European Philosophy* (London: Verso, 1995).

—, 'States of grace: the excess of the demand in Badiou's ethics of truths', in Peter Hallward (ed.), *Think Again: Alain Badiou and the Future of Philosophy* (London: Continuum, 2004), pp. 106–19.

—, 'Uncategorical imperatives: Adorno, Badiou and the ethical turn', *Radical Philosophy*, 111 (2002), pp. 33–7.

Dewsbury, J. D., 'Unthinking subjects: Alain Badiou and the event of thought in thinking politics', *Transactions – Institute of British Geographers*, 32: 4 (2007), pp. 443–59.

Diderot, Denis, *Œuvres complètes: Édition critique et annotée*, vol. 7, ed. Jane Marsh Dieckmann (Paris: Hermann, 1976).

Douzinas, Costas (ed.), *Adieu Derrida* (Basingstoke: Palgrave Macmillan, 2007).

Drozdek, Adam, 'Beyond infinity: Augustine and Cantor', *Laval Théologique et Philosophique*, 51: 1 (1995), pp. 127–40.

Düttmann, Alexander García, 'What remains of fidelity after serious thought', in Peter Hallward (ed.), *Think Again: Alain Badiou and the Future of Philosophy* (London: Continuum, 2004), pp. 202–7.

Dufour, Dany-Robert, *On achève bien les hommes: De quelques consequences actuelles et futures de la mort de Dieu* (Paris: Éditions Denoël, 2005).

During, Élie, 'How much truth can art bear? On Badiou's "Inaesthetics"', *Polygraph*, 17 (2005), pp. 143–55.

—, 'Le ciel, Dieu, le divin: jeux interdits', *Critique*, LXII: 704–5 (2006), pp. 167–78.

Eagleton, Terry, 'Ideology and its vicissitudes in Western Marxism', in Slavoj Žižek (ed.), *Mapping Ideology* (London: Verso, 1994), pp. 179–226.

—, *Reason, Faith and Revolution: Reflections on the God Debate* (New Haven, CT: Yale University Press, 2009).

Ebguy, Jacques-David, 'Le travail de la vérité, la vérité au travail: usages de la littérature chez Alain Badiou et Jacques Rancière', *Fabula LHT (Littérature, Histoire, Théorie)* (2006). Retrieved from: http://www.fabula.org/lht/1/Ebguy.html. Last accessed: July 2010.

Eliot, Thomas Stearns, 'Leçon de Valéry', *Cahiers du Sud* (1946), pp. 74–81.

Esposito, Roberto, 'Chair et corps dans la déconstruction du christianisme', in François Guibal and Jean-Clet Martin (eds), *Sens en tout sens: Autour des travaux de Jean-Luc Nancy* (Paris: Galilée, 2004), pp. 153–64.

Feltham, Oliver, *Alain Badiou, Live Theory* (London: Continuum, 2008).

—, 'And being and event and . . .: philosophy and its nominations', *Polygraph*, 17 (2005), pp. 27–40.

—, 'Et l'être et l'événement et: la philosophie et ses nominations', in Besana, Bruno, and Oliver Feltham (eds), *Écrits autour de la pensée d'Alain Badiou* (Paris: L'Harmattan, 2007), pp. 107–24.

Feuerbach, Ludwig, *The Essence of Christianity*, trans. George Eliot (New York: C. Blanchard, 1855).

Fichte, Johann Gottlieb, *Introductions to the Wissenschaftslehre and Other Writings, 1797–1800.* ed. and trans. Daniel Breazeale (Cambridge: Hackett, 1994).

—, *Werke*, vol. 1 (Berlin: W. de Gruyter, 1971).

Ford, Russell, 'Book review: Ian James, *The Fragmentary Demand: An Introduction to the Philosophy of Jean-Luc Nancy*', *Continental Philosophy Review*, 40 (2007), pp. 107–11.

Fóti, Véronique M., *Vision's Invisibles: Philosophical Explorations* (New York: SUNY Press, 2003).

Foucault, Michel, 'Des espaces autres' (1984). Retrieved from: http://foucault.info/documents/heteroTopia/foucault.heteroTopia.fr.html. Last accessed: June 2010.

—, *Les Mots et les choses: Une Archéologie des sciences humaines* (Paris: Gallimard, 1990).

—, 'Of other spaces' (1984). Retrieved from: http://www.foucault.info/documents/heteroTopia/foucault.heteroTopia.en.html. Last accessed: July 2010.

—, *The Order of Things: An Archaeology of the Human Sciences*, trans. Alan Sheridan (London: Tavistock, 1970).

Fraser, Giles, *Redeeming Nietzsche: On the Piety of Unbelief* (London: Routledge, 2002).

Fynsk, Christopher, 'Foreword' In Jean-Luc Nancy (ed.), *Inoperative Community* (Minneapolis: University of Minnesota Press, 1991), pp. vii–xxxv.

Gall, Robert S., 'Of/from theology and deconstruction', *Journal of the American Academy of Religion*, 58: 3 (1990), pp. 413–37.

García-Düttmann, Alexander, 'L'évidence même', in François Guibal and Jean-Clet Martin (eds), *Sens en tout sens: Autour des travaux de Jean-Luc Nancy* (Paris: Galilée, 2004), pp. 143–52.

Gauchet, Marcel, *Le Désenchantement du monde: Une Histoire politique de la religion*, Bibliothèque des Sciences Humaines (Paris: Gallimard, 1985).
—, *The Disenchantment of the World: A Political History of Religion*, trans. Oscar Burge (Princeton: Princeton University Press, 1999).
Gaudemar, Martine de, 'Dieu le père ? (Histoire de la philosophie et psychanalyse)', in Charles Ramond (ed.), *Alain Badiou: Penser le multiple* (Paris: L'Harmattan, 2002), pp. 235–58.
Gaynesford, Maximilian de, 'Bodily organs and organisation', in Mary Bryden (ed.), *Deleuze and Religion* (London: Routledge, 2001), pp. 87–98.
Geroulanos, Stefanos, *An Atheism that is not Humanist Emerges in French Thought* (Stanford: Stanford University Press, 2010).
Gibson, Andrew, 'Badiou and Beckett: actual infinity, event, remainder', *Polygraph*, 17 (2005), pp. 175–203.
—, 'Badiou, Beckett et le postmodernisme', in Charles Ramond (ed.), *Alain Badiou: Penser le multiple* (Paris: L'Harmattan, 2002), pp. 421–36.
—, *Beckett and Badiou: The Pathos of Intermittency* (Oxford: Oxford University Press, 2006).
Gibson, A., 'The rarity of the event: on Alain Badiou', *New Formations* (2004), pp. 136–42.
Gillespie, Sam, *The Mathematics of Novelty: Badiou's Minimalist Metaphysics* (Melbourne: Re.Press, 2008).
Gillespie, Stuart, and Philip Hardie (eds), *The Cambridge Companion to Lucretius* (Cambridge: Cambridge University Press, 2007).
Gillespie, Stuart, and Philip Hardie, 'Introduction', in Gillespie, Stuart, and Philip Hardie (eds), *The Cambridge Companion to Lucretius* (Cambridge: Cambridge University Press, 2007), pp. 1–15.
Glendenning, Simon, *In the Name of Phenomenology* (Oxford: Routledge, 2007).
Glucksmann, André, *La troisième mort de Dieu* (Paris: NiL Éditions, 2000).
Goddard, Michael, 'The scattering of time crystals: Deleuze, mysticism and cinema', in Mary Bryden (ed.), *Deleuze and Religion* (London: Routledge, 2001), pp. 53–64.
Goldenberg, Mario, *A Conversation with Alain Badiou. Lacanian Ink*, 23 (2004), pp. 100–1.
Goodchild, Philip, *Capitalism and Religion: The Price of Piety* (London: Routledge, 2002).
—, 'Why is philosophy so compromised with God?', in Mary Bryden (ed.), *Deleuze and Religion* (London: Routledge, 2001), pp. 156–66.
Grant, Iain Hamilton, 'Prospects for post-Copernican dogmatism: the antinomies of transcendental naturalism', *Collapse* V (2009), pp. 413–51.
Grenz, Stanley James, *Renewing the Center: Evangelical Theology in a Post-Theological Era* (Grand Rapids, MI: Baker, 2000).
Guibal, François, 'Ouverture', in François Guibal and Jean-Clet Martin (eds), *Sens en tout sens: Autour des travaux de Jean-Luc Nancy* (Paris: Galilée, 2004), pp. 9–12.

—, 'Sans retour et sans recours', in François Guibal and Jean-Clet Martin (eds), *Sens en tout sens: Autour des travaux de Jean-Luc Nancy* (Paris: Galilée, 2004), pp. 59–104.
Guibal, François, and Jean-Clet Martin (eds), *Sens en tout sens: Autour des travaux de Jean-Luc Nancy* (Paris: Galilée, 2004).
Hägglund, Martin, *Radical Atheism: Derrida and the Time of Life* (Stanford: Stanford University Press, 2008).
—, 'The challenge of radical atheism: a response', *New Centennial Review*, 9: 1 (2009), pp. 227–52.
Hair, Lindsey, ' "I Love (U)": Badiou on love, logic, and truth', *Polygraph*, 17 (2005), pp. 127–42.
Hallett, Michael, *Cantorian Set Theory and Limitation of Size*, Oxford Logic Guides: 10 (Oxford: Clarendon Press, 1984).
Hallward, Peter, 'Alain Badiou et la déliaison absolue', in Charles Ramond (ed.), *Alain Badiou: Penser le multiple* (Paris: L'Harmattan, 2002), pp. 295–312.
—, 'Anything is possible: review essay on Quentin Meillassoux, *After Finitude*', *Radical Philosophy*, 52 (2008), pp. 51–7.
—, *Badiou: A Subject to Truth* (Minneapolis and London: University of Minnesota Press, 2003).
—, 'Depending on inconsistency: Badiou's answer to the "Guiding Question of All Contemporary Philosophy" ', *Polygraph*, 17 (2005), pp. 11–25.
—, 'Generic sovereignty: the philosophy of Alain Badiou – Badiou bibliography', *Angelaki*, 3: 3 (1998), pp. 87–112.
—, 'Introduction: Consequences of abstraction', in Peter Hallward (ed.), *Think Again: Alain Badiou and the Future of Philosophy* (London: Continuum, 2004), pp. 1–20.
—, *Out of This World: Deleuze and the Philosophy of Creation* (London: Verso, 2006).
Hallward, Peter (ed.), *Think Again: Alain Badiou and the Future of Philosophy* (London: Continuum, 2004).
—, 'Translator's introduction', in Alain Badiou, *Ethics: An Essay on the Understanding of Evil* (London: Verso, 2001), pp. vii–xlvii.
Hamacher, Werner, 'Ou, séance, touche de Nancy, ici (3)', in François Guibal and Jean-Clet Martin (eds), *Sens en tout sens: Autour des travaux de Jean-Luc Nancy* (Paris: Galilée, 2004), pp. 119–42.
Hamilton Grant, Iain, 'Speculative realism: presentation by Iain Hamilton Grant', *Collapse* III, Speculative Realism (Annex to Collapse II) (2007), pp. 334–66.
—, 'Psychoanalysis and the post-political: an interview with Slavoj Žižek', *New Literary History*, 32 (2001), pp. 1–21.
Hantaï, Simon, Jacques Derrida and Jean-Luc Nancy, *La Connaissance des textes, lecture d'un manuscrit illisible (Correspondances)* (Paris: Galilée, 2001).
Harman, Graham, 'On the horror of phenomenology: Lovecraft and Husserl', *Collapse* IV (2008), pp. 333–64.

—, 'On vicarious causation', *Collapse* II (2007), pp. 171–206.

—, 'Quentin Meillassoux: a new French philosopher', *Philosophy Today*, 51 (2007), pp. 104–17.

—, 'Speculative realism: presentation by Graham Harman', *Collapse* III, Speculative Realism (Annex to Collapse II) (2007), pp. 367–407.

Harpham, Geoffrey Galt, 'Doing the impossible: Slavoj Žižek and the end of knowledge', *Critical Inquiry*, 29: 3 (2003), pp. 453–85.

Hartley, Anthony (ed.), *The Penguin Book of French Verse: 4, The Twentieth Century* (Harmondsworth: Penguin, 1959).

Hebblethwaite, Brian, *Philosophical Theology and Christian Doctrine, Exploring the Philosophy of Religion* (Malden, MA, and Oxford: Blackwell, 2005).

Hegel, Georg Wilhelm Friedrich, *Hegel's Logic*, trans. William Wallace (Oxford: Clarendon Press, 1975).

Hegel, Georg Wilhelm Friedrich, and J. Carrère, *Correspondance*, vol. 1 (Paris: Gallimard, 1962).

Heidegger, Martin, *Being and Time*, trans. John Macquarrie and Edward Robinson (Oxford: Blackwell, 1973).

—, *Contributions to Philosophy (From Enowning)*, trans. Parvis Emad and Kenneth Maly (Bloomington: Indiana University Press, 1999).

—, 'Letter on humanism', in *Basic Writings: From* Being and Time *(1927) to* The Task of Thinking *(1964)*, ed. David Farrell Krell (London: Routledge and Kegan Paul, 1978), pp. 189–242.

—, *The Question Concerning Technology and Other Essays*, ed. and trans. William Lovitt (New York: Harper Torchbooks, 1977).

Heine, Heinrich, *The Romantic School and Other Essays*, ed. and trans. Jost Hermand and Robert C. Holub (London: Continuum, 1985).

Henry, Michel, *L'Essence de la manifestation* (Paris: Presses Universitaires de France, 1963).

Herbrechter, Stefan, 'Badiou, Derrida, and *The Matrix*: cultural criticism between objectless subjects and subjectless objects', *Polygraph*, 17 (2005), pp. 205–20.

Hewlett, Nick, 'Engagement and transcendence: the militant philosophy of Alain Badiou', *Modern and Contemporary France*, 12: 3 (2004), pp. 335–52.

Holbo, John, 'Critical discussion: on Žižek and Trilling', *Philosophy and Literature*, 28 (2004), pp. 430–40.

Hölderlin, Friedrich, *Selected Poems and Fragments*, trans. Michael Hamburger, ed. Jeremy Adler (London: Penguin, 1998).

Hollier, Denis, and Hilari Allred, 'The dualist materialism of Georges Bataille', *Yale French Studies*, 78: On Bataille (1990), pp. 124–39.

Hollywood, Amy, '"Beautiful as a Wasp": Angela of Foligno and Georges Bataille', *Harvard Theological Review*, 92: 2 (1999), pp. 219–36.

Hume, David, *A Treatise of Human Nature*, ed. Ernest Campbell Mossner (Harmondsworth: Penguin, 1985).

Husserl, Edmund, *Ideas Pertaining to a Pure Phenomenology and to a*

Phenomenological Philosophy, 1, General Introduction to a Pure Phenomenology, trans. F. Kersten (The Hague: Nijhoff, 1982).

—, *The Crisis of European Sciences and Transcendental Phenomenology: An Introduction to Phenomenological Philosophy*, ed., trans. and with an introduction by David Carr (Evanston: Northwestern University Press, 1970).

Hutchens, Benjamin C., *Jean-Luc Nancy and the Future of Philosophy* (Chesham: Acumen, 2005).

Imbert, Claude, 'Où finit le platonisme?', in Charles Ramond (ed.), *Alain Badiou: Penser le multiple* (Paris: L'Harmattan, 2002), pp. 357–74.

Jackson, Ken, 'The great temptation of "religion": why Badiou has been so important to Žižek', *International Journal of Žižek Studies*, 1: 2 (2007). Retrieved from: http://zizekstudies.org/index.php/ijzs/article/view/29/76. Last accessed: January 2010.

James, Ian, *The Fragmentary Demand: An Introduction to the Philosophy of Jean-Luc Nancy* (Stanford: Stanford University Press, 2006).

—, 'Incarnation and infinity', in Ignaas Devis Alena Alexandrova, Laurens ten Kate and Aukje van Rooden (eds), *Retreating Religion: Deconstructing Christianity with Jean-Luc Nancy* (New York: Fordham University Press, 2010).

Jameson, Fredric, 'Postmodernism and the market', in Slavoj Žižek (ed.), *Mapping Ideology* (London: Verso, 1994), pp. 278–95.

Jané, Ignacio, 'The role of the absolute infinite in Cantor's conception of set', *Erkenntnis*, 42 (1995), pp. 375–402.

Janicaud, Dominique, *Le Tournant théologique de la phénoménologie française*, ed. Jean-Pierre Cometti, Tiré à Part (Combas: Éditions de l'Eclat, 1991).

—, *Phenomenology and the 'Theological Turn': The French Debate* New York: Fordham University Press, 2000).

Jenkins, F., 'Humorous commitments and non-violent politics: a response to Simon Critchley's *Infinitely Demanding*', *Critical Horizons*, 10: 2 (2009), pp. 257–71.

Jennings, Theodore W., *Reading Derrida/Thinking Paul*, Cultural Memory in the Present, ed. Mieke Bal and Hent de Vries (Stanford: Stanford University Press, 2006).

Joeri Schrijvers, 'What comes after Christianity? Jean-Luc Nancy's deconstruction of Christianity', *Research in Phenomenology*, 39: 2 (2009), pp. 266–91.

Johnson, Alan, 'The reckless mind of Slavoj Žižek', *Dissent*, 56: 4 (2009), pp. 122–7.

Johnston, Adrian, 'From the spectacular act to the vanishing act: Badiou, Žižek, and the politics of Lacanian theory', *International Journal of Žižek Studies*, 1 (2007), pp. 1–40. Retrieved from: http://www.zizekstudies.org/index.php/ijzs/article/viewFile/1/1. Last accessed: January 2010.

—, 'Jason Barker, *Alain Badiou: A Critical Introduction*', *Theory And Event*, 6: 2 (2002).

—, 'There is Truth, and then there are truths – or, Slavoj Žižek as a reader of

Alain Badiou', *International Journal of Žižek Studies*, 1 (2007), pp. 141–85. Retrieved from: www.zizekstudies.org/index.php/ijzs/article/viewFile/10/26. Last accessed: January 2010.

Joubert, Claire, 'Badiou and the ethics of prose: revaluing Beckett' (Paris: Polart – Université Paris 8, 2004).

Kant, Immanuel, *Critique of Pure Reason*, ed. and trans. Paul Guyer and Allen W. Wood, *The Cambridge Edition of the Works of Immanuel Kant* (Cambridge: Cambridge University Press, 2000).

—, *Critique of the Power of Judgment*, trans. Paul Guyer and Eric Matthews, ed. Paul Guyer (Cambridge: Cambridge University Press, 2000).

—, *Lectures on Ethics*, trans. Louis Infield (Indianapolis: Hackett, 1980).

Kay, Sarah, *Žižek: A Critical Introduction*, Key Contemporary Thinkers (Cambridge: Polity, 2003).

Kearney, Richard, *Anatheism: Returning to God after God* (New York Columbia University Press, 2010).

Kendall, Stuart, 'Unlimited assemblage: Editor's introduction', in Georges Bataille, *The Unfinished System of Nonknowledge* (Minneapolis: University of Minnesota Press, 2001), pp. xi–xliv.

Kenney, E. J., 'Lucretian texture: style, metre and rhetoric in *De Rerum Natura*', in Stuart Gillespie and Philip Hardie (eds), *The Cambridge Companion to Lucretius* (Cambridge: Cambridge University Press, 2007), pp. 92–110.

Kenny, Anthony, *The God of the Philosophers* (Oxford: Clarendon Press, 1979).

Kerszberg, Pierre, *Critique and Totality* (Albany, NY: SUNY Press, 1997).

Kervégan, Jean-François, 'Un hégélianisme sans profondeur', in François Guibal and Jean-Clet Martin (eds), *Sens en tout sens: Autour des travaux de Jean-Luc Nancy* (Paris: Galilée, 2004), pp. 25–38.

Keynes, John Maynard, *The Collected Writings of John Maynard Keynes*, vol. 9 (London: Cambridge University Press for the Royal Economic Society, 1972).

Kierkegaard, Søren, *Concluding Unscientific Postscript to Philosophical Fragments*, trans. Howard Vincent Hong and Edna Hatlestad Hong (Princeton: Princeton University Press, 1992).

Kirsch, Adam, 'The deadly jester', *The New Republic* (2008). Retrieved from: http://www.tnr.com/article/books/the-deadly-jester. Last accessed: December 2009.

Kosky, Jeffrey, 'Georges Bataille's *Religion without Religion*: a review of the possibilities opened by the publication of *The Unfinished System of Nonknowledge*', *Journal of Religion*, 84: 1 (2004), pp. 78–87.

Kotsko, Adam, *Žižek and Theology*, Philosophy and Theology (London: T&T Clark, 2008).

—, 'Žižek's flawed "magnum opus"', *Journal for Cultural and Religious Theory*, 8:1 (2006), pp. 106–13.

Koyré, Alexandre, and Raïssa Tarr, *Du Monde clos à l'univers infini*, Collection Tel 129 (Paris: Gallimard, 1973).

Lacan, Jacques, 'A theoretical introduction to the functions of psychoanalysis in criminology', trans. M. Bracher, R. Grigg and R. Samuels, *JPCS: Journal for the Psychoanalysis of Culture and Society*, 1: 2 (1996), pp. 13–25.
—, *Écrits* (Paris: Éditions du Seuil, 1966).
—, *Le Séminaire, livre XVII, L'Envers de la psychanalyse*, ed. Jacques-Alain Miller (Paris: Seuil, 1991).
—, *Le Triomphe de la religion précédé de Discours aux Catholiques*, ed. Jacques-Alain Miller and Judith Miller, Camp Freudien (Paris: Éditions du Seuil, 2005).
—, *The Four Fundamental Concepts of Psychoanalysis*, ed. Jacques-Alain Miller, trans. A Sheridan (New York: Norton, 1981).
Laclau, Ernesto, 'An ethics of militant engagement', in Peter Hallward (ed.), *Think Again: Alain Badiou and the Future of Philosophy* (London: Continuum, 2004), pp. 120–37.
Lacoue-Labarthe, Philippe, 'Poésie, philosophie, politique', in Jacques Rancière, *La Politique des Poètes* (Paris: Albin Michel, 1992), pp. 39–63.
—, Untitled discussion of Alain Badiou's *L'Être et l'événement*, *Cahiers du Collège International de Philosophie*, 8 (1989), pp. 201–10.
Lacoue-Labarthe, Philippe, and Jean-Luc Nancy, *L'Absolu littéraire: Théorie de la littéraire du romantisme allemand* (Paris: Éditions du Seuil, 1978).
Lacoue-Labarthe, Philippe, and Jean-Luc Nancy, *Le Mythe Nazi* (Paris: Éditions de l'Aube, 1991).
Lacoue-Labarthe, Philippe, and Jean-Luc Nancy, 'Le «retrait» du politique', in Philippe Lacoue-Labarthe, Jean-Luc Nancy et al., *Le Retrait du politique* (Paris: Galilée, 1983), pp. 183–200.
Lacoue-Labarthe, Philippe, and Jean-Luc Nancy, *Le Titre de la lettre: Une Lecture de Lacan* (Paris: Galilée, 1990).
Lacoue-Labarthe, Philippe, and Jean-Luc Nancy, *Retreating the Political*, ed. Simon Sparks (London: Routledge, 1997).
Lacoue-Labarthe, Philippe, and Jean-Luc Nancy, *The Literary Absolute: The Theory of Literature in German Romanticism*, trans. Philip Barnard and Cheryl Lester (Albany, NY: SUNY, 1988).
Laffoucrière, Odette, *Le Destin de la pensée et 'la mort de Dieu' selon Heidegger*, Phaenomenologica (The Hague: Martinus Nijhoff, 1968).
Lalande, André, *Vocabulaire technique et critique de la philosophie* (Paris: Presses Universitaires de France, 1956).
Landes, Donald A., 'Le Toucher and the corpus of tact: exploring touch and technicity with Jacques Derrida and Jean-Luc Nancy', *L'Esprit Créateur*, 47: 3 (2007), pp. 80–92.
Laruelle, François, 'La Décision philosophique', *Cahiers du Collège International de Philosophie*, 8 (1989), [loose inserted leaf].
Lavaud, Claudie, 'Badiou lecteur de Saint Paul', in Charles Ramond (ed.), *Alain Badiou: Penser le multiple* (Paris: L'Harmattan, 2002), pp. 375–90.
Lawlor, Leonard, *The Implications of Immanence: Toward a New Concept of Life* (New York: Fordham University Press, 2006).

Lazarus, Sylvian, 'La politique entre singularité et multiplicité', in Charles Ramond (ed.), *Alain Badiou: Penser le multiple* (Paris: L'Harmattan, 2002), pp. 191–206.

Lecercle, Jean-Jacques, *Badiou and Deleuze Read Literature* (Edinburgh: Edinburgh University Press, 2010).

Lecercle, Jean-Jacques, 'Badiou's poetics', in Peter Hallward (ed.), *Think Again: Alain Badiou and the Future of Philosophy* (London: Continuum, 2004), pp. 218–31.

—, 'Cantor, Lacan, Mao, Beckett, même combat', *Radical Philosophy*, 93 (1999), pp. 6–13.

Lennon, Thomas M., 'Theology and the God of the philosophers', in *The Cambridge Companion to Early Modern Philosophy*, ed. Donald Rutherford (Cambridge: Cambridge University Press, 2006), pp. 274–98.

Lévinas, Emmanuel, *De Dieu qui vient a l'idée* (Paris: J. Vrin, 1982).

—, *Of God who Comes to Mind*, trans. Bettina Bergo (Stanford: Stanford University Press, 1998).

—, *Sur Maurice Blanchot* (Paris: Fata Morgana, 1975).

—, *Totalité et infini: Essai sur l'extériorité* (La Haye: M. Nijhoff, 1961).

—, *Totality and Infinity: An Essay on Exteriority*, trans. Alphonso Lingis (Pittsburgh: Duquesne University Press, 1969).

Locke, John, *An Essay Concerning Human Understanding*, ed. Pauline Phemister (Oxford: Oxford University Press, 2008).

Lyotard, Jean-François, Untitled discussion of Alain Badiou's *L'Être et l'événement*, *Cahiers du Collège International de Philosophie*, 8 (1989), pp. 227–46.

Macherey, Pierre, 'Le Mallarmé d'Alain Badiou', in Charles Ramond (ed.), *Alain Badiou: Penser le multiple* (Paris: L'Harmattan, 2002), pp. 397–406.

Mackenzie Jr., Louis A., 'To the brink: the dialectic of anxiety in the Pensées', *Yale French Studies*, 66, The Anxiety of Anticipation (1984), pp. 57–66.

Maddy, Penelope, 'Believing the axioms', *Journal of Symbolic Logic*, 53: 2 (1988), pp. 480–511.

Magnard, Pierre, *Le Dieu des philosophes* (Paris: Éditions de la Table Ronde, 2006).

Malabou, Catherine, 'Pierre aime les horranges', in François Guibal and Jean-Clet Martin (eds), *Sens en tout sens: Autour des travaux de Jean-Luc Nancy* (Paris: Galilée, 2004), pp. 39–58.

Maniglier, P., and D. Rabouin, 'A quoi bon l'ontologie? Les mondes selon Badiou Alain Badiou, Logiques des mondes', *Critique*, 63 (2007), pp. 279–94.

Manoussakis, John Panteleimon, *God after Metaphysics* (Bloomington: Indiana University Press, 2007).

Marchart, Oliver, 'Nothing but a truth: Alain Badiou's 'Philosophy of Politics' and the left Heideggerians', *Polygraph*, 17 (2005), pp. 105–25.

—, *Post-Foundational Political Thought: Political Difference in Nancy, Lefort, Badiou and Laclau* (Edinburgh: Edinburgh University Press, 2007).

Marion, Jean-Luc, *Being Given: Toward a Phenomenology of Givenness*, trans. Jeffrey L. Kosky (Stanford: Stanford University Press, 2002).
—, 'De la « mort de Dieu » aux noms divins: l'itinéraire théologique de la métaphysique', *Laval théologique et philosophique*, 41: 1 (1985), pp. 25–41.
—, *Dieu sans l'être* (Paris: Fayard, 1982).
—, *Étant donné: Essai d'une phénoménologie de la donation* (Paris: Presses Universitaires de France, 1998).
—, *God without Being*, trans. Thomas A. Carlson (Chicago: University of Chicago Press, 1995).
—, *L'Idole et la distance: Cinq études* (Paris: B. Grasset, 1977).
—, *Reduction and Givenness: Investigations of Husserl, Heidegger, and Phenomenology*, trans. Thomas A. Carlson (Evanston: Northwestern University Press, 1998).
—, *Réduction et donation* (Paris: Presses Universitaires de France, 1989).
—, *The Idol and Distance: Five Studies*, trans. Thomas A. Carlson (New York: Fordham University Press, 2001).
—, *Constellation de la philosophie* (Paris: Éditions Kimé, 2007).
Martin, Jean-Clet, 'Le murmure des pierres', in François Guibal and Jean-Clet Martin, *Sens en tout sens: Autour des travaux de Jean-Luc Nancy* (Paris: Galilée, 2004), pp. 105–18.
Martin, Stewart, 'Cul de sac, review of Jacques Rancière, *The Politics of Aesthetics* and Alain Badiou, *Handbook of Inaesthetics*', *Radical Philosophy*, 131 (2005), pp. 39–44.
May, Todd, 'Badiou and Deleuze on the one and the many', in Peter Hallward (ed.), *Think Again: Alain Badiou and the Future of Philosophy* (London: Continuum, 2004), pp. 67–76.
—, *Reconsidering Difference: Nancy, Derrida, Lévinas, and Deleuze* (University Park, PA: Pennsylvania State University Press, 1997).
Meillassoux, Quentin, *After Finitude: An Essay on the Necessity of Contingency*, ed. and trans. Ray Brassier (London: Continuum, 2008).
—, *Après la finitude* (Paris: Éditions du Seuil, 2006).
—, 'Contingence et absolutisation de l'un', *Métaphysique, ontologie, hénologie*, Université de Paris I (2008).
—, 'Deuil à venir, dieu à venir', *Critique*, LXII: 704–5 (2006), pp. 105–15.
—, 'Histoire et événement chez Alain Badiou', *Marx au XXIe siècle: L'Esprit & la lettre*, Université de Paris I (2 February 2008). Retrieved from: http://www.marxau21.fr/index.php?option=com_content&view=article&id=83:histoire-et-evenement-chez-alain-badiou&catid=39:badiou-alain&Itemid=62. Last accessed February 2010.
—, 'L'Inexistence divine: Essai sur le dieu virtuel', thèse de doctorat, Paris I (1997).
—, 'Métaphysique et fiction des mondes hors-science', *Le Mois de la science-fiction de l'ENS*, ENS Paris (November 2006).
—, 'Nouveauté et événement', in Charles Ramond (ed.), *Alain Badiou: Penser le multiple* (Paris: L'Harmattan, 2002), pp. 39–64.

—, 'Potentiality and virtuality', *Collapse* II (2007), pp. 55–82.
—, 'Spectral dilemma', *Collapse* IV (2008), pp. 261–75.
—, 'Speculative realism: presentation by Quentin Meillassoux', *Collapse* III, Speculative Realism (Annex to Collapse II) (2007), pp. 408–49.
—, 'Subtraction and contraction: Deleuze's remarks on *Matter and Memory*', *Collapse* III (2007), pp. 63–107.
—, 'Temps et surgissement ex nihilo', *Colloque: Autour de 'Logiques des mondes'*, ENS Paris (November 2006).
—, 'Time without becoming', CRMEP Research Seminar, Middlesex University, London (8 May 2008).
Melzer, Sara E., 'Codes of space in the Pensées', *French Review*, 51: 6 (1978), pp. 816–23.
Merleau-Ponty, Maurice, *Le Primat de la perception et ses conséquences philosophiques: Précédé de Projet de travail sur la nature de la perception (1933); et La nature de la perception (1934)* (Grenoble: Cynara, 1989).
—, *Le Visible et l'invisible. Suivi de Notes de travail* (Paris: Gallimard, 1964).
—, *Signs*, trans. Richard C. McCleary (Evanston: Northwestern University Press, 1964).
—, *The Primacy of Perception, and other Essays on Phenomenological Psychology, the Philosophy of Art, History and Politics*, ed. James M. Edie (Evanston: Northwestern University Press, 1964).
—, *The Visible and the Invisible: Followed by Working Notes*, ed. Claude Lefort, rans. Alphonso Lingis (Evanston: Northwestern University Press, 1968).
Michal, Thomas, 'Book review: Opposed to blurring on every level', *International Journal of Baudrillard Studies*, 3: 1 (January 2006). Retrieved from: http://www.ubishops.ca/baudrillardstudies/vol3_1/mical.htm. Last accessed: July 2010.
Michel, Andreas, 'Differentiation vs. disenchantment: the persistence of modernity from Max Weber to Jean-Francois Lyotard', *German Studies Review*, 20: 3 (1997), pp. 343–70.
Michon, Cyrille, 'Il nous faut bien un concept de Dieu', *Critique*, LXII: 704–5 (2006), pp. 92–104.
Milbank, John, 'Only theology saves metaphysics: on the modalities of terror', in Connor Cunningham and P. M. Candler Jr (eds), *Belief and Metaphysics* (London: SCM Press, 2007), pp. 452–99.
—, 'The shares of being or gift, relation and participation: an essay on the metaphysics of Emmanuel Lévinas and Alain Badiou'. Retrieved from: http://theologyphilosophycentre.co.uk/papers/Milbank_Metaphysics-LevinasBadiou.pdf. Last accessed January 2010.
Miller, Adam, 'An interview with Alain Badiou: "Universal Truths and the Question of Religion"', *Journal of Philosophy and Scripture*, 3: 1 (2005). Retrieved from: http://www.philosophyandscripture.org/Issue3-1/Badiou/Badiou.html. Last accessed: January 2010.
—, *Badiou, Marion and St Paul: Immanent Grace*, Continuum Studies in Continental Philosophy (London: Continuum, 2008).

Montesquieu, Charles de Secondat, baron de, *The Persian Letters*, ed. and trans. J. Robert Loy (New York: Meridian Books, 1961).

Moreau, Pierre-François, 'Alain Badiou lecteur de Spinoza', in Charles Ramond (ed.), *Alain Badiou: Penser le multiple* (Paris: L'Harmattan, 2002), pp. 391–6.

Mount, B. Madison, 'The Cantorian revolution: Alain Badiou on the philosophy of set theory', *Polygraph*, 17 (2005), pp. 41–91.

Mullarkey, John, *Post-Continental Philosophy*, Transversals, ed. Keith Ansell-Pearson (London: Continuum, 2006).

Nancy, Jean-Luc, *A Finite Thinking*, ed. Simon Sparks (Stanford: Stanford University Press, 2003).

—, *A l'Écoute* (Paris: Galilée, 2002).

—, *À plus d'un titre, Sur un portrait de Valerio Adami* (Paris: Galilée, 2007).

—, 'Answering for sense', trans. Jean-Christophe Cloutier, in James J. Bono, Tim Dean and Ewa Płonowska Ziarek (eds), *A Time for the Humanities: Futurity and the Limits of Autonomy* (New York: Fordham University Press, 2008), pp. 84–93.

—, 'Ascoltando', in Peter Szendy (ed.), *Écoute: Une Histoire de nos oreilles* (Paris: Minuit, 2001), pp. 7–12.

—, *Au Fond des images* (Paris: Galilée, 2003).

—, *Being Singular Plural*, trans. Robert D. Richardson and Anne E. O'Byrne (Stanford: Stanford University Press, 2000).

—, 'Between story and truth', *Little Magazine* (2001). Retrieved from: http://www.littlemag.com/jul-augo1/nancy.html. Last accessed: July 2010.

—, 'Chromatic atheology', *Journal of Visual Culture*, 4: 1 (2005), pp. 123–8.

—, *Chroniques philosophiques* (Paris: Éditions Galilée, 2004).

—, 'Church, State, resistance', *Journal of Law and Society*, 34: 1 (1997), pp. 3–13.

—, 'Conloquium', in Roberto Esposito, *Communitas: Origine et destin de la communauté* (Paris: Presses Universitaires de France, 2000), pp. 3–10.

—, *Corpus* (Paris: Seuil, 1992).

—, *Corpus*, ed. and trans. Richard A. Rand (New York: Fordham University Press, 2008).

—, 'Corpus', in J. F. MacCannell and L. Zakarin (eds), *Thinking Bodies* (Irvine; CA: Stanford University Press, 1990), pp. 17–31.

—, 'Démocratie finie et infinie', in Giorgio Agamben et al., *Démocratie, dans quel état?* (Paris: La Fabrique, 2009), pp. 77–96.

—, *Des Lieux divins: Suivi de Calcul du poète* (Mauvezin: Trans-Europ-Repress, 1987).

—, 'Dies irae', in *La Faculté de juger* (Paris: Minuit, 1985), pp. 9–54.

—, *Dis-Enclosure: The Deconstruction of Christianity*, trans. Bettina Bergo, Gabriel Malenfant and Michael B. Smith (New York: Fordham University Press, 2008).

—, *Ego sum*, La Philosophie en Effet (Paris: Flammarion, 1979).

—, *Être singulier pluriel*, La Philosophie en Effet (Paris: Galilée, 1996).

—, *Hegel: L'inquiétude du négatif* (Paris: Hachette, 1997).
—, *Hegel: The Restlessness of the Negative*, trans. Jason Smith and Steven Miller (Minneapolis: University of Minnesota Press, 2002).
—, 'Identité et tremblement', in *Hypnoses* (Paris: Galilée, 1984), pp. 14–47.
—, *Juste impossible: Petite conférence sur le juste et l'injuste* (Paris: Bayard, 2007).
—, *L''il y a' du rapport sexuel*, Incises (Paris: Galilée, 2001).
—, *L'Adoration, Déconstruction du christianisme 2* (Paris: Galilée, 2010).
—, 'L'Espèce d'espace pensée. Préface', in Benoît Goetz (ed.), *La Dislocation: Architecture et philosophie* (Paris: Éditions de la Passion, 2002), pp. 11–13.
—, *L'Expérience de la liberté* (Paris: Galilée, 1988).
—, *L'Impératif catégorique*, La Philosophie en Effet (Paris: Flammarion, 1983).
—, *L'Intrus*, Lignes Fictives (Paris: Galilée, 2000).
—, *L'Oubli de la philosophie*, La Philosophie en Effet (Paris: Galilée, 1986).
—, *La Communauté affrontée*, La Philosophie en Effet (Paris: Galilée, 2001).
—, *La Communauté désœuvrée*, nouvelle édition révisée et augmentée, Détroits (Paris: Christian Bourgois, 1999).
—, *La Comparution (politique à venir)*, Détroits (Paris: Christian Bourgeois, 1991).
—, 'La Comparution /The compearance: from the existence of "communism" to the community of "existence"', trans. Tracy B. Strong, *Political Theory*, 20: 3 (1992), pp. 371–98.
—, *La Création du monde, ou, La Mondialisation*, La Philosophie en Effet (Paris: Galilée, 2002).
—, *La Déclosion: Déconstruction du christianisme 1* (Paris: Galilée, 2005).
—, *La Pensée dérobée* (Paris: Galilée, 2001).
—, *La Remarque spéculative*, La philosophie en effet (Paris: Galilée, 1973).
—, 'Laïcité monothéiste', *Le Monde*, 2 January 2004.
—, *Le discours de la syncope I, Logodaedalus* (Paris: Aubier-Flammarion, 1976).
—, *Le Partage des voix*, Débats (Paris: Galilée, 1982).
—, *Le Poids d'une pensée, l'approche* (Strasbourg: Éditions de la Phocide, 2008).
—, *Le Poids d'une pensée*, Trait d'Union (Sainte-Foy, Quebec: Éditions Le Griffon d'Argile, 1991).
—, 'Le Portrait (dans le décor)', in *Cahiers Philosophie de l'art* (Paris: Institut d'Art Contemporain, 1999).
—, *Le Regard du portrait* (Paris: Galilée, 2000).
—, *Le Sens du monde*, La Philosophie en Effet (Paris: Galilée, 1993).
—, *Les Muses*, La Philosophie en Effet (Paris: Galilée, 1994).
—, 'Mad Derrida: *ipso facto cogitans ac demens*', in Costas Douzinas (ed.), *Adieu Derrida* (Basingstoke: Palgrave Macmillan, 2007), pp. 17–33.
—, 'Mad Derrida', Adieu, Derrida: A series of lectures held in commemora-

tion of Jacques Derrida, marking the launch of the Birkbeck Institute for the Humanities, Birkbeck, University of London, Friday, 6 May 2005.

—, *Noli me tangere: Essai sur la levée du corps* (Paris: Bayard, 2003).

—, *Noli me tangere: On the Raising of the Body*, trans. Sarah Clift, Pascale-Anne Brault and Michael Naas (New York: Fordham University Press, 2008).

—, 'Of divine places', in *The Inoperative Community*, ed. Peter Connor, trans. Lisa Garbus, Peter Connor, Michael Holland and Simona Sawhney (Minneapolis: University of Minnesota Press, 1991), pp. 110–50.

—, *Philosophical Chronicles*, trans. Franson Manjal (New York: Fordham University Press, 2008).

—, 'Philosophie sans conditions', in Charles Ramond (ed.), *Alain Badiou: Penser le multiple* (Paris: L'Harmattan, 2002), 65–79.

—, 'Philosophy without conditions', in Peter Hallward (ed.), *Think Again: Alain Badiou and the Future of Philosophy* (London: Continuum, 2004), pp. 39–49.

—, 'Postface', in Martin Crowley, *L'Homme sans* (Paris: Lignes, 2009), pp. 181–4.

—, *Sur le commerce des pensées*, Écritures/Figures, ed. Michel Delorme (Paris: Galilée, 2005).

—, 'Technique du présent: essai sur On Kawara', Paper presented at the *Cahiers-Philosophie de l'art*, 1997.

—, *The Birth to Presence*, trans. Brian Holmes et al. (Stanford: Stanford University Press, 1993).

—, 'The calculation of the poet', in Aris Fioretos (ed.), *The Solid Letter: Readings of Friedrich Hölderlin* (Stanford: Stanford University Press, 1999), pp. 44–73.

—, 'The confronted community', trans. Jason Kemp Winfree, in Andrew J. Mitchell and Jason Kemp Winfree (eds), *The Obsessions of Georges Bataille: Community and Communication* (Albany, NY: SUNY Press, 2009), pp. 19–30.

—, *The Creation of the World, or, Globalization*, trans. François Raffoul and David Pettigrew (Albany, NY: SUNY Press, 2007).

—, *The Experience of Freedom*, trans. Bridget McDonald (Stanford: Stanford University Press, 1993).

—, *The Gravity of Thought*, trans. François Raffoul and Gregory Recco (Atlantic Highlands, NJ: Humanities Press, 1997).

—, *The Ground of the Image*, trans. Jeff Fort (New York: Fordham University Press, 2005).

—, *The Inoperative Community*, ed. Peter Connor, trans. Lisa Garbus, Peter Connor, Michael Holland and Simona Sawhney (Minneapolis: University of Minnesota Press, 1991).

—, *The Muses*, trans. Peggy Kamuf (Stanford: Stanford University Press, 1996).

—, *The Self-Deconstruction of Christianity: An Open Discussion with Jean-Luc Nancy*. European Graduate School EGS, August 2000 [cited 30

August 2005]. Retrieved from: http://www.egs.edu/faculty/nancy/nancy-self-deconstruction-of-christianity-2000.html. Last accessed: January 2010.

—, *The Sense of the World*, trans. Jeffrey S. Librett (Minneapolis: University of Minnesota Press, 1997).

—, *The Truth of Democracy*, trans. Pascale-Anne Brault and Michael Naas (New York: Fordham University Press, 2010).

—, *Tombe de sommeil* (Paris: Galilée, 2007).

—, 'Tout est-il politique?', *Actuel Marx*, 28 (2000), pp. 77–82.

—, 'Un Jour, les dieux se retirent . . .', Pharmacie de Platon (Bordeaux: William Blake, 2001).

—, 'Une Pensée au partage des eaux', *Le Monde*, 11 March 2005.

—, *Une Pensée finie* (Paris: Galilée, 1990).

—, *Vérité de la démocratie* (Paris: Galilée, 2008).

—, *Visitation (de la peinture chrétienne)*, Lignes fictives (Paris: Galilée, 2001).

Nancy, Jean-Luc, and Jean-Claude Conésa, *Être, c'est être perçu* (Paris: Éditions des Cahiers Intempestifs, 2000).

—, and Thomas Ferenczi, 'Un entretien avec Jean-Luc Nancy', *Le Monde*, 29 March 2005.

—, and B. C. Hutchens, 'The future of philosophy. Interview', in B. C. Hutchens, *Jean-Luc Nancy and the Future of Philosophy* (Chesham: Acumen, 2005), pp. 161–6.

—, and Abbas Kiarostami, *L'Évidence du film* (Brussels: Yves Gevaert, 2001).

—, and François Martin, *NIUM* (Valence: École Régionale des Beaux Arts, 1998).

—, and Jérôme-Alexandre Nielsberg, 'L'athéisme, essence des monothéismes', *L'Humanité*, 24 May 2005.

Nault, François, 'La déconstruction et le jeu de l'athéologie (Nietzsche, Bataille, Derrida)', *Studies in Religion*, 27: 3 (1998), pp. 277–94.

Newman, S., 'Polemics Alain Badiou', *Contemporary Political Theory*, 7 (2008), pp. 225–8.

Nicolacopoulos, Toula, and George Vassilacopoulos, 'Philosophy and revolution: Badiou's infidelity to the event', *Cosmos and History: The Journal of Natural and Social Philosophy*, 2: 1–2 (2006). Retrieved from: http://www.cosmosandhistory.org/index.php/journal/article/viewFile/35/69. Last accessed: January 2011.

Nietzsche, Friedrich Wilhelm, *The Anti-Christ, Ecce Homo, Twilight of the Idols, and other writings*, ed. Aaron Ridley and Judith Norman, trans. Judith Norman (New York: Cambridge University Press, 2005).

—, *The Gay Science: With a Prelude in Rhymes and an Appendix of Songs*, trans. Walter Kaufmann (New York: Vintage Books, 1974).

Noys, Benjamin, 'The provocations of Alain Badiou', *Theory Culture Society*, 20: 1 (2003), pp. 123–32.

Nussbaum, Martha Craven, *The Therapy of Desire: Theory and Practice in Hellenistic Ethics* (Princeton: Princeton University Press, 2009).

O'Donnell, Liam A., 'Saint Paul: apostle, militant, communist', *Cosmos and*

History: The Journal of Natural and Social Philosophy, 2: 1–2 (2006), pp. 345–9.

Osborn, Eric Francis, *Tertullian, First Theologian of the West* (Cambridge: Cambridge University Press, 1997).

Osborne, Peter, 'Alain Badiou's *Being and Event*', *Radical Philosophy*, 142 (2007), pp. 19–29.

Pascal, Blaise, *Pensées*, trans. A. J. Krailsheimer (Harmondsworth: Penguin, 1986).

Pearson, Keith Ansell, 'Pure reserve: Deleuze, philosophy, and immanence', in Mary Bryden (ed.), *Deleuze and Religion* (London: Routledge, 2001), pp. 141–55.

Peperstraten, Frans van, 'Displacement or composition? Lyotard and Nancy on the trait d'union between Judaism and Christianity', *International Journal for Philosophy of Religion*, 65: 1 (2009), pp. 29–46.

Pinson, Jean-Claude, 'De l'athéisme poétique aujourd'hui', *Noesis 7, La philosophie du XXe siècle et le défi poétique* (2004), pp. 255–70.

Plato, *Laws*, ed. Benjamin Jowett (New York: Dover, 2006).

Plato, *The Republic*, ed. G. R. F. Ferrari, trans. Tom Griffith (Cambridge: Cambridge University Press, 2000).

Pluth, Ed, 'The Pauline event: review of *Saint Paul: La Fondation de l'universalisme*', *Theory and Event*, 3: 3 (1999). Retrieved from: http://muse.jhu.edu/journals/theory_and_event/v003/3.3r_pluth.html. Last accessed: July 2010.

Pluth, Ed, and Dominiek Hoens, 'What if the other is stupid? Badiou and Lacan on "logical time"', in Peter Hallward (ed.), *Think Again: Alain Badiou and the Future of Philosophy* (London: Continuum, 2004), pp. 182–90.

Popper, Karl R., *Unended Quest: An Intellectual Autobiography* (London: Routledge, 2002).

Power, N., 'Which anarchism? On the advantages and disadvantages of infinity for (political) life: a response to Simon Critchley's *Infinitely Demanding*', *Critical Horizons*, 10: 2 (2009), pp. 225–40.

Poxton, Judith, 'Embodied anti-theology: the body without organs and the judgment of God', in Mary Bryden (ed.), *Deleuze and Religion* (London: Routledge, 2001), pp. 42–50.

Protevi, John, 'The organism as the judgment of God: Aristotle, Kant and Deleuze on nature (that is, on biology, theology and politics)', in Mary Bryden (ed.), *Deleuze and Religion* (London: Routledge, 2001), pp. 30–41.

Quadrio, P. A., 'Speaking to the people: Critchley, Rousseau and the deficit in practical rationality', *Critical Horizons*, 10: 2 (2009), pp. 209–24.

Ramond, Charles (ed.), *Alain Badiou: Penser le multiple, Actes du Colloque de Bordeaux 21–23 octobre 1999* (Paris: L'Harmattan, 2002).

Ramond, Charles, ' Système et traduction chez Alain Badiou', in Charles Ramond (ed.), *Alain Badiou: Penser le multiple* (Paris: L'Harmattan, 2002), pp. 525–40.

Rancière, Jacques, 'Aesthetics, inaesthetics, anti-aesthetics', in Peter Hallward (ed.), *Think Again: Alain Badiou and the Future of Philosophy* (London: Continuum, 2004), pp. 218–31.

—, 'Esthétique, inesthétique, anti-esthétique', in Charles Ramond (ed.), *Alain Badiou: Penser le multiple* (Paris: L'Harmattan, 2002), pp. 477–96.

—, 'Les démocraties contre la démocratie', in Giorgio Agamben et al., *Démocratie, dans quel état?* (Paris: La Fabrique, 2009), pp. 95–100.

—, Untitled discussion of Alain Badiou's *L'Être et l'événement*, *Cahiers du Collège International de Philosophie*, 8 (1989), pp. 211–25.

Redfern, Walter, 'Introduction to Michel Tournier, "Gilles Deleuze"', in Mary Bryden (ed.), *Deleuze and Religion* (London: Routledge, 2001), pp. 199–200.

Regnault, François, 'Logique de l'assentiment', in Charles Ramond (ed.), *Alain Badiou: Penser le multiple* (Paris: L'Harmattan, 2002), pp. 339–54.

Renouard, Maël, 'Les mondes crepusculaires. Alain Badiou et la melancolie', *Critique*, 63 (2007), pp. 295–308.

Renouvier, Charles, *Esquisse d'une classification systématique des doctrines philosophiques* (Paris: Bureau de la Critique Philosophique, 1885).

Reul, Sabine, Thomas Deichmann and Slavoj Žižek, 'The one measure of true love is: you can insult the other', *spiked*, 15 November 2001. Retrieved from: http://www.spiked-online.com/articles/00000002D2C4.htm. Last accessed: January 2010.

Reynhout, Kenneth A., 'Alain Badiou: hidden theologian of the void?' *Heythrop Journal*, July (2008), pp. 140–62.

Ricœur, Paul, *Le Conflit des interprétations: Essais d'herméneutique* (Paris: Seuil, 1969).

—, *The Conflict of Interpretations: Essays in Hermeneutics*, ed. Don Ihde (London: Continuum, 2004).

Robbins, Jeffrey W. (ed.), *After the Death of God* (New York: Columbia University Press, 2007).

Robbins, Jeffrey W., 'Introduction: after the death of God', in Jeffrey W. Robbins (ed.), *After the Death of God* (New York: Columbia University Press, 2007), pp. 1–26.

—, 'The politics of Paul', *Journal for Cultural and Religious Theory*, 6: 2 (2005), pp. 89–94.

Rorty, Richard, 'Anticléricalisme et théisme', in Santiago Zabala (ed.), *L'Avenir de la religion. Solidarité, charité, ironie* (Paris: Bayard, 2005), pp. 45–66.

—, 'Feminism, ideology, and deconstruction: a pragmatist view', in Slavoj Žižek (ed.), *Mapping Ideology* (London: Verso, 1994), pp. 227–36.

Rorty, Richard, Gianni Vattimo and Santiago Zabala, 'Quel avenir pour la religion après la métaphysique?', in Santiago Zabala (ed.), *L'Avenir de la religion. Solidarité, charité, ironie* (Paris: Bayard, 2005), pp. 87–136.

Ross, Kristin, 'Démocratie à vendre', in Giorgio Agamben et al., *Démocratie, dans quel état?* (Paris: La Fabrique, 2009), pp. 101–22.

Rothenberg, Molly Anne, Sennis Foster and Slavoj Žižek (eds), *Perversion and*

the Social Relation, *The Universal Exception: Selected Writings, Volume Two* (London and Durham, NC: Duke University Press, 2003).
Salanskis, Jean-Michel, 'Les mathématiques chez x avec x = Alain Badiou', in Charles Ramond (ed.), *Alain Badiou: Penser le multiple* (Paris: L'Harmattan, 2002), pp. 81–106.
Sartre, Jean-Paul, *Being and Nothingness: An Essay on Phenomenological Ontology* (London: Routledge, 1969).
—, *Critique de la raison dialectique; précédé de, Questions de méthode*, ed. Arlette Elkaïm-Sartre (Paris: Gallimard, 1985).
—, *Critiques littéraires: Situations 1* (Paris: Gallimard, 1947).
—, *L'Être et le néant: Essai d'ontologie phénoménologique* (Paris: Gallimard, 1996).
—, 'Existentialism and humanism', in Stephen Priest (ed.), *Basic Writings* (London: Routledge, 2000), pp. 26–57.
—, *The Problem of Method*, trans. Hazel E. Barnes (London: Methuen, 1963).
Schmitt, Carl, *Political Theology* (Cambridge, MA: MIT Press, 1985).
Schneider, Laurel C., *Beyond Monotheism: A Theology of Multiplicity* (London: Routledge, 2008).
Schoder, Raymond V., 'Lucretius' poetic problem', *Classical Journal*, 45: 4 (1950), pp. 177–82.
Schrift, Alan D., 'Nietzsche's French legacy', in Bernd Magnus and Kathleen M. Higgins (eds), *The Cambridge Companion to Nietzsche* (Cambridge: Cambridge University Press, 1996), pp. 323–55.
Schürmann, Reiner, *Meister Eckhart, Mystic and Philosopher: Translations with Commentary* (Bloomington: Indiana University Press, 1978).
Sharpe, M., ' "Critchley is Žižek": in defence of critical political philosophy', *Critical Horizons*, 10: 2 (2009), pp. 180–96.
Sharpe, Matthew, *Slavoj Žižek: A Little Piece of the Real*, Ashgate New Critical Thinking in Philosophy (Aldershot: Ashgate, 2004).
Sheppard, Darren, Simon Sparks and Colin Thomas, *On Jean-Luc Nancy: The Sense of Philosophy* (London: Routledge, 1997).
Simont, Juliette, 'Critique de la représentation et ontologie chez Deleuze et Badiou (Autour du «virtuel»)', in Charles Ramond (ed.), *Alain Badiou: Penser le multiple* (Paris: L'Harmattan, 2002), pp. 457–76.
Sinnerbrink, R., 'Neo-anarchism or neo-liberalism? Yes, please! A response to Simon Critchley's *Infinitely Demanding*', *Critical Horizons*, 10: 2 (2009), pp. 163–79.
Sinnerbrink, R., and P. A. Quadrio, 'Ethics of commitment, politics of resistance: Simon Critchley's *Infinitely Demanding*', *Critical Horizons*, 10: 2 (2009), p. 153.
Smith, Daniel W., 'Badiou and Deleuze on the ontology of mathematics', in Peter Hallward (ed.), *Think Again: Alain Badiou and the Future of Philosophy* (London: Continuum, 2004), pp. 77–93.
—, 'Mathematics and the theory of multiplicities: Badiou and Deleuze revisited', *Southern Journal of Philosophy*, 41: 3 (2003), pp. 411–50.

—, 'The doctrine of univocity: Deleuze's ontology of immanence', in Mary Bryden (ed.), *Deleuze and Religion* (London: Routledge, 2001), p. 167–83.
Smith, James K. A., *Who's Afraid of Postmodernism?: Taking Derrida, Lyotard, and Foucault to Church*, The Church and Postmodern Culture (Grand Rapids, MI: Baker Academic, 2006).
Stiegler, Barbara, 'Réceptions de la mort de Dieu', *Critique*, LXII: 704–5 (2006), pp. 116–28.
Stone, Gregory B., 'The nameless wild one: the ethics of anonymous subjectivity – medieval and modern', *Common Knowledge*, 12: 2 (2006), pp. 219–51.
Stramignoni, Igor, 'Badiou's nocturnal jurisprudence', *Cardozo Law Review*, 29: 5 (2008), pp. 2361–93.
Strathausen, Carsten, 'A critique of neo-left ontology', *Postmodern Culture*, 16: 3 (2006). Retrieved from: http://muse.jhu.edu/journals/pmc/vo16/16.3strathausen.html. Last accessed: July 2010.
—, 'The Badiou-event', *Polygraph*, 17 (2005), pp. 275–93.
Szczeciniarz, Jean-Jacques, 'L'Être ou la structure', in Charles Ramond (ed.), *Alain Badiou: Penser le multiple* (Paris: L'Harmattan, 2002), pp. 107–48.
Tarby, Fabien, *La Philosophie d'Alain Badiou* (Paris: L'Harmattan, 2005).
Taubes, Jacob, *The Political Theology of Paul*, ed. Aleida Assmann and Jan Assmann, trans. Dana Hollander (Stanford: Stanford University Press, 2004).
Taylor, Charles, *A Secular Age* (London: Harvard University Press, 2007).
Taylor, Mark C., *Erring: A Postmodern A/theology* (Chicago: University of Chicago Press, 1984).
—, 'Non-negative negative atheology: review of *How to Avoid Speaking: Denials* by Jacques Derrida', *Diacritics*, 20: 4 (1990), pp. 2–16.
Thury, Eva M., 'Lucretius' poem as a simulacrum of the Rerum Natura', *American Journal of Philology*, 108: 2 (1987), pp. 270–94.
Tiles, Mary, *The Philosophy of Set Theory: An Historical Introduction to Cantor's Paradise* (Oxford: Basil Blackwell, 1989).
Toscano, Alberto, 'A plea for Prometheus', *Critical Horizons*, 10: 2 (2009), pp. 241–56.
—, 'Against speculation, or, a critique of the critique of critique . . . a remark on Quentin Meillassoux's *After Finitude* (after Colletti)', Speculative Realism, Centre for the Study of Invention and Social Process, Goldsmiths, University of London, 27 April 2007.
—, 'Communism as separation', in Peter Hallward (ed.), *Think Again: Alain Badiou and the Future of Philosophy* (London: Continuum, 2004), pp. 138–49.
—, 'To have done with the end of philosophy', *Pli*, 9 (2000), pp. 200–38.
Toscano, Alberto, and Nina Power. 'Editors' introduction – think pig!', in Alain Badiou, *On Beckett*, ed. Alberto Toscano and Nina Power (Manchester: Clinamen, 2003).
Tournier, Michel, 'Gilles Deleuze', in Mary Bryden (ed.), *Deleuze and Religion* (London: Routledge, 2001), pp. 201–4.

Vahanian, Gabriel, 'The death of God: an afterword', in Jeffrey W. Robbins (ed.), *After the Death of God* (New York: Columbia University Press, 2007), pp. 163–78.

Vahnhoozer, Kevin, and Martin Warner (eds), *Transcending Boundaries in Philosophy and Theology: Reason, Meaning and Experience* (Aldershot: Ashgate, 2007).

Vainqueur, Bernard, 'De quoi « sujet » est-il le nom pour Alain Badiou ?', in Charles Ramond (ed.), *Alain Badiou: Penser le multiple* (Paris: L'Harmattan, 2002), pp. 313–38.

van Rompaey, Chris, 'Book review: a question of fidelity', *Cosmos and History: The Journal of Natural and Social Philosophy*, 2: 1–2 (2006), pp. 350–8.

Vanhoozer, Kevin, 'Once more into the borderlands: the way of wisdom in philosophy and theology after the "Turn to Drama"', in Kevin Vanhoozer and Martin Warner (eds), *Transcending Boundaries in Philosophy and Theology: Reason, Meaning and Experience* (Aldershot: Ashgate, 2007), pp. 31–54.

Vattimo, Gianni, 'A prayer for silence: dialogue with Gianni Vattimo', in Jeffrey W. Robbins (ed.), *After the Death of God* (New York: Columbia University Press, 2007), pp. 89–113.

—, *After Christianity*, trans. Luca D'Isanto (New York: Columbia University Press, 2002).

—, 'L'Ère de l'interprétation', in Santiago Zabala (ed.), *L'Avenir de la religion. Solidarité, charité, ironie* (Paris: Bayard, 2005), pp. 67–86.

—, 'Toward a nonreligious Christianity', in Jeffrey W. Robbins (ed.), *After the Death of God* (New York: Columbia University Press, 2007), pp. 27–46.

Verstraeten, Pierre, 'L'Apport de Badiou à la considération de la 8ème hypothèse du Parménide', in Charles Ramond (ed.), *Alain Badiou: Penser le multiple* (Paris: L'Harmattan, 2002), pp. 149–68.

Vining, Joseph, *From Newton's Sleep* (Princeton: Princeton University Press, 1995).

von der Luft, Eric, 'Sources of Nietzsche's "God is Dead!" and its meaning for Heidegger', *Journal of the History of Ideas*, 45: 2 (1984), pp. 263–76.

Wahl, François, 'Le soustractif', in Alain Badiou, *Conditions* (Paris: Éditions du Seuil, 1992), pp. 9–54.

—, 'Présentation, représentation, apparaître', in Charles Ramond (ed.), *Alain Badiou: Penser le multiple* (Paris: L'Harmattan, 2002), pp. 169–87.

Ward, Graham, *True Religion* (Oxford: Wiley-Blackwell, 2003).

Watkin, Christopher, *Phenomenology or Deconstruction?: The Question of Ontology in Maurice Merleau-Ponty, Paul Ricœur, and Jean-Luc Nancy* (Edinburgh: Edinburgh University Press, 2009).

Weber, Max, *Max Weber: Readings and Commentary on Modernity*, ed. Stephen Kalberg (Malden, MA; Oxford: Blackwell, 2005).

Weiss, Allen S., 'Impossible sovereignty: between "The Will to Power" and "The Will to Chance"', *October* 36: Georges Bataille: Writings on Laughter, Sacrifice, Nietzsche, Un-Knowing (1986), pp. 128–46.

Wilkens, Matthew, 'Introduction: the philosophy of Alain Badiou', *Polygraph*, 17 (2005), pp. 1–9.

Wittgenstein, Ludwig, *Tractatus Logico-Philosophicus*, ed. David Francis Pears, Brian McGuinness and Bertrand Russell, Routledge Classics (London: Routledge, 2001).

Woodiwiss, Ashley, 'Philosophy at the end of the world: the gospel according to Slavoj Žižek', *Books and Culture*, November/December 2006. Retrieved from: http://www.booksandculture.com/articles/2006/novdec/5.30.html. Last accessed: July 2010.

Wright, C., 'Resurrection and reaction in Alain Badiou: towards an evental historiography', *Culture Theory and Critique*, 49: 1 (2008), pp. 73–92.

Zabala, Santiago, 'Christianity and the death of God', *Common Knowledge*, 11: 1 (2005), pp. 33–40.

Zabala, Santiago (ed.), *L'Avenir de la religion. Solidarité, charité, ironie* (Paris: Bayard, 2005).

Zimmermann, Jens, *Recovering Theological Hermeneutics: An Incarnational-Trinitarian Theory of Interpretation* (Grand Rapids, MI: Baker Academic, 2004).

Žižek, Slavoj, 'A glance into the archives of Islam'. Retrieved from: http://www.lacan.com/zizarchives.htm . Last accessed: January 2010.

—, 'A plea for "passive aggressivity"', in *The Universal Exception: Selected Writings, Volume Two* (London and New York: Continuum, 2006), pp. 209–26.

—, 'Attempts to escape the logic of capitalism', in *The Universal Exception: Selected Writings, Volume Two* (London and New York: Continuum, 2006), pp. 137–50.

—, 'Badiou: notes from an ongoing debate', *International Journal of Žižek Studies*, 1: 2 (2007). Retrieved from: http://www.zizekstudies.org/index.php/ijzs/article/view/26/85. Last accessed: January 2010.

—, 'De la démocratie à la violence divine', in Giorgio Agamben et al., *Démocratie, dans quel état?* (Paris: La Fabrique, 2009) pp. 123–49.

—, 'Foreword: Halward's fidelity to the Badiou event', in Peter Hallward, *Badiou: A Subject to Truth* (Minneapolis, MI; London: University of Minnesota Press, 2003), pp. ix–xiv.

—, 'From proto-reality to the act: a reply to Peter Dews', *Angelaki*, 5: 3.1 (2000), pp. 141–8.

—, 'From purification to subtraction: Badiou and the real', in Peter Hallward (ed.), *Think Again: Alain Badiou and the Future of Philosophy* (London: Continuum, 2004), pp. 165–81.

—, *In Defense of Lost Causes* (London: Verso, 2008).

—, 'Move the underground: what's wrong with fundamentalism? Part II'. Retrieved from: http://www.lacan.com/zizunder.htm. Last accessed: January 2010.

—, 'Multiculturalism, or, the cultural logic of multinational capitalism', in *The*

Universal Exception: Selected Writings, Volume Two (London and New York: Continuum, 2006), pp. 151–82.

—, 'Neighbors and other monsters: a plea for ethical violence', in Slavoj Žižek, Eric L. Santner and Kenneth Reinhard (eds), *The Neighbor* (Chicago and London: University of Chicago Press, 2005), pp. 134–90.

—, 'Nobody has to be vile', *London Review of Books*, 28: 7 (6 April 2006), p. 10. Retrieved from: http://www.lrb.co.uk/v28/n07/slavoj-Žižek/nobody-has-to-be-vile. Last accessed: July 2010.

—, *On Belief, Thinking in Action* (London: Routledge, 2001).

—, 'Only a suffering God can save us. Section 1: Hegel', *Lacanian Ink* (2007). Retrieved from: http://www.lacan.com/zizshadowplay.html. Last accessed: July 2010.

—, 'Only a suffering God can save us. Section 2: Kierkegaard', *Lacanian Ink* (2007). Retrieved from: http://www.lacan.com/zizmarqueemoon.html. Last accessed: July 2010.

—, 'Psychoanalysis in post-Marxism: the case of Alain Badiou', *South Atlantic Quarterly*, 97: 2 (1998), pp. 235–61.

—, 'Religion between knowledge and *jouissance*', *Lacanian Ink* (2007). Retrieved from: http://www.lacan.com/zizsmokeonthewater.html. Last accessed: July 2010.

—, 'The antinomies of tolerant reason: a blood-dimmed tide is loosed'. Retrieved from: http://www.lacan.com/zizantinomies.htm. Last accessed: January 2010.

—, *The Fragile Absolute, or, Why is the Christian Legacy Worth Fighting For?, Wo es War* (London and New York: Verso, 2000).

—, 'The ignorance of chicken, or, who believes what today', *autraumaton*, Spring (2007), pp. 47–61.

—, *The Metastases of Enjoyment: Six Essays on Woman and Causality* (London: Verso, 1995).

—, 'The parallax view', in *Interrogating the Real: Selected Writings* (New York and London: Continuum, 2005), pp. 231–46.

—, *The Parallax View* (Cambridge, MA: MIT Press, 2006).

—, 'The prospects of radical politics today', in *The Universal Exception: Selected Writings, Volume Two* (London and New York: Continuum, 2006), pp. 237–58.

—, *The Puppet and the Dwarf: The Perverse Core of Christianity, Short circuits* (Cambridge, MA: MIT Press, 2003).

—, 'The Real of sexual difference', in *Interrogating the Real: Selected Writings* (New York and London: Continuum, 2005), pp. 330–55.

—, 'The rhetorics of power', *Diacritics*, 31: 1 (2001), pp. 91–108.

—, *The Sublime Object of Ideology* (London: Verso, 1999).

—, 'The three faces of Bill Gates', in *The Universal Exception: Selected Writings, Volume Two* (London and New York: Continuum, 2006), pp. 227–36.

—, *The Ticklish Subject: The Absent Centre of Political Ontology* (London: Verso, 2000).

—, 'The two totalitarianisms', *London Review of Books*, 27: 6 (2005). Retrieved from: http://www.lrb.co.uk/v27/n06/slavoj-Žižek/the-two-totalitarianisms. Last accessed: July 2010.

—, 'Welcome to the desert of the Real', in *The Universal Exception: Selected Writings, Volume Two* (London and New York: Continuum, 2006), pp. 267–88.

—, 'Why is Wagner worth saving?', in *Interrogating the Real: Selected Writings* (New York and London: Continuum, 2005), pp. 307–30.

—, 'With or without passion: what's wrong with fundamentalism? Part I'. Retrieved from: http://www.lacan.com/zizpassion.htm. Last accessed: January 2010.

Žižek, Slavoj, and Joshua Delpech-Ramey, 'An Interview with Slavoj Žižek "On Divine Self-limitation and Revolutionary Love"', *Journal of Philosophy and Scripture*, 1: 2 (2004), pp. 32–8.

—, Doug Henwood and Charlie Bertsch, 'I am a fighting atheist: interview with Slavoj Žižek', *Bad Subjects*, 59 (2002). Retrieved from: http://bad.eserver.org/issues/2002/59/zizek.html. Last accessed: January 2010.

—, and Milbank, John, *The Monstrosity of Christ*, ed. Slavoj Žižek, Short Circuits (Cambridge, MA: MIT Press, 2009).

Zupančič, Alenka, 'The fifth condition', in Peter Hallward (ed.), *Think Again: Alain Badiou and the Future of Philosophy* (London: Continuum, 2004), pp. 191–201.

—, *The Shortest Shadow: Nietzsche's Philosophy of the Two*, ed. Slavoj Žižek, Short Circuits (Cambridge, MA: MIT Press, 2003).

Index

Absenthéisme, 111, 113, 114
Absolute infinite, 27, 146
Actual infinite, 24, 25, 27–8, 30–1, 32, 47, 62, 68, 76, 77, 81, 86–7, 99–100, 104, 217, 226
Adoration, 13, 80, 81, 145, 181, 184, 192, 219–20
Agapē, 10, 13
Agathon, 119, 156, 179, 242
Altizer, Thomas, 120
Anselm of Canterbury, 100, 145–6
Aquinas, Thomas, 210
Archē, 35, 38, 65, 108, 112, 114, 116, 216–17
Aristotle, 24, 141, 158, 179
Aron, Raymond, 3
Ascetic atheism *see* residual atheism
Ataraxia, 110–11, 120, 122–3, 128n72
a/theism, 15, 38, 41, 42, 43, 47, 112, 114, 115, 120, 135, 140, 147, 162, 207, 215
Atheology, 12, 15, 21n63, 21n64, 51n29, 96, 111, 114–21, 123, 132–4, 168, 176, 178, 180, 196, 198n2, 213, 215, 216, 218, 236n23, 240, 241
Augustine, 27, 210
Axioms, 15, 27, 28, 29, 30, 32, 45, 47, 48, 52n38, 66–7, 82, 86, 87, 95, 96–111, 113, 117, 120, 121–3, 127n56, 132, 155, 157–62, 189, 191–2, 196, 197, 222–3, 224, 229, 233, 240
    Axiom of choice, 107–8, 127n56
    Axiom of infinity, 100
    Axiom of the empty set, 30, 100, 159

Bad infinity *see* Good/Bad infinity
Bataille, Georges, 118, 216
Beckett, Samuel, 88n9, 223, 229
Bensaïd, Daniel, 96
Blanchot, Maurice, 4, 114, 120–1, 192, 239
Bosteels, Bruno, 97, 103, 183, 221
Brown, Nathan, 144, 174–6

Call, the, 181–5, 190, 196–7
Camus, Albert, 3–4
Cantor, Georg, 25–8, 31–2, 47, 106, 146
Capital, 15, 81, 191, 213–15, 216, 217–18, 221, 223–6, 233
Caputo, John D, 10, 42, 56n80, 97–8
Child of Man, 13, 208–10, 220, 231
Christmas projection, 37, 39–40, 47, 81, 85, 87, 118, 216, 232, 240
Clemens, Justin, 103
Communism, 3, 15, 191, 213, 217–22, 224, 226–31, 233
Comte, Auguste, 2, 14
Contingency (in Meillassoux), 135, 139–40, 141–6, 149–62, 163n4, 165n18, 166n37, 173–5, 176, 208–9, 212–13, 224, 230–4
Correlationism, 140–1, 142, 150, 151, 158, 161

Critchley, Simon, 124n17, 168, 183–5, 191–2, 200n34, 201n60, 191, 192, 194–6, 206
Crowley, Martin, 77, 182–5, 212, 221–2, 236n29
Cunningham, Connor, 42

De Kesel, Marc, 108
Deconstruction, 8, 12, 13, 14, 34, 36, 38–47, 53n49, 58, 61, 73, 75, 80, 83, 85, 95–6, 112, 116, 120, 148, 217, 240
Deconstruction of Christianity, 12–14, 38–47, 61, 73, 75, 80, 82, 85, 95, 112, 116, 240
Dedekind, Richard, 31
Deleuze, Gilles, 28, 39–40, 46–7, 97, 105
Democracy, 99, 148, 167, 193, 213, 215–18, 226, 232
Demonstration, 15, 106, 155–61, 171, 172, 190, 241–3
Derrida, Jacques, 7–8, 28, 46–7, 73, 83, 85, 115, 120, 221, 240, 243n3
Descartes, René, 2, 4, 24, 25, 49n9, 70, 83, 122, 143n4, 156
Disenchantment *see* Enchantment/disenchantment
Disenclosure, 73, 82, 86, 95, 116
Dostoyevsky, Fyodor, 169

Empty set, 29, 30
Enchantment/disenchantment, 58, 60, 62, 64, 112, 224–5
Epicurus, 64, 110
Equality, 108–9, 182–4, 193, 197, 211, 214, 220, 221–3, 227, 229, 230, 232, 233, 239–40
Eschatology, 4, 5, 37, 185, 193–4, 197
Eternity, 24, 26, 64, 69–70, 71, 83, 143, 153, 190, 208, 210–11, 212
Ethos, 13, 177–85, 188, 197, 202n63, 217, 218, 229–30, 232, 233, 240
Event, 30, 52n38, 65, 71, 83, 90n40, 96–100, 106–8, 117, 140, 185–8, 189–93, 194–6, 204n87, 223, 228–9, 240

Ex nihilo, 143, 149, 173–4, 192, 208
Exhaustion of metaphysics, 35–6

Factiality, 135, 140–2, 143, 144–6, 147, 149, 150–3, 154, 155, 157–8, 159–61, 165n16, 171, 174–5, 207, 210–11, 240
Faith, 5, 7, 9, 15, 40, 66, 98, 107, 115–17, 120, 122, 123, 134, 136–7, 139, 145, 155–62, 188, 190–1, 193, 196, 197, 202n63, 227, 233, 240
Feuerbach, Ludwig, 2, 14, 25, 120–1
Finitude, 44, 61, 114, 179, 182
Foucault, Michel, 54n51, 141
Freedom, 109, 176, 179–81, 197, 227

Galilei, Galileo, 24–5, 106
Gauchet, Marcel, 112
Generic, the, 30, 43, 47, 52n38, 108, 110, 124n20, 222, 227, 230
Gibson, Andrew, 194
Globalisation, 214
Glucksmann, André, 42, 56n80
Good, the, 103, 106, 107–8, 109, 115, 170–1, 174, 179, 183, 207, 215, 230, 233
Good/Bad infinity, 27, 46, 68, 72, 75–6, 80, 113–14, 217
Grace, 32, 71, 97–8, 99, 195
Granel, Gérard, 116
Guibal, Francis, 120

Hägglund, Martin, 128n72, 243n3
Hallward, Peter, 23, 29, 45, 46, 51n32, 99, 102, 103, 108, 110–11, 143–4, 149, 175
Harman, Graham, 51n34, 144, 154–5, 163n3, 163n4
Hegel, Georg Friedrich Wilhelm, 38, 44, 46, 58, 59, 68, 75–6, 86, 88n4, 102, 114, 137, 145, 189, 209, 210, 243n4
Heidegger, Martin, 4, 5, 6, 8, 22, 34–5, 59, 62, 63, 67, 73, 74, 85, 87, 133, 137, 141, 159, 178–80, 195
Hermeneutics, 102, 120
Heterotopia, 33–4, 37, 48, 54n51
Historicism, 26, 31, 34, 36–7, 148

Hölderlin, Friedrich, 58–9, 73, 81
Human animal, 66, 71, 72, 82, 84, 189, 190, 229
Hume, David, 141, 153–5, 161, 169
Husserl, Edmund, 7, 10, 122, 140
Hutchens, Ben, 119
Hyperchaos, 144, 149–53, 154, 157, 166n37, 170, 172, 174–6, 195, 197, 199n14, 207–8, 231, 240–1

Idea, the, 3, 5–7, 15, 36, 60–72, 73, 78, 79, 82, 86, 87, 106, 115, 170, 226–30, 240, 242
Imitative atheism, 1–3, 5, 11, 22–3, 33, 37, 39–40, 42, 43, 46, 47, 61, 70, 73, 74, 76, 80, 82, 85, 87, 95, 96, 98, 107, 111, 114–18, 120, 134, 140, 141, 145, 147, 168, 169, 170, 178, 206, 210, 218, 220, 225, 229, 230, 233, 239, 241
Immanence, 6, 7, 28, 68, 72, 80, 105, 106–9, 110, 115, 119, 121, 133–5, 142, 148–9, 156, 209–11, 220, 240, 241
Immortality (in Badiou), 71–2, 169, 207–8, 211, 212, 222, 243n3
Inaccessibility, 15, 28, 50n28, 51n33, 51n54, 52n38, 60, 73, 82, 102–3, 114, 117, 118, 119, 122–3, 125n31, 126n32, 134, 135–6, 142, 149, 159, 171, 192, 225, 240
Inaesthetics, 63–7, 78, 79
Incarnation, 13, 59, 60–1, 67–73, 82–6, 112, 209, 224
Incommensurability, 1, 14, 37, 41, 79, 80, 84, 86, 152, 153, 180, 214, 217–18, 219–21, 223
Inconsistent multiplicity, 28–30, 41, 44, 45, 47, 51n34, 72, 110, 138, 159, 233–4, 240
Inexistence, 70, 144, 149, 155, 166n37, 172, 230–1
Infinity, 8, 22, 23–5, 26–8, 30–2, 41, 46–8, 48n7, 49n11, 52n40, 59–60, 61–9, 70–7, 79, 80–1, 82, 86–7, 95, 100–2, 103–4, 107–8, 110, 113, 114–15, 117–18, 127n56, 145–6, 173, 179–80, 185, 191, 207, 209, 214–17, 220

Intuition, 29–30, 104, 105, 160–2, 174, 209, 211, 234, 241

James, Ian, 84
Janicaud, Dominique, 10, 220
Justice, 2, 5–6, 8, 13, 15–16, 60, 162, 168, 170–6, 190, 194, 197–8, 206–9, 211–13, 216, 220–1, 222–3, 227, 229–30, 231–4, 240

Kant, Immanuel, 7, 24, 105, 115, 117, 122, 133, 140–1, 147, 154, 156, 160, 178–9, 185–6, 189, 192, 201n60, 243n4
Keynes, John Maynard, 215, 235n16

Lacan, Jacques, 28, 44, 49n14, 67n93, 126n32, 169, 188
Lecercle, Jean-Jacques, 66, 109, 201n60
Leibniz, Gottfried, 24, 156, 243n4
Lévi-Strauss, Claude, 49n14
Lévinas, Emmanuel, 8, 10, 45, 46, 183, 185–6, 188, 192, 201n60, 220
Lucretius, 63–4, 109–10, 119
Lyotard, Jean-François, 11, 28, 98, 103, 105, 108, 126n32

Mao Zedong, 46, 102
Marion, Jean-Luc, 9–10, 100–2, 117, 243n3
Marx, Karl, 3, 109, 122, 175, 170, 193–4, 213, 225–7, 235n12, 243n4
Merleau-Ponty, Maurice, 9, 83
Metaphysics, 7, 10, 23–5, 27, 33–7, 41, 43, 48, 63, 117, 135–41, 143, 145, 162, 177, 183, 215–16
Milbank, John, 51n33, 103, 108
Miracle, 3, 25, 96–7, 99–100, 103, 111, 122, 149–50, 170, 191, 193, 199n14
Monotheism, 30, 41–3, 53n49, 74, 111–14, 117, 120, 142
Mullarkey, John, 108
Mysticism, 7, 9, 32, 60, 62, 96, 119, 149, 160, 215

Necessity (in Meillassoux), 135, 137–47, 150–2, 154, 155–60, 162, 174, 209, 211
Newton, Isaac, 171
Nietzsche, Friedrich, 5–7, 9, 10, 16, 22, 26, 31, 49n13, 58, 59, 82–3, 93n67, 115, 118, 195
Non-contradiction, principle of, 141, 146, 150, 152, 153–4, 158, 165n15, 207, 241

Occupation, atheism of *see* post-theological integration
One, the, 23–5, 27–30, 31–2, 41, 44, 45, 47, 51n33, 52n38, 99, 100, 103, 109–10, 138–40, 146, 159, 191, 225
Open, the, 59, 60, 61–7, 73–82, 86, 121
Osborne, Peter, 96

Parasitic atheism *see* imitative atheism
Pascal, Blaise, 22, 49n9, 96, 98, 103, 132, 172–3, 190–1, 193, 197, 207
Paul the Apostle, 12, 20n61, 32, 38, 99, 108, 139, 190, 193–4
Plato, 2, 5, 6, 7, 11, 14, 25–6, 36, 38, 41, 42, 43, 44, 46, 59, 62, 63, 65, 72, 103, 105, 106, 107, 111, 115, 122, 143, 156, 157, 170–1, 193, 214, 222, 242, 243n4
Platonism of the multiple, 14, 41, 66, 69
Postsecular, the, 1, 10, 12, 14, 112, 117, 239
Post-theological, the, 12–13, 45, 59, 60, 63, 65, 69, 77, 80, 112, 115, 116, 119, 155, 181, 187, 198, 231–2, 239, 240, 241
Post-theological integration, 13, 23, 40, 48, 70, 71, 72, 79, 81–2, 86, 95, 98, 116, 133, 135, 148, 162, 196–7, 206, 210, 232, 240
Principle of insufficient reason, 117, 145, 146

Rancière, Jacques, 98, 103, 191, 192–3, 236n29

Rationality, 7–8, 11–12, 74, 102, 106–7, 136–7, 142–4, 146–8, 150–2, 154, 156–8, 160–2, 171, 173, 209, 212
Reason, 115–17, 135–7, 147–8, 155–6, 161, 178, 210, 241
  Hypothetical/anhypothetical reason, 157–9, 161, 242
Relativism, 135, 137, 138, 145, 211
Residual atheism, 3–11, 23, 28, 31, 40, 47, 58, 59, 60, 67, 70, 72, 73, 74, 75, 77, 79, 80, 81, 86, 87, 95, 99, 109, 113, 114, 117, 120, 133, 134, 145, 148, 149, 168, 184, 194, 197, 206, 225, 231, 233, 234, 239, 240, 241
Resurrection, 172, 174, 176, 190, 206–8
Revelation, 96–7, 111, 121–2, 136–7, 139–40, 155
Ricœur, Paul, 134
Rimbaud, Arthur, 186
Romantic infinite, 59–60, 79, 102
Romanticism, 23, 58–61, 67–9, 70, 72–4, 76, 78, 82–3, 87, 102, 159, 171, 225, 239
Rousseau, Jean-Jacques, 187, 188

Schelling, Friedrich Wilhelm Joseph, 68
Schmitt, Carl, 170
Sense (in Nancy), 15, 44–5, 77–8, 79, 85, 177, 179, 181, 219
  Badiou's critique of, 186–7
Singular plural, the, 45–6, 48, 61, 80, 84, 139, 177–81, 183, 196–7, 219–21, 224, 230, 233–4, 240
Spacing, 73–86, 95, 118–19, 121–2, 177, 212, 214, 216, 218, 240
Spinoza, Baruch, 105, 122, 137, 179, 243n4
Subject (in Badiou), 66, 70–2, 117, 227, 232

Tarby, Fabien, 105
Taylor, Mark C., 120
Technē, 83–5
Theological turn, 8, 10, 13, 220
Transfinite, 27, 47, 146
Trinity, 51n33, 103, 112

Truths (in Badiou), 30, 52n38, 61–2, 64–72, 86–7, 90n40, 95–7, 99, 102, 105–6, 108, 117, 188–96, 223–4, 226–33

Valéry, Paul, 63–5
Vattimo, Gianni, 10, 26
Violence, 66, 87, 101–2, 115, 117, 122, 160, 190, 201n60, 224, 228
Void, 29–30, 61, 64, 67, 95–6, 100, 103–4, 109, 123n6, 133, 159, 188, 233

Wager, 103, 107, 172–3, 185, 190–1, 197
Wittgenstein, Ludwig, 7, 26, 126n32

'yet without', 15, 74, 80–2, 86–7, 91n44, 240

ZFC Set theory, 28, 30–1, 50n27, 52n38, 99–100, 110, 145, 158, 226
Žižek, Slavoj, 12, 20n62, 93n67, 96, 194, 226, 233

EU representative:
Easy Access System Europe
Mustamäe tee 50, 10621 Tallinn, Estonia
Gpsr.requests@easproject.com

www.ingramcontent.com/pod-product-compliance
Lightning Source LLC
Chambersburg PA
CBHW052214300426
44115CB00011B/1684